The InsurTech Book

Library of Congress Cataloging-in-Publication Data

Names: VanderLinden, Sabine, editor. | Millie, Shân M., editor. | Anderson, Nicole, editor. | Chishti, Susanne, editor

Title: The insurtech book : the insurance technology handbook for investors, entrepreneurs and FinTech Visionaries /
    edited by Sabine VanderLinden, Shân M. Millie, Nicole Anderson and Susanne Chishti

Description: Chichester, United Kingdom : John Wiley & Sons, 2018. | Includes index. |

Identifiers: LCCN 2017057073 (print) | LCCN 2017059018 (ebook) | ISBN 9781119362241 (pdf) |
    ISBN 9781119362203 (epub) | ISBN 9781119362210 (pbk.)

Subjects: LCSH: Insurance. | Insurance—Technological innovations.

Classification: LCC HG8051 (ebook) | LCC HG8051 .I6165 2018 (print) | DDC 368—dc23

LC record available at https://lccn.loc.gov/2017057073

A catalogue record for this book is available from the British Library.

ISBN 978-1-119-36221-0 (paperback) ISBN 978-1-119-36224-1 (ePDF)
ISBN 978-1-119-36220-3 (ePub) ISBN 978-1-119-44456-5 (Obook)

10 9 8 7 6 5 4 3 2 1

Cover Design: Wiley
Cover Image: © pkproject/Shutterstock

Set in 10/13pt Helvetica LT Std by Aptara, New Delhi, India
Printed in Great Britain by TJ International Ltd, Padstow, Cornwall, UK

The InsurTech Book

The Insurance Technology Handbook for Investors, Entrepreneurs and FinTech Visionaries

Edited by
Sabine L. B. VanderLinden
Shân M. Millie
Nicole Anderson

Editor in Chief
Susanne Chishti

Contents

6. The Value Chain

7. Business Models

8. You Said Tech

9. InsurTech Futures

Preface

The FinTech Book – the first globally crowdsourced book on the financial technology revolution – was published by Wiley in 2016 and has become a global bestseller. It exceeded all our expectations, and, in the meantime, the book is available in five languages across 107 countries both in paperback, e-book, and as an audiobook. More than 160 authors from 27 countries submitted 189 abstracts to be part of the book. About 50% of all contributors were chosen to write for the final book. When we launched *The FinTech Book* during 2017 across the world, our authors and readers had many opportunities to meet in person, sign the books together at global book launch events, and deepen our FinTech friendships worldwide.

In 2017 we decided to extend our FinTech Book Series by writing three new books on how new business models and technology innovation will change the global asset management and private banking sector ("WealthTech"), the insurance sector ("InsurTech"), and regulatory compliance ("RegTech"). We followed our approach of crowdsourcing the best experts for you to give you the most cutting-edge insight into the changes unfolding in our industry.

The InsurTech Book is the first book taking this approach globally – a book that provides food for thought to FinTech newbies, pioneers, and well-seasoned experts alike. Let me introduce you to our contributors and authors.

The reason we decided to reach out to the global FinTech and InsurTech communities in sourcing the book's contributors lies in the inherently fragmented nature of the field of Financial Technology applied to insurance globally. There was no single author, group of authors, or indeed region in the world that could cover all the facets and nuances of InsurTech in an exhaustive manner. What is more, by being able to reach out to a truly global contributor base, we not only stayed true to the spirit of FinTech and InsurTech, making use of technological channels of communication in reaching out to, selecting, and reviewing our would-be contributors, we also made sure that every corner of the globe had the chance to have its say. Particularly those that have very distinct views as to where InsurTech is going and the unique challenges it faces due to the inherent building blocks on which insurance grew. Thus, we aimed to fulfil one of the most important purposes of *The InsurTech Book*, namely to give a voice to those that would remain unheard and to spread that voice to an international audience. We have immensely enjoyed the journey of editing *The InsurTech Book* and sincerely hope that you will enjoy the journey of reading it, at least as much.

More than 250 authors from 25 countries submitted 244 abstracts to be part of the book. We asked our global FinTech and InsurTech communities for their views regarding which abstracts they would like to have fully expanded for *The InsurTech Book*. Out of all these contributors, we selected 75 authors who have been asked to write their full article, which has now been included in this book. We conducted a questionnaire among all our selected authors to gain greater insight into their background and expertise. More than 70% of our authors have postgraduate university degrees (see Table 1) and strong domain expertise across many fields (see Table 2), and 77% of our authors had their articles published before.

Table 1: What is the highest educational qualification of our 75 authors?

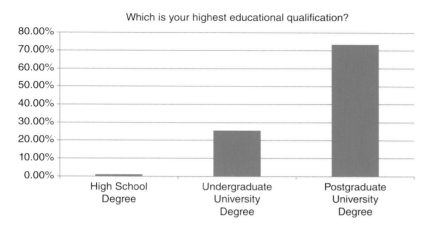

Which is your highest educational qualification?

Table 2: List all areas in which our authors have domain expertise; multiple choices were possible

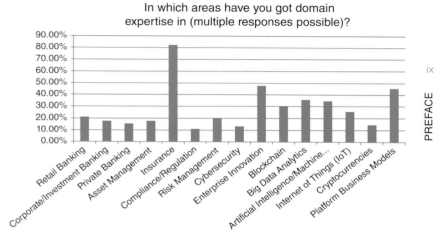

In which areas have you got domain expertise in (multiple responses possible)?

Tables 3 and 4 show that 35% of our authors are entrepreneurs working for InsurTech startups (many of them part of the founding team), 40% come from established financial and technology companies, and another quarter from service providers such as consulting firms or law firms servicing the financial services and insurance sectors.

More than a fifth of our authors work for startups with up to five people and another 35% for startups/small or medium-sized enterprises (SMEs) up to 50 people. Twenty-two percent of our authors are employed by a large organization of more than 1,000 employees.

In summary, we are very proud of our highly qualified authors, their strong expertise, and passion for InsurTech by being either entrepreneurs or often "intrapreneurs" in large established organizations who all are committed to playing a significant role in the global FinTech and InsurTech revolution. These remarkable people are willing to share their insights with all of us over the next pages.

Table 3: Authors selected the type of company they are working in

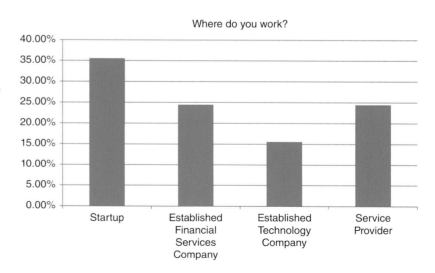

Where do you work?

Table 4: **Size of companies our authors work for**

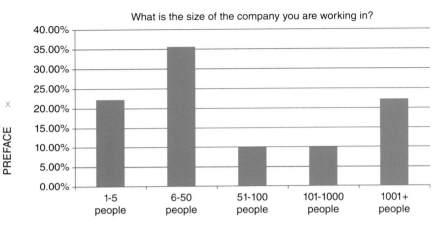

What is the size of the company you are working in?

Thus, this project would not have been possible without the dedication and efforts of all contributors to *The InsurTech Book* (both those who submitted their initial abstracts for consideration by the global FinTech community, as well as the final authors whose insights you will be reading shortly). In addition, we would like to thank our editors at Wiley whose guidance and help made sure that what started off as an idea, you are now holding in your hands.

Finally, I would like to thank the fantastic editors, Sabine VanderLinden, Shân M. Millie, and Nicole Anderson. Editing a crowdsourced book naturally takes several months and it was always a pleasure to work with their strong domain expertise and vision for the future of InsurTech globally!

Susanne Chishti
Co-Founder, *The FinTech Book* Series
Editor in Chief, *The InsurTech Book*
CEO and Founder FINTECH Circle and the FINTECH Circle Institute

Twitter: @SusanneChishti @FINTECHCircle
@InsurTECH_Book
LinkedIn: FINTECH Circle Group

About the Editors

Sabine L. B. VanderLinden

Sabine L. B. VanderLinden is the CEO and Managing Director of Startupbootcamp InsurTech, Europe's leading early-stage and independent accelerator for insurance technology startups, Rainmaking's corporate innovation and growth venture focused at the insurance and InsurTech spaces. She is also the founder of the Proposition Circle, an innovation advisory platform she uses to coach young businesses and advise investors. Mature startups in particular use this mechanism to get more personalized support and recommendations to grow their business.

At Startupbootcamp (www.startupbootcamp.org/accelerator/insurtech-london/), VanderLinden cultivates the expertise of a large group of leading insurers, investors, and mentors to bring the innovation of cohorts of promising startups across multiple geographies to market within a three-month period. At Rainmaking Innovation (www.rainmaking.io/), she leads corporate innovation within the insurance space to shape solutions to support insurers, brokers, and other insurance providers address core challenges and design innovation and execution initiatives that work.

Considered as one of the few leading women in InsurTech, VanderLinden ranks among the top 20 InsurTech influencers across a number of insurance influencer lists. She brings 20 years of senior positions and extensive operational and growth strategy expertise gleaned from her corporate innovation and startup acceleration activities working with global firms including IBM, FICO, Pegasystems, and SSP and hundreds of well-known financial services institutions for which she has developed unique growth strategies. She brings strong InsurTech expertise to these stakeholders, being one of the few influencers who identified InsurTech as a growth market in late 2014 and made InsurTech the

de facto term to acknowledge new ventures in the insurance and technology space.

She writes on the topics of strategic execution, InsurTech innovation, digital business models, and experience design to challenge current market practices and optimize value creation, and she is an international keynote speaker at conferences and thought leader on the topic of InsurTech.

An alumna of Sir John Cass Business School, where she earned her MBA, among her accreditations, she was awarded an Ovation Award for Outstanding Achievement, Breakthrough Thinking and Execution by IBM. She undertook advanced studies in mathematics and acquired five insurance examination accreditations from the Chartered Insurance Institute. She sits on the FinTech technology committee of the Monetary Authority of Singapore and is an advisory board member for TIA Technology. She is fluent in French and English.

You can reach Sabine on LinkedIn at www.linkedin.com/in/sabinevanderlinden/ and on Twitter via @SabineVdL

Shân M. Millie

Shân M. Millie is a hands-on innovation and strategic communications specialist, focusing on growth, service/product design, and corporate storytelling. She is a highly respected, extensively networked connector and commentator on and for UK General Insurance. Shân created the role of Tech and Innovation Associate for the Association of British Insurers (ABI), is Communications Entrepreneur in Residence for Startupbootcamp InsurTech London, and Founder Advisor for the British Insurance Brokers Association (BIBA) Innovation Group.

Shân enjoyed a successful media and content career, building and leading award-winning products, teams, and brands for professional audiences, including Treasury, Derivatives, Asset Management, Retail Banking, and, as Publishing Director of Insurance Times (2008–13), General Insurance. She identified the InsurTech "wave" early, and was personally instrumental in developing powerful platforms for incumbents and startups to connect ideas and people at a critical time for the fledgling InsurTech phenomenon, including designing one of the very first content programs and market-leading conferences dedicated to Innovation and Disruption for Insurance. A trusted industry mentor, Shân founded Bright Blue Hare, in May 2016, to work with startups, scale-ups, and established firms on partner relationships, customer and internal engagement, and sales, using the power of strategic communications. Bright Blue Hare also works with early-stage startups on a pro bono basis, advising seed round and startup companies on business model and value proposition design.

Shân's passion is to help individuals, teams, and firms work out and then tell their story – authentically, intelligently, and for maximum impact for customers, co-workers, and the bottom line.

Shân Millie is a board advisor, mentor, and facilitator, and a graduate of Christ's College, Cambridge University, UK. www.linkedin.com/in/shânmillie/ //@ SMMBrightBlueH//#WhatIsYourStory?//#Profit&Purpose.

Nicole Anderson

Nicole Anderson is a venture builder, investment (corporate venture, VC, family office and ICO) advisor. As a multiple time technology entrepreneur (CEO and Founder) and an innovation thought leader, she has gained an in-depth knowledge of crypto technologies, blockchain and digital identity. Passionate about technology business models that are challenging the status quo and providing greater inclusion for people globally, she has focused on the innovation intersection of emerging technologies and emerging markets both physical and virtual.

Voted Innovator of the Year 2017 by the South African Chamber of Commerce, Top 100 Women in FinTech 2016 by Innovate Finance, and included in the Power Women of FinTech 2015, 2016 and 2017, Anderson is also active in the London and European startup acceleration, incubation, and growth arenas working as an advisor and mentor to Level39, Startupbootcamp FinTech, London Tech Advocates – Women in Tech, and FinTech workstreams.

A founding member of FINTECH Circle Angel Network, the largest network of independent investors in FinTech in Europe, she has served as advisor to Microsoft Ventures London and been a multiple times judge for SWIFT Innotribe, the European and African FinTech awards, and BNP Paribas Global Hackathon.

Anderson serves as an industry thought leader and has featured on numerous panels and speaking circuits such as London FinTech Week, Rencontres Economiques (France), London's African Technology Business Forum, and FinTech Africa's annual conference. She is a contributing author to *The FinTech Book*, exploring the role of corporate venture as a catalyst for innovation in FinTech – www.thefintechbook.com – also published by Wiley.

She has an Honours Degree in Information Systems and Economics from the University of Witwatersrand, South Africa, and graduated from the Institute of New Economic Thinking, Barnard College, Columbia University, New York, specializing in the Economics of Money and Banking.

Editor in Chief
Susanne Chishti

(Twitter: www.twitter.com/SusanneChishti)

Susanne Chishti is the CEO of FINTECH Circle, Europe's first Angel Network focused on FinTech, InsurTech, WealthTech,

RegTech and Blockchain opportunities and the Founder of the FINTECH Circle Institute, a leading global peer-to-peer FinTech learning platform to acquire FinTech and digital skills. She is the co-editor of the bestseller *The FinTech Book*, which has been translated into five languages and is sold across 107 countries. Susanne is recognized in the European Digital Financial Services "Power 50" 2015, an independent ranking of the most influential people in digital financial services in Europe. She was selected as top 15 FINTECH UK Twitter influencer and as the UK's "City Innovator – Inspirational Woman" in 2016. Susanne is a FinTech TV commentator on CNBC and a guest lecturer on financial technology at the University of Cambridge.

After completing her MBA she started her career working for a FinTech company (before the term "FinTech" was invented) in the Silicon Valley 20 years ago. She then worked for more than 15 years across Deutsche Bank, Lloyds Banking Group, Morgan Stanley, and Accenture in London and Hong Kong. Susanne is an award-winning entrepreneur and investor with strong FinTech expertise. In 2017, Onalytica selected Susanne as the 13th most important FinTech Thought Leader globally. She is also a conference speaker at leading FinTech events globally.

FINTECH Circle is a global community of more than 100,000 FinTech entrepreneurs, investors, and financial services professionals globally. FINTECH Circle's advisory practice services clients including leading financial institutions such as BNP Paribas and UK's innovation agency NESTA, which appointed FINTECH Circle as partner for the £5 million Challenge Prize to work on Open Banking initiatives for SME Banking.

Susanne is a Non-Executive Director at two UK FinTech firms: Just Loans Group PLC (Alternative Lender) and RegTech Company Kompli-Global Ltd. In addition, she is on the Advisory Board of HandeFinMaker, a Chinese FinTech leader together with Nobel Prize winner Edward C. Prescott.

About FINTECH Circle

FINTECH Circle (www.FINTECHCircle.com) is a global community of 100,000 FinTech entrepreneurs, angel and VC investors, financial services professionals, and FinTech thought leaders, focusing on FinTech seed investing, education, and enterprise innovation. FINTECH Circle's CEO, Susanne Chishti, co-edited *The FinTech Book* published by Wiley, which became the first globally crowdsourced book on financial technology and a global bestseller across 107 countries in five languages.

Twitter: @FINTECHCircle

Instagram: @FINTECHCircle

About the FINTECH Circle Institute

The FINTECH Circle Institute (www.FINTECHCircleInstitute.com) is a peer-to-peer online learning platform, designed to empower finance professionals with the necessary digital skills to adapt to the rapidly changing industry. With board members ranging from traditional banks and FinTech experts, through to academics from leading universities, the platform offers practical bite-size courses on topics including WealthTech/Robo-banking, InsurTech, RegTech, Blockchain, Artificial Intelligence, Enterprise Innovation, and Startups. Every quarter, new bite-size classes are released online to ensure that members have access to the latest FinTech insights and industry experts working on the most cutting-edge FinTech innovations globally.

Twitter: @FTC_Institute

Join our LinkedIn Group to share your FinTech knowledge and learn from others:

www.linkedin.com/groups/8184397

Acknowledgments

After the global launch of *The FinTech Book* in 2016, we met thousands of FinTech entrepreneurs, investors, and financial services professionals who all loved the book and wanted to learn more how financial technology will change the global investment/ wealth management sector and private banking.

We came up with the idea for *The InsurTech Book* and spoke to our FinTech friends globally and everybody supported the idea. FinTech entrepreneurs across all continents were eager to share their powerful insights. They wanted to explain the new business models and technologies they were working on to change the world of finance. FinTech investors, "intrapreneurs", innovation leaders at leading financial institutions, and thought leaders were keen to describe their embrace of the FinTech revolution across investment management and private banking. Finally, our InsurTech visionaries wanted to share their vision for the future.

The global effort of crowdsourcing such insights was born with *The FinTech Book*, which became a global bestseller across 107 countries in five languages. We are continuing this success with *The InsurTech Book*. We are aware that this would not have been possible without the FINTECH Circle global community, the Startupbootcamp InsurTech community, and our own personal networks. We are very grateful to our global FINTECH Circle, FINTECH Circle Institute and Startupbootcamp communities of investors, lecturers, startups, mentors and corporates for joining us on www.FINTECHCircle.com and www.startupbootcamp.org and to Startupbootcamp as a global multi-disciplinary accelerator. Without the public support and engagement of our global FinTech community this book would not have been possible.

The authors you will read about have been chosen by our global FinTech and InsurTech community purely on merit; thus, no matter how big or small their organization, no matter in which country they work, no matter if they were well known or still undiscovered, everybody had the same chance to apply and be part of *The InsurTech Book*. We are proud of that as we believe that FinTech and InsurTech will fundamentally change the world of finance and insurance. The global FinTech and InsurTech community is made up of the smartest, most innovative, and nicest people we know. Thank you for being part of our journey. It is difficult to name you all here, but you are all listed in the directory at the end of this book.

Our publisher Wiley has been a great partner for *The FinTech Book* and we are delighted that Wiley will again publish *The InsurTech Book* in paperback and e-book formats globally. Special thanks go to our fantastic editor Gemma Valler. Thank you and your team – we could not have done it without your amazing support!

We look forward to hearing from you. Please visit our website www.insurtechbook.com for additional bonus content from our global InsurTech community! Please send us your comments on *The InsurTech Book* and let us know how you wish to be engaged by dropping us a line at learn@FINTECHCircle.com.

Nicole Anderson
Twitter: @NicoleAnMo

Susanne Chishti
Twitter: @SusanneChishti

Shân M. Millie
Twitter: @SMMBrightBlueH

Sabine L. B. VanderLinden
Twitter: @SabineVdL

What is InsurTech?

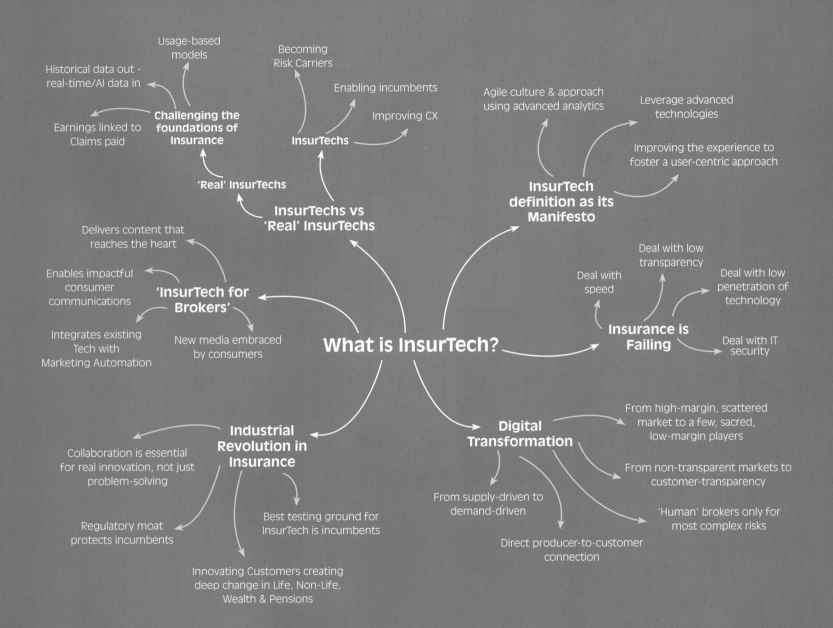

The six pieces selected for this section bring together the expected multiplicity of views, and provide a rich, informative, and engaging set of connected conversations exploring what InsurTech is, for whom, by whom, and why?

Valentino Ricciardi urges us to cut through the InsurTech "noise", setting out how the definition of InsurTech should be clear, simple, and comprehensive so that it actively shapes the vision of next generation talents and participation. Ricciardi's InsurTechs share the characteristics of early adoption of technology, digital by default, focused on specific niches and, most importantly, value creators – for customers, incumbents, or both.

Steve Tunstall also defines InsurTech as absolutely essential for insurance to remain relevant to the customer. His ruthless dissection of the failings of an industry he loves also asks us: insurance needs InsurTech, but does InsurTech need (incumbent) insurance? Tunstall explains how only 10% of corporate risk faced by the CEO finds relevance in insurance solutions today, and how current failings could lead to systemically low penetration in emerging economies. For him, InsurTech may not have all the answers, but certainly some of the *most* important ones, driven by digitalization.

For Alex Ruthmeier, the digital transformation of insurance is InsurTech. He sees four major transformative changes: customer transparency; direct-to-customer connection; a very few scaled players with low margins; and demand-driven (customer) focus. Ruthmeier's vision of InsurTech sees "human brokers" disappearing for all but complex risks, and more quickly than you might think.

Michael Jans also sees big challenges for brokers, but equally InsurTech as a huge opportunity for a broking rebirth. Writing from the perspective of the US, and its 40,000+ independent broker/agent firms, Jans envisions a near future of carriers shifting allegiances away from broker partners. He sees InsurTech as the route to delivering on that "peace of mind" customer promise at the core of the broker proposition, and the technology and scale to make the customer's "heart sing".

Jannat Shah Rajan posits a definition of InsurTech emerging from insurance's Industrial Revolution where innovating customers, increasing life expectancy, and change in life stages drive change in Life, Wealth, and Pensions, as well as Non-life. Her theory of a protective "regulatory moat" around incumbents makes it axiomatic for her that collaboration will be the order of the day. As she says, "Incumbents are the best testing ground for new InsurTech propositions." And lastly in this section, Karl Heinz Passler asks us to see not 1,200+ InsurTechs globally, but a segmented landscape of "InsurTechs" and "Real InsurTechs". He sees two distinct groups: the first, including those improving Customer Experience (CX); those enabling incumbents; and those becoming risk carriers themselves.

The second group are those Passler considers to be challenging the very underlying assumptions and foundations of insurance. He asks us to see "Real InsurTechs" as those eschewing historic data in favour of real-time and AI-generated data; those adopting usage-based models; and those linking corporate earnings to settling claims. These differing yet related and intertwined definitions share a common core in the belief that InsurTech is directly contributing to the reinvention of the way insurance is imagined, funded, constructed, and done.

InsurTech Definition as Its Own Manifesto

By Valentino Ricciardi
Insurance and InsurTech Knowledge Consultant, McKinsey & Co.

InsurTech is the new cool word within the vocabulary of the financial services, replacing the term FinTech, which established itself in the last years of 2000 when companies like Square, Transferwise, and Stripe accelerated the payments revolution launched by PayPal in the US and Alipay in China. However, I believe that InsurTech does not have yet a clear, agreed, and established definition.

An InsurTech definition should cover different concepts well beyond the idea of combining insurance and technology to include the native customer-centric approach, as well as the potential that technology has to enable incumbents' value chain or to disrupt incumbents' consolidated business models. This definition should be open and inclusive so as to host new and innovative technologies that are relevant both now and in the future. So *all* technologies at the forefront of insurance innovation, such as artificial intelligence, chatbots that enable H2C (Human to Customers) in distribution, as well as advanced analytics that are looking for the right use cases in the data-driven business of

insurance, need to fit and find their own space in the definition and concept of InsurTech, which has increased significantly, as shown in Figure 1.

Three Enigmas: Who? What? How?

Incumbents, startups, Venture Capital (VC) funds, and many other stakeholders are all players within the InsurTech field with their own agenda, perspective, and view of the InsurTech phenomenon. The fact that no shared definition was out there increased the temptation for stakeholders to come up with their own, based on *their* understanding of InsurTech. It often resulted in partial definitions, or definitions not yet shared and adopted by the insurance innovation community. This generated "noise" and hasn't helped to provide a clear understanding of the InsurTech phenomenon. A simple approach to get to a definition of InsurTech will be to find the answer to three simple enigmas: Who? What? and How?

The first question to address is: "Who is the subject, the engine of transformation within the insurance and insurance technology landscape? Is InsurTech identifying a specific type of startup, or a whole ecosystem of multiple companies operating in the domain of insurance technology?"

InsurTech, in its current common use of experts, practitioners, and bloggers, is identifying an ecosystem of many different companies that operate in the insurance technology domain. Those companies are early adopters of new technologies, digital by default and, most importantly, focused. InsurTechs are early adopters of innovative technologies such as big data, machine learning, cloud, and the Internet of Things, compared to the insurance incumbents, slowly evaluating and adopting. The early adopters are advantaged on this path by the fact that they are "digital by default", enabling innovation without the legacy of IT systems or overcomplicated procedures and operations.

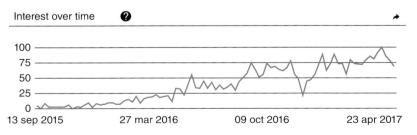

Interest over time

Figure 1: InsurTech interest over time based on Google research

Source: Data from Google Trends (September 2015 – June 2017)

Focus is another strong quality of the InsurTech, whose success is dependent on their concentrating on a specific line of business, area of the value chain, or client segment. There is no InsurTech so far that focuses on more than one line of business and customer segment at the same time. Successful InsurTech companies like Lemonade, Trov, and Oscar focused only on a specific line of business, i.e. Home, Property, and Health, respectively. The fact that they are looking for niches in the insurance business makes them more credible when they promise to challenge or help incumbents who are constrained by their size or other organizational factors.

Once we have in mind the concept of an InsurTech ecosystem it will be easy to define an "InsurTech company" as the company or startup that plays on this field. But they are not the only players in this domain; established, innovative players are fully entitled to be included. Arguably, the first InsurTechs were in fact the direct insurance companies that posed the initial threats to incumbents in the retail motor sector, such as Admiral in the UK and Geico in the US; the price comparison websites popular in the UK; or the IT and ERP system providers focused on insurance, like Guidewire and Tia Technology.

The second questions to address are: "What are those startups doing within the context of the InsurTech ecosystem? What is their primary goal?"

InsurTechs disrupt the traditional business model of incumbents developing innovative customer value propositions able to attract and engage clients, for example, they can enable full digital distribution of insurance products. Most often, InsurTechs enable the value chain of incumbent insurers offering innovative technologies and solutions to improve operational efficiency; for example, they can automate relevant processes across the value chain. However, our answer will remain partial if we don't add the primary goal of InsurTechs: to generate value either for customers, insurance incumbents, or both. Of course generating value is a "*sine qua non*" for any new industry that wants to ensure its own survival and sustainability to prosper over the long term. InsurTechs can focus either on generating value for clients by addressing their needs across the customer journey that

incumbents often fail to spot, or they can generate value for incumbents by addressing the pain points in their business and operative model that incumbents cannot improve efficiently.

The third and final question is "How are InsurTechs innovating the insurance business?" This question is crucial to understand what InsurTechs are doing that makes them different from incumbents.

There are at least three approaches that characterize the InsurTechs's way of working:

1. **Leverage the most advanced technologies.** The most innovative technologies are the core of any InsurTech's solution. InsurTechs are early adopters of innovative technologies and apply them to the insurance business, develop PoV, productize their solution, and offer it to insurance incumbents often creating the needs and the demand for a specific technology that the insurance business didn't perceive before. InsurTechs have a deep understanding of the technology they offer and it is not surprising that they find earlier than incumbents the best use cases and applications. It is equally unsurprising that technologies such as auto telematics, drones, or blockchain were brought to the market by InsurTechs rather than insurance incumbents.

2. **Focus on improving the experience to foster a user-centric approach.** InsurTech entrepreneurs' focus on improving the experience could be improving the purchasing journey of a customer, supporting underwriters during risk valuation, or helping loss adjusters in the loss assessment. Regardless, the InsurTech obsession is (and *must* be) improving the experience following a user-centric approach. InsurTechs improve customer centricity by developing new customer value propositions and products that simplify the clients' user experience in a sector that traditionally lags behind other industries in clarity and usability. The innovative push of InsurTechs in this field is fundamental to keep pace with clients that benchmark their purchasing experience

with digital channels such as Amazon, rather than with the traditional insurance agency experience. This obsession with user-centricity, however, also extends to "internal" users. In fact, InsurTechs that focus on the enablement of the incumbents' value chain develop their solution for employees with the same attention to usability and simplicity as the InsurTechs that improve incumbents' front-ends. The solutions that simplify and improve the underwriting process, the lead allocation mechanisms, and the claims management have an impact on the bottom line as relevant as the one that the InsurTechs focusing on customer experience have on the top line.

3. **Have an agile culture and approach and leverage advanced analytics to take business decisions.** InsurTech startups are very often developed by technology-driven entrepreneurs who are young and digital natives. They drive small and focused teams of motivated professionals that are more used to the tech startups' mindset rather than the mindset of consolidated financial institutions. They are not afraid to quickly develop, test, and bring innovations to the market following a lean and agile approach; they embed advanced analytics in their management practices and operations to generate insights and take business decisions on a day-to-day basis. They are also prepared for the idea of failing and learn from their failures as in the best tradition of Silicon Valley's startups.

The InsurTech Definition as its own Manifesto

The answers to my three enigmas are the essential elements to give a precise and comprehensive definition of InsurTech, which can be agreed upon by practitioners and will prove to be solid over time. Let's combine the elements and define InsurTech as follows:

> InsurTech is the ecosystem of focused, innovation-based companies (often startups) that generate value for clients and/or insurance incumbents by disrupting or solving problems across the insurance value chain through the engagement of technology by following a lean and user-centric approach.

This InsurTech definition should now be its own manifesto: it needs to be clear, simple, and comprehensive enough to show the direction of this evolving and promising domain to all entrepreneurs and insurance professionals wanting to engage with the InsurTech's ecosystem. This definition helps to cut through the noise and define those innovations and innovative business models that compose the InsurTech ecosystem. In fact, the concept of InsurTech wouldn't be possible without the goal of generating value for the clients or for the insurance incumbents; it wouldn't be possible without engaging technology or doing it without following a user-centric approach. I hope that defining a clearer "playing field" will shape the vision of the next generation of tech and insurance talents and attract them to participate in the transformation of the insurance industry, and the experience and value felt by its customers.

Why is Insurance Failing?

By Steve Tunstall
CEO and Co-Founder, Inzsure

The insurance industry provides amazing support to individuals, families, and businesses, often in their darkest times. Society truly benefits enormously from the proper running of the insurance sector. However, the benefits of insurance provide no immediate gratification to the purchaser. I will explain how the insurance community has historically addressed this issue. I will go on to consider why this has led to systemic weaknesses across the whole sector, which may now jeopardize an industry that I love – unless these challenges are addressed.

The Challenge

There is no tangible product delivered within most insurance transactions. The most risk averse individuals will buy it. The least risk averse will self-insure. However, no-one really wants insurance until they really need it. The customer only buys trust – or a promise of trust when times are hard. This tempts intermediaries to sell insurance using the tactics of fear and commoditization. Front-loaded commissions can lead to a tendency to secure sales irrespective of need. This propensity may lead to misrepresentation; it leads to dissatisfaction; temptation leads to fraud; suspicion and a breakdown of trust lead to dysfunctional claims systems; and so it goes. The cycle of fraud in the industry has undermined the true benefits of insurance for a long time.[1,2] The industry has no product other than trust. There is nothing else to take away from the transaction other than a promise. If the customer considers the promise to be compromised, there is nothing left.

The prolonged, cyclical soft market in insurance, coupled with an inflow of fresh capital during an unprecedented period of interest rates close to zero, has placed increasing pressure on bottom lines.[3] The unintended outcome has been that many in the sector have systematically underinvested in technology and innovation. The majority of these companies are left with systems, processes, and practices that would still be mostly recognizable by those that were working in the industry in the 1980s. While the insurance sector stagnated, changes across the business world and other industries were radical. It is only in the last decade or so that the world has enjoyed smartphones, social media, e-readers, YouTube, Google Maps, The Cloud, and virtual reality. Within the same time frame, the companies that dominated specific global markets have radically changed. We all know the GAFA (Google, Apple, Facebook, and Amazon) effect. Changes brought by Uber and Airbnb are arguably even more radical in the transport sector with autonomous driving as well as new approaches to accommodation and the renting market. Customer expectations have arguably changed forever. Already the protectionism in Financial Services is being disrupted by FinTech, and it is clear that insurers desperately need "InsurTechs" to remain relevant to the customer. The bigger question is perhaps whether InsurTech needs the incumbents in insurance. Before we address this issue let's step back and look at how we arrived here.

The History

Insurance and risk management techniques have been around for a long time. Methods for risk transfer were practised by Chinese traders as long ago as the third millennium BCE.[4] Modern insurance

---

[1] 8 worst insurance criminals of 2016, http://www.insurancefraud.org/hall-of-shame.htm; The car insurance industry is a disgusting racket 2015, https://www.spectator.co.uk/2015/10/the-car-insurance-industry-is-a-disgusting-racket/.

[2] Property/Casualty Insurance Cycle 2017, http://www.iii.org/fact-statistic/property-casualty-insurance-cycle.

[3] Peter L. Bernstein, Against the Gods: The Remarkable Story of Risk, 1998, http://www.goodreads.com/book/show/128429.Against_the_Gods.

[4] CNN-Anderson Cooper 360, Keeping them Honest: Insurance Battle, 2007, https://www.youtube.com/watch?v=IvPW087RiJ8.

is around 300 years old. Insurance companies help us all manage some of our risks. Whether personal or commercial, in exchange for a constant stream of premiums, insurance companies offer to pay a sum of money when a predetermined event occurs such as a natural catastrophe, a fire, or loss of life. An insurance company creates value by pooling and redistributing various types of risks. It does this by collecting liabilities (i.e. premiums) from all the companies that it insures and then paying them out to the few that actually need them. The insurance company can then effectively redistribute those liabilities to individuals or entities faced with some sort of event-driven crisis, where they will need more cash than they currently have on hand. As not everyone within the pool will actually suffer an event requiring the total use of all of their premiums, this pooling and redistribution function lowers the total cost of risk management for everyone in the pool.

Connecting Risk, Insurance, and Systemic Failure

The purchase of insurance products should be an important decision-making process for both individuals and companies. However, it is often an afterthought of last recourse, particularly after something goes really bad. Unfortunately, people tend not to like spending time thinking about the bad things in life. We all hope to live in a relatively benign environment. Arguably, human nature tends to allow personal and business risk protection methods to fall down the priority list. Unless we are jolted into action.

There is an old adage that insurance gets sold, it doesn't get bought. Over the years this has been the task of intermediaries – agents and brokers – who communicate directly with customers and explain why insurance is a good thing. When it works well, it's a tremendous partnership. When it doesn't work well, the customer feels they are getting poor or biased advice. As with many intermediary processes, there is little transparency as to who is really working for whom. If experience with claims is also problematic – either directly or indirectly – then the whole trust process is undermined. Both

individuals and organizations can question the merit of the solution and may seek alternative risk mitigation measures, which they feel are more trustworthy.

In personal lines this results in a lack of clarity of when and why insurance should be bought – other than because the law says so. There is an ingrained sense that insurers and their cronies will sell anything to anyone and then do anything to avoid paying claims. At times, it seems the primary drivers in the sector are anything except the customer. CNN[5,6] summarized the objective of insurers as "Delaying, Denial and Disputing" of legitimate claims. Surveys reveal that 25% of Americans now buy insurance with the deliberate intention of defrauding insurers. As Daniel Schreiber, CEO at Lemonade, puts it: "There is a reservoir of ill will against insurance companies. In the US most Americans perceive insurance as a necessary evil rather than a social good."[7]

In the corporate setting, the perceived lack of transparency and governance often translates into distrust in the buying process. The result is that insurance buying is frequently delegated to relatively junior and inexperienced employees who often have other things to do anyway. The purchase process can become a compliance-driven, commodity buy with little focus on the underlying reason for the policies, their coverage, and, most

---

[5] Washington Triple Damages for Unreasonable Insurance Denials 2007, Referendum 67, https://ballotpedia.org/Washington_Triple_Damages_for_Unreasonable_Insurance_Denials,_Referendum_67_(2007).

[6] What's Next in Insurance Tech? Lemonade CEO Daniel Schreiber at the Future of Fintech, June 2016, https://www.youtube.com/watch?v=ZYEYnFT3DCo.

[7] Global Insurance Industry Insights – McKinsey & Company, 2014, http://www.mckinsey.com/~/media/mckinsey/dotcom/client_service/Financial%20Services/Latest%20thinking/Insurance/Global_insurance_industry_insights_An_in-depth_perspective.ashx.

importantly, their security. The relatively low-level employee has a transactional relationship with a broker or agent. The relationship is muddied and sometimes dominated by internal purchasing teams who often have no idea how the transaction should be structured or why it might be important.

Everyone loses in this scenario. The individual is poorly prepared and/or served during traumatic life-changing events. The CEO whose company is in this mindset has missed a huge partnership opportunity. The broker or agent loses or ignores the chance to educate. There are huge benefits that can arise from a more robust debate and attitude to risk and insurance management. The underwriter and the markets behind the policies often have little or no idea of the quality of the risk protected. So, the market will provide something cheap and cheerful – particularly in the soft markets prevalent at the moment – and do everything in their power to delay or avoid paying claims if something goes wrong.

Insurance penetration rates in North America are arguably at their lowest ebb for decades and continuing to decline.[8] In the boardroom, insurance used to be relevant for perhaps 25% of corporate risk faced by the CEO in the view of the author. Nowadays that figure is below 10% according to research by Lloyd's of London. In emerging economies, where the phenomenon of insurance is only just getting going, scandals, performance failures, and consequent distrust mean that penetration levels under current models will likely never reach the levels in OECD countries.[9]

Transparency and Due Diligence: Where Can the Industry go from Here?

1. **Deal with low penetration of technology.** Insurance remains comparatively old fashioned when compared to the financial services sector generally. The failures of companies throughout the insurance stack to address technology issues are legion. Many insurance transactions remain mostly face-to-face and woefully inefficient. This is difficult to address. There is such a strong general distrust in the industry that many customers still retain a desperate need to look into the eyes of someone they hope will still be there in the event of a claim.

2. **Deal with low transparency.** Who gets paid what for the procurement transaction? There is almost no transparency in the insurance sector and a constant stream of high profile criticisms, both from within the industry[10] and investigations by global regulators,[11] show that there remains something intrinsically dirty and incestuous in the complete process that customers never get to see.

3. **Deal with low speed.** Placement takes a long time in insurance and usually involves extensive form filling. As discussed above, that's nothing compared to the demoralizing claims experience in many cases.

4. **Deal with low IT security.** The sector is well recognized as having comparatively weak data management processes compared to other areas of the financial services industry.

[8] Global Insurance Market Trends 2015 – OECD.org, https://www.oecd .org/daf/fin/insurance/Global-Insurance-Market-Trends-2015.pdf.

[9] Chubb's Greenberg on London brokers and US-China relations, April 2017, http://insuranceasianews.com/insights/chubbs-greenberg-on-l ondon-brokers-and-us-china-relations/.

[10] FCA launches antitrust investigation into aviation brokers, April 2017, https://www.ft.com/content/94c61531-69f1-389c-95f5-8c3ef0ac3464.

[11] Health insurer loses 6 hard-disk drives with records of 950,000 customers, http://www.computerworld.com/article/3026401/healthcare-it/health-insurer-loses-6-hard-disk-drives-with-records-of-95000-customers.html.

There have been repeated small-scale cases of data loss.[12] Fingers crossed there isn't a "Sony" moment imminent as this will do nothing to help the sector's already tarnished reputation with customers.

Does InsurTech have all the answers? That's debatable. But clearly change is imminent in some form or another and this book is a superb way to continue our self-critique as an industry.

---

[12] https://www.wsj.com/articles/SB125972626475872363; https://www .theguardian.com/money/blog/2015/jan/10/end-home-insurance-rip-off; http://www.news.com.au/lifestyle/health/health-problems/is-this-proof-health-insurance-is-a-rip-off/news-story/fdcdcbf90930bc64e-b8ad5297c277a82; https://www.iii.org/publications/commercial-insurance/how-it-functions/market-conditions-cycles-and-costs.

Digital Transformation in Insurance – Four Common Factors from Other Industries

InsurTech Facilitator and Co-Founder/Operations, ONE Insurance

and Dr Christian Macht
Board Member, VAI

We are living in the age of digital transformation. Like every age, it has its very own specifics, as well as effects for the economy and society. The authors have identified four common, underlying factors we see in common among already heavily-impacted industries. These factors are outlined with respect to their potential impact on insurance, which can be seen as a late adopter to the emerging technological and digital advancements:

1. From non-transparent markets to customer transparency.

2. Substitution of middle man – direct producer-to-customer connection.

3. From many scattered players with high margins to few scaled players with low margins.

4. From supply-driven (company focus) to demand-driven (customer focus).

Let's look at each of these in turn.

From Non-transparent Markets to Customer Transparency

In the past, customer market interactions, whether buying services or trading goods, were portrayed by the limited possibility to compare these with local agents or retailers. With the emergence of readily accessible information, this local focus widened and allowed for 24/7 active comparison and competition, e.g. via online direct sales or price comparison sites. In most Business to Customer (B2C) areas, the customer is now also able to validate a purchase intention based on peer reviews, which reduce again, at least perceived, uncertainty. The next level of transparency with the reduction of complexity – the matching of the customer's available data with an automated customized offering of products – is already market standard for industries like fashion, news, music, and movies.[1,2]

For the insurance industry, especially in the sales of Property and Casualty (P&C) and other standardized, self-explanatory products, this means a dramatic shift. Transparency of direct sales offerings should, in general, reduce principal–agent issues and information asymmetries and therefore cut into traditional intermediaries (agents/brokers). More available relevant information, e.g. reviews on after-sales performance, as well as stronger value-chain fragmentation and product specialization, will lead to even more holistic customer transparency as seen in price comparison sites like moneysupermarket, Check24, and GoBear. This will also be the case for complex and individual insurances as traditional impact balancing will be challenged and personal predetermination could lead to both personal and insurance predicaments and potentially stronger state involvement for basic coverage. Applying transparency already leads to major impact – sticking to the example of price comparison, this is evident for car insurance coverage where the customer journey nowadays typically starts online. This transparency of new digital intermediation will ultimately tip the scales.

[1] Phil Simon, *The Age of the Platform: How Amazon, Apple, Facebook, and Google Have Redefined Business*, Motion Publishing, 2011.

[2] Brad Stone, *The Upstarts: How Uber, Airbnb, and the Killer Companies of the New Silicon Valley Are Changing the World*, Little, Brown and Company, 2017.

Substitution of Middle Man – Direct Producer-to-Customer Connection

Digital advancements have allowed companies to offer products and services directly to the customer. Online platforms, ecosystems, and engines are the new middle man and they are substituting (parts of) the traditional supply chain and sales channels. In many industries new players have emerged, especially in retail, such as Amazon, Alibaba, and Rakuten, but also in, for example, aggregating transportation like Uber, Gett, and food delivery, e.g. UberEats and Takeaway.com. They started from excellent customer service and specialized products, finally expanding into various offerings and competing in all segments of previous offline-only intermediation.

Similar mechanisms will occur in the insurance (sales) industry. In a world where "online"/"cloud" is nowadays common for the consumer, intermediation will be based on, inter alia, social media profiling; automated recognition of needs; and guided, short, and simple customer data input. Easy to purchase (and cancel) products, direct- and event-based sales, and finally an automated real-time, traceable claims process will substitute the traditional broker. This is often talked about, but will finally happen at the latest in 2020, according to the authors' assumptions. Customers will ultimately not feel this shift directly as they get used to innovation and new market players like Lemonade, Trov, One, and Element quite quickly.

Within a future landscape of declining product margins due to rising price competition and increasing claims ratios, human brokers are not made for scale as they cannot monitor all potential trigger points of customers in a fragmenting coverage landscape. However, brokers will remain a trusted source of advice for complex products that will not entirely be sold online such as pension planning, luxury individual products, and for customers unfamiliar with online services – for the time being.

From Many Scattered Players with High Margins to Few Scaled Players with Low Margins

The aggregation of data and automated processes have enabled scalable digital business models that can easily survive with small product margins. Transparency and intermediation transformation has already resulted in fundamental change to many localized, fragmented players like taxi services, lottery, fashion retail, and web services. They previously enjoyed high relative margins (thanks to personal customer relationships, information asymmetries, and local protectionism), but rather low absolute profit due to normally small absolute business size (limited sales reach and scalability, especially the high ratio of fixed/semi-fixed cost vs. variable cost, risk averse funding principles, and the like). With ongoing digital transformation, the trend in impacted industries resulted in many of these small players losing margin or even running out of business. On the other hand, a few players emerged, who built large scaled businesses and now enjoy high absolute profits (or internal investment like Amazon) with low relative product margin. Especially in insurance, we still see a localized, fragmented market, with many small players scattered across all sectors, nearly all with fully integrated, self-built legacy-heavy value chains.

New players are, for example, pure white-label insurance carriers like Element or "insurance factories" like One that can be plugged into their business client's system with open application programming interfaces (APIs). Their focus will be on core business systems, i.e. underwriting and processing specialized, individual products – ranging from B2C to B2B2C, from unit size one to large scale roll-out – and could accelerate to industry leadership at unprecedented speed. Online, digital, social marketing, in combination with unparalleled pricing, provides the potential to overcome reach – however, still with the need of significant investment in areas most incumbents already "own". Transparency, digital intermediation, and scalability are individual facts that need to be reflected in governance, organizational structures, and company culture, the last being the greatest advantage for new entrants, and the hardest to transform for incumbents.

From Supply-driven (Company Focus) to Demand-driven (Customer Focus)

This trend aggregates an individual customer-centric focus to the company level. As product purchases will be channelled through, e.g., ecosystems, the primary point of contact and visibility of insurance companies will shift. The impact of focusing on the customer instead of the company is illustrated in Figure 1.

Product suppliers, as well as sales, are currently powerful, mostly vertically-integrated, independent units within larger incumbents. However, they will face the impact of becoming supply factories, providing on-demand, efficient services at lowest unit cost. It

will be critical to cater to customer demand whenever, wherever, and via whatever intermediation, through diverse but fully-integrated sales channels (via client relationship management (CRM) systems), whether directly attached to products (e.g. cars, electronics), external plug and play solutions, internal direct sales, or branded ecosystems. Insurance products will be developed from the customer's viewpoint, bundled, fragmented, and specialized, not solely following current rules of push-marketing.

Furthermore, insurance products will evolve, as customers demand varying coverage, all-in-one solutions, or integration of underlying services. Insurance providers will focus on protecting personal data and preventing identity theft in a dedicated digital vault, for example Deutsche Bank Digital Identity, and mobility providers will provide all-in services where the customer does not need to assemble the different steps. The trend of offering core services with satellites will create "security-service-ecosystems" with an integrated customer journey, where additional, external services will no longer be needed. Whether existing insurers integrate external digital solutions or build in-house is dependent on their size and willingness to invest the large sums needed, and their ability to attract the necessary talent.

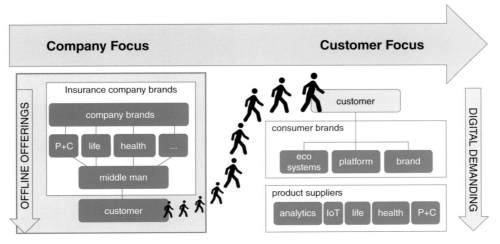

Figure 1: Shift from company focus to customer focus

Incumbents Will be Among the Winners

Innovation is not new in insurance. However, the current wave of digitalization is coming faster, is more fundamental, and – most importantly – is awash with new serious competitors. Hundreds of startups are emerging and billions of dollars are being bet on new technologies, as has been the starting point in many other industries. However, some incumbents are aware of the challenges they are facing and will transform themselves in order not to be overrun by new, innovative, or even disruptive players like AXA and Allianz. The flexibility to adapt to new technology, new customer demands, and unprecedented (external) ecosystems and platforms will be the winning formula for smaller players. Larger players will also have the option to stay relevant and profit from customers with greater willingness to pay for positively-perceived brands, but only on state-of-the-art digital offerings in a fully digitalized value chain. Challengers will also face many hurdles: high barriers of entry due to regulation, complex country specifics, high customer acquisition costs, and

(compared to the banking industry, for example) a currently still not deconstructed and easily accessible B2B offering along the whole insurance value chain (e.g. no "Carrier-as-a-service"). Between 2010 and 2016 the authors observed that most investment ultimately goes into customer acquisition, and only a smaller fraction into real digital and technological advancements like insurance industry specialized implementations of machine learning as demonstrated by Digital Fineprint. This should be a clear sign for incumbents that the race is on. However, with the right digital strategy, significant tech investments, and a talent and culture initiative, incumbents are in an excellent position. The remaining option of collaboration between incumbents and startups is tempting, but also hard due to difference in governance, speed, culture, acceptance of new technology, as well as sales and corporate-level buy-in. As the insurance industry is in absolute and relative money terms very attractive and currently not end-to-end digitalized, we will certainly see significant investment and many winning models. A few will ultimately emerge as fully-integrated digital champions – and reap the resulting high absolute profits and valuations.

InsurTech – Problem or Solution for Agents and Brokers?

By Michael Jans
CEO, Michael Jans Advisory

Twenty years ago, where would you have gone to find thousands of brokers gathered in one room? One of the national trade association conventions. Where would you go to find thousands of brokers today? At the technology conventions. Technology drives the insurance business. Even at the broker level.

And the biggest changes are yet to come.

Many brokers may not be aware – yet – but a lot of professionals and market experts are betting against them in the upcoming "technology tsunami" of InsurTech. Some predict that the gradual trend-line of slow erosion will become the rapid drop-off of disruption.[1] Clearly, some industry macro-trends leave legacy providers behind, such as buggy whip makers, for example. Others challenge us to wake up, catch up – and win.

What will the InsurTech revolution mean for today's broker channel? Most InsurTech investments are somewhere between "unfriendly" and "hostile" to today's incumbent broker. But not all. Some, in fact, help make the broker an important part of the InsurTech revolution. The right technology helps brokers fulfil the promise no other channel really makes. That's the promise of real people serving real people. It's the promise of human connectedness. It's the promise of personal advice and personal advocacy. And it's the promise of the comfort and confidence of having people on your side. This is the soft but powerful magic that binds a tribal species together: to be wired and connected at the deepest psychological level. Nonetheless, the threats are real.

The Rapidly Changing Insurance Consumer

Many of today's brokers are bewildered and bedazzled simply trying to keep up with today's insurance consumer. Ten or so years ago, this author's most requested report was called *25 Ways to Write a Killer Yellow Pages Ad*. Today that report withers on the vine of neglect. The insurance consumer of today probably can't find the yellow pages in their kitchen drawer. They are rarely separated from their smartphone.

No doubt, the numbers in the list below will be outpaced by the date of publication. (They usually are within weeks.) But they provide a glimpse into changing consumer behaviour (and a window into why so many of today's brokers are already worried they're being left behind).

In the US:

- 81% of consumers research online before shopping.[2]

- 88% trust online reviews as much as they trust personal recommendations from friends and family.[3]

- The average consumer reads between four and "52 or more" reviews before making a purchasing decision.[4]

---

[1] https://techcrunch.com/2016/05/02/insurance-brokerage-is-broken/.

[2] http://www.chainstoreage.com/article/study-81-research-online-making-big-purchases.

[3] http://searchengineland.com/88-consumers-trust-online-reviews-much-personal-recommendations-195803.

[4] Ibid.

- 98.4% check their email daily. 39% check it between 10 times and "throughout the day".[5]

- And, remarkably, they deliver 2,617 "discrete touches" – swipes, clicks, taps – to their smartphone daily.[6]

It's not a distant memory that the broker touched and nurtured their clients at the Rotary or the local youth sports league. They never dreamt that "digital marketing" would rank as a business skill, as necessary as quoting and selling. The growing gap – between today's digital savvy consumer and the broker – is the sweet spot that so many InsurTech startups want to dive into.

Rapidly Changing Technology – Can Brokers Keep up?

Clearly, new, attractive, and useful technologies are driving change in consumer behaviour. As far back as 2013, McKinsey & Company declared: "There are signs now … that the economics of the traditional agent model are beginning to unravel."[7] Some technologies, arguably, simply put the broker out of the insurance equation. Driverless cars. Technology-enabled sharing. Instant, mobile-assisted insurance. Products with insurance "baked in". In most cases, these leave the broker on the sidelines. The InsurTech revolution is frequently described as "InsurTech versus legacy"[8] – with the implication that traditional carriers will discover themselves to be bogged down in legacy habits and systems, while whipper-snapper startups sneak up and eat their lunch.

---

[5] https://www.mckinsey.com/…/mckinsey/…/agents_of_the_future_the_evolution_of_property_and_casualty_insurance_distribution.pdf.

[6] http://www.networkworld.com/article/3092446/smartphones/we-touch-our-phones-2617-times-a-day-says-study.html.

[7] https//www.iiaofil.org/Portals/0/Documents/FutureAgents_V_Final.

[8] http://insurancethoughtleadership.com/insurtech-vs-legacy-insurance-carriers/.

But the burden of legacy behaviour doesn't just infect carriers. Brokers suffer the same disease. In the US, for example, many brokers eagerly await the Reagan Consulting "Best Practices Study" for direction, but fail to see that it's a study of *historical behaviour, not innovation.* Forbes, Fortune, Inc., or Wired never highlighted the innovation of the broker channel for good reason. Gradual change and tradition were appropriate dogma … for hundreds of years. Misreading mega-trends can be deadly. The threats of InsurTech to the broker channel must be taken seriously:

- Some consumers want the convenience and efficiency promised by certain InsurTech business models. Just how many remains to be seen. It's less than 100%. But it's more than zero.

- The independence of the independent broker channel will deliver uneven responses. The independent channel has 40,000 firms in the US. Hundreds of thousands globally. Each one is led and managed by its own leadership. There's no "big boss" or corporate structure to say "do this". Some will rise to the challenge. Others will no doubt be left behind.

- Some carriers will shift allegiance. Many carriers boast of their "partnership" with the broker channel. Ultimately, though, their primary loyalty must be to their shareholders or their P&L. Brokers must be prepared for top-ranked carriers to experiment with more alternative distribution systems, especially as startups partner with existing carriers in order to overcome the difficult regulatory, actuarial, and underwriting barriers of the industry.

Adaptive Brokers have a Fighting Chance to Win

The broker channel is huge. Independent brokers write half of the world's insurance. Apparently, not just because "it's always been this way". More importantly, a sizeable demographic believes in it. It's their preferred "flavour" of insurance. Bain & Company's[9] 2014 research reveals the psychology behind the modern insurance consumer's purchasing decision:

- **Some want the best price.** Brokers generally lose that battle. The hyper-efficient direct channel dominates that battlefield. The emerging digital channel will soon challenge them.

- **Some want convenience.** No weekends? No evenings? Can't buy online? Not a bit convenient. Again, the direct channel wins this battle. But the digital channel threatens their lead here, too.

- **But many want peace of mind.** They care about the central value prop of insurance: *protection*. The emotional comfort of the local or expert broker delivers best on this promise.

What happens when brokers deliver on their "peace-of-mind" promise? The economic magic of loyalty. Loyal clients stay longer. They buy more insurance. They refer more friends and colleagues. What's that worth? According to Bain's research, loyal clients deliver a stunning 7X multiplier in lifetime customer value over low loyalty clients. And a 3X multiplier over neutral clients. But, as we observed earlier, the economics presents a stubborn dilemma. The current low commissions on most insurance prevent the kind of "reaching out" and networking that built the broker channel. It's not that Bob the Broker doesn't want to touch his clients more. He's upside-down when he does. Even more important, while his clients may value the "relationship", they don't want his phone calls. In 2015, Mblox's report, *Closing The Care Gap: The Insurance Industry Factor*, stated that 84% of consumers don't want phone calls from their insurance provider.[10]

This, it seems, is an unresolvable predicament for the broker channel. Enter "InsurTech for brokers". Simply put, InsurTech isn't just a challenge to the broker channel. It's a solution. McKinsey reports that InsurTech is focusing more on innovations in insurance distribution than any other category.[11] Certainly, most of it is disagreeable to the broker channel. But not all. What makes an InsurTech innovation supportive of the broker channel's inherent relationship-focused value proposition?

1. It replaces or supplements "old media" with the "new media" embraced by today's consumer, i.e. mobile-friendly email, SMS, personalization, etc. (The Direct Marketing Association claims email returns a 43:1 ROI.[12])

2. It integrates existing technologies – agency or broker management systems – with the new technologies of marketing automation. This "unlocks" the rich customer data currently stored in management systems – and allows it to be used to deliver ongoing value and create meaningful relationships.

3. It automates valuable tasks and communications – delivering "delight" to customer moments-of-truth throughout their customer journey. Brokers can easily deliver the loyalty-building touches and campaigns that support their underlying promise. Sophisticated systems can trigger meaningful communications based on the customer's constantly evolving journey. As they travel from "new customer" through stressful claims, account renewals, even birthdays, integrated marketing automation can help customers "feel the love" from brokers who otherwise would regretfully ignore them.

4. It delivers content that doesn't just reach for the wallet – but reaches the heart. Most brokers aren't prepared to become content marketers or copywriters. Effective solutions

---

[9] http://www.bain.com/Images/BAIN_BRIEF_Customer_loyalty_in_PC_insurance_US_edition_2014.pdf.

[10] https://www.mblox.com/wp-content/uploads/2016/04/Mblox-The-Insurance-Industry-Factor.pdf.

[11] http://www.mckinsey.com/industries/financial-services/our-insights/time-for-insurance-companies-to-face-digital-reality.

[12] https://www.mediapost.com/publications/article/109717/email-marketings-roi-probably-closer-to-130-than.html.

craft customizable messaging for the myriad of possible broker-customer touchpoints, from account rounding to nurturing newsletters to disaster preparedness and so forth. As Steve Jobs said, "... technology alone is not enough. Its technology ... married with the humanities that makes our hearts sing."

This is the promise of InsurTech for brokers. It's an equally compelling promise for the vast share of the market that cares about peace of mind and wants a broker to stand beside them: that we can make the heart of an insurance customer do the remarkable – *sing*.

The Best InsurTech May not be InsurTech

By Jannat Shah Rajan
Venture Capital Investor, AXA Strategic Ventures

InsurTech is broader than meets the eye, or proper noun in this case! Some might like to segment InsurTech from FinTech, and perhaps rightly so – FinTech has been associated thus far with banking activity: payments and foreign exchange has certainly evolved in the past two decades, during which time it is fair to say that InsurTech was neither a buzzword, nor was there much by way of advancement in the insurance industry. A wave of comparison websites emerged in the early 2000s,[1] as did strong niche non-life insurance brands such as Direct Line in 1991, followed by esure and Churchill in the UK, but none of this propelled the industry – price comparison and competition (all else remaining equal) could only lead to compressed combined ratios and compromised bottom-line performance, industry-wide. But for me, "financial institutions" encompass insurance companies since insurance is a financial arrangement, and naturally includes banks, asset and wealth managers, and all other participants in the financial industry. And so, for me, InsurTech, is a subset of FinTech, but we should be clear on what InsurTech literally means. It's about solving the problems of the US$5 trillion insurance industry[2] and innovating for the future of the industry. InsurTech players can either be directly active in the industry, or can equally provide services in and around it that make the experience of insurance a better one, not just for the customers but also for the providers. Banking kicked off its digital revolution first, but a deposit-taking institution has not nearly as many concerns as one who prices and takes on risk.

The Problems and Challenges of the Insurance Industry

The insurance industry is ripe for disruption and ready for evolution for a variety of reasons: consumer expectations, legacy systems, demographic changes, and – at least on a non-life and health basis – changes in consumer behaviour with respect to underlying assets. The new generation is moving away from asset ownership and the advent of customer-to-customer (C2C) marketplace models is enabling this. Even changes in the way people work means that remuneration and benefits are changing. There are numerous places in the value chain where technology can have an effect including: distribution, pricing and underwriting, big data for better risk models, claims handling, and reinsurance.

Incumbents and newcomers have an interesting dynamic in the insurance sector. While, in other industries, technological advance and new business models leapfrog and displace respective incumbents as the product or solution of choice, for example, entertainment streaming versus DVDs and VHS, the same thing does *not* happen in the insurance sector. Why? The regulatory environment is certainly a protective moat for top-tier insurers and a barrier to entry for InsurTech newcomers. To be a full-stack insurer, meaning one that does it all – the customer acquisition, the risk pricing, the underwriting, the claims processing – one needs to be backed by a balance sheet of regulatory capital. This cannot be built up overnight, but there are plenty of incumbents with the necessary capital that has been built up patiently over decades, even centuries. Incumbents are the best testing ground for new InsurTech propositions – they already have the capital and reserves, industry access and know-how, and a customer base that they are looking to retain.[3]

---

[1] http://www.theactuary.com/archive/old-articles/part-4/rise-of-the-motor-aggregators/.

[2] https://data.oecd.org/insurance/gross-insurance-premiums.htm.

[3] https://www.abi.org.uk/news/speeches/2017/04/huw-evans-speech-to-fca-project-innovate-insurtech-forum-28-march-2017/.

For insurers to remain competitive, they must think of ways to compete beyond price alone. Insurance purchases come with a range of reasons and timings, ultimately it is a grudge buy – it's either a regulatory requirement, conducted for reasons of risk aversion, or in some behavioural sense due to fear. InsurTech should seek to make it a better experience, and a convenient one at that. Incumbent insurers also tend to have back office challenges where pieces of the business do not communicate as well as they should, and could, if the systems were built today. This becomes apparent when we get to consumer touchpoints – policy purchase, potential claims, and renewals.

Is it all Problem-solving or is There Real Innovation too?

The world is full of opportunity to innovate: insurance is no exception. New product lines will be created, and, in doing so, the base expectation would be for them to be tech-enabled and agile. There are a couple of ways new product innovation will occur in the near term. New product lines, such as cyber insurance, will become more prevalent. They won't just be for large enterprise clients but will trickle down to the mid-market companies, SMEs, and even individual/ personal consumer policies. Most of us now have digital assets and could suffer a financial loss should these assets be breached, just as we would if we were to be robbed of our physical assets. Insurance companies will certainly want to provide for new business lines like these; but are they the right people to assess the risk? Does the existing insurance industry understand cyber risk? Chances are that they are not best placed to do this internally, just as a cybersecurity company isn't best placed to perform actuarial analysis, and this is where InsurTech would play a role. The future of new products such as cyber insurance relies on the partnership and collaboration of the insurance industry who can manage and provide capacity, and the cyber risk experts who can assess risk and help insurers to price. It doesn't stop here, though. As with other business lines, prevention will be a big focus and cyber companies are best placed to help manage risk and provide advice and services centred around prevention. Take, for example, health insurance, which is a

benefit insurance rather than a product that pays out in the event of a loss. Many insurers in the space are encouraging their customers to go to the gym, quit smoking, and are promoting a healthier lifestyle to ultimately improve their own claims payouts. The same preventative attitude can be taken to financial loss products by encouraging people to drive better and to be safer with their digital assets as per the earlier example of cyber risk.

New value-add services adjacent to insurance will make insurance more appealing to the customer. PropTech, AgTech, HRTech, and HealthTech, to name but a few, are well placed to provide additional services to the customer and be a new distribution, data collection, engagement, and prevention opportunity. Buzzmove in the UK is a tech-enabled home removals booking platform and part of the London PropTech ecosystem. After learning about your new home and moving your inventory, Buzzmove is in a great position to offer home and contents insurance, without the consumer coming to Buzzmove to necessarily purchase insurance – it is an added convenience.

New product types will also emerge. Insurers struggle to innovate with product types as they may not be cost-effective for them. Other financial products have undergone a wave of financial inclusion and the underbanked are slowly but surely being provided access into the financial system. App neo-banks such as Pockit, Monzo, and Revolut with more sophisticated and alternative know your customer (KYC) processes mean that more people can have bank accounts. The same can happen for insurance, but insurers struggle to access new customer bases and curate the right product. Customers may want access to a pensions, savings, or life insurance-type product, but the economics might not make sense when considering the size of premiums. InsurTech can play a big role here and there are already trends emerging with microinsurance for health policies, such as BIMA in Africa.

Where Does InsurTech Play a Part?

The best way for companies in and around InsurTech to help transform the industry is to collaborate. Many incumbents are open and willing to engage with the new crop to enhance their own service, such as AXA, Transamerica, American Family, Ping An, and Mass Mutual,[4] and they remain domain experts in their business lines to be able to advise in return. The regulatory moat means that for new InsurTech companies to do it all, becoming known as the "full-stack InsurTech", can be a slow, uphill, and capital-intensive burnout. Insurance companies have the balance sheets and the know-how – InsurTechs have the tech and a vision for where to steer the industry next.

InsurTech now and Going Forward

For many, InsurTech paints the picture of a full-stack insurer that solves and does all I have described as a digitally-native carrier, acquiring customers through the promise of better pricing and experience, while simultaneously giving more than just risk coverage to extract a better customer lifetime value. For me,

InsurTech is something broader and may, in some cases, make incumbents invisible and parametric. We may not even recognize a product, technology, or software to be transformative for the insurance industry; the best InsurTech might not be identified as InsurTech at all.

Insurance is undergoing an industrial revolution, and, in doing so, all aspects of the value chain will both evolve proactively due to InsurTech, and InsurTech will reactively produce new solutions to serve the ecosystem. Broadly speaking, the taxonomy will follow these pieces of the value chain (distribution, claims, underwriting, and so forth) and the different product lines across life, non-life, and health insurances. However, even this will evolve over time as new buzzwords and new industry-wide trends emerge.

As the automobile and mobility industry evolves, so will the corresponding insurance industry.[5,6] When increased life expectancies will translate into different staging and segmentation of life beyond simply studying, working, and retiring, so will the life, wealth management, and pensions industry. There's never been a better time to be in and around InsurTech.

---

[4] http://insuranceblog.accenture.com/insurtech-firms-are-starting-to-win-the-hearts-of-big-insurers.

[5] http://uk.milliman.com/uploadedFiles/insight/2016/Driving-for-Profit-2016.pdf.

[6] http://www.oliverwyman.com/our-expertise/insights/2015/nov/risk-journal-vol--5/revamping-business-models/beyond-loss-leader-strategy.html.

"Real" InsurTech Startups do it Differently!

By Karl Heinz Passler
Product Manager and Startup Scout, Basler Versicherungen

For decades, the insurance industry did business as usual. In 2010, a new kind of tech company started up in the vertical market and began to offer innovative, tech-based services to established risk carriers, intermediaries, and their customers. In 2017 the number of these so-called InsurTech startups skyrocketed to over 1,000 around the globe. On first impression, you can hardly distinguish InsurTech startups from one another. What are the key differences, and which have the potential to deeply change, or even disrupt, the insurance industry?

InsurTech Startups Take the Next Step

The term "InsurTech" is used to describe innovative, tech-driven ways of solving customer, operational, and business model problems in the insurance industry. InsurTech startups look at the industry as it is. They investigate the pain points that insurers, intermediaries, and their customers suffer from, and employ tech-driven solutions to ease those pains. These startups often observe successful technology-oriented solutions in other sectors, such as finance, and transfer them to the insurance sector.

These types of startups can be divided into three groups:

1. Startups improving the customer experience
2. Startups enabling incumbent providers
3. Startups starting as risk carriers.

Startups Improving the Customer Experience

Insurance customers have come to expect the same level of convenience from their insurance providers that they get from digital service providers such as Netflix, Amazon, and Facebook. Traditional insurance offers are not able to meet these changed requirements, as incumbents are still limited by their outdated administration systems.[1]

This creates opportunities for InsurTech startups acting as intermediaries on their own account to provide their policy-holders convenient services. Here are some examples: Check24 and CoverHound offer price comparisons for finding the lowest premiums; Bought by Many provides demand aggregation for obtaining special policies; PolicyGenius, Knip, and Clark provide digital brokerage to keep covers up to date. These startups give policy-holders an excellent customer experience tailored to their needs for convenience and low prices.

Startups Enabling Incumbent Providers

Most insurance providers underestimated the speed of technological progress and are now hindered from progressing fast enough by their legacy systems and their corresponding processes. This creates opportunities for InsurTech startups to enable incumbent insurance providers. This "self-help" can be found along the entire value chain:

- Simplesurance and KASKO provide online insurance self-service platforms that enable the delivery of cross-selling solutions for e-commerce stores and the delivery of new on-demand insurance products;

---

[1] http://insuranceblog.accenture.com/legacy-systems-a-roadblock-to-digital-innovation; http://www.insurancetech.com/unraveling-legacy-thinking-5-new-ways-to-think-about-insurance-technology/a/d-id/1314732.

- Bold Penguin, Virado, and massup support the online sale of white-label, low margin, niche financial products direct to customers or via brokers improving the quoting, binding, and servicing elements of new and existing policies;

- SPIXII and Insurista provide, respectively, automated insurance agent and messaging leveraging chatbots;

- Rightindem and Snapsheet provide friendly digital claims management platforms leveraging enhanced customer experiences;

- DreamQuark and others provide big data analytics and machine intelligence solutions that take advantage of stored data;

- DataRobot and Neosurance offer automated processing using artificial intelligence that identifies the best timely products.

These technology-based services enable incumbent risk carriers and intermediaries to better serve their partners and customers, reduce costs, and speed up and automate processes.

Startups Starting as Risk Carriers

With the arrival of the mobile Internet (strongly driven by the iPhone in 2007) insurance customers and sales partners developed solutions based on requirements that are difficult to embed within insurers' legacy systems and locked operations.[2] New full-stack InsurTech startups, powered with state-of-the-art technology, compete with incumbent companies in providing better products and streamlined and frictionless services. An acclaimed and respected example is Lemonade. Customers' distrust of risk carriers and their associated high premiums (due to fraud) is reduced by the application of behavioural science. In the case of Lemonade this includes the use of video interview-led claims, a flat-rate cost model, the use of artificial intelligence to automate and accelerate claim payouts, and donating left premiums post claims settlement to charitable organizations. Another case is Element (in founding as of the time of writing). The demand for simple

and transparent products and services by intermediaries and policy-holders prompted Element to equip the traditional business model of insurance with a more flexible product engine, letting distribution partners sell exactly the products they want.

Disruptive InsurTech Startups Take the Leap

Disruptive InsurTech startups challenge the industry's underlying assumptions. They re-evaluate the incumbent business model, based on the latest customer and technology insights. This approach leads to innovative and creative solutions, apart from those that are already well known. There are cases where they employ state-of-the-art technologies as basic building blocks for the delivery of superior products, and cases were they "only" augment their groundbreaking business models with technologies.

Other cases would include Disruptive InsurTech startups covering risks in new industries. Without the recent progress with digital technologies, such considerations would have been impossible.

These types of startup can be divided into three groups:

1. Startups offering superior products
2. Startups tapping into new markets
3. Startups running a new business model.

Startups Offering Superior Products

Farmers can control many factors of their operations, but they have no control over the weather. Unexpected weather and climate change are the cause of more than 90% of crop losses. The Climate Corporation (formerly known as WeatherBill)[3]

---

[2] Pages 3 and 6 of http://www.mckinsey.com/~/media/McKinsey/dotcom/client_service/Financial%20Services/Latest%20thinking/%20Insurance/Making_of_a_digital_insurer_2015.ashx.

---

[3] http://www.businesswire.com/news/home/20110228006841/en/WeatherBill%C2%AE-Raises-42-Million-Expand-Technology-Platform.

applies the latest technology solutions to remove weather-related risk in the agricultural sector. The unique technology platform continuously aggregates large amounts of weather data (big data) from multiple real-time and historic sources, combines sophisticated statistical analyses (artificial intelligence), and performs simulations in a cloud-based computing environment. The results are personalized (field-accurate) weather insurance covers, with automatically generated payments to farmers (without the need for field inspections) when unusual amounts of rain or snow happen, or a long drought occurs. Rather than providing region-based protection on historic data and approving claims manually, the field-accurate coverage and unique service of The Climate Corporation helps farmers protect their livelihoods. New startups are emerging with solutions able to deliver more precise assessments, like The Climate Corporation. One of these startups is Aerobotics, which utilizes advance technology to determine the health of farm land and therefore provide more accurate underwriting.

Startups Tapping into New Markets

The sharing economy (which enables prominent platforms such as Uber, Lyft, and Airbnb) leads to new customer requirements and services. Owners, renters, and lenders that use the services of the new economy look to be protected by timely available insurance for the things they want to see covered and the length of time needed for it. InsurTech startups offer innovative alternatives for commercial and private users: Slice offers pay-per-use insurance for on-demand workers (such as Uber drivers) and home-share insurance for hosts lending out their home (on Airbnb, HomeAway, and FlipKey). Cuvva enables users to purchase as little as an hour of insurance for those times you need to borrow a friend's car. The insurance is activated through a simple snapshot of the vehicle with their smartphone. Metromile partners with Uber to provide pay-per-mile coverage for personal rides with a seamless switch to a commercial per-mile car insurance plan for business rides. Trov is another solution that lets users (borrowers) buy insurance

for specific products (such as a laptop, camera, or bicycle) for a desired period of time. Trov users can turn protection on and off for various items through the simple swipe of the mobile app.

While the business of sharing is key to these business models, these companies offer new forms of insurance products that change individuals' appreciation for insurance. This allows customers to fill their protection gap and get insurance whenever needed, without committing to a long contract or interacting with traditional agents or brokers.

Startups Running a New Business Model

Customers are used to paying their premiums based on actuarial models estimating future losses, plus expenses and profit margins for the insurance provider. This traditional business model creates conflicts of interest between consumers and insurers, as fewer claims settled result in higher underwriting profits. LAKA created an innovative business model that aligns business and policy-holder interests. Customers only pay premiums based on settled claims and add an administration fee for the startup to cover its costs of operations. Moreover, their customers can be sure never to pay more than they would with a competitive offering, thanks to a cap on premiums (secured by a traditional reinsurer). To promote accountability and reduce fraudulent behaviour, users can progress into "better groups" with lower premiums to pay if they are able to protect their bikes more effectively. The team started to test their offering with bicycles. It intends to move to a wider range of product offerings over time.

The venture dissolves familiar conflicts of interest by running a new business model. It is no longer incentivized to refrain from paying out claims (by binding profits to incurred claims) or increase underwriting profits like traditional insurance providers. Thanks to the use of state-of-the-art technologies, the company can operate cost-effectively and deliver a superior customer experience.

Look Out for More

As new technologies emerge and customer behaviour changes, InsurTech and Disruptive InsurTech startups pursue different approaches with different results.

InsurTech startups improve the current industry structure by being bold at taking the next innovation step, often transferring tech-based solutions from other industries to the insurance sector – as per my earlier example of The Climate Corporation. They drastically improve customer experiences and enable established providers. Some start as digital tech enablers, others as full-stack carriers. Disruptive InsurTech startups take the leap and reinvent the way insurance business is done. They accomplish this by questioning underlying assumptions, re-evaluating them, and creating covers that are different from the known. They apply real-time data and artificial intelligence, cover only what and when it's needed, and link their profits with customer interests.

But this is not the end of the story. The next level of change will lead to unique cooperations among InsurTech startups but also among startups and incumbents. We have already seen this, with KASKO and Snapsure collaborating with the Swiss insurer Baloise, and there are many other relationships that will emerge once this book is published. Perhaps we will see the first example of an InsurTech and Disruptive InsurTech collaboration at the time this book is being published? A new level of new and old world cooperation would undoubtedly guide us into an exciting new era for insurance!

InsurTech
Now and
Next

2

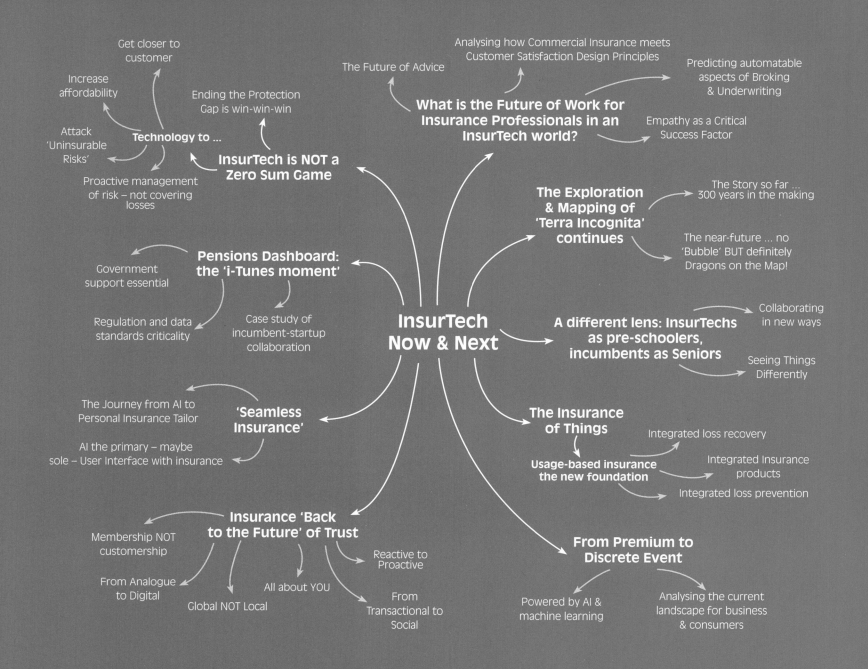

This part presents nine distinctive voices answering the brief "InsurTech Now and Next". Paolo Cuomo's "Cartographer's Dream" describes an analogy of InsurTech as Terra Incognita, a compelling but as yet unmapped world, being discovered, named, and classified beneath our feet. His view of this process of exploration, and what is held in store, does *not* include a bubble that bursts.

John Warburton envisions the impacts on people working in insurance, and specifically those working in Commercial Lines (CL) broking and underwriting. Looking at tech-driven change, Future of Work, Robotic Process Automation, and AI, his five-point action plan to enable CL brokers and underwriters to benefit proactively from technology exhorts them and us to build on their core professional strengths of tacit knowledge and empathy.

Neil Thomson offers up a personal and highly unusual lens to understand InsurTechs and their relationships with incumbents: look at them as preschool infants engaging with seniors, Thomson says, and learn from analogues in society. The next three contributions take the Internet of Things (IoT) – or Insurance of Things (InsoT), as Nick Bilodeau proposes – as the starting point for imagining the Next. Bilodeau posits next generation protection created by digital interconnectedness, integrated insurance products, loss prevention, and recovery support with usage-based insurance as the foundation.

Sylvia Michaelowski gives Personal Lines and Commercial Lines scenarios where insurance evolves, and is evolving, to support customers at specific moments and for specific risks, defined and chosen by them.

Henrique Volpi elaborates on a similar theme, albeit with a particular perspective, describing a "seamless insurance", and an inexorable progress from AI to AI Personal Assistant to Personal Assistant as Personal Tailor. Volpi's vision sees AI becoming the primary, if not sole, user interface (UI).

Yvonne Braun shares the story to date of the development of the UK's Pensions Dashboard Project, the "Tunes moment" for Pensions. The case study illustrates how using methods any InsurTech would recognize (tech sprints, collaboration, transparency, consumer centricity) has created success, but also the importance of regulation and legislation, including on data standards as critical to ultimate implementation.

Susanne Møllegard's chapter presents a positive vision for insurance where technology and coexistence in a sharing economy will bring back trust, and take the whole industry "Back to the Future". Her six mega-trends transforming the insurance sector include membership, social media impact, and digital self-service and global impact.

In the final chapter of this part, Nick Martin urges us to move beyond insular InsurTech debates to seize the opportunity to close both the protection and communication gaps; increase insurance affordability and penetration globally; and make yesterday's uninsurable risks insurable today. "New markets will emerge that expand the overall industry 'pie', not only to the benefit of all market participants, but more importantly, society at large."

A prediction for InsurTech Now and Next that we can all join in striving and hoping for?

A Cartographer's Dream – Exploring, and Mapping, the New Unknown

By Paolo Cuomo
Co-Founder, InsTech London

Overused as it is, the phrase "start of the journey" absolutely fits where the InsurTech world currently finds itself. This new world is so nascent that it was only during 2016 that we actually agreed on the portmanteau of "InsurTech" to describe it. (Having had a brief flirtation with "InsTech", and a minor diversion via "InsureTech".) It's not just the inconsistency in spelling that makes us feel like the cartographers of bygone years, but also the large parts of the map that are still blank. The maritime cartographers' phrase "Here be dragons" feels as apt when defining the roadmap for InsurTech in the early twenty-first century as it did when defining the shape of America and Australia in the sixteenth and seventeenth centuries. The unknown is as bewitching, the discoveries as exciting, the stories as apocryphal; but, fortunately, the dangers somewhat less. Yes, most of the first wave of InsurTech startups will, like Icarus, rise rapidly upwards, before crashing to oblivion, drowning plenty of venture capitalists' money in the blue seas of unachieved customer numbers. And, while those whose dreams are crushed by incumbents (or funding short-falls!) might feel like Britain's Captain Scott freezing to death in the Antarctic in 1912 there will be no real lives lost. Yes, our families may complain they never see us, but we're a quick Facetime away, rather than truly out in unexplored lands; and while a diet of pizza and flat whites may not help our cholesterol, at least the tomato sauce prevents scurvy.

I watched the late-nineties mobile and Internet boom as a somewhat disconnected observer, focusing on early jobs and struggling to name a true entrepreneur beyond Clive Sinclair or Richard Branson. But I'm just loving riding this InsurTech wave, with all the thrill of the hunt but no risk of being gored by a wild boar in a previously unexplored forest.

At the start of 2015 there was no InsurTech. There were indeed some fresh new companies smartly using technology to make a difference in the insurance space. But they were stand-out exceptions, glanced at with a combination of curiosity and confusion – not something that warranted the creation of a new noun. Bought by Many had been going for a while in the UK, having spotted the opportunities of social media to cluster like-minded customers – in effect a clever proxy to "big data analytics". Friendsurance had been operating a tech-enabled peer-to-peer insurance concept in Germany since the start of the decade.[1] InShared was running a "100% internet", "100% self-service" insurance company in the Netherlands.[2] These and other similar companies were blazing a trail, but they were so busy getting on with it that they didn't need a moniker to describe what they were doing. And when asked they simply offered "FinTech for insurance". So we sat there in 2015, at the centre of a multi-trillion-dollar, centuries old industry, seeing (or more appropriately "hearing") the assault of FinTech on the financial services world and wondered "What about us?"

Now, don't let people tell you insurance isn't innovative. Sure, the underlying product has stubbornly remained the same annual policy based on a small number of data points, and on the commercial insurance side, paper is still prevalent, but this is not an industry that doesn't know what technology is. Data analytics has been used since 1744 when life insurance contributions were first calculated by two Scottish clergymen using Jacob Bernelli's cutting-edge "Law of Large Numbers" – leading to what today is the multi-billion Scottish Widows investment company.[3] Commercial insurance had kicked off in London half a century earlier. As London sat at the centre of a global empire, coffee shops had become the social media of their day, and, as in the

---

[1] http://www.friendsurance.com/#section-about.

[2] https://www.linkedin.com/company-beta/575174/.

[3] http://www.the-insurance-network.co.uk/sight/bring-insurance-into-the-digital-age/.

twenty-first century, the network effect kicked in and there could only be a few winners. Edward Lloyd's coffee house on Tower Street became the place for ship owners to congregate and share information and ultimately identify ways to share risk that over time turned into the underwriting of insurance (risk-sharing individuals signed their names under the information about the risk and thus the term underwriter was born).[4]

While many elements of these 300-year-old models remain, the industry (or industries if you consider life insurance, health insurance, personal lines, and commercial lines as significantly different businesses) continues to evolve. Personal lines insurance embraced the Internet well before banking, with comparison websites being one of the big achievements of Web 1.0. There can be much discussion about whether comparison websites – with their focus on price above all else – have helped or hampered the consumers' coverage of their risks, but from a use-of-technology point of view, they were cutting edge. Evolution in commercial lines has been slower on the technology front, but the appetite of smart underwriters to look for ways to underwrite any new risk has always driven innovation. We live in a world of cyber attacks, data breaches, intricately connected supply chains, threats to planes from drones, driverless cars, virtual currencies, and commercial exploration of space, not to mention an increasing volume of "old" risks – catastrophic weather events, political unrest, and the like. Underwriters look for all sorts of ways to understand such risks better, requiring them to master everything from blockchain to firewalls to reusable spacecraft.

With such a dynamic industry, it was clear the "FinTech in insurance" map was not going to stay blank for too long and, indeed, as 2015 progressed the explorers were setting out. InsTech London[5] kicked off in April 2015 with a mere 20 individuals in an overpriced London wine bar. The speed of growth would have made many startups proud. The ecosystem blossomed through a virtuous circle of

explorers ready to head into the unknown, cartographers and ship builders supporting the journeys, and kings, queens, and emperors happy to fund the journeys in return for their share of any treasure. In their day, brave, arrogant, white men such as Columbus, Magellan, and Da Gama headed off funded by European sovereigns. Our wave of explorers is more diverse, often more modest, funded less by royalty and more by venture capital funds and incumbent insurers (plus parents, friends, and crowd-sourcing).

The startups have taken various forms. InsurTech companies, which developed innovative distribution models, are a principal focus on the personal lines side – ranging from chatbot front-ends to UBI (usage-based insurance) via robo-broking. Growing equally rapidly is a range of smart home and telematic products offering owners and insurers more information about their risks – in part as a risk reduction exercise, in part as a form of marketing differentiation. There are a few players looking to build full-stack personal lines insurers and take on the incumbent carriers, with Lemonade as the posterchild in early 2017, but most startups are smart enough to see that partnering with incumbents (especially those looking for ways around the challenges of internal innovation) is an easier way to scale.

On the commercial insurer side there is even less logic to building an end-to-end business. There is the well-trodden route of becoming an MGA (Managing General Agent) if you wish to create your own insurance company, and disrupting a value chain dominated by multi-billion-pound behemoths and nimble niche players is typically more than most want to bite off. Thus, most of the startups are looking to where the value chain is in need of a dose of smart, tech-enabled enhancement. We're seeing exciting point solutions such as low-cost satellite imagery to support the claims process (including views *before* the claim took place) from machine-learning enabled fraud detection, online news-site scraping to enhance underwriters' insight, and IoT-enabled monitoring of just about anything that moves or has sensors. To avoid overwhelming people,

_____

[4] https://en.wikipedia.org/wiki/Underwriting.

[5] www.instech.london.

InsTech London (a networking community I co-founded in 2015) coined the term TRAMBID to cover some of the key technologies – telematics, RPA (robotic process automation), augmented reality, machine learning, blockchain, IOT, and drones – and each of these is becoming increasingly prevalent at multiple points in the underwriting process.

Yes, there is the inevitable talk of bubbles and undoubtedly there are some daft ideas getting irrational funding, and some good ideas that, for a range of reasons, will fail. However, investors learned a lot from Bubble 1.0 and much of the InsurTech investment community "cut their teeth" in the world of FinTech over the last half decade. With the growth of InsurTech-focused investors,[6] and a community that is increasingly corresponding on the various new ideas, it is unlikely that any InsurTech-specific bubble will grow and then burst. Whether a general backlash against robots, AI, and use of data comes to pass, slowing the speed of change is clearly a far bigger question than merely insurance and InsurTech.

The successful explorers of past centuries are remembered as the winners in the canons of their age, while, with the exception of a few heroic failures such as Britain's Captain Scott, the losers rapidly descended into obscurity. As we reflect back in a decade's time on this current wave of frenetic change it will all seem so natural and obvious. Let us not forget, as we stand here right now, that the path yet to tread is shrouded in mist and without doubt "there be dragons" out there.

---

[6] https://www.linkedin.com/pulse/where-money-meets-insurtech-how-our-startups-being-funded-grant.

Where Does InsurTech Leave the People who Work in Insurance?

By John Warburton
Founder, Konsileo

> "Robots will take over most jobs within 30 years, experts warn."
>
> *Daily Telegraph, 13 February 2016*

> "According to our estimates, about 47 percent of total US employment is at risk. We further provide evidence that wages and educational attainment exhibit a strong negative relationship with an occupation's probability of computerization."
>
> *Carl Benedikt Frey and Michael A. Osborne*

> "The future of employment: How susceptible are jobs to computerisation?"
>
> *Oxford University, 2013*

> "If you don't think about and plan for the future of work then your organization has no future."
>
> *Jacob Morgan, The Future of Work, 2014*

The impact of robotic process automation (RPA) and artificial intelligence (AI) on employment is becoming a matter of significant public debate. There are commentators, such as Oxford University's Frey and Osborne, who foresee significant public policy challenges as up to 50% of roles are eliminated. There is also evidence that, especially in the transition, there is a very negative impact on wages, bringing with it further public policy and security challenges.

In some ways, there is room for pessimism. Some foresee a dystopian future where people are subordinate to either the machines themselves, or massive, coercive corporations. Consultants PwC talk about three "worlds" in the future: an "orange world" of small organizations specializing in particular markets or capabilities, a "green world" of companies with strong CSR (corporate and social responsibility) agendas; and a "blue world" of strong and (greedy) corporations. (See PwC, "The Future of Work – A Journey to 2022".) These scenarios are convincing and challenging because we can see the trends already starting, with the end of the "job for life", virtualization of our working lives, always-on technology, and normative changes in working culture.

Insurance, Technology, and the Future of Work

> "We have to accept the fact that our careers no longer go 'up' and we can't depend on one company to take care of us for life."
>
> *Josh Bersin, Forbes.com*

For insurance, technology-driven change has a very mixed history. Insurance was an early adopter of technology in the 1960s and 1970s and, as a result, was one of the first industries to experience the "legacy" challenges of innovating on very complex and difficult to understand processes and systems that were created at that time. As a result, employment in the industry has remained fairly steady, at circa 2.4 m in the US[1] and 305,000 in the UK.[2] We are, however, only part-way through what author Jeremy Rifkin has termed the "Third Industrial Revolution". InsurTech holds the promise of propelling insurance towards what Klaus Schwab, the World Economic Forum founder, has termed the "Fourth Industrial Revolution" where physical, digital, and biological worlds are fused.

---

[1] US Department of Labor, http://www.iii.org/fact-statistic/careers-and-employment.

[2] ABI Key Facts, www.ABI.org.uk.

The "future of work" issue in insurance is particularly difficult to manage, not only because of legacy issues, but also because of the intangible nature of what people in insurance actually do. At its core insurance is a promise to pay money if certain things happen. The insurance industry has grown up because:

- it's challenging to predict the likelihood of things happening (so the actuary came about);

- it's difficult to balance all the various factors and put a price on it (ditto the underwriter);

- it's hard to keep track of all the various promises made (hence IT in insurance);

- people don't know what risks they face (so the broker was needed);

- working out what is a fair compensation following an event is tricky (thus claims/loss adjusters);

- all these people need managers … and so on …

If all these tasks become more straightforward because robots/AI can handle the complex but repetitive elements, then (so the argument goes) the logic for people to be engaged in this work reduces considerably. Many believe that this wave of technology adoption will reduce employment as complexity is reduced and customers' demands for cleaner, low-touch experiences are met by InsurTech. So, what is the future of employment in the industry and which roles will survive and prosper?

The classic framework to understand the impact of "computerization" on work is that developed by Autor et al. in 2003, which is shown in Table 1. It talks about

Table 1: Predictions of task model for the impact of computerization on four categories of workplace tasks

	Routine tasks	Non-routine tasks
	Analytic and interactive tasks	
General Examples	• Record-keeping • Calculation • Repetitive customer service	• Forming/testing hypotheses • Medical diagnosis • Legal writing • Persuading/selling • Managing others
Insurance Examples	• Simple product quotation • Running actuarial models	• Decision making complex claims • Insurance broker fact find • Developing/designing actuarial models
Computer Impact	Substantial substitution	Strong complementarities
	Manual tasks	
General Examples	• Picking or sorting • Repetitive assembly	• Janitorial services • Truck driving
Insurance Examples	• Filing • Writing covernotes	• Bodyshop/repairs • Home emergency services • Installation/configuration IoT
Computer Impact	Substantial substitution	Limited opportunities for substitution or complementarity

Source: After Autor et al., The skill content of recent technological change: an empirical exploration, *Quarterly Journal of Economics*, 2003.
Note: Insurance examples added by author

"complementarities" between IT and various types of work; i.e. where technology enhances the effectiveness and productivity of the tasks as opposed to other tasks where technology can "substantially substitute" for labour. We can also imagine insurance tasks that will be similarly impacted. In broad terms, the routine tasks will tend to disappear and/or attract reduced wages over time while the non-routine tasks continue to attract reasonable remuneration. Since 2003, technology developments in AI will undoubtedly have moved some tasks from the right to the left-hand side of the chart below, e.g. truck driving and maybe medical diagnosis.

The key consideration, however, is that this analysis is conducted at a *task*, not a *role*, level. Obviously if a role exists to fulfil only one highly repeatable task within an industrialized process, then the role itself is at risk if the task is automated. This "deskilling" as a step on the road to an automation process has been a hallmark of much of the operational change in insurance, in common with nineteenth and twentieth century developments in manufacturing. Like more modern manufacturing techniques built on six-sigma and self-organizing teams, insurance organizations are now starting to wake up to the value of empowering teams to manage their own efficiency and effectiveness – this tends to prove particularly effective where tacit knowledge and empathy are most critical. This mix of tacit knowledge and empathy will continue to drive fulfilling careers in insurance.

Commercial Insurance Broking and Underwriting – Technology as Enabler to Excellence

Much of the InsurTech activity in the early wave has focused on accelerating the process of automation of routine activity. The most obvious opportunities for this are in personal lines (i.e. for consumers) where straightforward opportunities for improvement in user experience and efficiency exist. In addition, consumers in many markets have demonstrated that they are willing to self-serve. In the market for commercial insurance, the case is less clear cut and the market is not necessarily automatable, as shown in Figure 1.

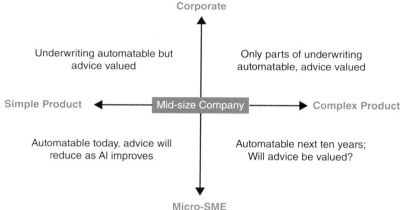

Figure 1: Opportunities for automation

Source: Konsileo, PKF Littlejohn

There are a number of factors that both accelerate and retard the commoditization of commercial insurance underwriting, as shown in Figure 2. In essence, the desire and economic imperative of insurers to actively commoditize the market is retarded by both clients' and brokers' desire to retain human contact in the process as companies get larger and/or more complex.

The slowness of "e-trade" and resistance to commoditization tends to be viewed negatively, but an alternative interpretation is that market participants perceive alternative, non-rational benefits in the current trading relationships. Within this inertia may well be the seeds of a source of enduring strength in the commercial insurance market and employment within it. It suggests that empathy, longstanding relationships, and tacit knowledge have an economic value to clients. In this regard,

Demand side: brokers and clients		Supply side: insurers	
Accelerating factors	Retarding factors	Accelerating factors	Retarding factors
• Increased requirements for automated data exchange with insurer, from brokers • Client self-service takes off, therefore insurers are in control of the entire process • Trading between individual underwriters and brokers is discouraged, through solus and panel arrangements • Increased familiarity with technology	• Broker software houses unable to provide correct data and rich data • Clients with more complex risks value advice and expect wide insurer choice • Open market trading relationships preferred by individual brokers and underwriters • Brokers trust individual underwriters more than the firms they work for, and will follow them if they move insurer	• Insurers seek cost savings • Deployment of Artificial Intelligence to deal with complexity of rating models and expert judgement • Appetite for investment in new technology in commercial rises	• Insurer economics are more sensitive to poor underwriting decisions than higher operating expenses • Data is heterogeneous and there is high complexity of the underlying data set • Investments might focus on automation of the administration processes and leave underwriters in place

Figure 2: Factors affecting commoditization of underwriting in commercial insurance

Source: Konsileo, PKF Littlejohn, "Future of Commercial Insurance Broking", Chartered Insurance Institute, April 2017

the development of the commercial market adheres to the customer satisfaction product design principles of Noriako Kano (Attractive quality and must-be quality, *Journal of the Japanese Society for Quality Control* (in Japanese) 1984), much used by companies such as Amazon and which talk about:

1. **"Must-be attributes"** or threshold requirements that are expected and cause dissatisfaction when not present (e.g. in insurance not losing instructions, accurate documentation).

2. **"One-dimensional attributes"** that cause satisfaction when present and dissatisfaction when absent (e.g. easily contactable insurance broker).

3. **"Attractive attributes (or delighters)"** that are not expected but appreciated (examples could include additional digital tools for clients to understand their risk or additional analysis work undertaken by brokers).

The challenge is that much of the process innovation in the industry has tinkered with "must-be" or "one-dimensional" attributes in order to save cost. This means that many clients see changes in a negative light. Similarly, the relatively small number of "delighters" often become commonplace over time (e.g. claims tracking) and there is not a pipeline of true innovations to sustain delight. This lack of innovation in customer experience, alongside the intrinsically challenging and heterogeneous nature of commercial insurance, goes a long way to explaining the slow take-up of self-serve and new propositions in commercial insurance. Figure 3 sums up the client considerations in evaluating new propositions. Clients balance the convenience versus risk of advice together with their perception of the challenges of self-serving insurance. The risks are perceived as relatively low for small businesses but increase exponentially as businesses get larger.

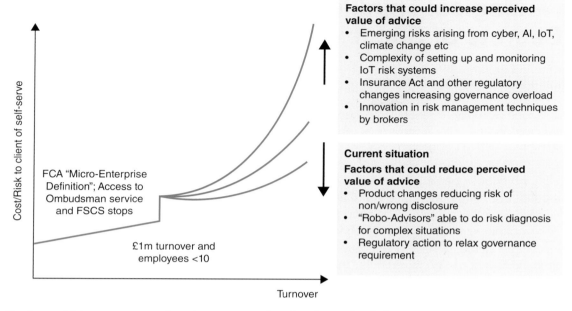

Factors that could increase perceived value of advice
- Emerging risks arising from cyber, AI, IoT, climate change etc
- Complexity of setting up and monitoring IoT risk systems
- Insurance Act and other regulatory changes increasing governance overload
- Innovation in risk management techniques by brokers

Current situation
Factors that could reduce perceived value of advice
- Product changes reducing risk of non/wrong disclosure
- "Robo-Advisors" able to do risk diagnosis for complex situations
- Regulatory action to relax governance requirement

FCA "Micro-Enterprise Definition"; Access to Ombudsman service and FSCS stops

£1m turnover and employees <10

Cost/Risk to client of self-serve

Turnover

Figure 3: **Factors that could increase and reduce perceived value of advice**
Source: Konsileo, PKF Littlejohn

Manifesto for the Individual Broker or Underwriter

The impact of technology on the careers of individual underwriters and insurance brokers means that they should:

1. Develop skills that require creativity and tacit knowledge in execution (i.e. are not routine).

2. Have client relationships that rely on empathy, not just on an asymmetry of information or market access.

3. Use technology to help them deliver client value by either delighting clients with the technology or freeing up time for empathetic interactions.

4. Use data to support judgements and expertise development.

5. Be flexible in the way they work, where they work, and in their relationships with colleagues.

Insurance broking and underwriting – the people who work in insurance – have every chance to become the professional service that they strive to emulate. However, a transformation in the attitude of practitioners to their role and in the support that they get from the organizations they work for will be required.

InsurTechs – Magical Thinking and Other Secrets of Success

By Neil Thomson
Strategic Sales Director, Freelance InsurTech Consultant

Much has been written about the disruptive threat of InsurTech and how traditional insurance as we know it will come to an abrupt end. I don't believe this to be true, in fact I think the opposite. I see InsurTechs mixing it up with insurers, producing some very exciting opportunities. Insurance has never been better and the future of insurance is looking very good! But, is this really the case? Can InsurTechs and the traditional insurer thrive together, be stronger together, grow together? This chapter explores the InsurTech vs. insurer relationship from a different perspective, and discusses the wide spectrum of opportunities that can be driven out of this collaboration. Using shared experience and learnings, barriers to innovation can be overcome to deliver better customer propositions.

The development of InsurTech continues to accelerate at a pace and the impact on insurance and wider communities is now a global phenomenon. Although InsurTech doesn't have an official birth certificate as such, the term InsurTech is thought to have been first used in July 2015.[1] This means we can successfully date InsurTech at the time of writing as being just over two years old. It may feel that InsurTech has been around for a long time but it's only just blown the candles out on its second birthday cake! We refer to humans just over two years old as "preschool infants".[2] I believe there are a lot of shared characteristics between infants and InsurTechs, and that analysing these shared characteristics (see Table 1) can give us great insight into understanding how InsurTechs have become so successful.

Table 1: Developmental characteristics shared between InsurTechs and infants

Behavioural Characteristics	Infants	InsurTechs
Very demanding	Y	Y
Know what they want	Y	Y
More importantly, know what they DON'T want	Y	Y
Immediate gratification, want it NOW, not tomorrow	Y	Y
Imagination runs wild, demonstrate use of "magical thinking"	Y	Y
No boundaries or limitations when it comes to idea generation	Y	Y
Challenge the status quo and ask Why? Why? Why?	Y	Y
Fast and agile	Y	Y
Don't take "no" for an answer	Y	Y
Limited patience	Y	Y
Focused on the present and future NOT the past	Y	Y

As you can see, quite a lot of these developmental characteristics are shared between InsurTechs and infants. These behavioural characteristics go a long way to explain the successful "rise and rise" of InsurTechs.[3] They know what their customers want, their imagination runs wild, they are not patient, and they always challenge the status quo. If comparing infant and InsurTech characteristics gives us insight into their success, what about looking at traditional insurer characteristics? Bearing in mind that some insurers are over 300 years old and therefore "off the scale" in terms of human development milestones, if InsurTechs can be likened to two-year-old infants then perhaps we should

---

[1] http://www.instech.club/wp-content/uploads/2016/10/SBC-InsurTech-PwC-InsurTech-Trend-Report-.pdf.

[2] https://www.willistowerswatson.com/en/insights/2017/05/quarterly-insurtech-briefing-Q1-2017.

[3] http://www.slideshare.net/FTPartners/ft-partners-research-prepare-for-the-insurtech-wave.

be comparing insurers with seniors! Perhaps describing insurers as seniors goes part of the way to explaining their current challenges. Being a senior is no bad thing: seniors are well established, have the benefit of experience, have the benefit of hindsight, and therefore generally know what works and what doesn't work. Although the benefit of experience is a strong one, insurers are being held back in other ways, notably by ageing legacy technology systems. These ageing legacy systems may have been fit for purpose in the late nineties (the era of Netscape browsers, Palm pilots, mini-disc players, and Tamagotchi) but they struggle to compete in today's world, let alone tomorrow's.

Insurers do know what their customers want but they struggle to react, and are not agile; they are often weighed down by heavy cost bases, bureaucracy, and legacy technology. One way in which insurers are hurdling these barriers is by mixing it up, with InsurTechs and working together. Digital Partners, Munich Re's global venture established in May 2016, has established partnerships with nine companies: Blink, Bought By Many, Jetty, Next Insurance, Simple Insurance, Slice, So Sure, Trov, and Wrisk. In 2017, Aviva Ventures invested £5m in Neos, the first company to combine smart home technology with home insurance in the UK.

What can 300-year-old insurers learn from three-year-old InsurTechs?

Before examining this further, I'd like to highlight a wonderful example from outside insurance – indeed outside business – of how mixing up groups can produce opportunities. The Providence Mount St Vincent care home in Seattle is both a care home for the elderly and a preschool nursery. Five days a week, children aged from six weeks to five years interact with Mount St Vincent's residents, whose average age is 92. Activities range from musical hour to story time to art classes. Workers at the care centre describe having the whole spectrum of life present and describe it as a joy and challenge to always be together.[4] The mixture of preschool infants completely transforms the elderly residents, stimulating mental and physical activities. The infants are happy, comfortable, and innovative, always coming up with new ideas to play, have fun, and be happy. A movie entitled *The Growing Season* released in 2017, has been made about Providence Mount St Vincent. The movie title is a reference to the fact that these two groups of people – the preschoolers and the seniors – come together so perfectly well in the "present state". This to my mind is similar to the mixing together of InsurTechs and traditional insurers. The InsurTechs are agile, inquisitive, and their imagination is not held back; they are constantly challenging the status quo and developing new and better propositions. The characteristic of asking "why? why? why?" is a dominant feature in their approach to disrupting the existing insurer model. And, despite a general perception that InsurTechs are a threat to traditional insurance, there are many examples of collaboration between the seniors and infants, generating value through the development of new propositions. Industry leaders like MetLife, Aviva, AXA, Allianz, and XL Catlin have recognized the importance of collaborative efforts, launching dedicated incubators.

When considering the insurance landscape cocktail, InsurTechs and insurers are not the *only* ingredients to throw into the mix. We also need to consider the entrepreneurs and investors. There's currently a tremendous investor interest in InsurTech and investors – following the money! The mixing of investors and entrepreneurs; the InsurTech upstarts and their wild imaginations; and traditional insurers, with their extensive customer base and large financial backing, makes a perfect cocktail and the financial gains potentially massive. Investors are looking for companies to create value by solving big problems and not just tinkering around the edges of an existing insurance company or systems. Investors will follow the money and invest where they see large potential gains. With a proliferation of new ideas and new startups, the companies with big ideas that can produce a step change will be chosen by the investors in an "X Factor" fashion. The ideas or companies with

─────────────

[4] http://www.seattletimes.com/seattle-news/education/retirement-home-meets-day-care-at-providence-mount-st-vincent/.

this "X Factor" will be chosen to be coached and nurtured. The others will be asked to "go home" or walk the lonely path of trying to "go it alone". InsurTechs and investors are keen to prospect every link in the insurance chain and no doubt this will lead to much wider disruption. InsurTechs and their new propositions will dig deep to extract costs and improve the customer experience, simplifying all processes, lessening friction, empowering and delighting customers, and even making the claims process pleasurable. Walking through London in Spring 2017 with my children, I saw for the first time "The Thumb". Artist David Shrigley's sculpture is a 23-foot-high hand with a long thumb cast in bronze, and was occupying the fourth plinth in Trafalgar Square. It's proper name is "Really Good"; the sculpture represents positivity and the best of us, and is designed to present a message of optimism, about making the world a better place. I think Shrigley's "The Thumb" neatly summarizes the current InsurTech and insurance landscape: it's all about positivity, and making the world a better place, through imagination and expertise.

"INSoT" – The Insurance of Things and the Proliferation of Protection

By Nick Bilodeau
Head of Marketing, Insurance, Canada, American Express

The insurance industry is about to get a lot more interesting. Much has been written in recent years about the increasing integration of the Internet, technology, and data into all parts of life and everyday objects.[1,2,3] And beyond the literature, looking at what's already in the market, it's quickly becoming apparent that this will profoundly change the way we live. From FitBit activity trackers and Nest learning thermostats, to even smart fridges that provide real-time grocery lists and smart mirrors that offer customized skincare routines, we're already beginning to get an early glimpse of what's to come.

So, what does this all have to do with insurance? Over time, this growing digital interconnection – commonly referred to as the Internet of Things (IoT) – will have a knock-on effect, enabling a wide range of value-adding benefits and services across many industries as it continues to evolve. Insurance will ultimately be a part of these benefiting industries and will increasingly become more broadly integrated into our day-to-day lives – in

what could by extension be referred to as the "Insurance" of Things (or INSoT).

An INSoT world will bring about the next generation of protection. It will be a world in which sensors, real-time big data, and advanced analytics blend with policy-holder profiles to produce a more profound and holistic understanding of customers, their environments, and risks in need of coverage. This deeper level of understanding and interconnectivity will in turn support the broader delivery of protection and risk mitigation, whether in new forms of insurance products, loss prevention, or recovery support.

Integrated Insurance Products

On the product side, our device-oriented and data-sharing society will enable insurers seamlessly to provide consumers with ongoing opportunities for protection. Product offerings will be personalized and relevant, and many will be built to also help influence behaviour positively and improve lives.

Take Usage Based Insurance (UBI) for instance. Though UBI has been around for over a decade,[4] advances in technology are expected to significantly increase market penetration, moving UBI from a small niche to the commonplace and making "pay-as-you-drive" much more prevalent over the next decade.[5] Mobile apps and factory-installed telematics in cars will help layer live driving behaviour data into driving histories and provide more customized rates tailored to an individual's own driving habits. Leading auto insurers like Progressive, Allstate, and State Farm already have

[1] A. T. Kearney, Internet of Things 2020: A glimpse into the future, https://www.atkearney.com/documents/4634214/6398631/A.T.+Kearney_Internet+of+Things+2020+Presentation_Online.pdf/af7e6a55-cde2-4490-8066-a95664efd35a.

[2] EY, Internet of Things: human-machine interactions that unlock possibilities, http://www.ey.com/Publication/vwLUAssets/ey-m-e-internet-of-things/$FILE/ey-m-e-internet-of-things.pdf;

[3] PwC, Sensing the future of the Internet of Things, http://www.pwc.com/us/en/increasing-it-effectiveness/assets/future-of-the-internet-of-things.pdf; McKinsey & Company, Internet of Things, http://www.mckinsey.com/global-themes/internet-of-things/our-insights.

[4] Constandinos X. Mavromoustakis et al. (eds), *Advances in Mobile Cloud Computing and Big Data in the 5G Era* (2017).

[5] Usage-based insurance expected to grow to 142 million subscribers globally by 2023, IHS says, http://news.ihsmarkit.com/press-release/automotive/usage-based-insurance-expected-grow-142-million-subscribers-globally-2023-i.

programs in place and many others are following suit.[6] UBI is also expected to increase accessibility by allowing previously uninsurable or difficult to insure drivers to get coverage through new monitored coverage programs. Such programs will help teach these drivers better driving behaviours and in turn give them the opportunity to earn better premiums.

In life and health, wearables will make possible ongoing risk profiling and "pay-as-you-live" pricing. Life insurance policies, for instance, will not only provide protection and peace of mind, but also help you live longer. Leveraging gamification principles and technology, policies will be designed with dynamic premiums that vary based on factors like eating habits (gleaned and tracked through food content recognition apps), as well as activity levels and vital signs, captured and tracked through connected health devices. Early forms of this are currently available, with carriers such as John Hancock and Zurich having programs that offer discounts for meeting fitness targets and adopting other health benefiting activities.[7,8]

And as digitally derived efficiencies in distribution, underwriting, and administration reduce costs and improve integration with other industries, we'll also see a significant growth in on-demand small-

ticket insurance offerings. From locking in low gas prices at the pump to getting incremental life coverage at the airport minutes before take-off, highly personalized and context-relevant solutions will be woven into everyday life.

Integrated Loss Prevention

But data in an INSoT context won't only be leveraged to better understand customer needs and offer personalized products. Just as importantly, it will be put to use to drive early loss detection and risk prevention, and ultimately to reduce the frequency and severity of accidents and claims. Connected cars, homes, health devices, and the ability to connect virtually anything else will allow for real-time monitoring, feedback, and mitigating measures.

This is where the lines defining roles and responsibilities around prevention will get increasingly blurred across industries. It's where partnerships between very different types of organizations will become a lot more prevalent. And it's also where insurance companies will need to evolve the most – from being reactive payers of claims to proactive and collaborative providers of loss prevention support.

Beyond influencing prevention through product and pricing constructs, insurance companies will work directly and indirectly with manufacturers, tech firms, utility companies, public sector entities, and a variety of other organizations to gradually form an intricate network of risk mitigating functionalities. Together, they'll implement ongoing monitoring systems, anticipate and identify potential problems, and then proactively address them before customers are even alerted of any issues. A good example of an initial start on this type of ecosystem within the property insurance space is a recent partnership between Willis Towers Watson, a global risk management, insurance brokerage, and advisory company, and Roost, a smart home technology company. Together, the

[6] NY Times, Lower your car insurance bill, at the price of some privacy, https://www.nytimes.com/2014/08/16/your-money/auto-insurance/tracking-gadgets-could-lower-your-car-insurance-at-the-price-of-some-privacy.html; Usage based insurance global market grew by 32% in 2016 to 14 million policies, says PTOLEMUS UBI Quarterly Dashboard, http://www.businesswire.com/news/home/20170518005743/en/Usage-Based-Insurance-Global-Market-Grew-32-2016.

[7] PR Newswire, John Hancock introduces a whole new approach to life insurance in the U.S. that rewards customers for healthy living, http://www.prnewswire.com/news-releases/john-hancock-introduces-a-whole-new-approach-to-life-insurance-in-the-us-that-rewards-customers-for-healthy-living-300062461.html;

[8] Life insurance customers to get cash back for meeting health goals, http://www.irishtimes.com/business/technology/life-insurance-customers-to-get-cash-back-for-meeting-health-goals-1.3102980.

two companies plan to create a home telematics consortium with other organizations to help the industry make the most of IoT. The consortium will focus on aggregating and analysing household data in order to determine how effective home telematics devices are in reducing water and fire related damage.[9]

What kind of innovations might we ultimately see as a result of new loss prevention ecosystems? We could see things like weather report feeds and home foundation humidity instruments working together to keep an eye on an approaching thunderstorm. They could, for instance, regulate a connected basement sump pump should water levels rise too quickly and notify homeowners, plumbers, and an adjudicator to minimize and document damage if something fails.

We could also see commercial transportation fleets further leverage telematics and sensors to better monitor vehicle mechanical components and geolocations to enhance maintenance servicing. For example, sensors could identify engine troubles and trigger maintenance stops, which could be automatically scheduled and remotely coordinated while vehicles are on the road, in order to prevent breakdowns and potential traffic accidents. Though the full integration required to make this happen isn't yet available, companies like Cisco and Sierra Systems are already providing notable fleet solutions[10] that help transportation companies track vehicles, monitor items like tyre pressure, as well as map and reconfigure routes.

---

[9] Willis Towers Watson and Roost to establish home telematics consortium of U.S. carriers, https://www.willistowerswatson.com/en/press/2017/05/willis-towers-watson-roost-establish-home-telematics-consortium.

[10] Cisco Fleet Management Solution, https://www.cisco.com/c/dam/en/us/products/collateral/se/internet-of-things/at-a-glance-c45-735852.pdf; Leveraging the IoT Revolution in Fleet Management, https://www.sierraw-ireless.com/applications/automotive-and-transport/fleet-management/#/Fleet%20Management.

Integrated Recovery Support

A data-driven insurance industry will also give rise to enhanced claims service levels and more proactive incident management. The aim will be to help relieve customers of much of the effort associated with claims submission through the use of automation and simpler processes.

As smart objects, smart contracts, and blockchain technology take hold over the coming five to ten years, we could see things like claims submissions, diagnosis, reporting, and service provider coordination become fully automated. This would result in speedier processing, payments, and recovery, not to mention increased transparency and customer satisfaction.

As an example, the same sensors that will facilitate UBI and incentivize safer driving will also be leveraged to notify third parties should an accident occur. They'll detect the incident, send for help (e.g. an ambulance, the police, a tow truck), and then convey the right information to the right people (e.g. who's in the vehicle, medical histories, emergency contacts, etc.). Drones could then be used to begin claims adjusting by assessing the scene and taking pictures to document damage (something that's already being piloted by some insurers). Should an injury be involved, a medical claim would automatically be submitted, loss of income coverage initiated, and appointments with rehabilitation specialists scheduled.

What's Next?

While we've only scratched the surface on the impact IoT will eventually have on the insurance industry, it's clear there's a lot of change to come. And though technology will eventually enable this pervasive and seamless integration of insurance into our daily lives and though we've already begun to see some of the changes take place, it will take time for it to materialize fully. It will require widespread, real-time big data integration across a broad spectrum of diverse but interrelated products and services. What's more, historically slow to change regulations and privacy controls in some regions will ultimately need to be adjusted to accommodate a substantially different approach to and level of information exchange. Fortunately (or unfortunately for the unprepared), we're not talking about decades, but rather over the next five to ten years. And in some cases, we may even come to see some regions speed up adoption by mandating elements of INSoT, such as UBI, as they prove to lead to higher levels of safety.

The course of these changes will also alter industry dynamics. In addition to insurers establishing operating partnerships across other traditionally unrelated industries like manufacturing and retail and expanding into newly developed parts of the market, such as geolocation software development and sensor analytics, they'll also be confronted by new competitors – likely data-proficient entrants and common household names like Google, Amazon, or Facebook. To cope, some insurers will seek to specialize and narrow their focus as the scope of insurance broadens. Others will leverage scale, grow with the expanding value chain, and seek to develop missing capabilities in order to properly compete. For some these capabilities will be developed in-house. For others they'll involve unique acquisitions and mergers between insurers and, most likely, tech companies.

Whatever the approach and exact path to bringing INSoT to reality, we're certain eventually to see an industry that is completely reimagined and forever transformed.

From Insurance Premium to Discrete Event

By Sylvia A. Michalski
Strategic Advisor, S. Michalski Consulting

The insurance industry, $4+ trillion globally according to a 2016 global insurance markets report published by Allianz,[1] is considered to be one that hasn't changed for over 75 years, with companies developing newer business models focusing on the areas of distribution, policy comparison, and coverage. Consumers often purchase insurance policies, whether home, life, auto, etc., paying premiums without an understanding of what their policies covered or excluded. Businesses also purchase various insurance policies to cover their operations, whether for general liability, errors and omissions, etc. They can insure themselves on a very broad level to mitigate risk. Startups in the UK, US, China, and Germany are showing alternative ways to have insurance coverage: buying groups; pay-by-mile for autos; crisis crowdfunding; social risks (marriage, child safety); this includes paying back a portion of premiums. London-based Bought By Many, an InsurTech firm that uses social media and search data to sell insurance, focuses on consumers' insurance (via buying insurance as collective groups) for specific requirements such as pet insurance, gadget insurance, or private health insurance. Startups are also focusing on creating new offerings for business buyers, small and large, with better digital offerings, and focusing on specific sectors, from insuring startups in their specific growth phase, or focusing on specific occupations and sectors such as consultants, restaurants, etc.[2] Examples of companies offering differentiated insurance offerings include:

- Metromile – US startup offering consumers to pay by the mile to drive their vehicle.
- Lemonade – US startup offering consumers to buy insurance paying into a common claims pool offering to pay unclaimed pools to the customer's charity or social cause.
- TongJuBao – Chinese startup offering peer risk sharing in such areas as family marriage, missing children, and family unity.
- Insureon – US startup offering digital insurance offerings to small-to-medium businesses providing quotes within 15 minutes to various industry verticals such as retail, restaurants, IT, consulting, health care, to name only a few.

What is clear about the newer companies offering target insurance offerings is that consumers will be able to focus on direct needs when necessary, as opposed to having no option but to accept blanket coverage that leads potentially to overcoverage. Metromile targets low mileage drivers, stating the 65% of all drivers overpay to subsidize high mileage drivers, potentially saving their target customer up to US$500 yearly.

The insurance industry is moving from general coverage to discrete events, whether this means covering only specific areas, for example, life events, and allowing consumers and businesses the benefit of insurance coverage while managing premium costs.

Evolving Insurance Options – Consumer Discrete Events

New business models are offering consumers alternative insurance coverage simply based on a unique personal situation tied to a discrete event taking place, whether for a day, a month, or other, exclusively *consumer-defined* time parameter. Specific consumer scenarios listed here illustrate the ever-changing options available, but in truth the scenarios are endless (subject to specific national and state regulatory restrictions):

---

[1] Kathrin Brandmeir, Dr Michaela Grimm, Dr Arne Holzhausen of Allianz, Global Insurance Markets – Current status and outlook up to 2026.

[2] 2015 BAIN Global Digital Insurance Benchmarking.

- Air travellers who fly infrequently, frequently, or take multiple-leg trips
As an air traveller, should I insure any flight that I take or all flights or insure those that are likely to be cancelled or delayed? Will I have the data to be informed, whether about weather, the carrier's operations record, or other events that may impact flight cancellations and/or delays to influence my decision to purchase insurance coverage or not?

- Car drivers who drive infrequently or frequently
Should I seek insurance coverage for part-time driving based on number of hours or number of miles? Does the premium cost truly take into account my driving record or driving area to determine the likelihood of an accident or theft? Should I require someone who borrows my car to pay to insure themselves whether they drive the car for two hours or a day? Should I insure my vehicle as part of a group?

- Renters or homeowners who have varying amounts of personal possessions
What should I insure – all personal possessions or specific ones? Should I purchase buyers' assurance coverage on newly purchased items, or not even consider? Should I seek insurance coverage to qualify for a rental lease with or without a co-signer? There are some good examples of InsurTech already at work for consumers in this way. Insurer AXA has worked with several European startups to offer more innovative coverage for consumers, including French carpooling insurance startup BlaBlaCar, Spanish home exchange community MyTwinPlace, and peer-to-peer German insurer Friendsurance.

Evolving Insurance Options – Business Discrete Events

New insurance companies like Germany-based Simplesurance Group and US Next Insurance offer businesses digital platforms to shop and compare insurance policy options, including offering specialization in specific professions. More innovative insurance companies such as AXA are offering coverage based on parametric policies to insure against specific weather events for several industries. With the deployment of sophisticated models and analytics, insurance carriers may begin to offer businesses insurance based on specific discrete events defined as those with the likelihood of causing operational hindrance and financial loss, among other areas. The Climate Insurance Group LLS owned by US-based Climate Corporation offers parametric insurance policies reducing farmers' risks by crossing agriculture with big data analytics. The following list identifies some specific business scenarios illustrating real business need for the insurance buyer, and which may become available in the insurance-buying process:

- Weather events – forecasted events or natural disasters
As an agricultural business, do we insure against all forecasted weather events or some in case of drought or excess rainfall? As a retail business, do we insure for the potential impact of weather on seasonal sales? Should countries plan for natural disasters to finance funds post-catastrophe for some, or all, weather events?

- Security events – internal and external
Businesses face disruption to operations from internal and external events, whether hackers attempting to steal information and customer data or employees committing company policy violations. Do businesses start to insure for cybersecurity even if they have installed the most sophisticated infrastructure that would likely prevent such attacks?

Businesses routinely insure themselves with policies covering cyber liability, general liability, key officers, and directors' and officers' liability because this is mandatory. The analogy is similar to consumer scenarios, though: how much coverage is needed and what is the likelihood that discrete events will take place? There are some good examples of InsurTech supporting commercial insurance in this way: Indio, a US-based startup, developed a workflow management platform for traditional commercial insurance brokers that automates the manual processes of retrieving quotes from different carriers and processing insurance applications from clients. Brokers utilizing the Indio platform gain access to a connected commercial insurance marketplace, centralized quoting, and digital tools to interact with the end-client.

Today's evolving insurance, powered by data and analytics, gives multiple options and coverage (full or partial) for consumers and businesses to mitigate risk. Established insurance companies are partnering more frequently with startups to offer better digital experiences – it's happening here and now. However, as technology in AI and machine learning take greater precedence and are more widely adopted, even more sophisticated models will be developed to offer highly-specialized insurance coverage for consumers and businesses alike. The journey from insurance premium to discrete event will be complete, but it is most definitely already part of InsurTech: Now and Next.

Further reading

CB Insights, The insurers most actively investing in startups across the Internet of Things, 10 May 2016.

CB Insights, Who's who in the rise of small business insurance tech startups, InsurTech Insights, 22 November 2016.

Peter G. Colis, The new-world insurance agent, Techcrunch.com, 16 April 2016.

Sam Friedman, Insurance is ready for an upgrade, TechCrunch.com, 10 July 2016.

Jean-Francois Gasc, Insurtech point the way to major changes in the insurance industry with their internet of things, The Accenture Insurance Blog, 15 November 2016.

Elena Mesropyan, 31 P2P insurance startups capitalizing on the power of virtual communities, Let's Talk Payments, 25 January 2017.

Esther Val, Meet the insurers of the sharing economy business model, Sharetribe.com, Marketplace Academy, 1 March 2017.

Seamless Insurance: The Time is Now

By Henrique Volpi
Author, InsurTech Entrepreneur and Co-Founder, Kakau

The connected world and digital transformation is impacting every industry. The insurance industry is no exception and encounters its own revolution now. From peer-to-peer platforms, on-demand contracts, and wearable devices, the focus has shifted significantly to the user and the user experience. For hundreds of years the industry was somewhat provider-centric – the concerns centred around loss ratio and profitability. And for hundreds of years the relationship was analogue, bureaucratic, and unfriendly. From the customer's perspective the system is entirely broken: policies are expensive, claims processes are long and complex, and it takes too long for the customer to get paid. There is no trust between incumbents and their customers. In the case of commercial customers, a significant share of the claims regulation ends up being discussed in arbitration boards.

InsurTechs are starting to change this scenario, providing new products, digital channels, and an approach overtly centred around the user experience. Customers are becoming "users" and benefiting from the digital transformation with blockchain, machine learning, chatbots, and cloud-based solutions such as Lemonade, Trov, and Oscar. What comes next? *Seamless Insurance*. Deriving from the term "Seamless Banking" first coined in 2015 by futurist Anders Sorman-Nilsson,[1] we envision a "Seamless Insurance" concept, where one should be able to sign for on-demand policies on the go, with dynamic pricing and through fully digital channels. Since every possible appliance with which you interact is connected, you will buy your car insurance in your car just before you set off on the drive; get travel insurance at the terminal before you travel; and home insurance through your connected refrigerator when you learn about a possible thunderstorm. Seamless Insurance does not require the customer to visit or engage with a branch office, agent, bank, or retail store.

It is easy to foresee how seamless the experience would be for banking or insurance in a hyper-connected world with virtual reality, beacons, drones, and augmented reality. Imagining your brain being integrated with an AI platform, which will enable you not only to order an insurance product, but also to calculate relevant risks, values, and options, is perhaps harder – but will be a reality by the mid-2020s.[2] That AI-driven seamless insurance journey has already started with automated bots replacing error-prone and process-driven tasks, in many cases very repetitive ones such as claims and servicing tasks, initially on the consumer side and then in more complex commercial lines, where humans interact with machines. Indeed, the claims process is a clear candidate for full automation with no human intervention required long term, using chatbots and bots in general as enabling technology in addition to robotic process automation. Lemonade in the US; Trov in Australia, the US, and the UK; and Zhong An Insurance in China are good examples of where advanced technologies are used to transform processing experiences. Various startups are integrating the bots with machine learning platforms and anti-fraud solutions creating a much faster and better user experience and achieving even greater results for the insurers in terms of rates of fraud. Lemonade combines these capabilities to settle customer claims in three seconds. The claims bot is not only replacing entire teams through advanced predictions and analytics, but also providing a digitally enabled experience from one single place of interactions. Most large insurance incumbents do not have anti-fraud solutions of this sophistication, exclusively dedicated to the digital channel. This makes such bot-led solutions an obvious choice for differentiation in the world of digital.

[1] https://www.youtube.com/watch?v=Nn0HckduXOc and http://www.speakersconnect.com/anders-sorman-nilsson/.

[2] www.neuralink.com.

AI as Insurance PA

As chatbot solutions evolve with the enhancements of machine learning-led platforms, they start to move up the value chain to deliver enhanced customer engagements while relying less on humans. By initially automating necessary but tedious process tasks, bots are gradually becoming assistants for every necessary task. Information, policy changes, and cancellations along with the claims process will become natural tasks to be executed with the help of "chatbot solutions". However, in this evolving scenario, since every piece of interaction now is being performed via a digital medium, and the data are constantly being stored and analysed, the bot will then give advice around products, dates, risks, and opportunities, like mega digital comparison helpers or robo-advisors within the parameters of regulatory frameworks. We can imagine that just as you hire an Uber car to go to the airport, the insurance PA is going to propose that you get coverage for your trip to the airport, even if the car is using its autonomous driving option. As you approach boarding, the PA will offer travel insurance for you, and any family members travelling with you. Because all relevant big data and the digital footprint are simultaneously and instantaneously analysed, the PA will curate the product with very specific coverage for malaria since your vacations include a stop in areas of risk in South America. It is even more powerful to have the PA integrated with your past interactions with other providers (including former insurer incumbents' legacy systems).

PA as Tailor

That is where analogue meets digital: where your current digital behaviour and past interactions intersect. Integrating the current digital data with the historical, your PA will be able to offer a specific dynamic price based on your profile, and yours alone. Group risks will be long gone; products will be tailor-made, informed by huge quantities of relevant data, to meet the very specific needs of that unique individual. This means that users should benefit from a great reduction in premium cost, since individuals subsidizing a specific age or risk group will no longer exist. Dynamic pricing with the use of online telemetry and big data is a game changer for both the user and

the insurer. This augmented insurance experience will mean nothing less than the process of retiring actuarial science as we know it. Let us all call this new actuarial science Actuarial Science 2.0 – where pricing make sense!

AI as the New UI

From interacting with your vehicle, to ordering insurance products for potential future default to your microwave, there is no real limitation to the augmented insurance experience. AI in insurance becomes the new user interface. Customers will rely on their PA – most likely giving it a charming name – for all customer experiences and tasks to be accomplished. In fact, it becomes a much better experience, since the PA knows everything about you, whether historical or online contextual data. It is thus able to provide the best recommendations for you and you alone. This is what we call true personalization. On the flip side, traditional insurers and InsurTechs will attract your PA's attention by focusing on the exact criteria of the segment to which you belong with solutions or products that are presented exactly when needed and supported with the most precise pricing. Consumers will benefit from a fluid offer-response process to acquire new relevant products coming to market; providers will acquire customers faster and retain customers better through the increased precision of their interactions.

What about Seamless Insurance for Commercial Insurance?

AI for Precision Agricultural Insurance is a great example of the possibilities. We have already seen early entrants such as The Climate Corporation. More recent innovations have emerged with the likes of Farm Dog, Farmers Edge, and Aerobotics.[3] In the race to chase greater agricultural production, variety of

---

[3] http://farmdog.ag/; www.farmersedge.ca/.

technologies are becoming key drivers to improve production volume and quality, support more precise underwriting, or eliminate irrelevant activities in the claims environment. Think of IoT devices, intelligent apps, drones monitoring, and satellite imagery helping producers make real-time decisions regarding every aspect of their land and cropping. Precision Agriculture will help the world produce better quality crops in larger volumes. However, as farmers know, there are no guarantees of success in the farming business: every year, extreme weather and disease have a significant impact on crops. Agriculture is in fact a multi-year business. So insurance is paramount for producers to keep their business healthy when outside factors such as tornados can destroy their production in an instant. AI integrating with existing Precision Agricultural technologies, and an insurer's operational systems, could not only disseminate fairer prices based on location, geography, and production patterns, but also provide valuable recommendations to predict future requirements around crops and pest control. Precision Agricultural needs a range of Precision Insurance offerings that captures the history of production but also incorporates real-time telemetry to better service the industry.

The Time is Now

While they may sometimes look as if they come from sci-fi books, technologies that allow seamless and frictionless interactions are already available and used in many adjacent sectors. The only challenge is that they are actually used in silos. Our experience of using Facebook M's chatbot, Echo's Alexa, and Jawbone's wearables is becoming gradually ubiquitous. So the challenge for insurers and innovators is how properly to curate these different pieces and, more importantly, work out how you design the architecture to deliver Seamless Insurance. There is no one correct answer. Companies are likely to be going through a process of trial and error, resulting in some inevitable mistakes. When you have the user at the centre of your process and product design, it may take longer to achieve the right outcomes, but better products and solutions will be built as a result. Insurers and innovators should take advantage of emerging technologies and fluid on-demand workforces, and be the catalyst of a profound economic transformation. The time is now.

The Potential of a Pension Dashboard Infrastructure for UK Pension Savers

By Yvonne Braun
Director of Long Term Savings, ABI

Voice-controlled, AI-enabled technology is fundamentally reshaping our experiences of shopping, entertainment, consuming information, and using financial services.[1] The UK FinTech industry is one of the most innovative in the world, and seen by government as an important part of building a highly-skilled, highly-productive economy, and helping consumers make full use of their own data.[2]

Yet this wave of innovation and open data seems largely absent from retirement savings. Of course, some pension companies have developed snazzy apps, such as MyAviva, to pick just one example, making it much more straightforward for their customers to get up-to-date information about their pension savings and offering useful tools to help with decision-making. But much customer interaction in the pension space is still paper-based, particularly in the world of trust-based and defined benefit (final salary) pension schemes.

This was not necessarily a problem in a world where people spent decades in a job, and where final salary schemes were the norm for many workers. Back then, a worker could retire in one month, receive their last pay slip, and receive their first final salary pension payment the next month, with virtually no need to engage with the process. But the labour market in the UK has changed fundamentally over recent decades. Outside the public sector, defined contribution (DC) schemes are now the norm, and membership of DC schemes has now eclipsed the membership of defined benefit (DB) schemes.[3] The government's auto-enrolment reforms introduced in 2012 mean that all employers must set up and pay into a workplace pension scheme for their workers. This extremely successful policy means that at the time of writing there are over 7 million new savers in workplace pensions, estimated to rise to 10 million by the time the policy is fully rolled out in 2019.

This means millions of pension pots are created as people move jobs, and every new employer automatically enrols them into their pension scheme. The government estimates that people will have 11 different jobs throughout their career so many people will potentially gather 11 or more different pension pots in the process. The ABI's very conservative estimate is that there are currently well over 60 million pension pots in the UK. As pensions are rarely at the forefront of people's minds, and even less so when moving to a new house, many lose track of their pension savings. The Department for Work and Pensions estimates that there is about £400 million in lost pension money.[4]

In addition to this macro backdrop, there are also universal, well-established behavioural factors that work against engagement with pensions: present bias and ostrich behaviour mean we don't like to engage with difficult decisions about the long term – and making decisions about saving for retirement is a perfect example of that.[5] As a result, research has demonstrated time after time that many

---

[1] https://www.forbes.com/sites/robertadams/2017/01/10/10-powerful-examples-of-artificial-intelligence-in-use-today/2/#390a68783c8b.

[2] https://www.gov.uk/government/speeches/our-fintech-industry-can-power-prosperous-future-article-by-philip-hammond and https://www.gov.uk/government/news/digital-strategy-to-make-britain-the-best-place-in-the-world-to-start-and-grow-a-digital-business.

[3] The Pensions Regulator, Corporate Plan 2017–2020, p. 9.

[4] https://www.gov.uk/government/news/government-reforms-to-stop-savers-losing-mini-pension-pots and https://www.gov.uk/government/news/new-pension-tracing-service-website-launched.

[5] Ideas 42, Freedom and Choice in Pensions: A Behavioural Perspective, 2015.

people have very little connection with their pensions – a survey found that three in five (59%) workers with pension savings have no idea how much they have saved for their retirement.[6] At the same time, life expectancy has increased, which is fantastic news but begs the question how we will fund our longer lifespan. All these factors point in the same direction – we need to take much more responsibility for our financial health after work, and start engaging with our retirement savings.

This is where the pension dashboards project comes in: it seeks radically to improve the consumer experience of pension savings, by enabling consumers to see all their pension entitlements – including the State Pension – in a single place of their choice online. It is a "must" to engage with millennials, and there are international examples, e.g. Scandinavia,[7] for inspiration.

The UK's pension dashboard prototype project is an interesting case study of a new vision for UK pensions made real with technology, collaboration between industry and technology partners, transparency, and innovation.

The Pension Dashboard Prototype Project

When the previous Chancellor George Osborne announced at the Budget in March 2016 that the industry would "design, fund and launch a pension dashboard by 2019", the ABI and our members were delighted. We had already worked with the Money Advice Service and a number of others on the pension dashboard alpha project.[8] We volunteered to manage a project leading to a prototype in March 2017. In the summer of 2016, HM Treasury established a steering group with representatives from all parts of the sector and two independent members. In September 2016, the pension dashboard prototype project was formally launched by the Economic Secretary to the Treasury. The purpose of the dashboard was framed as enabling consumers to gain a holistic view of all their pension pots. This would help ensure that consumers don't lose touch with their pensions, can get a sense of their overall preparations for retirement, and empower them to make decisions.

The prototype project would, over the nine months to March 2017:

- agree and document the design of an initial back-end infrastructure for pensions dashboard data sharing;

- build and demonstrate a basic working prototype of such an infrastructure using anonymized customer data and a digital ID; and

- learn lessons on challenges and potential solutions that can be deployed for the subsequent development of an industry-wide dashboard infrastructure.

More widely, it was the aim of the project to create a dashboard prototype to demonstrate the end-to-end infrastructure to connect multiple pension schemes with pension dashboards. The focus of the prototype was to show that the "plumbing" works. The user interface was important only in so far as it demonstrates that all of the connections are working.

The project approached this task in three phases. Once all contributors had been signed up, a discovery phase identified the needs of users, explored technology and other constraints, and agreed the scope of the project, the data standards, and architecture for the prototype, as well as identity standards and customer stories.

The project also tendered for "development partners" – technology companies to actually build the infrastructure. In the development phase, the development partners built the

---

[6] https://bandce.co.uk/survey-finds-that-three-in-five-people-do-not-know-how-much-they-have-in-their-pension-savings/.

[7] See, for example, the Swedish dashboard at www.minpension.se/.

[8] Creating a Pensions Dashboard. Pensions Finder Alpha White Paper, 2016.

required technology in a series of sprints. The project published prototype data standards documented with the assistance of Origo, and these common protocols (or APIs) enabled all parties working in the prototype project to interoperate.

Finally, in the demonstration phase, the prototype was demonstrated to ministers, and the project held a series of inclusive, open events to demonstrate the working of the prototype, invite stakeholders' comments, and share lessons learned. This included a "tech sprint" event for experimentation with the prototype to explore its potential and innovative ideas for the future after 2019.

Collaboration as the Key Ingredient

The key ingredient for the success of the project has been collaboration. The dashboard concept has much in common with the Open Banking program,[9] but the pensions sector is much more diverse and fragmented than banking, with around 40,000 schemes, two different regulatory regimes, and public sector provision. It was critical, therefore, that the project be truly cross-industry. We assembled 16 contributors to finance the project and support it in a number of working groups to take key decisions, which were then taken to the steering group. They come from all parts of the pension sector: Mastertrusts such as B&CE (The People's Pension), NOW: Pensions and NEST; third-party administrators such as Aon Hewitt and Willis Towers Watson; DC pension providers such as L&G, Aviva, Standard Life, Fidelity, Prudential, LV=, Zurich, Royal London, and Scottish Widows; closed book provider Phoenix; and a single large employer scheme, the HSBC pension scheme. We also involved the Pensions and Lifetime Savings Association to ensure the views of defined benefit and trust-based schemes are represented in the project.

---

[9] www.openbanking.org.uk/.

Collaboration has also been key in the development phase. Twenty-one technology companies bid on a pro bono basis for the project. The project chose six companies: Runpath, Experian, Aquila Heywood, Origo, ITM, and Safran. They worked together building two parallel prototypes, both displaying the information in the same user interface.

The structure was the same for both prototypes: a pension finder service sits between the schemes and the user interface. It acts as the messaging hub that directs queries out from the dashboard to the pension schemes, and funnels pension information back to the dashboard. Both prototypes also undertake identity verification to the assurance standard required by the Department of Work and Pensions to release the state pension information. In both cases, a pension finder service connects with pension providers either directly or through integration service providers. We believe those ISPs will have an important role to play in the industry-wide implementation to assist schemes that may not have data available in easily readable formats.

Transparency

Another important principle for the project has been transparency. The project has been running challenge panels right from the start to give different parts of the market access to its work. In the discovery and development phases, the project held four challenge panels for FinTech companies, pension providers, defined benefit schemes, including in the public sector, and consumer representatives to test the prototype's scope and understand stakeholders' key concerns, as well as begin a dialogue on governance. All our material, as well as a film showing how the dashboard prototype works, is available at https://pensionsdashboardproject.uk.

Innovation

Finally, innovation was key, as befits a project sometimes described as the "iTunes moment" for pensions on social media.

There is no monopoly of wisdom on what pension dashboards should look like, and that the "plumbing" should eventually allow different dashboard providers to engage people in different ways. And we saw how this could happen for real at the TechSprint event in April 2017. The TechSprint was part of HMT's FinTech Week 2017[10] and brought together eight teams of 21 leading technology firms with consumer groups and industry experts to develop ideas for how pension dashboards can revolutionize retirement planning, using the dataset from the prototype as a starting point. One team designed a service that would compare an individual's pensionable income to others at a similar age and socioeconomic profile and tell them how they compared to their peers, and where they should be in order to achieve an adequate replacement rate in retirement. This was presented as "acting your age" and the service encouraged users to take action.

Another team focused on presenting a timeline view of pensions data delivered by employers, not providers, and cross-referencing the user's pension records against their employment history from their LinkedIn account to identify gaps and help them find lost savings. A third team built a product to allow people to bring together the past, present, and future in a personal profile to connect their pension savings with their passions and build a sense of ownership and understanding.

From Prototype to a Live Service by 2019

To deliver the promise of the dashboard, coverage is key. We believe consumers will only use dashboards if they are comprehensive. Consumers need to see their State Pension, DC pensions, and DB pension, both in the public and the private sector.

A "coalition of the willing" approach will not deliver this coverage. Many trust-based schemes, but also some contributors, have been clear that they will not prioritize making data available unless there is legislation or regulation requiring them to do so. The regulatory framework for the dashboard infrastructure must strike a balance between innovation and consumer choice and protection. Dashboards must *not* become a vehicle for scammers or lead generators. Finally, a governance body or implementation entity is needed to establish data standards, data security, and data sharing agreements, as well as proposing a commercial model, all to be tested with stakeholders. This governance structure needs to be commercially savvy, enable innovation, and command consumer trust.

Perhaps most importantly, the project needs the continued backing of government. Given the fragmentation of the UK pension landscape, leaving the project to the industry without government support might eventually bring about a dashboard infrastructure, but it is likely it would take far longer, and be much less comprehensive. There is a huge prize within our reach – government support, coupled with industry collaboration, innovation, and transparency can deliver it, making a positive difference for millions.

---

[10] https://www.gov.uk/government/news/fintech-week-2017-celebrating-britains-status-as-global-fintech-hub.

Six Mega-trends that Will Take Insurance Back to the Future

By Susanne Møllegaard
CEO and Co-Owner, Process Factory

The insurance industry started out as a safety net among peers. Over time the help has become organized, leading first to mutual insurance companies and later to stock insurance companies. As much as this development has led to a greater degree of professionalism, it has also led to a kind of alienation. Furthermore, there is a problem with the basic structure of the insurance products, since the interests of the insurer and the insureds are not aligned. Broadly speaking, the insurer will be better off if premium levels are maximized and claims costs are minimized, whereas the opposite will be true for the insureds.

Basically this has led to a situation of mutual mistrust between the involved parties. The lack of trust inspires the insureds to act with caution when notifying a claim or even to fraudulent behaviour, and the insurer to apply strict underwriting rules, complicated insurance terms, and costly claims processes. The consequences are high cost levels leading to high premium levels and low customer satisfaction.

The great news is that all this is about to change.

A number of mega-trends today are influencing the insurance industry in ways that many consider will bring back trust (see Figure 1). Paradoxically enough, the old-fashioned trust mechanisms are recreated by the application of modern technology and modern ways of coexisting in the sharing economy, bringing the industry "back to the future".

Mega-trend 1: From Reactive to Proactive

The main focus of insurance is reimbursing the costs after the occurrence of an incident. Despite experimenting with claims

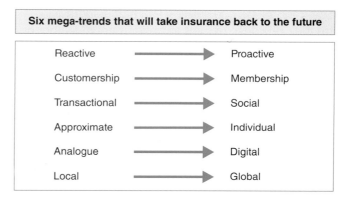

Six mega-trends that will take insurance back to the future

Reactive	→	Proactive
Customership	→	Membership
Transactional	→	Social
Approximate	→	Individual
Analogue	→	Digital
Local	→	Global

Figure 1: Six mega-trends that will take insurance back to the future

prevention initiatives mostly motivated by a wish to reduce claims cost, no traditional insurer has yet come up with game changing initiatives.

From a customer perspective, however, claims prevention is preferable to claims coverage, and with the perspectives of the Internet of Things (IoT), we see the rise of the proactive insurance policy that aligns the interests of the insurer and the insured. We see startups taking this trend seriously, replacing traditional insurance with claims prevention services using smart wireless sensors to detect fires, water damages, and break-ins. An example is the British InsurTech startup Neos teaming up with international specialist insurer Hiscox to offer a new type of home insurance that combines protection and insurance in new and forward-thinking ways. California-based Omada Health is another great example. They provide clients with a box of gadgets to monitor health, weight, activity level, etc., thereby focusing on reducing the risk of various chronic diseases before focusing on reimbursements. And we see car insurers such as Swedish insurer Moderna and global insurer Discovery using telematics to help drivers improve their driving style and avoid risks. You could say that these intelligent products are a two-edged sword. They open up new types of risks while at the same time providing us with new ways to monitor and prevent risks.

This mega-trend offers possibilities that can help traditional insurers transform their business models to better meet customer needs. But it also creates entry points for a new type of competitor coming from industries producing or selling these intelligent products. We are used to thinking of insurance as a stand-alone product, but, in the future, claims prevention coverage is likely to be just another built-in property from many offered by the product.

Mega-trend 2: From "Customership" to Membership

The increasing professionalism and customer orientation in the insurance industry has led to a greater distance between insurer and insured, because a customer only buys a product or a service from a vendor and is not obliged to offer any more than a payment for the product or service.

A membership, on the other hand, is empowering and engaging. A member brings more than money into the relationship. Often you cannot become a member of a club or union unless you qualify for it or perhaps even go through prescribed rituals. Being a member commits you, makes you obliged to the rest of the club or union, and demands of you that you follow the agreed set of rules.

Peer-to-peer initiatives have become increasingly popular among startups across the world, industrializing this trend by offering tech platforms where groups of peers can find each other and share their risk. The peer factor tends to increase trust, which hopefully results in less safeguarding and a lesser degree of fraud, which in turn allows the insurance provider to reduce costly internal control structures. The Berlin-based Friendsurance and the French Inspeer were among the pioneers of peer-to-peer insurance, but on a global scale we now see more than 30 InsurTech startups offering different peer-to-peer models. In the purest form we see examples such as the British Cycle Syndicate. However, in most cases, the business model involves some kind of reinsurance and premium payback model.

Among the startups to follow are the Chinese TongJuBao, focusing on social risks such as marriage safety insurance, and Teambrella, a Russian bitcoin-based peer-to-peer insurance platform.

Mega-trend 3: From Transactional to Social

Transactional systems lead to a highly structured customer interaction that can be perceived as rigid. The system is not really created to fit individual purposes, making the insured feel small and trapped.

In the future we will see customers choosing insurance by recommendations from trusted connections, because people in general trust family, friends, and connections, but distrust an unknown sales person. The selling process is in fact going to be outsourced to your existing customer or third parties delivering a meaningful interface to the customers. The consequence is that an insurer's only way to influence the selling process is by interacting with customers and "customers-to-be" in the social realm.

The change towards engagement and social networks is prominent in many areas of our lives today. Engaging in social networks is a conversation, not a one-way communication. We see new players creating platforms for social interactions and supporting their clients by sharing valuable tips and knowledge, responding to concerns and questions raised in a peer group, thereby showing themselves as a relevant and trusted partner that helps with so much more than just the insurance they offer. UK-based Bought by Many is a great example. They have introduced a platform that helps people with special insurance needs to connect and seek better insurance conditions. Bought by Many uses social media to get in contact with customers and facilitates dialogues with customers about the design of insurance products

Social also means being close to the customer, knowing their needs, and involving them in developing both the products and the digital solutions used for the social interaction.

Mega-trend 4: From Approximate to Individual

Most models used for product development and price setting are based on historical and anonymized data about different groups of customers defined by a number of criteria (e.g. age, address, claims history, size of house, type of car). As a result, the product and price offered to customers is at best an approximation of their needs and risk. In a way it is just like selling clothes by offering one size only. Sometimes it fits, sometimes it doesn't. And the likelihood is that everyone at some point experiences a lack of fit, which is annoying and also creates uncertainty. In fact this is how most insureds perceive their policy today.

With the huge amount of data available from the things we own, the roads we travel, the people we know, and the activities we engage in, this situation is changing. We have already seen startups offering the first examples of what we can call on-demand or pay-per-use insurance, a flexible type of insurance that offers coverage based on the actual needs and actual conduct of the insured. One example is motor insurance, where the premium is calculated based on mileage, position, and driving style. Metromile is an American InsurTech startup that has launched a pay-per-mile car insurance. Octo Telematics from Italy is also worth keeping an eye on. They offer their analytical technology to insurers, allowing them to relate to risk in new ways.

Other examples could be travel insurance and personal accident insurance that are linked to the GPS positions of the insured and turn on/off insurance such as the American startup Trov for personal belongings where the insured can add and remove belongings on the list of items covered based on here-and-now needs.

The main advantage is clearly that the insured only pays for the relevant insurance during the relevant time needed, yet feels certain of having the right protection.

Mega-trend 5: From Analogue to Digital

This is probably the most obvious mega-trend. Everything is going digital and the interesting point is that it can enable trust. Given the opportunity to self-service, customers tend to feel more in control due to a higher level of transparency and less dependency on the insurer's internal and (often bureaucratic) procedures.

Most established insurance companies still have a long way to go to get there due to old and inflexible legacy systems and complicated product structures. We haven't seen true self-servicing platforms, handling the entire customer life cycle from the acquisition of the insurance to filing a claim digitally, offered by incumbents in the insurance industry. In reality, human beings are still needed to handle larger parts of the primary customer processes.

New competitors, however, start with the vision of a truly digital self-servicing platform aided by augmented intelligence and very little human interaction. We can expect to see a rise in the number of new insurance providers offering digital self-service platforms. In the beginning, their focus will be on narrow products, but gradually we will experience them expanding their businesses. American Lemonade is one of the startups that has put a lot of effort into creating a digital platform using AI, chatbots, and a lean app.

An important point is that being digital is not just about operational efficiency within the insurance company. This mega-trend is first and foremost about the customer's experience and about offering customer solutions that guarantee speed, transparency, and trust.

Mega-trend 6: From Local to Global

Today's insurance is still local, with local demands and regulations leading to local products and processes. It can be difficult to imagine that this will change, but don't be fooled. Startups think global and will go for elements in the value chain that are ripe for new business models and new technological solutions, just like we have seen in a number of other businesses.

Many people probably instinctively limit themselves to thinking that the solutions arising from the other five mega-trends will be limited to local initiatives, but look what has happened to payments, house rental, telephony, and the rest. On the horizon, we see new competitors targeting parts of the value chain in the insurance industry, offering global platforms for brokers, peer-to-peer insurance, on-demand insurance, telematics solutions, and smart products to aid claims prevention. They offer transparency, speed, and trust. Key values that seem to have been neglected over the last couple of decades in the industry-wide hunt for big scale and professionalism. Luckily enough, the shift in technology and the promise of the sharing economy now make it possible to revive these important values thus bringing us safely back to the future.

InsurTech – Not a Zero Sum Game

By Nick Martin
Fund Manager–Insurance, Polar Capital

The insurance industry could be on the brink of moving from being capital rich to capital poor as new technologies rapidly expand the pool of insurable risks. Innovative, open-minded, and agile companies will transform yesterday's uninsurable exposures into profitable growth opportunities that will further the industry's critical contribution to the resilience of global communities. InsurTech startups are making progress but have yet to fully appreciate the scale of the opportunity. Incumbents who seek partnership with innovative startups are more likely to embrace it.

Time to Move Beyond the Current InsurTech Debate

The current InsurTech debate is all too often based on the premise that the shiny new startups will win at the expense of the tired old incumbents. The conversation centres around changing distribution models and improved customer centricity. However, InsurTech is so much more than a few cool new apps seeking to displace tired incumbent products. By leveraging emerging technologies and introducing new ideas from outside the industry, InsurTech can help incumbents further enhance the critical role insurance plays in society. It is often forgotten that insurance acts like oil that greases world trade and economic activity while providing the first line of protection to vulnerable people and communities in their times of need.

The Overlooked Multi-billion-dollar Market Opportunity

Swiss Re reported that in 2016 there were US$175 billion of economic losses[1] from natural catastrophes and man-made disasters in line with the inflation-adjusted average of the previous ten years. However, the level of insured losses in 2016 was US$54 billion, meaning the insurance industry only picked up 31% of the damage bill. 2016 had a "protection gap" of US$121 billion and the longer-term record is no better. Swiss Re calculate that, in terms of ten-year rolling averages, insured losses grew by 4.6% between 1991 and 2016, and economic losses by 5.6%.[2] InsurTech startups today, which focus on improving the customer proposition in some way, might well succeed, eating someone else's lunch. However, the potential gains that come from providing solutions to close the protection gap are magnitudes higher (the figures just cited are for property risks only; the opportunity is even greater when adding in similar protection gaps for life and health insurance). The societal benefit extends much beyond pure company profit. Increasing insurance penetration is key to improving global resilience against the rising level of economic and humanitarian risks associated with catastrophic weather and climate-related hazards, particularly in middle/low-income countries.

Using Technology to Close the Protection Gap

At The Economist Insurance Summit conference in 2016, Tom Bolt, then of Lloyd's of London, noted that an increase of 1% in insurance penetration can lead to a 13% drop in uninsured losses and a 22% drop in taxpayers' share of the loss. When the benefits

[1] P3 Swiss Re sigma report 2/2017.
[2] P7 Swiss Re sigma report 2/2017.

of increasing insurance penetration are so obvious, what is stopping the industry making yesterday's uninsurable risk insurable today? There are three main factors:

- The insurance product is not affordable (especially relevant to developing and emerging markets).
- The insurance product is unavailable as the industry cannot sufficiently price the risk given excessive, unmodelled, or unknown exposures.
- There is a "communication gap" leading to a lack of awareness and appeal of the product, often due to a lack of customer centricity and/or excessive product complexity. This is all too common in mature markets.

There is a real opportunity for InsurTech companies to work with the insurance industry in addressing these system "blockages", that if unlocked would drive increased demand, and grow the overall insurance premium "pie". Rising penetration can lower premiums and thus create a virtuous circle.

Let's look at each of the three factors in more detail.

Making Insurance More Affordable

In the last ten years (2006–2015) less than 60% of the premium paid by US policy-holders for commercial risks was used to pay claims.[3] The balance was eaten away by a high level of transaction costs including claims settlement, acquisition, and administration. Embracing technology can lower the cost of information gathering as well as improve its quality, benefiting both insurers and policy-holders. Traditional information asymmetries will disappear.

Many InsurTech startups have business models looking to lower excessive distribution costs, thereby increasing affordability to a

greater percentage of the buying population. In 2016 the World Bank assisted in the launch of a government-backed insurance scheme in Kenya to offer help to agricultural workers in the face of flooding and drought conditions.[4] One program obtains data from satellites to estimate the availability of pasture on the ground and triggers a payout to participating farmers when pasture availability falls below a predetermined threshold. This innovative use of satellites as well as the ability to collect crop yield data through mobile phones is expected to lead to similar schemes being used throughout Africa. Mobile phones also can act as a payment mechanism for a continent where the lack of banking facilities is still common.

Making Yesterday's Uninsurable Risks Insurable Today

In a world of accelerating innovation, it is often forgotten that insurers are the original data companies. The industry has made considerable progress in the use of data analytics. In the past, for example in the soft market of the late 1990s, the industry was characterized more by boom and bust pricing cycles but today the magnitude of rate change is much more muted, with better data enabling a quicker reaction to unexpected rises in loss costs. We are just at the beginning of this data journey. Insurers have the opportunity to enhance their existing data sets significantly, through new external sources such as sensors and IoT (Internet of Things), social media and drones. Better insights, powered by big data and predictive analytics, lead to an improved understanding of risk, a necessary condition for insurers to begin to address some of the key concerns of commercial insurance buyers today. They often care more about intangible assets such as brand and

[3] Dowling & Partners & SNL Data.

[4] http://www.artemis.bm/blog/2016/03/17/world-bank-backs-index-insurance-scheme-to-assist-kenyan-farmers/.

reputation than the physical plant and machinery assets on which much of today's insurance offering is based.

There is a long held belief that insurers have to own all their underwriting data, as that is part of their competitive advantage. Tomorrow's winners will be those who realize you simply cannot own all the data that you now require, and have let go of the traditional business model. Partnerships and working with people from outside the industry will become ever more important.

How InsurTech Can Help Close the Communication Gap by Improving Customer Centricity

Collectively the insurance industry is trying to do more to close the protection gap. In 2016 the Insurance Development Forum (IDF)[5] was launched. The IDF is a partnership between the insurance industries supported by international organizations including the World Bank. Their mission is to incorporate the industry's risk management expertise into governmental disaster risk reduction and give insurance a larger role in providing resilience to communities globally.

At the 2016 International Insurance Society annual conference, IDF Chairman Stephen Catlin noted: "We talk about innovation and new products. The reality is we are not even selling well the product we know and love dearly." The less insular InsurTech community with their diverse skillsets, often from outside of the insurance industry, can help insurers start to address the obvious misunderstanding consumers, governments, and regulators share of the social value of the insurance product. At the same conference, Sam Maimbo, a manager in the World Bank's Group Finance and Markets Practice, noted that he spends 70% of his time explaining what the industry has to offer as he sits between deep technical insurance teams and the public sector.

Addressing this "communication gap" has parallels with many InsurTech business models that focus on better customer engagement. Furthermore, technology is an enabler for the traditional insurance industry model to move from one of post-loss reactive reimbursement to one of proactively managing down customers' risks. The latter model of risk prevention is significantly more valuable and can change insurance from the grudge purchase that many customers view it as today. Increased personalization of the product will further the appeal.

The insurance industry has a tremendous opportunity not only to help itself but also the global community. The current size of the protection gap is a failure of the industry and any companies that can help address it will not only be first movers in new markets but will also add social value and resilience to vulnerable communities. Many argue that currently there is an abundance of capital in the insurance industry. However, if the industry fully embraces the power of technology and enhanced data analytics, that abundance of capital turns into an abundance of opportunity. In short order, the industry will go from capital rich to capital poor and provide profitable growth opportunities for those companies who lead the way. The most successful insurers will likely be those who embrace innovative, nimble startups through partnerships. The startups may feel they can go it alone but they need help from incumbents who are skilled at navigating a highly regulated and complicated ecosystem. Given that the industry sells nothing more than a promise to pay, startups would be foolish to overlook the power of a trusted brand.

Through reduced costs and better efficiency, technology can be an enabler to make insurable what was previously uninsurable. New markets will emerge that expand the overall industry "pie" not only to the benefit of all market participants but, more importantly, to society at large.

InsurTech is not a zero sum game.

---

[5] www.idf.org.

The Founder's Journey

3

Not too Big to Fail

- Only 12 percent of companies that were in business in 1955 are still alive today

- The average life span of a business created in 1955 was 55 years. It is today less than 10 years

- It takes two years for a new venture to scale-up to $1bn
  - Volumes of $1bn size new ventures:

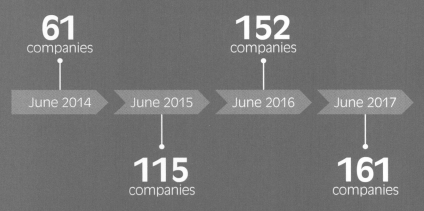

61
companies

152
companies

June 2014 → June 2015 → June 2016 → June 2017

115
companies

161
companies

- Top 5 ventures: Uber, Didi Chuxing, Xiaomi, Airbnb, Palentir
- Not to fail means:
  - Being clear on customer strategy
  - Team diversity
  - Processes must be challenged
  - Keep it simple
  - Accept when it cannot be done
  - And celebrate every success

Expertise of The Future

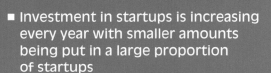

- The two most likely areas for R&D innovation within the next 5 to 10 years will include software and services

- Investment in startups is increasing every year with smaller amounts being put in a large proportion of startups

- Corporate and InsurTech leaders bring different set of capabilities to their respective business:

Corporates	InsurTechs
Structure	Skills & Ability
Process	Knowing when to say "no"
Culture	Working Charter
Expertise	Can do attitude
Relationships	Operate in Chaos
Assess & Deploy	Test & Learn

By combining such capabilities, incumbents and InsurTechs will develop ecosystems where they can coexist to mitigate risk for people and businesses

In this part, we address the founder's journey. Regardless of whether we address founders who have been in business for decades or nascent ones, no organization is infallible in times of change.

While some well-known global brands learned this too late, today no incumbent business can afford to ignore emerging market realities and avoid adapting their internal business practices to thrive within a fast-paced marketplace.

Embedding entrepreneurial mind-sets, strong internal cultures, lean developments, and innovative execution approaches are on the lips of many business owners, regardless of whether these leaders are mature or new ones. They want to deliver leaner, faster, cheaper, more relevant, efficient, and engaging products and services that stand the needs of changing generations and survive current market dynamics.

Emerging business leaders understand that they have two options. They can diverge and become disruptive from their more mature peers or converge and collaborate with them. Still, regardless of the competitive slant selected, true values, principles, and beliefs are required to support small teams of hand-picked and talented individuals focused on achieving set vision, mission, and goals.

Like their younger driven market counterparts, incumbent players are learning to reconfigure their businesses to embrace easily disruptive innovations and lean methodologies to deliver inexpensive and precise solutions that bring their business into the next century. They will hunt and publicly unveil solutions and offerings that help them grow and achieve differentiation and competitive advantage. Nonetheless, they must also be open to learning from the tumultuous journeys of those young founders, and remember that in times of uncertainty, considering win-win agreements with those younger players can yield massive benefits.

In this part, the founders share their path towards execution and differentiation as they learn to strengthen their operational understanding of the use of artificial intelligence, telemetry, and genomics among other emerging technologies, despite internal barriers.

Not too Big to Learn not to Fail?

By Ruth Polyblank
Head of SME and Digital, Chubb Insurance
Company of Europe

The Insurance Landscape: Introducing the Status Quo

Perhaps the most fundamental lesson from the collapse of the subprime market and the subsequent global recession must be that no institution is infallible. Neglecting to act when needed is the only thing that stands between an organization and its risk of failure, regardless of its market position, prestige, or pedigree.

Incumbent and established insurance organizations – whether insurers, brokers, loss adjusters, or claims corporations – are often criticized for failing to innovate or disrupt the insurance market and perhaps this is not without reason.

From the death grip of inadequate legacy platforms and a "that's how we've always done it" mind-set to antiquated protocols designed by overly conservative and hierarchical internal committees, the status quo largely remains intact, particularly in the still heavily intermediated commercial insurance market where barriers to entry remain high.

Yet the industry press is littered with bold pledges from incumbents launching "exciting" new initiatives that promise to innovate, to "digitalize", or to disrupt. If what we are reading is correct, incumbents have numerous vehicles for change and we are on the verge of seeing the impact of these upon their balance sheets and dated customer experiences, in a meaningful way akin to other innovative industries like Healthcare, which, according to PwC's 2016 Global Innovation 1000 Study,[1] will pass both the computing and electronics industries to become the largest overall industry

by R&D spending. However, the sum of all these efforts is not yet tangible and is likely to be in the magnitude of incremental change rather than wholesale transformation.

Anecdotally, innovation seems to be constrained to improving a single process, *distribution or experience*, and much of this work is incubated outside of the main business in a separate hub, often located in a hipster postcode. Which also leads to the question: why are modern business practices like business-led IT not being adopted as broadly or with the level of penetration they should, to ensure that large organizations remain relevant?

Why Innovation is More Difficult for Incumbents?

Innovation requires an organization's ability to distance itself from the status quo. It is about starting from a blank sheet of paper and focusing the attention of the business on a specific outcome, usually the customer. However, for incumbents there is safety in the known. As an industry we make decisions based upon historical data. Separating ourselves from all the things we know have made us profitable is difficult, and the business of innovation can lack hard evidence of success. In addition, the incentive for change can appear underwhelming; the industry has seen many threats come and go and speculation of a huge disruptor waiting in the wings has been in play for some time. And habituation to this threat has kicked in.

Mind-set is key to successful innovation, and when that is threatened with change, while some may embrace it all heartedly, others, whether individuals or whole teams, will wed

[1] Barry Jaruzelski, Volker Staack, and Aritomo Shinozaki, PwC, Software-as-a-catalyst, *Strategy+Business,* 85, Winter 2016, Global Innovation 1000 Study, Reprint 16409.

themselves to how things are currently done as a defense to this change. Culture and acceptance of change are fundamental but since employees are often conditioned to eliminate risk and cling to a process for safety, this can be one of the most difficult challenges to overcome.

It is this reluctance that makes many processes inside large organizations unfit for purpose when it comes to innovation. The traditional insurer's procurement process, supported by RFPs or Requests for Proposals, and a tech startup's engagement process are both as star-crossed as prospective partners could ever be in how they operate, especially if you then also add in the due diligence required by most IT departments and potentially lengthy legal contract negotiations that might ensue, should they make it through the financial and credit checks.

It is counter-intuitive to stop doing something that has previously been successful or, at least, has not had a negative outcome. The tipping point from *cash cow* to *dog* is never clear or even predictable, so it's understandable that organizations cling to the masterplan until the proverbial fat lady begins warming up. Instead of a millennial style FOMO (Fear Of Missing Out), organizations are plagued with the rather more corporate FOF (Fear of Failure) but innovation is not for the fainthearted nor for the lacklustre.

Is it reasonable to expect boardrooms with little or no appetite to trail-blaze when the results are unpredictable to say the least and the duration of their personal career plan may consist of only single digit numbers? This difficult-to-turn vessel, the huge steamship that is our insurance sector, has been built over many generations based on sound and safe decision-making and processes that mitigate risk. It is therefore unsurprising that turning this boat around is going to take a while – and that's assuming that the course will not change direction again, mid-manoeuvre.

In short, incumbents are not innovating because they are reluctant to move away from the blueprint. Their decisions are based on experience. However, the experience of those decision-makers often doesn't include innovation or change management. This, coupled with an institutional and inherent fear of failure, means resistance to change.

A Mismatching Exercise

And so there is an inherent insurance innovation mismatch: idealistic startups who build great experiences with a customer that stands at the centre of their decision-making process but who often struggle to secure fundamental insurance underwriting capacity or significant bottom-line results. And incumbents who have a wealth of underwriting expertise and capability, but struggle to take it to market, adopt agile working practices, change mind-sets, and embrace new technologies (at least without diluting them by anchoring them to legacy systems). Together the two components would undoubtedly prove extremely powerful.

Imagine a startup with the resources of a large insurance group or equally an incumbent with the agility and out-of-the-box thinking of a startup.

Right under our Noses?

Let's set aside the cultural change that is required by an incumbent to identify and implement innovation or transformative change. Instead let's look at the significant advantages that your average incumbent has.

The key to success is to play to your strengths. Incumbents have phenomenal resources. It's not just about the size of your war chest, existing distribution, and internal experts across legal, HR, marketing, and sales who provide advice. Unlike other existing potential entrants, the wealth of underwriting expertise and data mean that, in theory at least, the incumbents are the best placed to innovate.

Successful innovation in other industries focuses on delivering significantly better customer experiences by connecting suppliers of services and customers in the simplest way possible.

So, how does an incumbent innovate the way they take their substantial insurance experience and capacity to those who wish to transfer risk away from their own balance sheets?

How do we Learn not to Fail?

Well, there is no single right answer but there is certainly a wealth of behaviours and actions that, if adopted, will significantly improve the chances of success:

1. **Leading from the front.** Senior executives will need to sponsor innovation efforts and be prepared to be challenged and create new precedents when issues are escalated to them.

2. **Enabling intrapreneurs.** Find forward-thinking, customer-focused employees and empower them to innovate and challenge. Intrapreneurs can offer the incumbents a vision and a roadmap to bring about change from within but they will need authority and support if they are to be successful. The strongest candidates may not be the most obvious, and are just as likely to perform in the marketing or actuarial department as in underwriting.

3. **Customer strategy is king.** Ensure that a sound commercial customer strategy underpins your innovation objectives, so that it isn't innovation for innovation's sake. Let the opportunity be your guide, not the capability of the technology.

4. **Create diverse teams.** Innovation requires a broad range of skillsets unlikely to be found in similar groups of employees; diverse perspectives and experience aid problem-solving.

5. **Challenge your processes.** From appointing new suppliers to simplifying the due diligence review, ensure your processes are proportionate to the risk and allow empowered employees to get things done.

6. **Don't overthink it.** Adopting agile working, using proof of concepts, and minimum viable product development mean that you can afford to learn on the job rather than be dictated to by your cost vs. benefit analysis.

7. **Celebrate successes.** Creativity can be infectious, especially where there is tangible benefit. Sharing success stories creates a more positive and open innovation culture, which will assist future initiatives.

8. **Accept that there are limitations.** Not every employee will engage with innovation nor do they need to. Not every initiative will be successful and not every launch will deliver. The key is to learn from the failures and apply the successes again and again.

Learning not to Fail

Indeed, it is not that incumbents are too big not to fail – that has already been proven. But are they too big to change and avoid extinction?

There is cause to remain wholly optimistic and look forward to an insurance ecosystem where InsurTech startups, new entrants, and the incumbents coexist to mitigate risk for people and businesses, allowing customers to make their own choices about how they put this protection in place.

How exciting that the insurance industry could be a case study for the innovating incumbent.

In essence, the mild irony is that the way large incumbents can prevent failing is to accept and embrace a degree of failure.

Insurance Expertise, Family, and Integrity – The Story of SPIXII's Founding Team

By Alberto Chierici
Co-Founder and CPO, SPIXII

Renaud Million
Co-Founder and CEO, SPIXII

and Emma Pegg
Marketing Executive, SPIXII

SPIXII is a London-based tech startup, founded by Italian-born Alberto Chierici (Alberto C.), French engineer Renaud Million, and Italian-born computer scientist Alberto Pasqualotto (Alberto P.).

Our aim? We want to redefine the relationship that exists between insurers and their customers, and make the process of dealing with insurance simple and transparent.

How are we doing this? We are working with insurers to build an automated digital agent, supported by artificial intelligence technology and behavioural economics. This will help insurers provide a seamless digital experience for their customers.

We all know that we need insurance. But when insurance has been sold from a place of fear, insurers often become the villains rather than the heroes in helping customers live more safely and securely. As SPIXII navigates its second year as a young startup, here are some of the lessons we've learnt while building a company whose core premise is to revolutionize the insurance industry.

Defining the Target

Our adventure began in 2012 with friendship. Renaud, my co-founder, was convinced that the current approach used to sell insurance was outdated, and should start with a clear understanding of the customers' needs. He, in agreement with many of his friends and other digital customers, felt the pain of buying insurance. Renaud started to explore a new concept, which gradually materialized when he discussed the idea with me, Alberto C.

Renaud and I were both training to become actuaries when we met at an actuarial insurance tutorial. We clicked immediately. Renaud explains:

> Alberto C. was the first person I talked to, who shared a similar passion for insurance and a belief that insurance products could be sold differently. For the next two years, we bounced ideas off each other. Yet, it wasn't until 2015 – when insurers were beginning to prioritize digital initiatives through transformation projects and explore trends otherwise only seen in Silicon Valley – that we knew it was time to act.

Reality hit. I realized that, even though we were just about to qualify as young actuaries while working respectively for one of the top five consultancies, we had to take this opportunity by the horns. In order to do that, we had to drop out of one secure career and move into a far riskier one.

In May 2015, while participating in a Hackathon weekend in which we won an "Incubation prize", Renaud and I named our first idea "Safer". Despite declining the offer to move to Munich to develop it further, we believed this offer showed us we were going in the right direction. After being accepted into a startup accelerator in December, we left our jobs. And in January 2016, we registered the company. Our first real defining moment was when we left the office and began talking to people.

Renaud would tell you that "as tech-oriented people, it wasn't easy to start conversations with strangers. But after interacting with individuals in coffee shop queues and on the street, we found that people gradually understood the value of our offer once we touched upon their pain points."

During those highly engaging discussions we identified our first target segment: young professionals. This segment quickly expanded to "digital consumers": people who buy almost exclusively with their smartphones and whose first reaction when buying insurance is to message a friend or family member for advice. We realized if we were able to create technology that acted just like this, we would be onto something big.

So, my first piece of advice is this: before developing technology for a specific customer segment, talk to them so you can understand their concerns as much as possible. Identify their pain points; what problems do your customers face in day-to-day life? How can your technology help? Your business has a far greater chance of success if it can articulate these pain points clearly and compellingly. Only then will your target audience be able to gain awareness of your value.

Establishing the Working Charter

Right at the start of our journey, we decided to establish a working charter: a set of principles that would guide us in all aspects of the business. Renaud, Alberto P., and I met in Milan in December 2015 to discuss what it would take to start SPIXII. We discussed our likes, dislikes, strengths, weaknesses, and core values: namely, friendship, professionalism, a sense of family, openness, trust and respect, as well as entrepreneurship and constant curiosity. These values became benchmark principles, to be encapsulated by everyone in our team. From this point on, we felt like and acted as a family. As Alberto P. described, "we were three brothers with a shared father: our common vision for SPIXII".

We found that once we agreed these brand values with such clarity and transparency, it became easier for us to attract talent that fitted within these attributes. As Renaud points out, "in a young startup, there's no time for comfort or stability. The connection you have with the people around you is vital to manage the ups and downs of startup life."

Ask any founder and I'm sure they'll say the same thing: your first hires are incredibly important for the future of your business. We found that by using our shared values as a foundation, we could attract like-minded individuals who fit our company culture.

Our First Hires

Our first strategic hire was Johannes Windus, who joined our team as Business Development Manager. After studying insurance at university and working in sales, Johannes shared our frustration with the way insurance was sold: out of fear rather than trust. While working in Germany, he wrote a paper on how digital agents could transform the insurance industry. And when he read a review in *The Financial Times* – "Ten fintech start-ups that are causing a stir in insurance"[1] – he sent us an email the very next day. Three days later, we met him in Munich. A week and a half later, he was in London to help us with our business development efforts.

Friedrich Roell is SPIXII's back-end developer. After meeting Renaud through mutual friends, he resigned from his job to join the company. While based in Munich, he spends two to three weeks a month in London, and describes working with SPIXII as a highly rewarding "intense and emotional adventure".

The Importance of Adapting, and Saying "No"

Integrity underpins SPIXII's working charter. Yet, when budgets are tight and the future uncertain, it can be a challenge to stick to these underlying principles. For Renaud, "one of the biggest challenges for a startup is to balance its long-term vision with its short-term survival tactics. The decisions to say 'no' are always the most difficult to take."

---

[1] O. Ralph, Ten fintech start-ups that are causing a stir in insurance, *Financial Times*, https://www.ft.com/content/db833e5a-6eb1-11e6-a0c9-1365ce54b926.

As many young startups know, our ability to drive traction is often linked to our ability to raise funding. Very early on during our startup journey, an incumbent company presented us a contract with terms that were difficult for us to accept. They wanted us to run a proof of concept for very little financial returns in exchange for a three-year exclusivity agreement. While the incumbent would have helped SPIXII become a recognizable brand, it was clear that our company values were completely misaligned. The combined exclusivity and lack of financial reward meant that this contract could have put our business into jeopardy.

So, How Can Startups Afford to Say "No"?

To my mind, the answer is simple. You have two ways to go about it. First, accept a bad deal in exchange for very little money and sink your business a few months down the line. Or, risk sinking your business quicker, but based on a decision made from calculated gut instinct. This is similar to betting on the great product you have built, as well as the relationships you've established in the industry over the years.

Another one of our life-changing decisions was not to raise capital. My belief is that there is a myth fuelled by questionable press, venture capital, accelerator ecosystems, and business schools that the road to success must always be the same: an entrepreneur has an idea, assembles a team to develop that idea, acquires angels or venture capital funding to bring the idea to market and scale, then goes and builds "the next big thing".[2]

However, not all founders are born equal. Some want to jump onto the funding bandwagon, aspire to create a business that delivers shareholder value, fund it and sell it to the highest bidder, then

move onto the next venture. Others genuinely want to create a successful business that creates value for customers.

Did you know that less than 1% of businesses are venture fundable?[3] In both of the above scenarios, entrepreneurship is a requirement; value must be delivered to customers to generate revenues and profits. We've found that the best way to finance your business is through the revenues you generate from your customers and their feedback, at least at first.

In addition, once an investor takes a chunk of your business at seed or pre-seed stages, it's likely that they'll ask you to stick to your original plan. Of course, good venture capitalists are always happy to back startups that pivot if this makes sense. But, as extensive research by Dr John Mullins shows, this is rarely the case.[4,5,6] You risk losing your investor's support, particularly in today's risk-averse European seed capital market (as compared with the more mature US investing market).[7] As a startup it is essential that you aim to remain agile.

For insurers, we understand that fragmented operational environments have created challenges to fully embed a customer-first culture. High operating costs and low margins are the status

[2] See blog from leading Silicon Valley entrepreneur Sramana Mitra at www.sramanamitra.com.

[3] https://www.forbes.com/sites/dileeprao/2013/07/22/why-99-95-of-entrepreneurs-should-stop-wasting-time-seeking-venture-capital/#3c54b-b1246eb.

[4] J. Mullins and Randy Komisar, *Getting to Plan B: Breaking Through to a Better Business Model* (Boston: Harvard Business Press, 2009).

[5] J. Mullins, *The Customer-Funded Business: Start, Finance or Grow Your Business with Your Customers' Cash* (Jersey City: John Wiley & Sons, 2014).

[6] J. Mullins, *London Business School*, http://www.london.edu/faculty-and-research/faculty/profiles/m/mullins-j#.WSBqwhPyuRs.

[7] D. Rao, Why 99.95% of entrepreneurs should stop wasting time seeking venture capital. Forbes, 2013, https://www.forbes.com/sites/dileeprao/2013/07/22/why-99-95-of-entrepreneurs-should-stop-wasting-time-seeking-venture-capital/#3c54bb1246eb.

quo for today's insurers. However, we also know that digital experiences powered by intuitive digital agents yield significant benefit for those who want to take advantage of it.[8]

Ultimately, your business is only as strong as the people behind it. It is thus vital that you outline your values early, then use them to attract talent and create a team that operates in sync, without losing the values and passion that brought it together. Powered first by the friendship built among the co-founders, then by the values shared across the team, we find a people-first approach to business mirrors our mission to put the human back into insurance.

[8] A. Deleger, A Match Made in Heaven – Chatbots and Insurance Services. Stanfy, 2017, https://stanfy.com/blog/chatbots-and-insurance-services/.

Disrupting Car Insurance – Drivies App Makes Driving More Fun, and Insurance Fairer

By Laura García García
Chief Product Officer and Co-Founder, Drivies

Jesús Bernat
Chief Technical Officer and Co-Founder, Drivies

and Dr José Luis Blanco
Chief Data Officer and Co-Founder, Drivies

Emerging Usage-based Insurance

Digitalization, big data, the sharing economy, and connected and self-driving cars are all testaments of an ongoing revolution that will change traditional ways of doing things, and impact in particular the insurance market – from risk estimation, tariff assessment, and insurance distribution to customer engagement.

The wide adoption of the smartphone in our daily lives has converted devices into behavioural proxies, which, combined with big data technologies, provide significant improvement in ways to estimate risks for car insurance, and enriching socio-demographic-based tariffs with driving data. This is not new but the telematics black box has become a roadblock to mass market adoption.

Drivies: A New Approach to Usage-based Car Insurance

Following a Telefónica intrapreneurial initiative, the authors created Drivies. Drivies estimates driver risk by assessing

each user's actual driving patterns, and then offers fairer car insurance prices through a prepurchase scoring model. The app leverages gamification techniques including competition theory, comparison among users, and social networking interactions. By providing detailed information of the user's driving activities and its evolution overtime, Drivies creates a compelling value proposition for each driving user, and a higher-quality acquisition channel for insurers.

Unlike many other app-based telematics solutions, the Drivies business model relies on identifying the best drivers first, before they buy a policy, and not an app that estimates and adjusts the tariff post-sale. This enables the delivery of risk selections and telematics tariffs that are based on true driving behaviours.

Furthermore, Drivies plays well in a marketplace environment. Thanks to collaborative arrangements with local brokers, the app provides insurance options from the main car insurance companies, from low-cost offers to high-value ones. However, the risk profiling data that is collected is exploited in an exclusive way by one single insurance company at any point in time. This way, users are offered a wide variety of preferred insurance brands, coverages, and prices to choose from (including a differential telematics tariff, with better prices for good drivers), while the differential value of the knowledge capture through telematics data is preserved for that specific insurer.

A compelling value proposition is also critical for any app to succeed in our app-saturated times. Most app-based telematics solutions are purely focused on one single insurance proposition – meaning that they focus on providing an optimized price for good driving. However, such price-driven messaging is only relevant for those drivers closer to their renewal date. It also attracts price-driven users, who are typically more prone to churn.

Drivies' value proposition is actually focused on helping drivers make the most of their driving. The app offers relevant driving information to enable the driver to improve their driving and compete with others for good driving. It also helps the driver earn discounts based on their app usage. The insurance discount is a secondary advantage for Drivies' users. Such strategy helps us capture high-value customers, who are not entirely price-led.

Technical Differentiations

Building an app that automatically records a driver's driving patterns creates a series of challenges.

The app must:

- automatically detect the start and the end of a user's journey;
- handle any positions a mobile phone may be placed into;
- distinguish the different driving manoeuvres (e.g. accelerations, braking, mobile phone manipulation, cornering, etc.);
- minimize battery consumption;
- assess whether the driver is driving or not.

To overcome these technical challenges, we have decided to use accelerometers and gyroscopes (if present), while minimizing the use of a global positioning system (GPS), since a GPS is a main source of energy consumption on the device.

Accelerometers measure the acceleration forces acting over the mobile device, while gyroscopes measure the rotation speed, which is used to find out one's driving orientation.

When the solution is being deployed, the app may face additional problems:

- Different vendors produce different personalization for the Android operating systems in particular: the same version of an operating system can behave differently on various types of phones depending on the manufacturer.

- Drivies must work behind the scenes. Current versions of the operating systems can create limitations to those background modes.
- Drivies is currently able to overcome many mobile phone-related challenges. Still, battery-related issues exist and our goal is to continuously strive to optimize usage.

Our Spanish Beta: Lessons Learnt 18 Months Post-Launch

Drivies was launched in the Spanish market in July 2015 as a beta concept. Since then, more than 125,000 drivers have downloaded the app, and 24,000 of them have requested a car insurance quote through the app. Almost 40 million kilometres and 3 million journeys have been tracked and analysed through the app.

Product: The Value of Using Fast Iterations and Clear Key Performance Indicators (KPIs) to Optimize Performance

Drivies was developed following lean startup methodology. We constantly iterated and tested our concept to validate our key hypothesis for success, and we still do. A new version of the app is released every two weeks, enabling us to introduce new features or to remove those features that have proved a hindrance to app performance. All customer acquisition activities are tracked on a per-channel, per-week basis and adjusted according to one of our main KPIs: cost per acquired driving user. We use A/B testing to compare new user experiences, functionalities, and marketing messages. These metrics would be useless without the tracking of additional parameters: user acquisition (cost per user), user retention (ratio of users that use the app for at least two weeks), and lead conversion (ratio of users that buy a policy through the app). The application of lean startup and lean analytics brought relevant improvements in Drivies. Figure 1 shows the cohorts of Drivies' drivers (percentage of users who drove from day 1), and Figure 2 highlights the evolution of our monthly active drivers since January 2016.

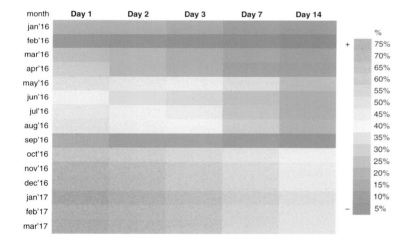

Figure 1: Driver cohorts

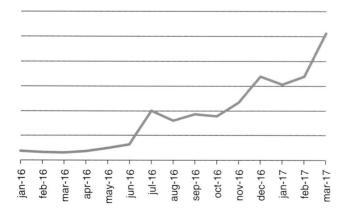

Figure 2: MAUs evolution

Despite targeting genders equally, more than 70% of Drivies' users are male.

Drivies started with a three-insurer marketplace. We quickly learned that to optimize our sales conversion we needed to open the application to more insurers to offer more options to end-consumers. Today, Drivies works with over 20 insurers. The Drivies app offers a variety of interaction options (chat), prices, offers, and adverts (top recommendations) to the users of the app. These have been pivotal to increase our sales.

Information Brings Unique Insights

App-based insurance telematics, and emerging machine learning techniques, provide great opportunities to enhance risk assessments. They could also potentially disrupt the global insurance market

The data we collected unveiled unique pieces of information from users' demographic, driving and claims patterns, behaviours, and habits. Attitudes and preferences are reliable predictors of risk. They are actually just as useful indicators as one's driving skills or one's demographics. Drivies has changed the way we think about risk, how we compute it and evaluate our customer base at Telefónica. We know that risk assessment is imperfect. However, we also know that one can assess the risk for specific policies from reviewing data patterns across a limited number of days through the app. Our insight is constantly evaluated and updated.

Figure 3 shows how our models have evolved when introducing these new sources of information. We can clearly rank user profiles and policies based on the level of risk. And as we gain more insights we discover new patterns more rapidly.

As the telematics data brings continuous updating to our models, we can systematically evaluate the stability and confidence of our results. This is the power of dynamic data analysis.

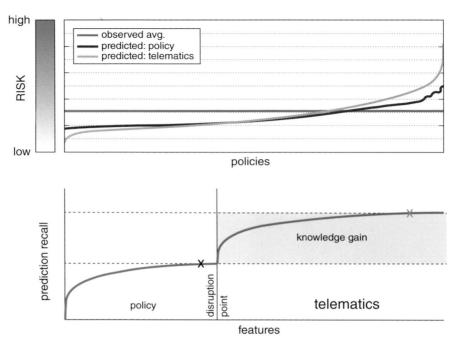

Figure 3: Improvement in risk prediction thanks to telematics

There is more to the data we collect than the information it provides. Quality and size are two additional parameters we monitor.

For any big data problem, data structuring and monitoring is a big issue, as well as a great opportunity. As the amount of data constantly increases, the number of analyses that need to be covered rapidly expands, but also our learning capabilities. This enables reliable business insight extraction and facilitates data quality and reliability checks that were previously impossible.

Figure 4 shows several maps of Spain describing the car insurance industry in 2014. In chart (a) we display the rate of claims incurred associated with different regions, whereas in chart (b) we highlight the distribution between insured versus registered vehicles. There are large oscillations from one region to the next. This means either that some regions gathered a high number of insured vehicles with low claims ratio or that the demographic data is biased. Chart (c) shows policy owners based on declared address areas based on policy information. Because pure demographic-based approaches are biased and do not capture the right set of information, good risks are unlikely to get the tariffs they deserve. Our pilot overcame this limitation and identified where the actual driving took place. This is depicted in chart (d).

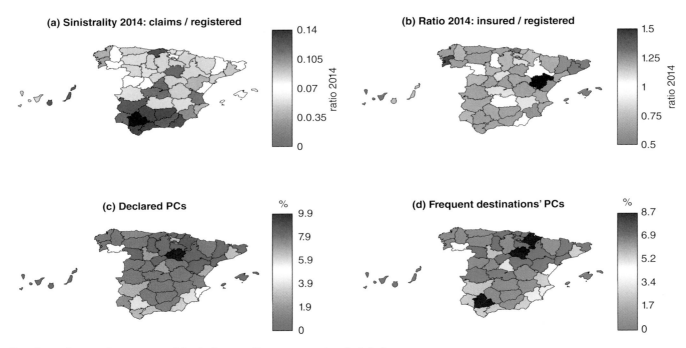

Figure 4: Declared car demographic information vs. actual driving areas

Sources: Data from Spanish Traffic Department, Dirección General de Tráfico, Micro Datos 2014; Spanish Association of Insurance and Reinsurance Institutions (UNESPA), Informe Anual 2014

Conclusions

Drivies demonstrates that an app can not only be a good assessor to measure the driving behaviours of driving app users, it can also significantly improve the assessment of the potential inherent risk embedded within specific risks, on a per-user basis. By leveraging concepts such as gamification, Drivies has shown itself to be a unique asset to acquire high-value consumers and serve them well.

Genomics 101 – The Search for a Better Life Expectancy Predictor Leads GWG Life to a Science Lab

By Jon Sabes
CEO, Life Epigenetics and CEO, GWG Holdings, Inc

When I first visited the human genetics and biostatistics lab at the University of California at Los Angeles (UCLA) in 2015, life insurance was not on the mind of the researchers. While the genomic revolution that began decades earlier raised the spectre of insurance underwriting based on our genetic code, no one seemed to be paying much attention to the more recent epigenetic revolution and its implications in predicting mortality and lifespan.

That autumn day, I had an appointment to meet Dr Steven Horvath,[1] the unassuming German immigrant who, as a UCLA professor, had developed the technology that came to be known as "Horvath's Clock", a predictor of human mortality that promised to be far more accurate than anything coming before. Dr Horvath is a recognized expert on ageing who has focused his research on finding the root causes of ageing encoded in the DNA molecule. In 2013, he reported he had found that human cells have an internal "biological age" and "biological clock" at the DNA molecular level that is indicative of the ageing process. His work was hailed as groundbreaking and featured in the scientific journal *Nature*.[2] It was research that caught the eye of my brother Steve – he has a PhD in chemistry and he flagged it for me. That's what led me to California, armed with the idea that this research could help the business I had co-founded in Minneapolis.

It was fitting that we would be the ones to make the connection between his research about lifespan and life insurance: at GWG Life,[3] our entire business is based on estimating the lifespan of the people whose life insurance policies we buy. We are a secondary market life insurance company; we purchase policies from seniors who no longer want, need, or can afford them, and we pay them a lot more than the originating insurers will. We hold the policies and continue making premium payments until the policy-holder's death when we receive the policy benefit – sometimes policy-holders sell only a portion of the benefit while others sell the entire policy's benefits to GWG Life and other companies in this secondary market.

It's a small part of the US$20 trillion life insurance industry, but it uses the same principles of risk assessment and pricing the biggest insurance carriers have always used. Our part of the business is based on the fact that large life insurance carriers offer only small cash values to policy-holders when they most need them. On the other side of this transaction, consumers benefit from our business, and you can understand why when you see that we have paid out almost US$400 million directly to policy owners, compared to the US$26.1 million in surrender values offered by insurance carriers for the very same policies.

By 2015, when I went to California, we had become convinced that the process of determining the risk in a life insurance policy was in desperate need of reinvention. Historically, the life insurance, long-term care insurance, and annuity industries have used "medical evidenced-based underwriting" to assess, select, and price risk in order to operate their businesses profitably. Medical evidenced-based underwriting is exactly what it sounds like – an underwriter can draw blood and review an individual's medical data and family history to create a view of the insured's health profile in order to appropriately select and price the risk. Ironically, while the biggest single determinant of a policy's price is whether an applicant is a smoker, the test to determine whether someone smokes is highly

---

[1] https://www.biostat.ucla.edu/people/horvath.

[2] http://www.nature.com/news/biomarkers-and-ageing-the-clock-watcher-1.15014.

[3] www.gwglife.com/.

inaccurate and insurance carriers are left to rely on self-reporting from applicants.

So, I was at UCLA that day to find out if Dr Horvath's research was precise enough to apply to our business and give us a better way to determine how long policy-holders are likely to live. I intuitively knew that if it turned out to be true, that Dr Horvath could more accurately predict individual all-cause mortality, the implications would go far beyond the life insurance secondary market business.

The meeting started slowly. When I asked him if he had ever heard of the life insurance business, he surprised me by saying, "No, I haven't." I then asked him if he had been to Las Vegas, to which he said "Yes, I have." The Las Vegas analogy provided us some common ground to discuss the calculated risk the life insurance business takes on its policies. Think of it like this, I told him, "we are looking for a way to access the 'down card' of life expectancy in a real-life game of Black Jack." Knowing how close the dealer is to 21 – in effect, the policy-holder's life expectancy – would be a game-changer for us, to continue the gambling analogy, something he instantly understood. After an hour of sharing information, he pledged to contact us when his research reached the point of being able to provide the kind of predictive intelligence we needed and I went back to Minneapolis, convinced we were on to something.

Meanwhile, I began pouring over the science to understand what Horvath was exploring. The study of chemical modifications to the DNA molecule that reveal ageing, among other things, is known as epigenetics.[4] Epigenetics is the study of how the DNA molecule's instructions are translated into the production of proteins that make us who we are. In other words, while scientists unravelled the sequence of our DNA molecular code in 2003 following a 13-year, publicly funded project that cost US$2.7 billion,[5] in many ways only

now are they beginning to understand how that code translates into our individual makeup. Dr Horvath's epigenetic research has focused on methylation sites on our DNA in order to study the genetic and epigenetic determinants of ageing and mortality. In layman's terms, methylation is the change to genes that can be caused by environmental factors ranging from smoking to air pollution.

It is important to add here that the epigenetic research does not look at DNA, factors that are unchanged from birth and are unaffected by lifestyle and environment. Instead, epigenetics focuses on the methylation levels of the biomarkers that offer clues to whether someone is ageing more rapidly or more slowly than average, producing their "biological age".

It's pretty complex science that, in 2015, was still on the frontier of the epigenetic revolution. In the fall of 2016, I got the call I was waiting for: Dr Horvath had made a breakthrough and he wanted us to have it.

The breakthrough was exactly what we were looking for. After a statistical analysis of over 13,000 individual DNA samples that included over 3,000 mortalities, Horvath had found a specific set of DNA methylation-based biomarkers that were predictive of individual risk of all-cause mortality (all-cause mortality is a statistical assessment of deaths for any reason that researchers use as part of their analysis of life expectancy).

The implications of Horvath's discovery[6] were simple and profound: for the first time, individual lifespans could be estimated with significantly greater precision across large groups of people. And if we could apply the methodology to our business, we could, in fact, make better decisions on which life insurance policies we should purchase. We quickly optioned the technology from UCLA and, in announcing it to the world, I published a white paper about

---

[4] http://www.whatisepigenetics.com/what-is-epigenetics/.

[5] https://www.genome.gov/10001772/all-about-the--human-genome-project-hgp/.

[6] https://labs.genetics.ucla.edu/horvath/dnamage/.

what we were doing that I named "My Secret Master Plan" in homage to the entrepreneur I greatly admire, Elon Musk.

So what does it mean for our company, GWG Life, and the life insurance industry? Since optioning the technology in November 2016, we began working to find out how quickly we could integrate it into our business and apply it to new products and services. We began to gather genetic information from policy-holders by requiring cheek swabs from anyone who submits a policy to us, a very simple method to gather the material we need for analysis. In January, we hired Dr Brian Chen who was Dr Horvath's first author on his most important work and who had been working at the National Institute on Aging. Dr Chen began analysing the cheek swab samples and conducting research of our own on the implications of this technology. From the start, we believed there was value alone in simplifying the process: replacing blood samples with cheek swabs policy-holders can gather themselves saves time and money. Our analysis had also shown that we only needed to increase the accuracy of lifespan prediction by a small amount to improve the current system, but we believe much greater improvements are on the horizon. The data Dr Chen is analysing holds the promise of a deep understanding of how individuals age.

We are now more convinced than ever that this biomarker technology is at the intersection of the two cresting trends of InsurTech and the epigenetics revolution and provides the means of more inexpensive and precise life insurance products for consumers. There is immense promise in applying it to create more precise and improved life insurance products in mature markets, and in new markets where traditional medical evidence-based underwriting has been impractical or impossible. We believe that gathering genomic information will create an easier and more precise method of underwriting insurance that will, in time, become the industry standard.

We believe our corporate lineage is fitting as it was the very existence of the life insurance secondary market that drove Elizur Wright, the "father" of the modern life insurance era, to reinvent the industry by establishing regulations that require insurance carriers to provide surrender values to consumers and maintain statutory capital. And it's the secondary market that will, once again, drive another reinvention of the industry, and this time the reinvention will come from technology and market forces.

Internation-
alizing
InsurTech

4

InsurTech is a global phenomenon

GERMANY
- 1980–2017 – premiums have risen from $38bn – $108bn
- $200BN in annual revenue is still in the hands of the incumbents

CHINA
- A global insurance leader where 92% of insurance sales are online
- Internet insurance wrote premiums of just under $25 million
- Property and casualty insurance companies collected $12 billion in premiums from online sales
- A pioneer in cyber insurance – and leading in the way in regulation

LATAM
- The life insurance protection gap is estimated at $7TRN (SIGMA – World insurance 2015)
- Most are uninsured – consumer insurance represents less than 3% of the average GDP across the region
- Brazil leads having had the first digital brokers since 2012

TURKEY
- Seen a rise of 47% in FinTech investment in 2016
- 65 authorised insurance and retirement pension companies exist (39 non-life, 8 life, 17 pension, 1 reassurance)
- 81% of the vehicles but only 31% of homes are insured for compulsory earthquake insurance category

InsurTech is truly a global phenomenon. The activity and opportunity are diverse and distributed. And, like most areas of FinTech, are driven by specific market needs, demographics, or pressure points.

This part explores fascinating accounts from both mature and less developed markets, infused with case studies and cutting-edge data, which brings to life the vibrancy in this space across the globe.

Mature markets in Europe such as Germany are marked by their traditional incumbents such as Allianz and Generali. But this landscape is being changed by new market entrants such as Check24, WeFox, and TreeFin, who are taking advantage of the "gap" created by classic players trying simply to manage legacy infrastructure.

The global and undisputed InsurTech market leader is China, where 92% of insurance sales are online. This is propelled by smartphone adoption, regulatory openness, and mass urbanization, which are serving as significant drivers. The tech giants Baidu, Alibaba, Tencent, and Jongdong are leading the charge across all insurance lines.

Other markets such as Turkey, which, despite significant political instability and greater potential economic isolation, race towards a viable FinTech hub, especially in the Sharia finance world, which is marked by some great technology innovation.

Developing markets such as Latin America and South and East Africa are serving as fertile ground for technology innovation to thrive. Satellites, drones, and the Internet of Things are much needed to serve rural communities. InsurTech innovators such as Turtlemint in India and Acre in Africa are case studies to consider.

This part also reflects the global thought leadership of our authors, who without the opportunity given by *The InsurTech Book*, might not have had the platform to share their valuable experiences and knowledge with the world.

Internationalizing InsurTech – A Global Phenomenon in Different Markets

By **McKenzie M. Slaughter**
Founder and CEO, Prohaus Group

and **Telly V. Onu**
Impact Ecosystem Innovator and Managing Partner, Prohaus Group

The insurance industry has remained the same since its inception and has significantly lagged behind banks in adopting financial innovations. Recently, new players have offered new ways to underprice risk, creating new types of premiums and servicing consumers in a tightly regulated on-demand economy. This chapter will expose the reader to the impact of these new technologies on reorganizing specific points in the value chain and in unlocking new innovative business models, which will ultimately benefit both customer and the insurance industry, and will serve as a mechanism to internationalize and decentralize the resulting InsurTech innovations.

Introduction

Over the years, incumbent insurers have been able to implement incremental improvements around online customer servicing. New entrants are demonstrating that this approach is no longer sufficient.

As it relates to risk and underwriting, insurance firms compete with each other, in part based on their ability to replace that uncertainty with (in aggregate) remarkably accurate estimates outcomes. Years of fine-tuning these estimates have resulted in actuarial tables that mirror aggregate insured behaviour and conditions. The standard insurance underwriting techniques are still quite costly and time consuming due to the manual nature of data collection and processing. In life insurance, for example, an insurer will typically spend approximately one month and several hundred dollars underwriting each applicant.

Clearly there must be a better way. New forces are impacting the value chains of a number of industries such as financial services and insurance. This causes a reconfiguration of the way in which insurance is delivering value to customers through new and innovative business models and/or technologies. Airbnb and Uber provide on-demand collaborative services, a trend that is one of many, disrupting how the insurance industry develops and markets products to the on-demand economy's unique customer base.

With new and emerging technologies unlocking the power of large amounts of data, digitalization of the production processes, interconnectivity along the value chain and within the value network, and an overall new digitally enhanced customer experience, the entire insurance industry has the potential to reorganize itself leading to even more transformative business models. Examples include insurers' use of specific telemetric sensors and other elements of the Internet of Things (IoT) to underwrite and price policies in a matter of seconds due to the real-time nature of the data being analysed, as is the case with auto insurance. Other examples include the application of robotics and AI (artificial intelligence) and analytics that can improve service turnaround times by reducing the need for intervention as well as provide radically different experiences for customers through faster claims settlement, easier onboarding and renewals, and fraud controls to name but a few. This lowers premiums for customers, increases revenue, and lowers costs for insurance companies, making them even more competitive

For the first time in over a decade, the insurance industry has seen a proliferation of new players offering new ways to underprice risk, creating new types of premiums and servicing consumers in a tightly regulated on-demand economy.

Key Value Drivers of InsurTech

With intergenerational customer centricity fuelling the disruption, Gen X and millennials are redefining the manner of engagement in the industry. In accordance with a study by PwC, in 2020, millennials and Gen X will control more than half of all investable financial assets or about US$30 trillion. Eighty percent are weary of traditional non-transparent brick and mortar financial services providers and prefer using online channels. Millennials want to be in control of their finances and are extremely cost conscious. This generation has grown up with the digital experience offered by companies such as Google, Amazon, Facebook, and Apple. They expect the same level of information transparency and social customer experiences used to making purchase decisions from their financial services providers. They are now faced with an insurance industry that is stuck in a time warp of highly intermediated, vague products through high-cost and low-service channels. In summary, transparency, simplicity, and attractiveness are facilitating the emergence of InsurTech as a viable industry of its own.

Uncovering Opportunities in the Insurance Value Chain

A quick look at the critical pieces of the insurance value chain can show the tremendous impact and opportunities for new technologies:

Marketing, sales, and distribution. The distribution model is moving online, market boundaries are blurring, and business-to-business and business-to-consumer products have the ability to cross borders enabling the internationalization of products and services and leading to changing dynamics in the global ecosystem. As we shall see later, the utilization of technologies such as the distributed ledger system can create a global decentralized insurance system.

New business underwriting. New pricing models are based on new value configurations such as peer-to-peer sharing. Underwriting also involves new risk-based models leveraging big data, personalized products, and innovations such as usage-based insurance.

Policy and claims management. Digital claims handling, including automated assessments and fraud detection, and online/self-servicing of claims are all opportunities that InsurTech can offer in transforming data.

Payments. While payment innovation has been a focus within the finance sector, very little has been done to apply some of these payment or "PayTech" innovations to the insurance value chain. These include the use of mobile wallets that can be also incorporate risk pooling models, peer-to-peer insurance models, and streamlined payments, among others.

Customer service. With smart devices everywhere, consumers demand more contextual real-time information to facilitate their decision-making. There is also a high expectation for a seamless, frictionless experience. There is a need for end-to-end digital transformation along the customer journey with multiple touchpoints. Technology such as AI is being applied to either assist customers or in contextualizing all this data in a manner the customer can understand in real time.

Product design, development, and management. This allows insurance companies to repackage existing products that could be on-demand or modular and deliver them using online and mobile channels or in a different manner. It also allows for the development of new digital products and services and the personalization of products.

Future Applications: GAME Changing Technologies to Further Scale InsurTech

Decentralized Ledger Technology

As mentioned earlier, one area that has the most potential in internationalizing insurance is the famous decentralized ledger technology known as blockchain technology. Made famous by the increased adoption of digital currencies, it has the potential to facilitate cross-border risk underwriting through its transparent distributed database. The blockchain's ability to send, receive, and store information has the underlying power to disrupt the way businesses process digital transactions in insurance. The implications of this are significant as it is not only transparent but highly secure. This fosters trust, which means that any asset, whether tangible or intangible, can be assigned ownership and the transference between parties. This has the power to simplify back office claims processes and therefore reduces the costs of transactions, which can in turn reduce the premiums for customers. While still in the early stages, the use of this technology and resulting use of the ledger and decentralized network could create many new products and services. On the one hand, using smart contracts can not only support claims management when it is used as a register of claims, but linking this ability with insurance as applied to collateral for lending can work very effectively in increasing access to finance.

By incorporating a layer of AI into smart contracts, one can see on the horizon an almost autonomous delivery of insurance, which can be effective in usage-based insurance.

Peer-to-Peer (P2P) Insurance

Much as crowdfunding disrupted the financing of SMEs, the power of the decentralized ledger technology and smart contracts can transition new models of insurance, such as P2P insurance into a new digital age. Peer-to-peer insurance empowers policy-holders to receive a greater portion of the premiums rather than the private wealth managers working for insurance companies. There are a growing number of startups that are adopting peer-to-peer and pooled methods to offer insurance.

A couple of examples are Mindful Society and Guevara, which are alternative insurance offerings utilizing share pools to access complementary health providers and cheaper auto insurance premiums. This uses the policy-holders' social capital to replace underwriters P2P, while the use of smart contracts can increase the speed of claims processing by better matching the demand between consumers and the online marketplace.

Conclusion

Overall, insurance firms are not investing enough in change to keep pace with the InsurTech trend and its transformation opportunities. In many cases, traditional insurers are being displaced by new players that are reliant on digital business models. The easy accessibility of cloud and mobile technologies as well as big data is changing the enterprise landscape. It is these new players that have found ways of becoming global players with their ability to scale these startups. The resulting impact would result in a unique InsurTech industry, with its own rules and norms. Will the industry catch up?

Increasing Access to Insurance in Developing Countries

By Susan Holliday
Principal Insurance Specialist, IFC

The Role of Insurance in Economic Development

Insurance, pensions, and savings support sustainable development in a number of ways:

- Allowing enterprises to take on more risk and create new businesses and jobs.

- Providing a safety net for individuals, families, and communities.

- Acting as an economic multiplier. Insurers can deploy assets into the local economy and support infrastructure and housing.

- Supporting the development of capital markets as insurers can invest their own funds and their customers' savings.

- Protecting against natural disasters and promoting food security.

Penetration of Insurance is Lower in Developing Countries

The penetration of insurance in developing countries measured by premiums to GDP is on average just 2.9% compared with over 7% in the US and higher in some European countries. Ironically this means that the most vulnerable people are often the least protected. To give just one example, more than one third of the world's poor live in low-income countries, which represent 70% of the most natural disaster-prone countries. The average direct loss from such "nat cats" is 2.9% of GDP, and can be as high as 12% as we saw in the Thai floods in 2011, whereas in industrialized countries the average loss is only 0.8% of GDP. The life insurance

protection gap is estimated (SIGMA – World insurance 2015) at US$7 trillion in Latin America and US$32 trillion in South and East Asia. In many cases, if the main earner dies or is unable to work, there is a devastating effect on their dependants, which in turn puts a strain on local communities.[1]

Affordable, Accessible, and Appropriate

The challenge before us today is how to provide protection that is affordable, accessible, and meets the needs of the individuals, families, and communities in developing countries. This is easier to talk about than achieve, but nonetheless technology is opening up new possibilities all the time and this is an exciting growth opportunity for the insurance industry. I would even go so far as to say that, as with payments and some other aspects of banking and lending, solutions from developing countries can help insurers transform their business models in more mature markets.

In order to gain traction, insurance products need to be affordable, accessible, and understandable. Technology can help achieve all of these. Traditionally many insurers shied away from mass market consumer and small commercial risks in developing countries on the basis that it was impossible to make any money. Technology can cut out costs, both in "manufacturing" and in "distribution", and this possibility will only increase further as areas like artificial intelligence (AI), new methods of authentication, use of algorithms for underwriting, mobile payments, etc. develop further.

Typically, insurance products are seen as very complicated, even by experts like me! In some cases, there is a view (rightly or wrongly) that there is a lot of small print, put there in order for the insurer to avoid paying the claim. While protecting against fraud is important in being able to make policies affordable, the insurance

---

[1] Swiss Re Sigma, World insurance in 2015: steady growth amid regional disparities, http://www.swissre.com/library/sigma3_2016_en.html.

has to be understandable and meet a real need. Otherwise people will not buy insurance unless it's compulsory, which is not usually the case in developing countries. This is an opportunity to design simpler products, where it is more obvious when a claim in triggered, without the need for lengthy form filling or delays.

There is a huge need for financial education, in both mature and developing countries. This can be seen as a precondition to the successful adoption of insurance. The importance of face-to-face communication by trusted sources cannot be overemphasized. However, technology still has an important role here. Agents and brokers can be provided with technology on phones or iPads to improve customer service and make the sales process more efficient. Advice can be given online or via mobile, both in terms of the insurance itself but also for areas such as health or what to do in case of weather-related events, for example. Gamification techniques can also help educate people about insurance and risk and drive better behaviours, in terms of risk prevention, exercise, etc.

Technologies Applied to Insurance in Developing Countries

I would broadly categorize the main insurance related technologies as follows:

- Fully digital insurer – regulated risk carriers;

- Online brokers/advisors – often regulated as intermediaries;

- Aggregators and platforms – such as price comparison sites;

- Process improvers – dealing with one part of the value chain such as claims, payments, or doctor consultations;

- Data and analytics – support insurers but also other sectors such as hospitals, auto manufacturers;

- Other – the catch-all, but includes the important areas of drones, satellites, wearables, mobile health, agriculture, and weather tech.

These apply equally to developing and mature markets, but in some cases it may be easier to gain traction in developing countries as there is less of an incumbent legacy.

Examples of Technology

While we are only starting to see how technology can transform the insurance industry, I would like to offer a few examples of what can be done.

MicroEnsure – Use of Mobile Phone Distribution and Bundling to Increase Insurance Penetration

MicroEnsure is an IFC investment, which partners with insurers and distributors to provide innovative insurance solutions to bottom-of-the-pyramid people in emerging markets. A recent product to be launched was the digital health service, TONIC, in Bangladesh. TONIC was launched through Telenor's mobile operator, Grameenphone. It offers four main services: health and lifestyle advice, access to a doctor on the phone at an affordable rate, discounts on services at hospitals, and a hospital cash product with claims paid directly to mobile wallet. This is an example of many of the ways that technology can deliver solutions in emerging markets, which both makes healthcare more accessible and cheaper and also relieves pressure on local resources due to saving on travel and hospital services.

Hellas Direct – New Fully Digital Insurance Company in Greece

Hellas Direct was founded in 2012 to offer motor insurance at a better price and with better customer service in Greece, where the economy remains under severe strain following the financial crisis. Hellas cuts out brokers (thus saving the hefty commissions involved) and sells policies directly by phone, online, or mobile. Underwriting is done by algorithms, so can be updated in real time, customers are offered different policy durations ranging from 30 days to a year, and claims are typically settled in a couple days making use of photos and videos from mobile phones and potentially even drones. The company has an app that can monitor driving behaviour and used gamification by launching a competition to identify the "best driver in Greece", which should improve road safety. They also offer ancillary services such as roadside assistance and a network of garages to ensure cars are repaired efficiently and costs are controlled. This model increases the interaction between the policy-holder and the insurer and reduces the risk of fraud. This is a good example of using the most modern technology to provide competitive pricing and excellent customer experience in a market that is still very old fashioned, and with the potential to move into other types of insurance.

Turtlemint – Online Broker in India

Turtlemint is an online broker offering motor insurance for cars and two wheelers, health, and term life. As well as comparing prices, Turtlemint focuses on identifying the key priorities of the customer, such as being able to use your local hospital, and finding the best fit. It also provides education about risks, insurance, safety, and health. Some of the interesting features of Turtlemint are that the site is directly linked with insurance companies' sites so you can buy a policy straight away; however, there is also an option to talk to an agent and many of Turtlemint's users are company agents who are using it for lead generation, or point of sale agents (who represent multiple companies). This means that the company can also impact the 80% of the Indian insurance market that is still offline, or those who prefer to continue to go through an agent. They use Facebook messenger as a communication tool, which is popular in India as many people have phones that do not have

a lot of memory and tend not to use apps. However, they also offer an app for agents as well as consumers, which provides fast processing of claims as well as access to ancillary services like roadside assistance. The company intends to add other lines of insurance such as travel, home, and crop as well as savings products in due course.

ACRE Africa – Applying Technology to the Needs of Small Farmers

One of the earliest examples of technological innovation in the insurance sector in developing countries was Kilimo Salama in Kenya. A joint venture between the Syngenta Foundation for Sustainable Development, Safaricom, and UAP Insurance, the product provided parametric cover based on rainfall. This model used various innovative technologies at all stages. The product was sold by community agriculture shops and seed distributors and if the farmer chose to buy the insurance, the stockist would scan the barcode on the bag of seeds corresponding to seed and fertilizer brands available for insurance at subsidized rates using an app on their mobile phone. The app would calculate premium payable, capture client details, and send policy confirmation via SMS. This was transmitted to the insurer, calculating the coverage amount and the premium. Communication was done by text message, and premiums and claims were settled using the M-PESA mobile wallet. The rainfall and other climate data were measured using solar-powered weather stations and the payments based on a widely used Water Requirement Satisfaction Index. The initial policy was designed so that if the crops failed due to weather, the farmer would receive a payout to enable them to buy more seeds to plant for the next harvest. The first version covered seeds for maize but subsequently the products have been extended to cover other crops, other inputs, such as fertilizers, and the harvest outputs. The product was also picked up by micro lenders, who made buying insurance a requirement to get a loan and this added considerably to the growth.

Conclusion

We can see that technology is already being used in many ways in developing countries to enable simple, affordable, and accessible products. While there are always local nuances, the ideas discussed here are certainly transferable to other markets. There are challenges to reach scale, not least the need for education about risk and insurance and advice. Furthermore, because these are new areas and in many cases involve collaboration between different sectors, it is important that regulation supports these innovations and they do not get caught up either in unintended consequences or in regulatory frameworks so onerous that they destroy the economics. It is, however, clear that technology is key to the advancement of accessible and affordable insurance in developing countries and can unlock many benefits both for consumers and the insurance industry.

Insurance in China

By Robert Collins
COO, Crossbordr

China is the second biggest insurance market in the world by premium volume, having surpassed Japan in 2016. With favourable macro-economic conditions prevailing, and a massive population of 1.4 billion people, the Chinese insurance market has grown dramatically. Nonetheless, the penetration rate for insurance in China remains low compared to Western measures. This leaves plenty of headroom for growth in the China market.

InsurTech in China

The Chinese market presents tremendous opportunities for InsurTech. China is a proven leader in the world of InsurTech. Internet insurance companies in China wrote premiums of just under US$25 million.[1] Property and casualty insurance companies in China collected US$12 billion in premiums from online sales – a total of 92% of online insurance sales were from the websites of non-life insurers.[2]

Millennials and Generation Y customers accounted for the majority of online insurance sales: 47% were born in the 1980s while 33% were born after the 1990s – the most active online users buying insurance online are young families.[3] While many other markets are embracing innovation and technology at a strong pace, China will rise to be the world leader in InsurTech.

---

[1] End of year 2015. CNNIC; IResearch; McKinsey.

[2] End of year 2015. Asian Insurance Review.

[3] 2016, Analysis of Internet Insurance Customer Conduct, Ant Financial Services Group and CBNdata.

Why Can China Become the Leader in InsurTech?

Most developing countries cannot claim to be leading players in technology, where the technology meets at the intersection of an age-old industry, such as insurance. Yet, China can rightly make this claim in InsurTech. How did China become such a fast growing, dynamic InsurTech market? This is due to the confluence of factors that have coalesced within China for InsurTech to develop so swiftly. They include: the growth in online penetration, booming e-commerce platforms, the increasing impact of social media, mobile telephony – with more than 50 million smartphone users in China – the rise of the middle class, mass urbanization, insurance industry deregulation, and a younger generation of Chinese consumers.

Early Regulatory Support

The Chinese insurance regulators played an important role in the rise of InsurTech. Before the word "sandbox" became a term to describe a regulatory establishment that supports development of InsurTech, the China Insurance Regulatory Commission (CIRC) was encouraging experimentation on a national basis.

In the year 2012, the moniker for InsurTech did not exist. Yet, CIRC designed legislation to support the development of online insurance. Most notably, CIRC enacted the so-called Internet Insurance Law in October 2015, which superseded an earlier law from 2012. With an accommodative regulatory environment, China built a solid foundation for InsurTech.

Ecosystem Power Players: BATJ

A discussion on China's fast growing InsurTech market is not complete without an understanding of the role of China's technology giants, commonly referred to as BATJ. It is an acronym for Baidu, Alibaba, Tencent, and Jingdong. Baidu is China's dominant search company; Alibaba owns Alipay and the e-commerce marketplace, Tmall; Tencent owns the wildly popular WeChat brand – a smartphone service provider with a "we can do everything app"; and Jingdong, also known as JD, is a big e-commerce platform player.

So, what does this have to do with InsurTech? Everything. BATJ know they have significant advantages over the industry incumbents – especially massive amounts of data. And they have access to distribution and can accelerate social engagement, too. The major technology giants have a strong desire to participate in China's booming financial services market – with insurance seen as an area that is ripe for disruption.

World Leader in InsurTech

ZhongAn Online Property & Casualty Insurance Company is catching significant growth waves in China. ZhongAn reported online premiums of more than US$375 million in 2016, an increase of 49% over 2015. This young and ambitious unicorn (unicorns are companies with valuations higher than US$1 billion) is setting the pace for online insurance. ZhongAn is more than the first online insurance company in China – it is an innovation powerhouse. The company is a full-stack digital insurer powered by an open, scalable cloud-based core insurance platform providing high-speed, high-volume service outputs that are in demand by China's consumers.

ZhongAn was born in 2013, by the joining of two Chinese technology giants – Alibaba and Tencent – and Ping An Insurance. (Ping An is a market leader in insurance.) At the end of March 2017, ZhongAn had cumulatively sold more than 8 billion policies to 582 million customers since its formation. The company ecosystem extends to 300 network partners. ZhongAn has very effectively used its first-mover advantage to become the challenger insurer in China. As such, ZhongAn has the potential to own 5% market share of the property and casualty market.

The company excels at product design and quick delivery of new products – often under two months. The company is adept at developing innovative scenario-based insurances, some of which are disruptive. These products are popular among ZhongAn's target customers – the younger generation of Chinese born in the 1980s and 90s.

The company markets over 300 products. A magical product designed by ZhongAn covers visitors to Shanghai Disneyland should they encounter excessive rain or heat. The company uses real-time government weather reports to trigger a payment to compensate visitors for a rained-out day at the park. Another product is flight delay – it pays compensation to passengers that don't depart on time. On many of its scenario-based products, claim payments are made directly to the insured's bank account – so-called parametric payments. ZhongAn is also pioneering innovative women's cancer products, too, by prescreening potential risk factors through voluntary DNA testing.

The firm will continue to blaze new trails in innovation with the help of ZhongAn Technology – a sister company focused on innovation. "ABCD" is ZhongAn's acronym for artificial intelligence, blockchain, cloud computing, and data, which it will enlist to keep ahead of the intensifying competition. It's all part of its master plan to commercialize new technologies to drive new growth. ZhongAn is likely to have its sights on the big prize – China's colossal auto insurance market.

Other Chinese InsurTechs

This market is fast becoming the hot bet for innovation in InsurTech, helping to shed China's "follow fast" image. While ZhongAn may be the new darling of InsurTech in China, the next batch of industry startups is already emerging.

Is there a Zendrive or Metromile near-equivalent in China? Yes, there's OKChexian. (Chexian means auto insurance in Chinese pinyin.) With its patented, smartphone-based telematics technology app name OKDrive, it offers not only customized pricing, but predictive modelling capabilities, too. And through OKScore – China's first auto insurance scoring methodology – driver behaviour can be assessed across five key dimensions. They also market a few clever and popular products to relieve pain points for Chinese drivers, including parking ticket and traffic jam protection plans.

You can't talk about InsurTech in China without mentioning TongJuBao (P2P Protect). They created a marketplace community that shares social risk among its buying group members. In this way, the community bridges the trust gap that's usually found in the traditional market relationships between the insurer and the customer. They bring interesting products to the Chinese market, including a novel child protection plan — missing children are a concern in China – as one of their more popular offerings. The company also offers protection against divorce, by providing a fixed monthly indemnity to help a member to reorganize their life. Looking ahead, P2P Protect plans to expand internationally, starting in Europe and the US.

Other InsurTech firms in the market worth mentioning include Huize Insurance, an online insurance marketplace, and Xiaoyusan, an online life platform, which claims three million users. There are also newcomers such as An Xin Insurance and Yi An Insurance – two domestic online insurers that will be worth watching. The market will no doubt closely follow the progress of the new Allianz-Baidu joint venture upon the launch of Bai An Insurance.

China's Biggest Opportunity?

Digital health in China is yet another big prize in the insurance market. The healthcare market is projected to grow to US$1 trillion by 2020. Expanded opportunities for private health insurance have arrived as the government deregulated the market. Not surprisingly, private investment has brought new business models and technology-led innovation to the Chinese digital health market.

Ping An is a hugely successful diversified financial services firm. It is one of three large private health insurers in China. It is very focused on the digital health market. Interestingly, its most notable investment outside of China is in digital health – Oscar Health Insurance. Ping An Haoyisheng (Ping An Good Doctor) is the leading digital health platform in China. The company states it has more than 120 million registered users. Many of these healthcare platforms offer online health insurance products alongside other services such as medical appointments, medical advice, and consulting. Good Doctor is the mightiest of the unicorns in digital health so far, but other Chinese technology giants have their sights on this big prize, too. Recently, Tencent added to its growing collection of online healthcare companies with an investment in Haodaifu Online. It also owns a stake in two others: We Doctor Group and Miaoshou Doctor.

Looking Forward...

The future for InsurTech in China is very bright. By 2022, China's middle-class population is projected to exceed 600 million – nearly twice the size of the population of the US. Chinese consumers are on the rise and embracing the Internet of Everything. China is a rapid-growth market and remains underpenetrated for insurance. Groundbreaking innovation is thriving in China as insurance startups and incumbents embrace new technologies – think ZhongAn Technology as an innovation engine for its sister insurance company, new business models sprouting up from P2P Protect to OKChexian to Ping An Good Doctor, and newly created products abound – some wrapped with parametric solutions – the list goes on.

Most notably, one of China's market leaders, Ping An Insurance, is the leading light in InsurTech, too. The exceptional performance and determined leadership demonstrated by Ping An bodes well both as a source of inspiration and a challenge for other Chinese insurance incumbents. In the coming years, the Chinese insurance industry will see many more growth waves from InsurTech firms. Some will remain ahead of incumbents and startup companies alike.

Seven Things Insurers and InsurTechs Need to Know about the German Insurance Market

By Dr Robin Kiera
Thought Leader and Founder, Digitalscouting.de

There's a simple rule for winning against the best soccer team in Germany, Bayern Munich: don't play soccer against them. Play chess. The same principle also applies to incumbent insurers and InsurTech companies in Germany. The most successful InsurTechs in Germany don't challenge the incumbents at their game – they invent new rules that make the situation unpredictable. This chapter sheds light on the playing field of incumbents and InsurTechs: the insurance market in Germany.

1. The German Insurance Market is a One-stop Shop

The German insurance industry, led by Allianz and followed by Talanx, Generali, R&V, and Debeka, is by far not the largest national market. Compared to the largest market in the world, the US$1.3 trillion market, Germany only generates US$208 billion annual revenue.

But here's the good news: the German insurance market is primarily regulated on a national level. Unlike other large markets, there are few legal differences between the 16 different states. Once you enter the market anywhere, you are ready to go nationwide. It's a one-stop shop.

2. Incumbents in Germany: a Success Story with Underlying Problems

Over the last four decades, incumbents in Germany have set impressive records. From 1980 to today, the yearly amount of premiums of direct insurers has risen from US$38 to 208 billion, and the proportion of premiums compared to GDP has risen from 4.57% to 6.2%. At first glance, these numbers[1] indicate a strong and stable industry.

But a closer look reveals troubling details. From 1980 to today, the number of insurers has decreased by 33%. Moreover, the average age[2] of agents is alarmingly high:[3] 48.8 years – in some cases well over 50. Studies have shown that, over time, the customer base of an agent converges to the social demographics of that agent. In the case of an ageing sales force, it is likely that the customer base is ageing too. Considering that the most lucrative insurance contracts are sold in the age cohort from 25 to 45, a lot of incumbents in Germany are sitting on a ticking demographic time bomb – especially since new players in the market target precisely the profitable customer cohort. However, the decades of success and great recent KPIs could cloud the judgement of industry veterans managing incumbents today.

---

[1] GDV, Versicherungsbeiträge, http://www.gdv.de/zahlen-fakten/branchendaten/ueberblick/#versicherungsbeitraege.

[2] Versicherungsbote, Altersschnitt der Versicherungsvertreter bei 48,8 Jahren, published on 26 March 2014, http://www.versicherungsbote.de/id/4793492/Versicherungsvertreter-Vermittler-Alter-Nachwuchs-Durchschnitt/.

[3] Versicherungsbote, Versicherungsvertrieb – Nur jeder zwanzigste Vermittler jünger als 30 Jahre, published on 4 September 2015, http://www.versicherungsbote.de/id/4827965/BKV-ermittelt-Versicherungs-branche-ueberaltert/.

3. InsurTechs in Germany: a Success Story, but no Disruption – Yet

Even though in 2016, only about US$82 million[4] was invested into German InsurTechs, several InsurTech companies have developed exciting business models and digital products and services along the value chain. There are marketplaces such as Check24 (founded by Heinrich Blase and Eckhard Juls) or Getsurance (Johannes and Victor Becher). Some InsurTechs focus on digital insurance management systems, such as Clark (Christopher Oster), Wefox (led by Julian Teicke), Knip (Dennis Just and Christina Kehl), and Treefin (Andreas Gensch and Reinhard Tahedl). There are also direct insurers or companies working with tied agents, such as Haftpflichthelden (Stefan Herbst, Florian Knörrich, and Jan Schmidt) and Ottonova (Roman Rittweger) – and don't forget the cashback approach of Friendsurance (Tim Kunde and Sebastian Herfurth). Several InsurTechs offer sales tools and targeted insurance, such as Massup (Fabian Fischer) or Kasko (Nikolaus Sühr and Matt Wardle). Last but not least, several InsurTechs were founded as part of the company builder Finleap (Jan Beckers, Ramin Niroumand, and Hendrik Krawinkel).

Nevertheless, the largest parts of the annual US$200 billion German insurance market are still in the hands of the incumbents. While we have seen several innovations by InsurTechs in Germany, not one has disrupted the market – yet.

4. The Technological Legacy of Incumbents Binds Billions of US Dollars

If you want to ruin the mood of a C-suite of a German insurer, mention "legacy". Since most German insurers have focused for decades on

generating record-breaking revenue by focusing on thousands of agents and brokers, the IT department was perceived as a service and cost centre. Different silo departments were ordered to develop individual solutions. This led in most cases to a highly fragmented, expensive IT landscape with limited performance. German insurers invest billions of US dollars in maintaining and developing their legacy systems using so-called "run the business" budgets. And if you compared such budgets to budgets focused on transformational activities, a lot less of these are invested in innovative digital products and services.

5. Incumbents' Cultural Constraint Wastes Uncounted Resources

Most insurers in Germany are over 100 years old, and were founded with strong top-down hierarchies and command-and-control structures. Over time, these fossil organizations developed cultures reflecting their structures. In most incumbents, this heritage still exists today. Here's a personal example: I witnessed a project manager from an agile e-commerce company taking over her first project at a midsize German insurer. Due to the disastrous status of the project, she reported a red light. Eventually, the CIO called her personally, making it clear that she should immediately change "red" to "green", "because it did not look good". Needless to say, she did it – even though this did not improve the project. Incidents like this explain the big portfolios of melon projects at incumbents: green on the outside, red on the inside.

In addition, there are C-suites employing private chefs, separate entrances, and VIP elevators. For the rest of the employees, bloated rules regulate the size of offices, access to the Internet, or the help of assistants according to one's rank. This culture affects the performance of organizations. I once witnessed the founding of a digital unit led by an almost 60-year-old industry veteran. Instead of pushing the project, he spent the first weeks

---

4 Deutsche Startups, "82,4 Millionen flossen 2016 in InsurTech-Start-ups", published by the ds-team on 26 January 2017, https://www.deutsche-start-ups.de/2017/01/26/824-millionen-flossen-2016-insurtech-start-ups/.

designing his new business cards and celebrating his new title, among other things. No question that this fossil manager led the digital multi-million-dollar project right off a cliff.

Another phenomenon is the HiPPO Syndrome: the Highest Paid Person's Opinion. Who, when working for an incumbent organization, has not witnessed meetings where subject matter experts fall silent out of fear of contradicting a C-suite or senior vice president who presents his or her non-expert opinion?

In contrast to this, over the last decades, new, agile organizations have developed. Here the CEO participates with the intern in group exercises, demonstrating the eradication of formal hierarchy. Teams – especially in the development of digital products and services – organize their work independently. Input from individual employees is a part of daily business. Deviation from a process is considered creativity, and failure learning. Success stories from around the world have shown that agile organizations possess several advantages. Production is more customer-oriented, faster, and cheaper.

A century ago, fossil principles may have helped to form a US$200 billion industry. In the era of digital revolution, these principles have become cultural legacies, wasting resources and impeding modernization.

6. Incumbents Have One Strategic Advantage, but They Need to Use it

In contrast to their several disadvantages, incumbents possess one central advantage over InsurTechs: gigantic amounts of knowledge and a century of experience supported by the capture of customers' needs, bound in terabytes of historical data.

The possibilities are endless. Imagine, for example, an insurer using sophisticated data analysis and designing artificial intelligence models to provide customers with valuable digital products and services. Imagine using big data analysis to calculate risks and crushing pricing – making high-cost coverage available to underinsured parts of society. Imagine an insurer calculating buying or cancellation probabilities and designing strategies to support selling automatically or countering the cancellation of policies with concise, omnichannel communication. All this could increase revenue significantly, but more importantly it could change the way insurance is perceived: from being a necessary evil to the social good it once provided. There is a saying: "If you're still improving candles, you're not likely to develop a light bulb." To embrace digitalization's unique opportunities, incumbents need to invest dramatically in their technical and cultural modernization. It's not enough to digitalize with fossil tools, methods, and manpower – and large portfolios of melon projects. New methods, tools, and skills need to be used for true cultural change.

7. Insurance in Germany is Like the Bundesliga

One question remains: will new players such as InsurTechs or diversifying tech companies be able to conquer the large customer base of the incumbents with exciting digital products and services before the incumbents catch up?

I believe that the insurance industry in Germany is like the Bundesliga. Every season, certain teams like Bayern Munich are on top. Then there are the teams always struggling at the bottom of the league (for example, my favourite, Hamburg Sports Club). And every season, some teams do surprisingly well or surprisingly badly. Most likely, this will be the case in the German insurance industry too. Most top insurers will prevail. Others will struggle. We will see some positive and negative surprises. InsurTechs will establish themselves in the industry. At the same time, more and more traditional insurers will disappear faster and faster, because technical and cultural legacy prevents modernization the customers demand.

The insurance market in Germany has not yet been disrupted. But the underlying change in customer behaviour and customer expectation is dramatic. If you want to beat Bayern Munich, don't play soccer against them. Some incumbents are slowly beginning to realize that they need to stop playing their fossil game and start to play the agile one. They are preparing or pursuing dramatic changes while other incumbents still plan to wait and see. As in soccer, the latter will lose.

Considering the state of the industry, well-funded InsurTech companies can challenge the status quo. This also applies to diversifying tech companies and first-moving incumbents. Maybe this is a once-in-a-century chance in which large changes in the German insurance market are possible – for the benefit of the customer. An exciting time for all of us.

In summary, the most successful InsurTechs in Germany don't challenge the incumbents at their game – they invent new rules that make the situation unpredictable. This chapter shed light on the playing field of incumbents and InsurTechs: the insurance market in Germany.

InsurTech in Turkey – Challenges and Opportunities

By Melike Belli
Market Development Manager, Cybertonica

Introduction

The Turkish FinTech ecosystem has been growing and attracting global interest since the beginning of 2016. Recent developments have brought banks, financial services incumbents, FinTech startups, investors, policy-makers, regulators, experts, and professionals closer together in a stronger ecosystem. In 2016, FinTech startups raised US$29 million compared to US$4.6 million in 2012, and 47% of the total startup investment was made into them. FinTech is now the top investment category in Turkey.

In a report published by Deloitte and Global FinTech Hubs Federation in 2017, Turkey's financial centre, Istanbul, is listed as a "new" FinTech hub among 44 cities across the world.[1] Most of the 200+ FinTech companies operating in Turkey are based in Istanbul. A majority of these startups provide innovative payment and digital banking solutions. A closer look at the players in the FinTech ecosystem reveals that the number of startups operating on the InsurTech scene is very low.

Insurance in Turkey: The Industry Overview

The insurance sector is regulated by the undersecretariat of Turkish Treasury. As of March 2016, there are 65 authorized insurance and retirement pension companies in Turkey (39 non-life, 8 life, 17 pension, 1 reassurance).[2] Multinational companies, such as Allianz and AXA, are strong players in the insurance industry. Currently, Allianz is the market leader of the non-life insurance segment while Ziraat is dominating the life insurance segment.[3] Motor insurance, health insurance, home insurance, life insurance, and the compulsory earthquake insurance are the main products offered in the Turkish insurance market.

During our interview, Accenture Turkey's Digital Transformation Senior Manager, Cansen Ergun, stated that the total premium production increased by 41% between 2010 and 2015. However, compared to peer countries, the Turkish insurance market is still underpenetrated as total premiums as a percentage of GDP represent only 1.4%.[4]

In our interview, Accenture Turkey's Digital Country Lead, Erdal Guner, mentioned that unlike the banking industry, which has multiple customer segments, there are two main customer types in the Turkish insurance sector: individual customers and business customers.

Cansen Ergun explained that customer ownership lies with insurance agents for most of the products and insurers remain relatively passive in customer segmentation as they don't possess sufficient information to make a detailed analysis. However, she added, they do leverage banks' customer segmentations (corporate, retail, affluent, etc.) for products sold through bancassurance.

---

[1] Deloitte, A tale of 44 cities – Connecting Global FinTech: Interim Hub Review 2017, April 2017, London: Deloitte, http://www2.deloitte.com/content/dam/Deloitte/uk/Documents/Innovation/deloitte-uk-connecting-global-fintech-hub-federation-innotribe-innovate-finance.pdf.

[2] T.C. Basbakanlik Hazine Mustesarligi, Sigorta ve Reasurans Sirketleri ile Emeklilik Sirketlerinin Ruhsat Sahibi Oldugu Branslari Gosterir Tablo, March 2016, Ankara: T.C. Basbakanlik Hazine Mustesarligi, https://www.hazine.gov.tr/tr-TR/Sayfalar/Sigorta-Sirketleri.

[3] Investment Support and Promotion Agency of Turkey (ISPAT), Financial Services Sector in Turkey, June 2016, Ankara: Investment Support and Promotion Agency of Turkey, http://www.invest.gov.tr/en-US/infocenter/publications/Documents/FINANCIAL.SERVICES.INDUSTRY.pdf.

[4] Ibid.

While Turkey is advanced in digital banking, insurers are lagging behind in technology usage.[5] However, Cansen Ergun shared that customer behaviour has been evolving along with the rise of digital connectivity: customers need and demand greater transparency, quicker access to information, price and service comparison platforms, and reliability, urging insurers to utilize digital channels.

The Turkish InsurTech Ecosystem

According to Start-ups.Watch, there are 12 active InsurTech companies that have raised US$2.1 million in the last two years, showing that the InsurTech market is untapped in Turkey.

Most of these InsurTech companies, such as Sigortam.net, Sigortayeri, and Sigorta Dukkanim ("sigorta" means insurance in Turkish), are aggregators; they are comparison websites providing customers with quotes from different insurance providers. Other than aggregators, there are data and risk analysis companies like Reidin and UrbanStat; policy management companies such as PolitaSIS and Polibis; and risk management companies like Globit and Risklator operating in the market.[6]

Main Challenges

There are several reasons why the insurance industry has not yet fully embraced technology, and why InsurTech has a tiny share in the Turkish FinTech market:

1. Individual insurance customers are generally sceptical towards insurance companies, and their trust in insurers and awareness in relation to having insurance policies are quite limited. Most customers don't realize why they need insurance, don't clearly know what they are buying or understand the terms and conditions, and think that they haven't been given the right information about the products. Moreover, in Turkey, the more income an individual has, the greater their willingness to have an insurance policy. Recent data show that even in the compulsory insurance categories, the expected results have not been achieved. While in the compulsory traffic insurance category 81% of the vehicles are insured, in the compulsory earthquake insurance category only 31% of homes are insured.[7]

2. Insurance products are sold via two main distribution channels: insurance agents selling 63% of non-life insurance products, and banks selling 79% of life insurance products (mostly with their credit products).[8]

At the same time, the current proportion of insurance policies that are being sold purely on digital channels is very low. Insurance companies neither promote digital channels enough nor lead customers to use them. In our interview, Erdal Guner said:

Insurance companies in Turkey consider insurance agents as their "main customers" since agents are crucial distribution channels. They are less willing to bypass agents and communicate with customers through digital channels as they don't want to upset their agents holding the relationship with them.

Cansen Ergun also commented:

InsurTech start-ups in Turkey can remove the intermediaries in acquiring and retaining customers after having enough capital

---

[5] M. Belli, Banking and FinTech – Developing a FinTech Ecosystem in Istanbul, February 2016 (Istanbul: Interbank Card Center of Turkey), http://bkm.com.tr/wp-content/uploads/2016/02/Banking-and-FinTech.pdf.

[6] M. Belli, The Turkish FinTech Ecosystem – Progress Report 2016. February 2017, Istanbul: Interbank Card Center of Turkey, http://bkm.com.tr/wp-content/uploads/2017/02/Progress-Report-FinTech-2016.pdf.

[7] Sigorta Bilgi ve Gozetim Merkezi, Turk Sigorta Sektoru Yukselise Gecti, March 2016, https://sbm.org.tr/tr/BasindaSBM/Sayfalar/turk-sigorta-sektoru-yukselise-gecti.aspx.

[8] Insurance Association of Turkey, Insurance Association of Turkey & Turkish Insurance Market, April 2016, http://www.internationalinsur-anceforum.com/wp-content/uploads/2015/11/TSB-xprimsunumakif.pdf.

and getting a license to operate. However, the power of agencies in the current model means higher barriers to entry for InsurTech start-ups.

3. Current regulation, access to capital, and gaining a licence to operate are the challenges facing new entrants in the insurance sector. Erdal Guner stated:

> I believe that the first successful InsurTech initiatives in Turkey will come from large incumbents that can focus on innovation easily as they already hold the licence and have the capital to operate. However, after gaining its licence, if an InsurTech start-up can come up with an innovative model around service business, it will have a chance to succeed before the large insurance companies.

4. Cansen Ergun mentioned that InsurTech is a very new phenomenon in Turkey and many insurance companies don't know much about InsurTech. Therefore, there should be reports, trainings, and conferences explaining the benefits of collaborating and engaging with InsurTech startups.

InsurTech Opportunities

The insurance and InsurTech market in Turkey is promising and can offer many opportunities for innovative startups:

1. The low insurance penetration suggests that the market is still untapped and has a huge potential to grow. According to the CEO of Zurich Insurance Group Turkey, Yilmaz Yildiz, the industry has been attractive to foreign investors (e.g. Lloyd's of London's interest in entering the Turkish market[9]) as average total premiums constitute only 1.5% of GDP, and, compared to EU averages, Turkey's US$30 billion insurance sector can increase fivefold to US$150 billion.[10]

2. Located between Europe and Asia, Turkey offers significant opportunities for incumbents and investors. It is a dynamic country with 80 million inhabitants and its large tech-savvy young population is open to adopting new technologies to meet their financial needs, including insurance.

3. Most global insurers, such as Allianz and Aviva, already have operations in Turkey and can contribute to the development of InsurTech startups by either collaborating with them or investing in them. This could improve the InsurTech ecosystem as there will be more startups entering the space and raising investment.

4. Recently, some incumbents have realized the opportunities in this underpenetrated market and have been driving innovation to meet growing demand. PwC Turkey Insurance Industry Leader, Talar Gul, stated that new technologies are on the agenda of insurers and they have been investing in innovative solutions improving the quality of their infrastructure.[11] Sharing his observations on the trends affecting insurance providers, Erdal Guner observed:

> Digital and InsurTech are hot topics for insurance companies in Turkey. They are interested in learning and understanding new technologies that can transform and improve the way they do business: They are talking about the successful InsurTech start-ups around the world and having multiple projects on how to use technology to improve efficiency (such as using chatbots in operations).

> Cansen Ergun stated that digital transformation has been effective in multiple areas, such as products (development efforts mostly in connected services like telematics, connected health, etc.);

---

[9] Business Insurance, Lloyd's of London interested in entering Turkey, March 2016, http://www.businessinsurance.com/article/00010101/STORY/160609918/Lloyds-of-London-interested-in-entering-Turkey.

[10] World Finance, Turkey's insurance industry has $150bn potential – Zurich Turkey CEO, March 2017, http://www.worldfinance.com/markets/insurance/turkeys-insurance-industry-has-150bn-potential-zurich-turkey-ceo.

[11] Dunya, "Kaygili ama cabalayan bir sektorumuz var", October 2015, http://www.dunya.com/gundem/kaygili-ama-cabalayan-bir-sektorumuz-var-haberi-295495.

distribution channels (utilizing apps and social domains, developing digital channels engaging with customers more often, directly, and quickly); and operations (including robotics process automation, claim submission through digital platforms, aggregators, etc.).

5. Erdal Guner thinks that there are opportunities for startups in the Internet of Things (IoT) space, such as connected health, connected cars, or connected homes. However, their innovative solutions need to be different from the existing insurance-only offerings; they should bring added value to Turkish customers and include an insurance policy, assistant services, and other valuable services in their model.

Conclusion: Unlocking the Potential

There is a high and untapped potential in the Turkish insurance and InsurTech market. The growing young and digital/tech-savvy population requires sophisticated financial products and services meeting their needs and expectations well. We can expect that, in the near future, the digital transformation of the Turkish insurance industry will be triggered, insurance and the InsurTech market will boom and start to grow quickly, and more insurance products will be sold via traditional and digital channels.

InsurTech in Latin America – The Promise of Insurance for Everybody?

By Denisse Cuellar
FinTech and StartUps Partnerships Manager, Banco de Creditor BCP

Talking about the insurance market in Latin America is quite a challenge because the adoption of insurance on the continent is quite low. Unlike the US or Europe, where buying an insurance policy is common and straightforward, in Latin America this is a painful process and in many cases a luxury. The insurance market represents less than 3% of the average GDP in the region, compared to more than 10% in the US and Europe; Chile and Brazil are the exceptions with slightly more than 3%.[1] (Something important to note in understanding this region is the supremacy of car insurance: life, health, or travel insurance policies are not very attractive to the Latin American customer yet.) But change is happening. The insurance market is growing steadily in the region, and is positively changing Latin Americans' lives.

With Internet penetration at approximately 67% and 63% for Brazil and Mexico, respectively (statisca.com), unsurprisingly, then, InsurTech adoption in the region is also very modest. Combined with low insurance penetration in the region, it is obvious that the digital revolution could only benefit the market. However, as with any market, digitization is just one consideration. Innovation is another. Although not mature and in early growth stages, Latin American InsurTech appears to be adopting a customer-centric approach.

---

[1] EY, 2017 Latin American insurance outlook.

The InsurTech Movement in Latin America

ComparaOnline was the first digital broker in Chile and in the region when it launched in 2009. The startup began as an auto insurance price comparison site but because it initially faced a high demand among those who wanted to know more about the products, it pivoted to take in advisory and selling. Today, ComparaOnline now has a presence in Colombia and Brazil. Last year, the company was selected among the top 100 leading global innovators by KPMG.

To be a relevant actor in the region, it is necessary to be in Brazil. After all, Brazil leads the Latin American insurance market and it was here, in 2011, that the first digital brokers appeared in the shape of Bidu and Minuto Seguros. Minuto Seguros, the biggest online broker in the region, decided to take the risk of approaching the insurance market differently by focusing on the relationship with the customer. The startup created its own platform, connected to several insurers, to provide products with the best prices and a digital policy-issuing process. In addition, their customer service is one of its strengths and has grown rapidly, confirming that the Brazilian consumer values advisor support in the buying cycle and will choose providers accordingly.

From 2016 onwards, some disruption emerged in the Latin American insurance market focusing on selected niches. ToGarantido, a broker of microinsurances that targets the low-income class using online and offline channels, is a great example, and also an example of insurance for inclusion that places the bet on very small prices to attract more clients. Youse is an InsurTech focused on millennials, giving their customers the ability to build and purchase their own insurance service with an app. Youse's business goal is to attract a generation that has never been interested in buying an insurance policy. Early signs show that they are succeeding and that keeping the insurance market more transparent in services and prices does enable the insurance industry to convince and attract new clients. Youse uses no intermediaries to sell its services, although this is still under review with the Regulator. In Peru, the InsurTech wave is at an even earlier stage but the first contender in the country is Seguro Simple, a digital broker that is disrupting the Peruvian insurance market. Alongside the disruptive activities, a sign of growing maturity is the beginning of consolidation: for example, Red Segura and AsegurateFacil, the two biggest online brokers in Colombia, launched in early 2009 and in 2015, respectively, decided to merge to create Busqo, thus becoming the biggest broker online in Chile with almost 70% of the whole Colombian market.

What about the Internet of Things (IoT) in Latin America? We have two examples of IoT in insurance. In Brazil, Thinkseg is an InsurTech that has an app that follows the client's driving to assess how a good driver he or she is and offers differentiated pricing. Thinkseg also provides a platform to small brokers who are not yet digitalized. In Argentina, SnapCar is an InsurTech that has a device in the car to collect information and measure the way in which users drive: it measures acceleration, braking, turning, speed, distance, mapping, and driving time and this information generates a score that determines the user's savings in their premiums. We can expect to see more of these developments, not least because there are supplier partners able to support insurers, brokers, and others to develop their digital capabilities.

Segutrends.com in Mexico, VisionX in Brazil, and WAN in Uruguay offer tools to accelerate the digital transformation of the insurance sector in the region.

Other Actors Building the Latin American InsurTech Ecosystem

Local insurers also have a role to play in fostering the InsurTech ecosystem in Latin America. Certainly, although less active than the banks, the insurance companies have started to develop initiatives to work with startups, including accelerators. In Brazil, Porto Seguro created Oxigenio, an accelerator program to partner with local InsurTechs. International reinsurer Munich Re's acceleration program MundiLab, based in Spain since 2016, is open for Latin American InsurTechs to participate and give them exposure to the European market. On the investment side, Porto Seguro, the leading insurer in Brazil, has also created Porto Capital, a venture arm to invest in startups. In Colombia, Sura Group, in partnership with Veronorte, has also created an investment arm for InsurTechs that can have synergies with Sura Group business. Collaboration is key in this ecosystem. If the insurers are focusing on customer centricity, InsurTechs can only be allies. After all, all the relationship with the customer is done through the customer services of the digital brokers.

Finally, Latin American InsurTechs need to have an eye on new technologies. The insurance market can be disrupted very easily by artificial intelligence, blockchain, machine learning, and the like. InsurTechs need to know what the future of their sector is! As a Latin American InsurTech, the challenge is to find the right balance between technology and human interaction. Despite the challenges to overcome, InsurTechs are giving a new face to the Latin American insurance market, a new face that will encourage the underinsured consumers here to place their bets on, and their trust in, the sector. The best outcome is for consumers to believe that everyone should, and can, have access to the right insurance for them, at the right price, and at the right time. This is the promise of InsurTech – insurance for everybody.

InsurTech Trends – Why Regionalization Matters

By Vasyl Soloshchuk
CEO and Managing Partner, INSART

and Dr Yuri Kartashov
CEO, Euclid Research Centre

The insurance industry is transforming at a fast pace. This is primarily due to the impact of a variety of breakthrough technologies, such as cloud computing, the Internet of Things (IoT), telematics, the blockchain, and artificial intelligence (AI). Insurance services have been modified to satisfy customers' expectations and need for lower costs, increased transparency, and high processing speed.

Due to differences in the development of societies in various parts of the world, prospects for each trend differ significantly. We explore what prospects each trend of InsurTech has and how they may evolve depending on regional differences.

Peer-to-Peer (P2P) Insurance

The P2P model is not new to the insurance industry. It has existed for hundreds of years; now devices and the Internet have made it possible to find people with similar insurance interests, help them get into communities, and organize insurance coverage.

A couple of years ago this stream seemed to be truly disruptive, but in reality it has not been as impactful an option as originally thought. The reasons for this are:

- People are not willing to make their insurance claim history available to strangers, despite being in the same insurance community.

- Policy-holders need to govern and assess risk potentials for other members of their community, otherwise they will not be protected against fraudulent insurance claims.

- Government regulatory frameworks need to be worked around in many countries to protect the interests of policy-holders and maintain the stability and reliability of insurance companies.

Referring to the Hype Cycle, it seems as though the P2P insurance model is going to experience a "trough of disillusionment", and only some of today's startups will succeed in reaching the "plateau of productivity".

However, P2P insurance has every chance to rise in developing countries where the population has strong family and community ties, especially in rural areas. Technology infrastructure is gradually increasing; this enables P2P insurance companies (e.g. Shacom in Taiwan, Wesura in Columbia, and Riovic in South Africa) to reach uninsured regions and use the opportunities there.

In Eastern Europe, people still don't rely on banks and prefer to unite into communities and deal jointly with the validity and size of payments. This has enabled P2P insurance companies such as PRVNÍ KLUBOVÁ (in the Czech Republic) and Teambrella (in Russia) to grow and become successful.

Yet the missing link is scale and data. And herein lies an opportunity. Unless there is a reformulation to the optimal equilibrium between a prudent risk-assessment mechanism and the number of pool members, P2P insurance will remain unstable.

Microinsurance

Today, this term is generally used to define insurance services for low-income populations. Microinsurance provides a mechanism by which to protect people against particular aspects of their lives, such as accidents, death in the family, natural disasters, poor harvest, business bankruptcy, etc. This model of insurance will continue to grow in markets in developing countries.

The significant obstacle to microinsurance distribution is the absence of relevant communications channels. To reach target customer segments, microinsurance providers (e.g. Democrance in the United Arab Emirates, Kilimo Salama in Kenya, and UBL Omni Term Life Insurance in Pakistan) are increasingly integrating mobile phones.

One further aspect that may inhibit the dissemination of microinsurance is the fact that the regulatory environment needs to adapt faster to a changing market landscape and become more flexible. They must also support and encourage insurance companies to develop microinsurance schemes.

Blockchain

Blockchain allows (mostly financial) transactional information to be securely maintained and quickly validated based on distributed ledger principles. In the insurance industry, blockchain enables risk mitigation and fraud tolerance, better transparency, and enhanced data access, as well as time and cost savings.

Using the blockchain may empower specific insurance models, such as P2P insurance (e.g. Dynamis in the US) and microinsurance (e.g. Helperbit in Italy), to bring transparency to these new products. The most market-ready solutions could be constructed using a blockchain stack, where claims validation is electronically simple, like flight delay or cyber attacks.

However, today, insurance can benefit from using blockchain within traditional business components, such as AXA's recent backing and acquisitions. This could become widespread in developed countries such as the US, UK, and Australia.

With the penetration of technology into remote, less-developed regions, insurance companies that use blockchain will have enormous potential to grow there. However, this growth will take some years, due to the present high reliance on paperwork in real-world processes.

Telematics, Biometrics, and IoT

Telematics was expected to transform insurance with car telemetry. However, apart from the young driver market, few policy-holders have yet shown interest in the benefits of the pay-as-you-drive approach, which uses a policy-holder's driving habits to level up, mostly reducing the cost of insurance. Still, as propositions are refined to really offer value-added services to customers, interest and market coverage will go on developing and expanding, and will eventually come to cover a larger share of customers.

Stimulated by insurance companies, technology companies will develop more sophisticated devices that will allow them to predict risks, thereby preventing or more accurately assessing damages not just in the field of car insurance, but also homeowners' insurance (e.g. protection against a leaking water pipe) and health insurance (e.g. tracking a person's activity and health). Although the EU adheres to solidarity principles (pricing cannot be based on genetic predisposition or gender differences), in developed countries, including China, insurers are beginning not only to monitor the state of health, but also to conduct consultations with medical specialists online.

In technologically underdeveloped countries, telematics may grow in popularity, mainly due to devices and applications that have already proven their efficiency in other locations. The main restriction here is cost: it is not viable to install black boxes in cars when the former costs at least twice the value of the insurance premium; insurers would be better off spending their budgets on motivating traffic law enforcement agencies than on playing around with technologies for collision prevention.

Lack of regulation concerning the use of data and personal data protection also impedes wider penetration of such devices. For example, there are no specific regulations for the use of telematics or biometrics in countries such as Indonesia, Malaysia, the Philippines, etc.

The evolution in this direction has a strong flavour of the big data age, which breaks the boundaries of the traditional actuarial techniques that used to apply to insurance.

On-demand Insurance

On-demand insurance allows policy-holders to quickly insure their life, health, homes, objects (equipment, jewellery, etc.), and vehicles for a short time using a mobile application. This type of insurance is very promising and is popular among users, because it allows them to insure their belongings temporarily when necessary, while saving significantly.

There are two emerging models:

- On-demand insurance is commonly considered against a marketing backdrop, in terms of "saving costs", seeing "insurance as a gadget" or as "smart insurance", etc. Indeed, the tech stack here only brings an operational frequency boost, retaining all the classic risk-quantification and pricing principles. But there is exposure, presumably in cases where people "just happen" to switch on the cover before an accident happens.

- On-demand insurance is impacted by adverse selection: the lower the cost of the coverage for high-risk events, the poorer the insurer will be.

Cyber Insurance

Significant amounts of sensitive information are gained and stored on servers and in the cloud globally every day. To prevent data breaches and mitigate risks, cyber insurance has been added to the agenda. However, today it is difficult to provide an adequate assessment of risks associated with cyber attacks, their financial implications, and ways to settle insurance claims because the regulators are also playing catch-up. China is becoming a pioneer

in this segment, and is trying to regulate the rules of cyber insurance at the legislative level. In the near future, it is expected that more countries will try to lay down rules for cyber insurance.

Conclusion

The development and implementation of new technologies in the insurance field appear to have been less rapid than was expected several years ago. However, the following points can be made in summary:

1. Developed countries (e.g. the US, UK, and EU countries) are the most innovative. We expect to see further development of new insurance models using blockchain, telematics, IoT, wearables, as well as on-demand insurance. However, no abrupt changes are expected; instead, the evolution will be systematic.

2. In poor and developing countries in Central Africa, Asia, and South America, using mobile channels has become the easiest way to distribute insurance, conduct risk assessments, and make insurance payments. There, microinsurance has the most potential.

3. P2P insurance may be distributed more widely in regions with strong community ties. The absence of tools for risk assessment and claims settlement has become the biggest impediment to using blockchain platforms to transparently communicate risks.

4. Advanced risk assessment and mitigation technologies (based inclusively on all the benefits of the big data age) applicable to insurance will include satellites that link to hotspots such as wearables, connected cars, and IoT.

5. New trends could emerge from the domain of insurance/risk data-aggregation solutions, including online risk prediction, stock market for data, etc.

InsurTech will come to concentrate more closely on improvement, optimization, and upgrading of existing insurance business processes, rather than giving birth to "new insurance" supernovas.

Collaborative Innovation: Observe – Partner – Invest

5

Collaboration could become disruption

If insurers don't take advantage of the opportunities presented by InsurTech, someone else will

Smart technologies allow for collaborative inter-insurance claims settlement ecosystem

1/3 in a 2017 survey would switch to Amazon, Google or Facebook if they offered insurance, traditional insurers

Partnerships will only work if win-win relationships can be created

Constantly look 'outside-the-box' to initiate, leverage, and redefine relationships with customers, suppliers, competitors, and complementors

One platform in one click:
Assessing the strength of an innovation idea:
1 Offering
2 Target market
3 Infrastructure
4 Compliance needs
5 Data needs
6 Collaboration viability in the business

Think InsurTech culture before InsurTech adoption

- The challenge is how to make new ideas work in an organization whose ways of operating haven't really changed and neither has its ability to embrace change

- The reality is that InsurTech cannot solve any of these problems but its successful adoption can be significantly undermined by them

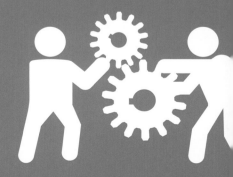

What is your objective?

9 ways insurers and brokers can respond

	Set up an **internal innovation team**	Build a **scalable technology stack**	Build your **own digital propositions**	Create a **"digital lab"**	Build a **"technology buffet"**	**Accelerator / Incubator**		**Invest in startups**	
						Build your own	Sponsor	Direct	Via third party
Effect cultural change	✓✓	✓	✓	✓					
Change existing processes	✓	✓✓	✓✓	✓✓	✓✓	✓			
Access better technology	✓	✓✓	✓	✓✓	✓✓	✓✓	✓✓	✓	
Direct financial return						✓	✓	✓✓	✓✓
Illustrative examples	Munich Re	Munich Re Aviva	XL Catlin Ageas	Aviva Sompo Digital Lab	Oxbow Partners Zurich	Swiss Re MundiLab	AIG Admiral Ergo	Transamerica Axa XL Catlin	Aviva Old Mutual InsurTech Venture Partners

B3i is an insurance industry Blockchain initiative launched in October 2016 by Aegon, Allianz, Munich Re, Swiss Re and Zurich

Collaboration in the world of innovation is essential. Innovation requires openness and connectedness across internal and external innovators. Two qualities that corporates, based on their institutional culture, struggle with.

In this part, we look at how insurers embrace open innovation – the processes they implement; the talent they hire or empower; the programs they design and test; and of course the types of partnerships they look for.

Authors Tshidi Hagan, Roberta Rizzo, and Bjorn Cumps all explore formalized models that support the collaboration needs of enterprises with the value gained from new market entrants and FinTech startups.

Much is said about the rise of innovation centres to service financial institutions. Dorota Zimnoch pays specific attention to how some of these capital intensive and highly diverse environments operate and thrive.

Partnerships are a key theme. The types of partnerships span innovation sources such as accelerators and incubators as well as co-investors and even other insurers. Partnering is commonplace in the technology industry but in insurance it is far less prevalent. However, there are some excellent examples of working partnerships described here, which pay specific attention to commercial, operational, and legal considerations.

Intra-organizational collaboration is a big theme too and includes how leadership can work to incentivize staff but also what cultural triggers are key to help make corporate innovation sustainable and embedded in how people view intrapreneurship. Particularly interesting are Willie Pienaar's insights into how classic change management models are being stretched to mould open innovation best practice.

Finally, Denis Thomas does make some sound recommendations on how competition and collaboration can often exist as a continuum to gain from combined strengths. This part is packed full of fascinating and evolving case studies – a chapter that everyone can relate to and gain value from.

The Corporate Collaboration Opportunity in InsurTech

By Tshidi Hagan
Program Director, Startupbootcamp InsurTech

Collaboration facilitates the development of a promising InsurTech sector. Through API-enabled back office technology, Munich Re Digital Partners is bringing more propositions to market, speedily and flexibly. Blue Marble, B3i, and Gen.Life demonstrate how shared R&D produces intellectual property for joint benefit but requires minimum resource investment. Cooperative incubation models are surfacing and global insurance accelerators such as Startupbootcamp and Plug and Play are proving that collaborative acceleration is a low risk/high return approach for embedding outside-in innovation. And on the investment side, Jerusalem Venture Partners, Eos Venture Partners, and Touchstone Ventures address the pitfalls of traditional corporate venture capital (CVC) and venture capital (VC) by leveraging the expertise of handpicked partners.

Background

Although internally run IT transformation programs, R&D labs, incubators, accelerators, and CVC funds are useful in upgrading dated technology systems, offering a customized exploration function, ingraining an internal culture of ingenuity, and leveraging advanced technology to develop customer-centric products, etc. When managed internally, these initiatives can be constrained by high upfront capital investment requirements and exorbitant operating costs, scarce skills, a limited network of subject-matter experts, mentors and investors, and delayed or slow delivery. The recent rise and accomplishments of collective InsurTech-focused corporate innovation models convey the compelling benefits of cooperation as explained further in this chapter.

Collaborative Digitalization

Digitalization: "the use of digital technologies to change a business model and provide new revenue and value-producing opportunities."

Insurers face the daunting task of remaining relevant in a digital age of high consumer expectations, rapid product development and adoption, and condensed customer acquisition cycles. Further, they seek to provide a seamless and consolidated multi-channel and multi-product experience for their customers and this requires system upgrades, reformed process design, data management, and strong analytics platforms.

When this is coupled with the inevitable challenges of automating or digitalizing manual processes across the entire insurance value chain (i.e. integration and migration complexities, lengthy project timelines, high costs of execution) then the benefits of leveraging the resources of suitable partners are illuminated.

Munich Re Digital Partners ("Digital Partners") was founded in May 2016 to allow the business to form more frictionless partnerships with startups developing InsurTech solutions. By setting up an independent vehicle, with a distinct and funded mandate combined with an API-enabled platform, Munich Re has ensured the venture's ability to swiftly and flexibly absorb external capabilities to address ongoing business challenges and exploit arising opportunities. As a result, one year since launching, Digital Partners has already publicly disclosed nine partnerships with startups creating bespoke property and casualty insurance and health insurance propositions. Among its partners are Jetty, Simplesurance, and Trov.

Since these partnerships are gaining rapid traction, it's anticipated that going forward more incumbents will replicate Munich Re's digitalization approach.

Collaborative R&D

R&D: "a series of exploratory initiatives pursued to improve existing or develop new products and business practices from the ground up."

As demonstrated here, some incumbents concede that emerging business models and technologies require cooperation among multiple industry players to yield sustainable and viable R&D results.

Blue Marble Microinsurance was launched in June 2015 by eight leading insurers and reinsurers to explore commercially viable microinsurance models to drive financial inclusion. Consortium members share costs, talent, and various execution risks to support the ideation, incubation, acceleration, piloting, and scaling of new ventures. Blue Marble currently has six ventures at different stages of acceleration across emerging markets. The most developed is a pilot launched in November 2016 providing drought protection insurance to 335 smallholder maize farmers in Zimbabwe.

B3i is an insurance industry blockchain initiative launched in October 2016 by Aegon, Allianz, Munich Re, Swiss Re, and Zurich to explore the ability of blockchain technologies to increase efficiencies in the exchange of data between reinsurance and insurance companies. At the end of 2017 the Blockchain Insurance Industry Initiative B3i announced it had expanded, with 23 new brokers and re/insurer entrants, which will help with B3i's upcoming market testing program.

Since 2016 Gen.Life has been creating a Software-as-a-Service (SAAS) platform that enables insurers to create an intelligent digital capability across the entire insurance value chain. Gen.Life aims to act as the R&D centre of excellence for its insurance partners in exchange for an annual R&D licence fee. In return, the insurers gain access to Gen.Life's AI and blockchain expertise and that of its partner startups; as well as Gen. Life's highly scalable, adaptive, and intelligent technology stack.

It will be interesting to observe the relative success of all of these initiatives and how this influences future corporate R&D efforts.

Collaborative Incubation

Incubation: "the gestation of ideas that yield a return over the long-term into commercially viable propositions through the provision of a vast array of business support facilities, resources, and services for up to 36 months."

Many organizations have delayed their adoption of cooperative incubation models due to concerns regarding IP ownership, data security, the development of generic vs. customized propositions, etc. However, due to the extensive capacity, facility, and resource commitments required to set up an internal incubator (e.g. AXA's Kamet), the sustainability of this autonomous incubation approach is being questioned.

As a result, we are starting to see cooperation between incubation specialists and incumbents struggling to advance early-stage ideas into commercial propositions independently. Since November 2016 Fintech Circle Innovate joined forces with the Cape Innovation and Technology Initiative to provide a tailored incubation as a service offering to African financial services players in line with global industry best practices. Further, in February 2017 Worry+Peace teamed up with Mohara to launch an incubator to offer business development, product design, regulatory, and technological support as well as domain expertise and mentorship to UK-based insurance distribution startups. More recently, Exponential Ventures (MMI Holdings' disruptive innovation arm) launched a financial wellness incubator in partnership with Anthemis Group, dedicated towards identifying business opportunities, refining business models, sourcing talent, and scaling startups.

It's expected that more coalitions of this nature will surface in the future to support the development of more cost-effective and efficient incubation methodologies.

Collaborative Acceleration

Acceleration: "the rapid advancement of early stage startups into commercial ventures through a structured three-month curriculum supported by a meticulously assembled network of subject-matter experts, mentors, and investors."

One of the more successful examples of fruitful cooperation has been observed in the collaborative acceleration of InsurTech startups.

Global Insurance Accelerator (GIA), based in Des Moines, Iowa, led the pack and was launched in February 2015. GIA's support base comprises 180 mentors and 10 investors (who are all US-centric insurance carriers) and, together, they've been instrumental in the graduation of 18 startups who have collectively raised approximately US$2 million as at April 2017.

In June 2015 Startupbootcamp InsurTech followed suit primarily supported by 15 renown corporate partners (mostly insurers and reinsurers) who leverage their combined resources to fund the accelerator's operations, mentor the startups, and explore various commercial opportunities with them. Further, the accelerator provides access to Startupbootcamp global's extensive network of over 2,000 mentors, more than 1,000 investors, and another group of 130 program partners (financial institutions, retailers, data providers, government agencies, etc.) working across 20 international programs. So far 20 startups are alumni of the program, and as at April 2017 some of them had jointly raised more than $20 million in follow-on funding.

Plug and Play Insurance (PPI) is a Silicon Valley-based accelerator that was introduced in April 2016. PPI brings together 38 leading reinsurers, insurers, brokers, and automakers to support the fast-tracked development of insurance technology solutions by early- and growth-stage startups. To date, PPI has 48 startups in its portfolio and the first cohort has already jointly raised at least $39 million.

Although it's early days, these accelerators are adding meaningful and measurable value to all their key stakeholders.

Collaborative Investment/CVC

Corporate VC (CVC): "a subset of VC in which established organizations make tactical equity investments into startups that are creating solutions that address existing business challenges or exploit emerging growth opportunities."

Since 2015 a more cooperative approach to CVC has been developing and, so far, four distinct models have surfaced. The first model involves investments by incumbents in sector-focused third-party managed funds to gain access to market insights and a pipeline of various commercial opportunities. Old Mutual's and Intesa San Paolo's investment in Apis Growth Fund I and Transamerica Ventures' investments in FinTech Collective and Lerer Hippeau Ventures possibly mark some of the earliest signs of this approach.

The second model entails partnerships between CVCs and specialist early-stage investors and is best demonstrated by Exponential Ventures' investment partnerships with Anthemis Group, 4Di Capital, and Startupbootcamp InsurTech. Within a year of launching, Exponential Ventures has invested in six financial wellness startups and holds an interest in Startupbootcamp InsurTech's accelerated startups.

The rapid emergence of VC funds that predominantly or solely invest in InsurTech startups encapsulates the third model. Their proposition gives investors access to vast domain experience and tried-and-tested early-stage investment expertise. Most are positioned to target insurers as limited partners, e.g. Eos Venture Partners, InsurTech Venture Partners, MTech Capital, ManchesterStory Group, etc., while others, like Annexus Ventures and InsurTech VC, operate as closed funds open to co-investing.

The final model is best captured by Touchdown Ventures' (Touchdown's) VC as a service approach. They leverage their reputable CVC track record and employ proven industry techniques to run bespoke CVC funds that allow their clients to maintain complete control over the investment process and, as such, produce precise outcomes tailored to each client's unique objectives.

All these investment models have the potential to enable incumbents to produce tangible strategic and financial results from early-stage investments.

Conclusion

The case studies cited successfully demonstrate that, notwithstanding various constraints including the potential for lengthy negotiation cycles, high execution risk and misaligned priorities, collaboration creates opportunities to bring cutting-edge products and services to market rapidly, cheaply, distinctly, flexibly, and compliantly by leveraging the expertise, experience, and resources of each member within the partnership.

Competition vs. Coopetition in the Insurance Market

By Denis Thomas
Associate Director, KPMG

Disruption via technology has been rampant in the fields of media and entertainment but technology has taken a while to latch on, especially within financial services. Banking is currently undergoing disaggregation via several modules that were once core, such as payments and lending. Insurance is at its nascent stage and rife for disruption as several players continue to compete and bite into each other's profit margins.

Competition vs. Coopetition

"I'm going to destroy Android, because it's a stolen product. I'm willing to go thermonuclear war on this."

This quote from Steve Jobs is just a glimpse into how nasty competition can get. This was partly needed and partly not. Do we need similar levels of competition within the insurance space? Can we remain profitable and compete in today's dynamic, technologically disruptive arena? Can all players in an ecosystem equally consider all options and invest in ideas with a high probability of success? No, it would be impractical to even think so! Ideally, we need to spread our investments wide and far and rely on experts within subdomains that complement our overall strategy and vision.

If we follow this thinking and extrapolate this thought further, there are several venues available within coopetition[1] that could

---

[1] Coopetition is the act of cooperation between competing companies; businesses that engage in both competition and cooperation are said to be in coopetition.

benefit both parties, the simple premise of collaboration between business competitors. Coopetition can help in the following areas broadly:

1. **Overcoming product development costs**
   New product development and customer acquisition costs almost always rank among the highest spent categories in many industries. The strategic importance of new products is far more critical now in the insurance market as those customers who preferred the ease of behaviour-led discounts and portfolio manageability are staying less and less glued to a single insurance company. From a technology point of view, InsurTech entrants focus on new product development and can easily complement an existing insurance provider's portfolio. From an insurer's point of view, the due diligence steps for selecting a firm remain complex. Collaboration will benefit larger insurance companies as it reduces lengthy development costs and the associated time spent on testing and retesting specific solutions until they are market ready. It also reduces the time to market and overall marketing costs as customer-focused products are introduced sooner in the market. The collaborative approach for smaller players helps them overcome regulatory hurdles, which would otherwise have engulfed them in a downward death spiral, while slowly eating into their daily operating costs. The collaborative competitive approach helps reduce risks by educating newer firms about the possible risk scenarios and taking essential steps before and during development to ensure most if not all risks are mitigated.

2. **Collaborating and competing on a universal market**
   There is no doubt that competition in the global insurance sector will increase, driven both by InsurTech firms and technology giants. For example, Tencent Holdings' insurer unit is the latest to receive a licence, which enables the dominant operator of China's social network to sell insurance to WeChat's 900 million users. The time to prep our firms is now! The universal market of the future is inevitable and we should

prepare ourselves to embrace a universal market where patents, prices, and customers are exposed. The primary objective with exposing patents and collaborating with competitors serves an underlying cunning and greedy purpose even within a universal market – the ultimate goal of earning higher profits and eventually amassing enormous wealth for oneself. But how could a pie grow without additional dough? Dough in this case stands for talent, money, reach, and many correlated factors that directly impact the profitability and competitive relevance of a firm. The universal market provides easy access to larger distribution networks and equips insurance agents with abilities for quoting, binding, and issuing customized insurance products to target customers in minutes rather than hours, days, or weeks.

Some of the questions that will rise in a universal market scenario are:

- Who are the current players and how can we collaborate to maximize value?

- Which relationships are complementary to my firm and if I do collaborate what value would my firm derive?

- Who are my competitors in this space and can I really collaborate in a mutually beneficial way?

- How can I strengthen my firm's relationships with suppliers, customers, and integrators via the universal market?

- Can I use the existing network and knowledge to sustain my firm's competitive advantage?

These are only a subset of questions that might crop up in one's mind while participating in a universal market. We need to take cues from our environment and constantly look "outside the box" to initiate, leverage, and redefine relationships with customers, suppliers, competitors, and partners.

3. Awareness of entropy

The second principle of thermodynamics states that everything in the universe traverses from a state of order to one of disorder, and entropy is essentially the measurement of that change. One cannot compete and remain proficient in all areas, as it is practically impossible. This also implies that one can never rest on one's laurels, whether one is a firm or a person.

One way to remain aware of one's standing in the industry is by investing heavily on future research and development, keeping a tap on regulatory changes, and a close eye on competitor moves. Yet all this still might not help, as is evident from the Kodak and Nokia cases, known to our generation, who went from being respective leaders in their field to being non-existent. This wouldn't have been the case had they been aware of entropy in their environment via new entrants who were disrupting the space through touchscreens and digital cameras. This example is essentially the best argument in favour of collaborative competition.

4. Opportunities for up-selling and cross-selling

If an existing customer would benefit from a product that your competitor sells, or vice versa, there would be up-selling and cross-selling opportunities. This would eventually increase customer loyalty and satisfaction for both parties.

5. Competitive advantage

Coopetition helps with competitive advantage too as it provides quick access to additional skills that are currently missing within the existing firm, technological diversity, profitability, reputation, and knowledge sharing via access to a broader talent pool.

The involvement for coopetition can be more direct via investments or via an innovation centre, which brings me to my next topic on innovation centres and possible benefits for firms adopting similar practices.

The advantages to coopetition can be easily summarized, as shown in Figure 1.

The potential on return for investment D is much higher with the same amount of risk for A as is depicted by the two investments, A and D. The approach to collaborative competing exposes us to much better returns (positioning ourselves at D) while maintaining our risks at a minimum.

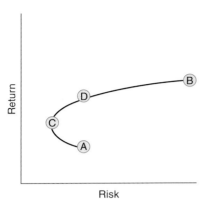

Figure 1: Efficient frontier

Innovation Centres and Incubation

The rise of innovation centres within technology companies and banks over the past few years is evidence enough to demonstrate and corroborate unequivocally the importance of investments in R&D. The very existence of IBM and GE over the years has been a factor in investing in relevant technologies that eventually helped them pivot their business model to suit the changing market needs. One can further optimize this route by studying efficient innovation centre designs prevalent across sectors and picking up cues relevant to the domain such as: innovation input and output subindex, overall global innovation index, and innovation efficiency ratio as outlined by GII (global innovation index) for ranking countries.

Innovation centres can benefit the participating firm via five primary masts as shown in Figure 2:

1. Fostering and tapping on existing talent within the pool.

2. Mentoring and monitoring probable ideas/firms that benefit the underlying firm's overall portfolio.

3. Building an entrepreneurial spirit among employees that would drive nimbleness and flexibility and gradually increase the firm's inherent risk-taking appetite.

4. Testing and ideating on product prototypes before they are officially launched into the market

5. Promoting cross-functional collaboration to resolve departmental and BU silos that arise from operating in a large conglomerate firm operating in several geographies.

This is merely a mechanism for a firm to stay more involved in the action and secure a "front row seat" into what is occurring within their domain or outside. It also helps them garner a fresh perspective to their otherwise myopic view on research and development within their organization. We are already witnessing a growth of innovation centres within the banking domain and it is about time the insurance industry caught on. I know we are pushing for coopetition as a growth strategy and incubation as a building block to achieve the same at our next strategic steering committee meeting.

What about you?

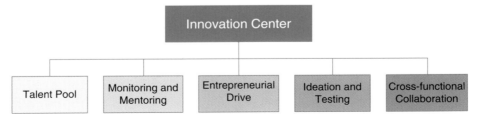

Figure 2: Innovation centres

Incumbent and InsurTech Collaboration via Open Innovation Strategy

By Dorota Zimnoch

Founder and MD ZING Business Consulting, Strategic Advisor, The Heart

The digital revolution has hit the insurance sector, with InsurTech disrupting the entire value chain and customer life cycle. The "I want it now" culture, increasing consumer needs, high competition, and changing regulations force incumbents to change. As quoted by Computerworld, "a survey of 2,005 British adults, conducted on behalf of GMC Software in March 2016, found that 85 percent of consumers with insurance would like their insurer to give them insight into how they could lower their premium, for instance by suggesting changes in behavior."[1]

Disruptive technologies offer the opportunities to redesign customer experience, create new products and value-added services, streamline internal processes, and increase operational efficiency.

The complexity of the insurance sector ecosystem, high barriers to entry, and potentially long return on investment allowed insurers to maintain a status quo for decades and keep new competitors away. Instead they focused on product and distribution strategies. In addition, the financial crises of 2008 impacted the reputation and trust of the industry. However, the digital revolution, the pressure from consumers, regulators, and competition, including the rise of InsurTech and tech giants, means that change in the sector is inevitable. PwC reported that cumulative 2010–2016 funding in InsurTech reached US$3.4 billion.[2] What PwC also found in the 2016 survey is that 74% of respondents fear disruption; however, only 43% have a strategy to address the challenge and 28% are willing to explore partnerships with InsurTechs.[3]

To stay in the game, insurers must respond with the most effective strategies to reinvent business for a digital age.

Internal Innovation

One such strategy is to foster innovation internally in the organization. From researching trends, benchmarking with competition and applying customer intelligence, through identifying customer needs, applying design thinking and user-driven innovation to implementing process improvements and redesigning business strategies – these are all examples of the corporate innovation toolkit (see Table 1).

One of the successful examples of such internal innovation is the Aviva Drive app that assesses user driving and rewards safe driving with discounts. Allianz offered its customers the MYClaim app enabling the filing of claims on mobile. An interesting approach to driving innovation and changing corporate culture has been taken by TransAmerica, which launched the innovation cafes for employees, who are called internally "tomorrow makers", encouraging them to brainstorm and work on innovative ideas.

---

[1] Computerworld, How UK insurers are embracing digital innovation with mobile apps, gamification and customer data analytics, 4 April 2016.

[2] PwC, 20th CEO Survey. Key findings in the insurance industry, February 2017.

[3] PwC, How Insurtech is reshaping insurance, 2016.

Table 1: Corporate innovation toolkit

Corporate innovation toolkit (examples)		
Creative thinking	**Idea management**	**Stage gate | NPD**
Training employees in problem solving techniques	Managing the process or idea collection, review, and implementation	Improving the decision-making process
Customer intelligence	**Design thinking**	**Process improvement**
Using ethnography, ODI, and other methods to discover unmet customer needs	Optimizing the design process	Leveraging Kaizen, Six Sigma, or other methods for data-driven quality design of products and processes
Trend research	**User-driven Innovation**	**Business models**
Understanding emerging patterns in society, tech, and markets	Engaging users in co-creating solutions and experiences	Designing and reviewing business model innovations
Competitive intelligence	**Technology scouting**	**Lean startup**
Benchmarking competition	Identification of potential technologies for competitive advantage	Fast validation of hypotheses

Source: The Heart Warsaw

However, learnings from other industries, particularly from the banking sector, show that internal innovation can take corporations only to a certain point due to several internal constraints. These include the speed of driving change in the organization, contradictory business priorities, and a limited talent pool and IT resources. The biggest blocker is a lack of innovation culture. According to the Willis Towers Watson survey of 200 senior-level executives within the insurance industry, 58% said insurance lagged behind other financial services organizations in implementing digital technologies and 74% of them believed their sector had failed to show leadership in digital innovation.[4]

For this reason, insurers are turning outwards searching for innovation and solutions that can enhance and accelerate their digital transformation.

Driving Innovation via Collaboration and Partnerships

Driven by individual business objectives, e.g. leveraging advantage of the first mover, acquiring technology or talent, expanding the value proposition, and developing new distribution channels, insurers adopt one or several models: buy, partner, invest.

Figure 1 summarizes nine different models of partnerships that we have identified while working with corporate clients at The Heart, and how insurers can maximize the results and extract most value from the technology revolution by cooperating with InsurTech. We acknowledge that this matrix is not exhaustive and, as the ecosystem is working on different deals and partnerships, that new models are likely to appear.

---

[4] Willis Towers Watson & EFMA Report. New horizons. How diverse growth strategies can advance digitalisation in the insurance industry, 2016.

Buy from Purchase or licence new technologies that give you a competitive edge	Purchase service	License technology	Co-development
Partner Launch new products and businesses on revenue-sharing basis	Offer bundling	White label	Co-branding
Invest Deal flow for your company's strategic or financial investments	Acquire	Investment	Merger & Acquisition

Figure 1: Collaboration models: buy, partner, invest

Source: The Heart Warsaw

Buy from Startups

Insurers can partner with InsurTechs by purchasing their services, licensing their solutions, or co-developing solutions.

One such example is YU!. It is a new insurance brand launched in Poland as a collaboration between Yanosik (telematics and communication company) and insurer Ergo Hestia. YU! collects data on user behaviour and, by applying artificial intelligence (AI), thus provides customers with personalized car insurance. New technologies allow YU! to offer a better customer experience at competitive pricing and for Ergo Hestia, the insurance provider, it opens a new distribution channel.

Cognotekt provides software as a service solution for insurers to automate personal lines claims. Currently operating on the German market, it provides automated windscreen protection.

Startups like Friendsurance or PolicyGenius act as independent online brokers offering customers unique and relevant customer experience, while providing insurers with an additional distribution channel.

Partner with Startups

Another strategy is to partner with InsurTechs, offering an InsurTech's services to customers by bundling offers or providing them on a white-label or co-branded basis:

- AXA Spain signed a partnership with SocialCar, a car-sharing platform for individuals. The cooperation provides the startup with more credibility, giving users full car insurance, while for AXA, again it provides a new distribution channel.

- Munich Re partnered with Trov, offering on-demand insurance in the US.

- Liberty Manual partnered with startup Canary, which provides home security solutions. As a result, customers can benefit from the enhanced savings under Liberty Mutual's Smart Home Discount Program.

- Digital Fineprint uses social media to help customers choose the best insurance. The startup partnered with MetLife to expand to Asia.

- Munich Re partnered with app-based insurance provider Wrisk and became its exclusive carrier for business underwritten in the UK, Europe, and the US.

- In late 2016, Hannover Life Reassurance Company of America entered into a global strategic partnership and invested in the Sureify Labs. As a result, Sureify's LifeTime platform was enhanced with the hr | ReFlex automated underwriting solution.

Invest in Startups

The third and probably most common strategy is to invest in startups. The majority of the world's largest insurers, such as Aviva, AXA, Allianz, AIG, MetLife, Generali, or XL Catlin, have established their own in-house venture capital funds and committed investment in startups. Forty-five percent of the Willis Towers Watson survey respondents state a preference for acquisitions to gain digital capabilities.

Allianz invested in Simplesurance in order to learn how to onboard customers in digital channels. Insurer IAG enhanced its value proposition for the fleet customers with the acquisition of CCS Innovation in Logistics, while Travelers expanded their digital distribution ability with the purchase of Simply Business, the UK's largest insurance broker.

How to Respond and Choose the Right Strategy?

At The Heart we help corporations to cooperate effectively with startups by using an open innovation strategy.

It starts with the corporation identifying its business objectives, which is probably the most critical factor of the whole strategy. What can work for one insurer, e.g. setting up a business accelerator, may not be the best strategy for another. The objectives should be clearly aligned with the expected impact, which could be incremental, adjacent, or transformative (see Table 2).

Business objectives determine the model of cooperation and help to prioritize solutions. For example, if a business would like to build closer engagement with customers it can partner or purchase an IoT or wearables startup and by monitoring customer behaviours and analysing data can enhance risk assessment capabilities and offer more personalized and relevant services.

Once the criteria for potential partnership are set the company can choose one or several ways to uncover the solution. From hackathons and a call for startups, through participation in demo days, to proactive search for solutions. A very interesting approach was taken by Unilever, which created the Unilever Foundry platform. The Unilever brands and business lines publish briefs on the platform outlining problems that need solving. The ready-to-scale startups are invited to submit their proposals on how to approach those challenges. In 18 months, the Unilever Foundry executed a hundred pilots with a 48% success rate. Another tactic could include development of

Table 2: **Open innovation strategy**

Innovation Strategy
Impact: Incremental | Adjacent | Transformative
Models: Observe | Work with startups | Invest in startups | Build startups

Challenges	Sourcing	Selection	Deals and legal	Execution
Hunting grounds	Monitor ecosystem	Selection	Speed	Pilot | PoC
Pressure and KPIs	Define needs	Co-creation	IP Management	Implement locally
Visibility	**Relations**	**Resources**	**People**	**Culture**
Single point of contact	Deal flow partners	Budgets	Top management support	Non-invented here
	Partner perception	Time and attention		Experimentation
	Relationship management tools			Role models and success stories

Source: The Heart Warsaw

corporate or sponsor accelerators, like W1 Forward InsurTech Accelerator or MetLife Accelerator Collab.

The alternative strategy is to search for startups proactively. While it may be tempting and appropriate to run scanning services in-house, and there are some who do it successfully, our experience shows that successful projects require full-time resources to be allocated to such projects. Prior experience in working with and evaluating startups is also important to ensure that the right criteria are applied to the search process. That is why many companies work with programs like Startupbootcamp or turn to hubs like The Heart for professional scouting services, which is usually more cost effective and faster.

The foundation of successful digital transformation and innovation requires support from top management, allocation of the right human resources and capital, and fostering an innovation culture in the organization. Above all, it is about building incumbent and InsurTech partnerships based on trust, leveraging the strengths of both sides, and encouraging "test and learn". And although not all the projects will end successfully, only by active participation in the ecosystem combined with a commitment to transformation will insurers be able to be relevant, respond to disruptions, and win the hearts of customers.

As the old African proverb says: "To go fast, go alone, to go far, go together."

A Collaborative Approach in the InsurTech World – One Platform in One Click

By Dr Roberta Rizzo
Senior Manager, EY

InsurTech is a simple word to summarize a complex mix of new technologies and disruptive business models in the insurance world; it is a new way to work, to improve customer satisfaction and internal/external collaboration, a new value chain. It is a process that combines different methodologies and strategies in an innovative vision where the focal point is the client or the community, as illustrated in Figure 1.

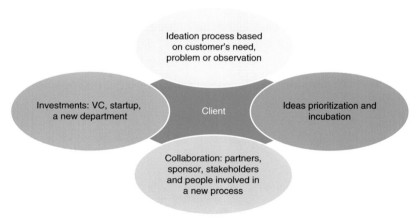

Figure 1: **InsurTech**

How Does this Model Work?

Think about you. What do you need in terms of protection? Do you want to protect your family, your car, or simply your piano or your tablet? What do you do to satisfy these needs? How can you secure your identity against fraud and cyber risks? How do you choose the best solution? Nowadays, we have a lot of new and innovative solutions to sort out these problems due to a proliferation of startups and the effects of digital transformation in (some) insurance companies but this is not enough. The tricky point is to have *the* solution to be able to allow an insurer to satisfy those needs in just one click. Data analytics enable the creation of interactive, mobile collaboration platforms, specific communities or ad hoc products, everything securely tracked and usable through the medium of, for example, blockchain technology. This is the future: one space where customers are the main sponsor and are able to engage in co-creation/ideation to shape a specific solution for a specific problem/need. All stakeholders involved must be able to incubate this first ideation process and produce, in a co-creation and collaboration space, a unique product/platform/solution to be detached from traditional market and company. This needs to be developed in a completely disrupted way (via a startup or new area/line of business) and must focus on customer needs. An example is shown in Figure 2.

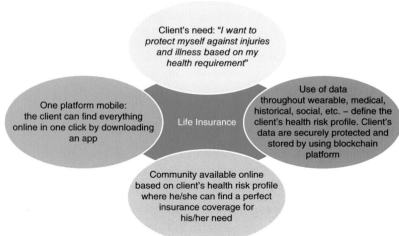

Figure 2: **Disruption of life insurance industry**

How to Manage the Collaboration Platform for an Innovative Project?

When an insurance company decides to move forward to develop a collaboration platform dedicated to their customers, the first problem is to shape the ideation process. This is aimed at transforming an idea into a project and to ensure this project is well managed and can solve the questions: is my idea innovative? Does it really solve a problem, disrupt a process, or develop a different value proposition? What kind of innovation do I want to create: "sustaining innovation" or "disruptive innovation"?

What is the business value? What about developing a business model canvas? How can I develop each phase of my project in one sheet, simply to engage others?

From Idea to a Project

1. Assessing an idea:

To assess which one of the three innovation types an idea relates to, it's important to answer some specific questions:

- *Offering.* Does the idea expand or enhance an existing offering or is it a completely new offering (within the company or elsewhere)?
- *Target market.* What is the target market? Is it an existing market the company is already in? Is it a new market?
- *Infrastructure.* Can the existing infrastructure be used for the idea, or are some enhancements required? Or is a completely new infrastructure required for the idea to work?
- *Compliance and regulatory.* Do we know the compliance and regulatory requirements for the idea? Are they already fully defined, somewhat defined, or are they unknown or not defined yet?

- *Historical precedents and existing data.* Is there existing data or historical information that can be used to help model financial projections/a return of investment? There may be none, some, or a solid amount.
- *Collaboration across business units.* To realize the idea fully, does it require various company business units or regions to coordinate efforts?

It is important also to analyse the three lenses of innovation applied to the idea in terms of desirability, commerciality, and feasibility, using a ratings system, in particular:

- *Desirability.* Is the idea something that either clients or your company want and need? Focus on the benefits and outcomes for clients or which your company want to achieve.
- *Profitability.* Is the idea commercially viable or will it become so? Is it something that will either generate new revenue or save money for the company?
- *Feasibility.* Is the idea technically feasible? Are there any new/early-stage technologies required that might influence the idea? Does the company have the expertise required?

Is the idea core, adjacent, or disruptive? Figure 3 outlines this clearly.

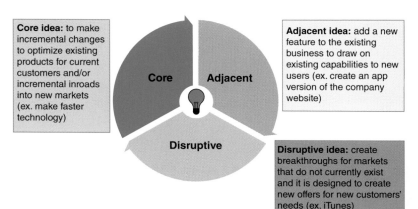

Core idea: to make incremental changes to optimize existing products for current customers and/or incremental inroads into new markets (ex. make faster technology)

Adjacent idea: add a new feature to the existing business to draw on existing capabilities to new users (ex. create an app version of the company website)

Disruptive idea: create breakthroughs for markets that do not currently exist and it is designed to create new offers for new customers' needs (ex. iTunes)

Figure 3: Core, adjacent, and disruptive ideas

A sample idea assessment tool is given in Figure 4.

Idea Assessment Tool

Idea Title		**FAO Sponsoring Idea?**	Select One (list)
Idea Owner		**Business Alignment via FAO?**	Select One (list)
Idea Owner Department Reporting	Select One (list)	**Type of Innovation**	Core OR Adjacent OR Disruptive (Pick one) (list)
Innovation Focus Area (FA)	Select One (list)		
Focus Area Owner (FAO)	Select One (list)		

Is this idea Core, Adjacent or Disruptive?		**Idea Owner**	**Focus Area Owner Assessment**
Offering	Does this idea enable a completely new offering or does it expand on/strengthen an existing offering?	Select One (list)	Select One (list)
Target Market	What type of market does this idea target? (Note: the "market" includes the customer group, geography, and customer problem solved)	Select One (list)	Select One (list)
Infrastructure	Can we use existing <name of the Company> infrastructure (e.g. retail branch network, stores, online channels, technology platforms, etc.) to deliver the offering created by this idea or do we need to build new infrastructure?	Select One (list)	Select One (list)
Compliance and Regulatory	How well defined and understood are the compliance and regulatory requirements associated with this idea?	Select One (list)	Select One (list)
Historical precedents and existing data	How strong are the historical precedents and existing data on which we can model financial projections for this idea's return?	Select One (list)	Select One (list)
Collaboration across business units	Does this idea require multiple <name of the Company> business units or regions to coordinate their efforts to realize the idea's potential?	Select One (list)	Select One (list)
Based on the answers above, how would you classify the innovation type of this idea?		Core OR Adjacent OR Disruptive (Pick one)	Core OR Adjacent OR Disruptive (Pick one)

COLLABORATIVE INNOVATION: OBSERVE – PARTNER – INVEST

How does the Idea score on the 3 lenses of Innovation?		**Idea Owner - Rating (1-5)**	**Focus Area Owner Assessment - Rating (1-5)**
Desirability: is this an idea that the client desires? Does it clearly articulate a client Pain Point or Opportunity?			
Client Opportunity (Gain)	Does the idea identify the benefits and outcomes clients want (new revenue, reduced costs, functional utility, required features, desired and unexpected gains). Is this a big opportunity? (Think in terms of moderate to huge)	Select One (list)	Select One (list)
Client Pain Points	Does the idea describe the frustrations, risks, problems, inhibitors and bad outcomes that are getting in the way of your clients if happen? How big of a pain is this? (Think in terms of Moderate to Extreme)		
Commerciality: what are the market size, revenue streams and cost elements?			
Market Potential	What is the scale of impact? How big is the potential size of the market for this idea?	Select One (list)	Select One (list)
Revenue Streams/Cost Saves	Does the idea articulate how value would be captured (revenue, cost save) and what price a client might be willing to pay?		
Cost Structure (approximately)	Does the idea outline the key cost elements required to deliver on the idea?		
Feasibility: how easy or difficult is it to develop and deploy a solution?			
Technical feasibility	From a technology point of view, how easy or difficult is it to develop a solution behind the idea? Are there any new, early stage technologies required? Does <name of the Company> have the technology expertise required?	Select One (list)	Select One (list)
Regulations/ Compliance/ Data Privacy	Are there key regulations, compliance and/or data privacy requirements to address? How easy or difficult will this be?		
Additional comments or supporting information about the idea			

Figure 4: Idea assessment tool

Value Strategy Framework

PRODUCT &/OR SERVICE

Benefits	Features	Experience
• What your product &/or service do • Tangible & intangible	• How your product &/or service work • Characteristics • KPI	• Customer assessment & test • Feeling of your product &/or service

CUSTOMER

Wants	Needs	Problems
• Emotional drivers of purchasing • Desirable features	• Rational drivers of purchasing • Solution driven	• Risk of switching to your product • Possible failures

Company:
Product &/or service:
Customer:

Figure 5: **Value strategy framework**

2. Preparing your value proposition and your business model canvas (see Figures 5 and 6).

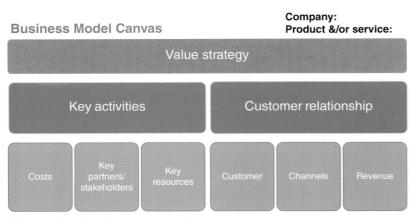

Figure 6: **Business model canvas**

3. Looking at your approach between different alternatives (agile, waterfall). You can use, for example, the Design Thinking Framework to learn about the customer for whom you are designing your project by observation and interview to know how you have to develop each feature of your idea (see Figure 7).

Design Thinking Framework

Figure 7: **Design thinking framework**

4. And finally, here is *the best approach* to be used (as shown in Figure 8), the right mix of different approaches to transform the idea into a project.

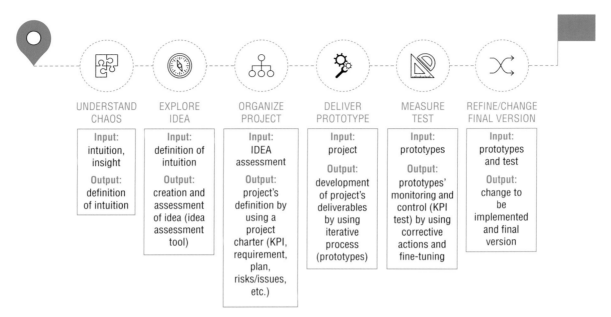

Figure 8: Different approaches to transforming an idea into a project

Conclusion

The "Digital Era" requires innovative solutions to be all-inclusive to guarantee a satisfactory experience for our customer not only by considering a traditional insurance offer but also by adding new features and choices to be more flexible, competitive, fast, and simple. To manage these changes, I suggest following some fundamental rules:

1. Change your internal company mindset to focus on digital strategy and innovative culture. Have a Chief Digital Officer or a Digital CEO.

2. Spread innovative knowledge and competence across departments and by talking directly with your customer to propose digital solutions.

3. Use the new framework as explained previously to manage digital projects by involving small and cross-functional teams and business units, committed to these projects, able to test and measure each prototype directly with customers and to implement changes and features quickly (every two weeks, for example).

To realize all of these goals there is one key word: collaboration. This is a must to exchange ideas, to build a creative and mixed team to manage projects, and to ensure a variety of perspectives. Because in the end:

Collaboration is important not just because it's a better way to learn. The spirit of collaboration is penetrating every institution and all of our lives. So learning to collaborate is part of equipping yourself for effectiveness, problem solving, innovation and life-long learning in an ever-changing networked economy.

Don Tapscott

Dating InsurTech Startups

By Prof. Dr Bjorn Cumps
Professor of Financial Services Innovation and FinTech, Vlerick Business School

Bye Bye Traditional Insurance?

Allianz & Simplesurance, Munich Re & Slice, Axa & Trov, Zurich & Cocoon, Manulife & Indico …

Love is all around in the world of InsurTech today. Both large corporates and startups have observed and learned from what happened and is still happening in FinTech: disruptive innovation does not necessarily equal "bye bye traditional insurance companies". Not all large corporate insurance companies will disappear and startups will not rule the insurance world. In fact, very few new players will manage to truly bring disruptive innovation as defined by Clayton Christensen:[1] "a product or service that takes root initially in simple applications at the bottom of a market and then relentlessly moves up market, eventually displacing established competitors." Most new players, in InsurTech too, will not be disruptive as such; however, they may change many different aspects of how the insurance sector operates today: new profit models and pricing structures, new products and features, new services, delivery channels, and client interactions. We see a clear trend towards creating better and more personalized client experiences, more client interactions, in-context services, real-time data-driven insurance solutions, microinsurances, claims prevention, and open collaboration (see Table 1). All of these can be valuable. All of these can fundamentally change the insurance sector. And all of them can be done in partnership between large corporates and new startups. InsurTech will not be the end of the large insurance corporates. But it will be the end of the traditional insurance operating model as we know it today.

---

[1] C. M. Christensen et al., "What is Disruptive Innovation", *Harvard Business Review*, December 2015.

Table 1: Traditional vs. new insurance model characteristics

Traditional Insurance	Insurance 2.0 – InsurTech
Claims handling	Claims prevention
Avoid client interaction	Stimulate client interactions
Know your risks	Know your customer and their risks
1-size-fits-all	Specific, personalized, sliced and diced
Insuring people	Insuring people and technology
Fat and gentle	Lean and mean
Manual and slow	Augmented, automated, and cognitive
Closed value chain	Open ecosystem
Product push	Client pull
Boring	Exciting

Dating and Relationships in InsurTech

Collaborative innovation is gaining importance in the insurance sector. Why? Because it makes good business sense. Large insurance corporates have scale, customers, capital, business and market knowledge, regulatory expertise, licences, and the resources startups can only dream of. Startups are innovative, agile, creative, focused, customer-centric, opportunity-driven, tech-savvy, and change-oriented. Sounds like we have a match! However, dating and building relationships is often more complicated than it sounds.

So are large corporates swiping across their InsurTech startups Tinder apps? We do see a lot of startup CEOs dressing up with suit and tie to meet with possible new corporate partners. But what are their intentions? We see at least four different types of partnerships currently emerging.

Figure 1 gives an overview.

Figure 1: Partnership models

- The horizontal axis indicates the *duration of the engagement* and makes the distinction between modular and flexible companies who team up for a short period and true partnerships for the long term.

- The vertical axis indicates the *intensity of the engagement* and indicates how much time, effort, and resources are being put in to make the relationship work.

If we zoom in on the four quadrants, each of which describes a different kind of relationship between startup and incumbent:

- **The Quicky.** In our research scan of the InsurTech landscape we identified many incubators and accelerators. The Swiss Re accelerator, launched in 2016, is a 16-week program to mentor startups. Allianz X hosts promising entrepreneurs for 100-day sprints to build new businesses. AXA has launched a €100 million InsurTech dedicated incubator called Kamet. These are just a few of many similar corporate incubators we identified. We categorized these initiatives as "The Quicky": startup and incumbent flirt with each other for a short period and with little true commitment to build a real relationship. Both in FinTech and InsurTech, large corporates want to get to know the startups better: how they work, how they think, what their culture is like, and how it can help their own employees to be more like the startups. Typically, the large corporate makes a selection of startups and provides them with

facilities, mentoring, and access to their knowledge and network. The commitment of both sides is often limited and so is the real value creation potential. However, if they prove to be interesting, this first fling can be the start of a more serious partnership.

- **The LAT (Living-Apart-Together).** Partners engage for the long term yet effort invested in the relationship is low, e.g. taking minority stakes or product/service referral partnerships. In this type of relationship both partners do commit to each other yet leave each other the breathing space to grow and each go their own way. Corporate venture capital investments of corporates in InsurTech startups are a good example of how to build a more long-term commitment (if done for strategic reasons and not only financial investment) without committing to real operational integration of both organizations. The recent funding round of One Inc. led by AXA strategic ventures is a nice illustration of how a corporate like AXA can follow a startup like One building a new SaaS platform (Software-as-a-Service) changing the insurance infrastructure. It can be a strategic option for the future. A cautious approach, building a relationship without having to see each other every day. Similarly, when the corporate and startup make referral agreements for products and services and each serves different customer segments with their complementary products there is little true operational integration needed.

The first two relationship types described are characterized by a low engagement intensity – limited time, effort, and resources are invested in the relationship and there is no real focus on operational integration. The next two types we identify are quite different and do focus more on operational interaction and integration between the partners.

Figure 2 will be used to discuss these partnerships further.

- **The Steamy Affair.** Both partners engage in a more operational partnership, focused on short-term mutual interest and benefits. What we currently see in the insurance sector is how business

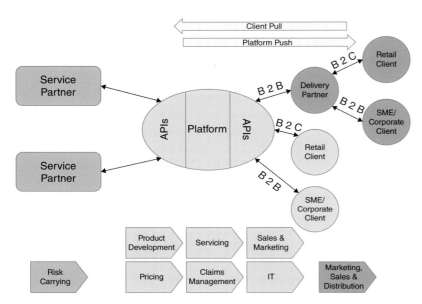

Figure 2: Towards new operating models in insurance

functions (risk carrying, product development, pricing, claims handling, and distribution) are being split up across different business partners. A nice example from our study is the operating model of a company like Qover with the ambition to become full-stack insurance providers, partnering with insurance capacity providers like Lloyd's (risk-carrying function) and selling both direct to clients or via an intermediary delivery partner. With such operating models, which are mostly flexible, API (Application Programming Interfaces), and cloud-based solutions, partners have a more "technical relationship", producing and consuming each other's APIs in an open and often platform-based setting. Partners do not necessarily need to know each other very well. A strong business architectural capability is at the basis of these kinds of "friends with benefits" models. Different dynamics will also coexist in these models ranging from customers and delivery partners who pull information from the insurance provider (on pricing, claims status, products, etc.) to platforms who push

opportunities and leads to possible new or existing partners out there who can try to convert the lead.

- **The Marriage.** Long-term partnership built on a solid foundation of mutual platform or deep and meaningful integration of both organizations. This can be through equal partnership or acquisitions. The most common example is a traditional large corporate acquiring an InsurTech company and integrating it into its own offering and operations. The acquisition of the UK InsurTech startup Simple Business by the US corporate Travelers is one example. Basically, the corporate buys not only the products and services but also the InsurTech partner's digital business capability to integrate it in its own business. However, as we all know, a marriage is not always easy. Especially in this case, where corporate and entrepreneurial cultures are quite different. We have already learned from FinTech that there needs to be a good balance between ring-fencing the entrepreneurial culture on the one hand and strongly blending and integrating the technological, infrastructural, and data components on the other.

Finally, much like in personal relationships, combinations of these four models are of course possible. Many corporates today combine the incubator/accelerator approach with corporate venture capital investments and/or acquisitions. Clearly, the insurance sector today has just hit puberty and partners are experimenting to see which approaches create most value. One major conclusion from our study is that partnerships will only work if win-win-(win) relationships can be created.

Based on what happened in FinTech and the first deals we analysed in the insurance sector, models with low-intensity engagement seem interesting yet not sufficient to deal with the changes we discussed in the table shown earlier in the chapter. Indeed, our first findings indicate that much more is needed than incubators or a financial stake. The high-intensity engagement models leading to successful new capability integration in existing corporates or new, flexible ecosystem operating models as discussed in the previous figure will be the leading partnership model for the InsurTech sector.

Altered Attitudes, Altered Outcomes – Collaborating for a Better Future

By Willie Pienaar
CEO, NuvaLaw

We've all heard the endless stream of lawyer jokes. Perhaps the most telling one is: how many lawyer jokes are there? Three, the rest are all true stories. But at the heart of these jibes at one of the oldest professions is the fact that many people still feel that lawyers are there, not as a means to protect the vulnerable and uphold justice, but simply to make money.

Unfortunately, insurance is often cast in the same light – a grudge purchase, painful, but unavoidable. Changing the construct of how insurers deal with disputes and claims has been a journey of collaboration, co-creation, and the understanding that there is a better way of doing things; a new methodology that works for the insurers, their shareholders, the professionals working in the industry, and, most importantly, the consumer. The journey begins with an altered attitude.

The Penny Drops

In 1992, I was working as a barrister in Cape Town. While the job was fulfilling, I soon realized that there was a significant disconnect. I knew that for a lawyer, time is money and we were all obsessed with billable hours. However, time was also costs incurred for our clients, and, in the end, the economy of the law (as it was practised) was often exactly what was standing in the way of access to justice!

Looking more closely at the challenge, it was clear that the problem was twofold: a lack of early exchange of information and a lack of time management. What we were missing was the ability to make informed decisions, based on structured information exchange.

This realization was later amplified when mediation began to make its mark as a highly efficient means of settling disputes. Successful mediation depends on an open exchange between parties. Where information is shared early in the process, this allows the parties to reach consensus far more quickly and, as a result, far more cost-effectively.

Change is Slow and Difficult

Taking this knowledge into the litigious insurance industry gave us the fertile ground to apply our new way of conducting business. Insurance is characterized by high-volume, low-quantum, high-cost, recurring disputes. In so many instances it made no sense to take these sorts of disputes through a complex, costly legal system. Of course, the challenge would be to convince business leaders who were entrenched in an environment that is notoriously competitive, that it was in their interest not only to try a new way of doing things, but also to collaborate between themselves.

The NuvaLaw founders quickly realized that the introduction of our digital negotiation platform for inter-insurance claims would require a mind shift from insurance company leadership, as well as sound evidence of its business benefits.

The Case Study

Fortunately, a project with the South African state-supported motor vehicle insurance fund gave two of the NuvaLaw founders more than 40,000 cases to prove its efficacy.

Using our expertise in alternative dispute settlement, and building a new process of information management, the team designed a solution that proved that a new way of engaging was not only possible, but profitable.

Our team was able to settle 76% of the contested cases – 70% of which were settled in the conciliation (first) phase. This was largely driven by structured exchange of information, which is such a vital part of our process. We also saw a reduction in settlement costs of 36%, with capital payouts 42% lower than the typical costs of litigated cases.

How We Won Them Over

Armed with this evidence we were able to win over five South African insurance companies. Their leadership realized that the early exchange of information, the abandonment of a hostile, litigious environment, and by using tested business rules and processes, we would significantly improve efficiencies. By driving down the collective costs of claims we were able to show that their focus should be on innovating their product offerings and carving out real market differentiation in the eyes of their customers.

For the claimant lawyers, meanwhile, we were able to use our substantial evidence to prove that while they might be earning 70% of their usual fees per claim, they could boost their volumes of settled claims and come out ahead of the game. After all, who wants to wait two to three years for a case to reach the courts?

Building a Future Based on Collaboration

The ongoing advancement of smart technologies has added significant impetus to our vision of delivering a truly collaborative inter-insurance claims settlement ecosystem.

So much has already been written about the technologies that are being rolled out and that are revolutionizing the platform economy. Whether it's blockchain, machine learning, or any other tech, the key

issue facing insurers is less about the technology and more about how they will adapt their thinking to unlock the next strategic wave of the ecosystem.

Unfortunately, this will need to happen sooner rather than later. With Alibaba already playing in the insurance space and Accenture warning that as many as a third of respondents in a 2017 survey would switch to Amazon, Google, or Facebook if they offered insurance, traditional insurers are feeling the pressure as never before. These companies have already built their ecosystems, and have been spending years investing in and partnering with smaller, innovative companies. More importantly, they have a captive, pre-existing customer base who trust them.

Accenture sums up our thoughts about ecosystems most eloquently:

> Winning insurers in the digital age will do much more than tick off a checklist of technology capabilities. They will be defined by their ability to evolve their corporate culture to take advantage of emerging technologies and of the new business strategies that those technologies drive.[1]

The Only Thing to Fear is Fear Itself

In our experience, the biggest obstacles to affecting a mind shift within the insurance and legal industries are pockets of resistance.

Heads of department within the insurance industry are often resistant to change. Understandably, many will cite the burden

---

[1] Accenture Technology Vision for Insurance 2016 People First: The Primacy of People in the Age of Digital Insurance. Downloadable at http://ins.accenture.com/rs/897-EWH-515/images/Accenture-Technology-Vision-for-Insurance-2016-Full-Report-POV.pdf.

of regulations and compliance as their reason. Protecting personal information, maintaining data integrity, and a lack of willingness to open our systems is holding us all back – unnecessarily so.

While security should remain a keen focus, the very nature of our claims settlement system creates a safe space. Information exchange is governed by explicit rules. What's more, the processes of voluntary arbitration and mediation are themselves governed by strict rules that are contractually guaranteed as confidential. This structured process forms the basis of a structured ecosystem.

The other challenge is that large multinational insurance companies are not known for their nimble business structures and can move at glacial speed when it comes to change. While this is certainly changing, it is still a hurdle that must be overcome. This is clearly a leadership challenge. It is up to the captains of industry to dictate the rate of innovation and change and it must be driven from the top down.

While the insurance industry is going through a digital revolution, it is not alone. The legal industry is facing its own disruption. This has been ably supported by the sharing economy, which has created lawyers on demand, in any jurisdiction, at a considerably lower cost. Focusing on the disruption, PwC noted in 2016:

> Overall, the impact of the sharing economy on legal services is only starting to play out. But it looks certain to drive significant change

in a profession that has seen little fundamental change to business models for many years. It's a development that no firm can afford to ignore.[2]

But it is not just the sharing economy that is driving change. The logical extension of this shift is to take the next step into the ecosystem economy. If the leaders of law firms realize they can't ignore the sharing economy, they should also understand the benefits of the ecosystem economy. The business benefits of collaborating with insurers on the platforms they are participating on, within the ecosystems they are operating in, will mean more work, saved jobs, and, ultimately, their future survival.

Until now, neither insurance nor the legal fraternity has had much incentive to change or indeed collaborate. But the pace of change and the rate of new competition will force their hands sooner than they think. Carefully aligning with the right strategic partners, making use of smart technologies, and adopting an altered attitude is the only way either industry will alter their outcome.

Today, NuvaLaw is winning over insurers in the UK, Europe, Africa, and Australasia. We will be working together to co-create a platform-based ecosystem, which will rely on collaborative technologies, processes, and mindsets to achieve equitable commercial outcomes – for the industry and, most importantly, for the customer.

---

[2] PwC, The future of legal services in a sharing economy, 2016, http://pwc.blogs.com/megatrend_matters/2016/12/the-future-of-legal-services-in-a-sharing-economy.html.

Think InsurTech Culture Before InsurTech Adoption

By Dimitri Anagnostopoulos
Partner, True North Partners

I love buzzwords. These days one can hardly have a conversation in a business context without using one: "FinTech", "InsurTech", "Big Data", "Innovation", "Disruption", "Disruptive Innovation" … the list goes on. One can fill whole sentences with supposedly very important messages, yet without really saying much, especially when there is no clarity on what these terms refer to. For example, if I read "InsurTech can be the driver of innovation for your business", I have to ask myself if that is really true. What does that mean for products or technologies in InsurTech? Is it because an idea is innovative or is it simply about efficiency? What if adoption doesn't really work? Specifically on the last point, I see two main challenges when looking at "InsurTech adoption". The first one is failure to implement the desired solution successfully. The second one is failure to actually achieve or realize the desired/planned benefits.

The drivers of these two challenges link back to organizational culture. Yet "culture" is such a generic term that can mean everything and nothing at the same time, unless you really break it down to practical issues, understand their nature, and identify how to address them.

When I speak at FinTech or InsurTech conferences, I always ask the audience what they are seeking to get out of the presentation. The answer is always the same: "to learn how InsurTech (or FinTech or big data, for example) can benefit our organization". Yet my presentations provide a different angle. I like to look at how technology can help an organization if it is ready for it. Technology does not solve every problem.

The use of technology in financial institutions is not new. What has changed is the pace at which ideas are generated and built, such as the Internet, digital enablement, and API platforms, to name only a few. Some have made technological development easier, cheaper, and more widely accessible. A lot of these ideas may be innovative (or disruptive), but frankly, many are simply introducing efficiencies (equally valuable, but let's not confuse efficiency with innovation). Thousands of startup companies have risen with new ideas or products. The trend we have seen until now in insurance is that these startups don't compete with insurers but rather try to partner with them and introduce their ideas to the industry. So the challenge for insurers is not the lack of ideas. In fact, ideas are developed at a much faster pace than the market can actually absorb. The challenge for insurers is that they need to look internally and prepare in a number of ways in order to tackle the two main challenges of InsurTech adoption.

Looking at the first hurdle, successful implementation, the challenge is how to make new ideas work in an organization whose ways of operating haven't really changed and neither has its ability to embrace change. The word "change" is probably the most important one to focus on when talking about InsurTech. Successful implementation of ideas (innovative or not) takes a lot more than simply partnering with startups or adopting their products. Proper integration in the organization requires effective change management across different functions including process, people, attitude, habits, and performance monitoring.

Many times I have seen companies referring to their "new ideas portfolios" as "fast lane projects", trying to portray a sense of urgency, efficiency, and agility. However, the speed with which stakeholders take decisions and even the key performance indicators (KPIs) driving/guiding decisions, are far from being adequate to drive fast lane projects to successful implementation. The requirement for multiple individuals' signatures (who evaluate decisions based on "silo objectives") and multiple committees' approvals points to a culture that lacks responsibility and accountability at the appropriate level. It naturally leads to slow decision-making processes and a tendency for inaction across the organization, which is conflicting with the "real-time" decision-making actions that "fast lane projects" require – especially when it comes to "pivoting" or "discontinuing" decisions during the development phase.

Obstacles to successful implementation exist in other ways. Risk aversion through activity that states "the more checks the better" might fail to recognize the source of problems in the end-to-end process. Resources capacity, lack of specialization or expert input, and the legacy of existing infrastructure are some of the additional challenges that can impose serious implementation risks, including internal departments being misaligned. Any new firm-wide implementation requires good communication across all levels and departments of the organization. If communication is insufficient (or inefficient) then implementation risk is likely to increase. These last examples might not link directly to "culture", but the fact that large organizations struggle with this, as a constant, means this can add "risk" and delay to project signoff and execution.

As already mentioned, failure of successful implementation is only one side of the problem. Failure to actually achieve or realize the desired/planned benefits is the other issue. And this could point to the following reasons:

(a) You might have chosen to implement a "weak" solution, and

(b) You might have implemented a solution in an "unsuitable" way.

Implementing a weak solution may be the result of inappropriate KPIs. For example, I have seen large portfolios with project ideas, out of which the ones chosen for implementation were the least related to strategy or clients' needs. There was a clear mandate from "the top" that successful implementation is measured by "timely delivery" of a project and "on budget". It had nothing to do with "tracking benefits after implementation" or relevance to the Client Value Proposition (it was simply assumed that benefits or CVP would be achieved). The outcome was that stakeholders, whose bonuses were based on the above, were simply choosing the projects that were less difficult and less risky to implement (i.e.

less probable to fail), regardless of their relevance to the business, the strategy, or the clients.

Remember that people manage their careers not their jobs. They try to promote the product (or action) that would get them to their bonus, regardless of whether this is the right one for the client, regardless of whether this increases client loyalty, whether it increases risk for the organization, or even if it is irrelevant to the overall strategy. This is an obvious misalignment between "InsurTech adoption objectives" and the way you have internally set individuals' success criteria.

Misaligned KPIs might not only result in choosing "weak" projects. They may have a longer-term impact to your organization as they will affect product offering, client value proposition, client loyalty, and ultimately revenues. The culture of "inward looking targets" (own revenue) rather than "outward looking objectives" (clients' needs) may incentivize wrong behaviour. For example, if we set KPIs that measure next quarter's revenues instead of client attrition or satisfaction, we do not promote a culture that tries to understand clients in depth and identify specific needs. We take decisions based on a static segmentation that describes an economic class, but fail to recognize other important characteristics within the same segment that could influence insurance needs (e.g. individuals' lifestyles). So, when the "InsurTech adoption objective" (client service) is measured and incentivized by the wrong drivers, there is a high risk of misalignment or failure to realize desired benefits.

A relevant example of this is the adoption of telematics solutions, and more specifically car tracking devices that record driving behaviour, which are failing to provide a sufficient answer to the question "are we really servicing our clients?" Failing to service clients will directly challenge the success of the initiative and the realized results. Early adoptions of telematics solutions are monitoring driving behaviour, reporting on ex-ante chosen risk parameters, and giving discounts to clients based on those. But where does this actually service clients? Does my InsurApp help me become a safer driver? Does my InsurApp assist me with active "driving protection" measures (which need 99.9% accuracy) or does it only report on passive "driving behaviour detection" (which needs 90% accuracy for underwriting purposes)? Analysing driving behaviour data 24/7 can certainly improve insights for risk underwriting, but from a client's perspective "bigbrothering", without active protection from distracted driving the moment I sit behind the steering wheel, is far from "servicing clients". Also, let's not neglect unintended behaviour from the client's side. Personally, I have discontinued such a telematics service – I almost had an accident twice, because cognitively I was trying not to "harsh-brake" and lose my discount (I was actually becoming a worse driver).

Adopting a telematics solution by spending a few millions is the "easy part" (assuming you have managed to solve the challenges of installation, car replacement, and service discontinuation). The difficult part is how to use the solution in a way that adds value to clients as well as assisting them to manage road risks actively. This would eventually facilitate a comprehensive CVP, creating loyalty through real differentiation for existing customers and attracting new ones.

Before deciding on any new ideas from the InsurTech ecosystem, it is important to acknowledge that innovation (or change) is not something you can simply buy. It needs to be part of the company's culture, a mindset that you need to understand and whose laws you need to harness. Clayton M. Christensen, in his book *The Innovator's Dilemma*, makes the analogy of the early days where humans tried to fly. Yet flight only became possible when people understood the laws of gravity, Bernoulli's principle, the concepts of drag, lift, resistance, etc. In a similar manner, do you understand all the potential stumbling blocks to innovation or change in your organization and are you prepared to understand them and address them in an effective way so as to mitigate similar "adoption risks" mentioned earlier?

The challenges of slow decision-making speed, and inappropriate KPIs, mentality, people, infrastructure, and other internal inefficiencies (by no means a comprehensive list) are not new, and none of them is the result of InsurTech penetration. They have all been around for many years. The reality is that InsurTech cannot solve any of these problems, but its successful adoption can be significantly undermined by them. It took the financial industry more than 10 years and not until the global financial crisis of 2008 to shift attention from "risk modelling" to the importance of "risk culture". We are experiencing a similar situation whereby insurance companies are focusing on InsurTech adoption while neglecting the enabler, InsurTech culture.

The Value Chain

The InsurTech start-up landscape

- More than 550,000 new start-up businesses were established on average per month in 2016. We estimate FinTech/InsurTech related start-ups to account for 30,000

- InsurTech start-ups have received $20bn of investment since 2004

- There are over 3,000 InsurTech start-ups:
  - A little less than 50% located in the USA
  - 30% in Europe
  - 20% in Asia and
  - the last 10% across Oceania, Africa and LATAM

- 1,000s of start-ups are emerging every month
  - 80% of start-ups are likely to fail
  - Of the 20% that remain alive, less than 1% of those that get founded become unicorns

Incremental innovation – Transforming the Value Chain

InsurTechs that leverage digital technologies to enhance the value chain can provide insurers with great headways over their competitors

- 33% of the start-ups funded between 2013 and 2015 had a focus on internal insurance processes. By 2016, this number increased to 61%

- Key processing areas include:
  - Internet-first business models (10%)
  - Distribution and customer engagement focused players (40%)
  - Underwriting and advanced scoring mechanisms (10%)
  - Digitization enablers (40%)

The new world of underwriting is behaviour centric

From Demographics parameters	To Psychographics parameters
Age	Personality
Gender	Interests
Income	Attitudes
Education	Opinions
Job class	Values

Data, Cyber Security & GDPR

On GDPR

- After the launch of GDPR, the penalty for a company's data breach is estimated at €20m or 4% of its global annual turnover or its upcoming financial results, whichever is the greater

- Small breaches will be fined at €10m or 2% of a company's global annual turnover or its upcoming financial results, whichever is the greater

On Cyber Security

- 65% of companies recognize that with the emergence of internet-first businesses and digital technologies, cyber risk exposure will increase exponentially during the course of the next two years

- Indeed, the impact of cyber risk on business disruption is 72% greater than to assets such as property, plant and equipment

- Digital assets are valued 14% higher than other assets

- The loss incurred from digital assets is estimated 30% higher than other assets

- However, organizations only insure 15% of their digital exposure – this includes businesses and government

- Those that have already been affected by cyber security breaches estimate the economic impact on their business averages $2.1 million

The authors in this part wanted to share their views as to why InsurTechs are becoming useful entities to re-engineer existing value chains, particularly at a time when insurance firms must invest significant time and effort to keep pace with current change.

You will find these articles cover the full set of insurance activities across the value chain, and other more targeted pieces that observe specific domains of expertise, such as microinsurance, products sold through smart devices or parametric insurance that drives frictionless experiences.

The authors start by reviewing an interpretation of the insurance value chain and offer improvement options and a method to identify those startups that will be the most suited to accelerate internal acceleration programs.

Advanced analytics is a key enabling driver of this change. One author asserts that insurers should go beyond basic demographic segmentation and infer individuals' psychographics through the use of very specific data sets that are able to improve the accuracy of risk assessments across pre- and post-sales engagement processes.

Micro-policies, or the process of cutting traditional insurance products into smaller, digestible, non-overlapping coverage elements, are at the beginning of their journey, particularly in industrialized markets. Another writer recognizes that reinsurance has changed relatively little in its fundamental form since it emerged from the Industrial Revolution. Still, it is believed that, like many other sectors, it will become more commoditized.

While insurers look for the secret sauce to improve their operations, many of the emerging recommendations point to more intuitive and "as-a-service" infrastructures able to offer and manage smaller bite-size risks or products, volumes of data, and connected systems.

The propagation of connected devices raises an ethical concern from our day-to-day data usage and digital collection, with emerging regulations forcing every organization and government agency to put the customer first, develop new data procedures, and determine these private and public companies' cyber security exposure and act upon it.

At the core of it all reside data and machine learning algorithms able to provide improved ways of determining and managing risks, moving products from a protection to a prevention status. It is believed that new models will require the creation of new data exchanges able to support large ecosystems of participants, and ease the delivery of transparent interactions.

A Four-Step Practical Guide to Build InsurTech Value Chain Ecosystems

By Dr Ivan Gruer

Associate Manager, Accenture, Technology

"Corporates have now wholesale outsourced R&D to the startup and venture community" is what Dave McClure, founder of 500 Startups, claimed at the CB Insights'[1] 2017 Innovation Summit. However, since more than 550,000 new startup businesses were established on average per month[2] in 2016, how could they support R&D developments within insurance companies and deliver significant value chain improvements?

This chapter intends to support the design of insurance value chains ecosystems that are valuable for both consumers and insurers, as well as to other key stakeholders relevant within the insurance value chain.

The InsurTech landscape is getting wider and wider where each InsurTech fixes a specific issue across the insurance value chain. With this four-step practical guide we intend to describe ways to identify and develop value chain improvements and then new business models by combining InsurTechs that leverage IoT, wearables, and blockchain capabilities.

To develop effective InsurTech value chain ecosystems, an organization needs to consider the following four steps:

1. Conduct startup-storming.

2. Organize startups' themes using the Kawakita Jiro method.

3. Scout for relevant solution(s) using the Quality Function Development matrix.

4. Select the right solution.

We will review each step in turn to identify those startups that may be the most relevant for your business.

Step 1: Conduct Startup-Storming

Startup-storming is the process under which an organization will research and identify startups that are emerging with the InsurTech landscape. At this stage, you will want to produce a list of InsurTech startups that potentially correlate with these challenges to solve within your insurance business. These will include the big names or usual suspects, but should also include those that may seem to be, at face value, less relevant. Such lists can be compiled by reviewing top venture capitalists' portfolios as well as the yearly intakes of accelerators' cohorts (e.g. 500 Startup, Startupbootcamp, and Techstars). They all have a thorough selection process. Once you have put together your list, you will want to capture the elevator introduction from each startup. Such statement highlights (1) what they are about and (2) which issues they want to fix.

For instance, Lemonade's vision statement is "a transparent instant insurance for renters and owners", while Fitsense's mission is "making insurance truly personal".

Step 2: Organize Startups' Themes Using the Kawakita Jiro Method

With a list gathering together hundreds of themes, it is likely you will get lost. Kawakita Jiro (KJ), a Japanese anthropologist, invented a method for organizing and classifying ideas into affinity groups.[3] This method facilitates group problem-solving efforts and focuses

---

[1] CB Insights, Startups Are The New Corporate R&D, January 2017, http://www.cbinsights.com/blog/corporate-vc-startup-innovation/.

[2] R. W. Fairle, E. J. Reedy, A. Morelix, and J. Russel, Startup Activity. The Kauffman Index, 2016, http://www.kauffman.org/kauffman-index.

[3] K. Ulrich, *KJ Diagrams*, The Wharton School, 2013, http://opim.wharton .upenn.edu/~ulrich/documents/ulrich-KJdiagrams.pdf.

on organizing a wide number of ideas into a limited number of groups. As a result, the idea selection process is improved and the problems solved better understood. Hence, startups are often grouped into affinity groups that link them together based on their core theme. Such groupings also ease the understanding of their capabilities.

Step 3: Scout for Relevant Solution(s) Using the Quality Function Development (QFD) Matrix

The QFD Matrix[4] links the affinity groups with measurable characteristics and key performance indicators (KPIs). For example, in insurance we have metrics like Average time to settle a claim, Loss ratio, Claim frequency, Underwriting speed, etc. The result is captured into a matrix where addressable consumers' needs are listed on the rows, while the KPIs metrics are listed on the columns.

We have simplified the explanation using a few exemplary startups.

Use the QFD matrix to evaluate, on a scale from 1–5, how much each startup could impact the insurance business; and the strength of the relationship between startups and a KPI to be measured using 9 for a strong relationship, 3 for an average relationship, and 1 for a weak relationship. The scores at the bottom of the matrix are calculated by adding each column from top to bottom, the product of the startup importance, and the strength of the correlation with the KPI.

As an example, consider the column "Average time to settle a claim" (see Figure 1). The absolute importance rating of 48 is calculated as follows: $(2 \times 9) + (5 \times 3) + (4 \times 1) + (2 \times 1) + (3 \times 3) = 48$.

The relative importance of a KPI provides a measurement of how much value could be created from a combination of startups. Comparing all the results, the absolute value of 48 for "Average time to settle a claim" has the lowest relative importance (3%). Whereas, "Revenue per policy holder" is the KPI that should be improved by combining the right startups.

Step 4: Select the Right Solution Using the Pugh Matrix

The purpose of the Pugh Matrix (see Figure 2) is to support a brainstorming session to discuss and debate the most relevant new business models: "Which are the KPIs with the highest scores and which appear across a number of startups?", "Which startup differentiates itself with just a few high rated KPIs?", etc. This approach facilitates the identification of new solutions and ensures that product managers can proactively share new relevant ideas. You will find below three examples that emerged from discussion.

Solution 1 – Personalization of a Health Insurance Product

Millennials and digital natives in industrialized countries have different life expectancies to those of Generation X mostly because of lifestyle. Consumers' needs change over time. This solution allows an insurer to gather the relevant data to develop and launch a health insurance product that a consumer can co-design with a simplified user interface. This goes beyond the concepts of instant umbrella, coverage on demand, or modular offers (e.g. Allianz1 by Allianz Italy).[5] Quotes are evaluated accordingly to personal lifestyle and behaviours as well as insights from different data sources, including wearables, doctors, and historical data. Related startups: Geniuschoice, Teambrella, Instanda, and Fitsense.

[4] G. Kecek and O. C. Akinci, Quality Function Deployment and an Application in an Insurance Company, *International Journal of Academic Research in Business and Social Sciences*, 2016, 6(4), http://hrmars.com/hrmars_papers/Quality_Function_Deployment_and_an_Application_in_an_Insurance_Company.pdf.

[5] https://www.allianz.com/en/press/allianz-journal/edition-01-15/150201_have-a-nice-day/.

Product ⤑
Sum ↓

Category	Product	Description	STARTUP IMPORTANCE	Revenue per policy holder	Average cost per claim	Average time to settle a claim	Loss ratio	Claim frequency	Renewal / retention	Underwriting speed	Number of referrals	Asset under management	Quotas vs production
WEARABLE & IoT	Quantifyle	Make a commitment, track momentum, earn rewards	3	3	3		3	3		1	9		
	Fitsense	Making insurance truly personal	5	3	3		3	3	3	3	1		3
ANALYTICS & AI	Orbital Insight	Understanding trends on earth	4		9		9	9	1	3			3
	Quantemplate	Insurance data integration and analytics	4	3	3		9	3		3		3	9
MOBILE APP	Snapsheet	Making a great claims experience	2	1		9			3				1
	Geniuschoice	Getting aware of what you eat	2		3		1	3	1	1			
OPERATIONS	Instanda	Insurance design and delivery within unprecedented timescales	5	9		3	3		9	9		3	9
	Gatehub	Personal asset wallet for instant payments and trading	1	1					1	1	1	9	1
P2P & EMERGING MARKET	Totohealth	Reduce maternal and child mortality and developmental abnormalities in early stages using mobile technology	3	1	9		9	9	1		3		
	Lemonade	A transparent instant insurance for renters and owners	4	9		1	1	1	9	9	3		3
	Bima	Using mobile technology to bring insurance to everyone	3	9					3	3	3		3
	Teambrella	Truly P2P insurance	2	9	1	1	3	1	9	3	9		3
HEALTH & LIFE	Practo	Appointments with doctors, medicines and clinical records in one secure APP	3	3	3		3	1			3		1
	Healint	Allowing doctors to take advantage of mobile devices & AI	3	3	9	3	3	3	3	3			3
	Myfuturenow	Taking control of the pension	4	9	3		3	1	3	3		9	9
		ABSOLUTE IMPORTANCE		222	155	48	180	127	160	162	90	72	186
		RELATIVE IMPORTANCE		16%	11%	3%	13%	9%	11%	12%	6%	5%	13%

Figure 1: QFD Matrix

Solution 2 – Smart Life Insurance Leveraging the P2P Pooling Model

We can extend the P2P concept beyond ventures such as Lemonade and Teambrella by equipping each peer with his own analytics tools to become familiar with the complexity insurance products. The risk of each new peer wanting to enter a pool will be measured from a variety of data sources and automated rules. This assessment will be used to decide whether to approve a party to a specific pool through clear decision support. For life insurance review, each peer will be able to gain the best advice by leveraging the peer associated to a dedicated portfolio. Related startups: PensionBee, Myfuturenow, Teambrella, and Orbital Insights.

Solution 3 – Micro-Health Insurance for Developing Countries

In this scenario, organizations can learn a lot from the microinsurance products that are being designed for the emerging markets. Those products are often supported by payment platforms able to accept the settlement of small premium amounts directly from mobile telecom contracts, particularly for those with no bank account. Such products connect a digital platform to local healthcare systems and telemedicine services, practitioners, patients, and drugs

providers willing to participate in the program. In many African countries, for instance, over 75% of the population have no access to basic medicines and would do well to access proper diagnosis, monitoring, and digital recovery services. Related startups: Bima, Jamii, Totohealth, and Practo.

A final assessment is delivered by reviewing the scores captured at the interception of the matrix. These are the −1, +1 or 0 meaning, respectively, worse, better, or equal results to the baseline reference. Your Pugh result is defined by adding all the scores

			Solution 1 - Self designed life insurance	Solution 2 - Smart P2P insurance	Solution 3 - Health insurance for dev. countries
WEARABLE & IoT	Quantifyle	Make a commitment, track momentum, earn rewards	1	−1	1
	Fitsense	Making insurance truly personal	1		1
ANALYTICS & AI	Orbital Insight	Understanding trends on earth	1	−1	
	Quantemplate	Insurance data integration and analytics	1	1	
MOBILE APP	Snapsheet	Making a great claims experience			1
	Geniuschoice	Getting aware of what you eat	1		
OPERATIONS	Instanda	Insurance design and delivery within unprecedented timescales	1	−1	
	Gatehub	Personal asset wallet for instant payments and trading		1	
P2P & EMERGING MARKET	Totohealth	Reduce maternal and child mortality and developmental abnormalities in early stages using mobile technology			1
	Lemonade	A transparent instant insurance for renters and owners		1	
	Bima	Using mobile technology to bring insurance to everyone	−1		1
	Teambrella	Truly P2P insurance	1	1	
HEALTH & LIFE	Practo	Appointments with doctors, medicines and clinical records in one secure APP	−1	1	1
	Healint	Allowing doctors to take advantage of mobile devices & AI	−1		1
	Myfuturenow	Taking control of the pension	1	1	
		PUGH RESULT	5	3	7

Figure 2: Pugh Matrix

from each row. These results estimate the level of innovation provided by each solution. Consider developing these solutions with the highest scores, leveraging an agile methodology, as they are indicative of solutions providing more value to customers.[6]

Conclusion

"Creative thoughts must always contain a random component."[7] Analysing capabilities developed by startups and learning from their success might be a great alternative to developing your own internal innovation initiatives.

Startups with great solutions give insurers and insurance providers great headway over their competitors and help high potential

ventures to prosper and grow since only 0.9% of startups that are founded (if they reach that stage) become unicorns.[8]

Creating new value-adding ecosystems was the purpose of this chapter. My intent was to share with you tools that can help you accelerate your ability to identify and work with the most relevant startup business models that are emerging daily. I believe that operating results will come from combining several startups rather than working with just one.

The cases of Lemonade and Teambrella have already created some level of discomfort within the insurance sector. What will it take for insurers to take a leap of faith to acquire those capabilities that will help them survive in a highly uncertain market?

[6] D. Leffingwell, *Agile Software Requirements: Lean Requirements Practices for Teams, Programs, and the Enterprise*, Addison-Wesley, 2011.

[7] Gregory Bateson, *Mind and Nature: A necessary unit*. Hampton Press, 2003.

[8] CB Insights, Venture Capital Funnel Shows Odds of Becoming a Unicorn Are Less than 1%, December 2015, https://www.cbinsights.com/blog/venture-capital-funnel/.

Sell Your Insurance at the Right Time – Consider Micro Policies

By Andrea Silvello

Co-Founder, Neosurance, Founder and Managing Director of Business Support

Even in today's connected world, insurance agents and brokers remain the most prevalent means to sell non-compulsory insurance coverage to potential customers. "Insurance is sold, not bought!", a sentence commonly heard in the InsurTech arena, is (and will remain) to my mind imperative for insurers to acquire and retain customers.

Due to contractual complexities and blurred understanding of claims terms, insurance buyers often find it difficult to grasp fully the value offered by the insurance products they purchase. The lack of customized offers that fit with new market realities and the needs of changing customer segments mean that many buyers end up underinsured or unaware that their requirements are not covered.

What is Expected of Insurers When it Comes to Creating an Effective Digital Customer Experience?

Many financial services institutions, including banks, have already developed complex applications supported by great user experiences that guide clients with their day-to-day banking needs. The best examples are the very popular online-only banks that have managed to attract clients without having physical agencies: a characteristic that is prized by younger generations (millennials and Generation Z), who are not so keen to deal with the inconvenience of traditional bank counters. Not to mention the retail industry, which was one of the first to meet the requirements of connected generations for real-time buying, meaning geo-location supported apps to promote personalized offers.

The key question is: why is the insurance sector so much slower at adopting digital capabilities, which can bring enormous benefits to the industry and to their clients? It is well known that insurers have encountered delays with their digital innovation programs due to the complexity of legacy systems. However, shifting customers' expectations together with an increased usage of digital channels are both forcing insurance players to focus on their innovation strategies.

Users today do not just go online, they live online. To be more precise, they experience an endless series of moments, hopping between the nonlinear sequencing of the offline and online worlds. These are competitive threats insurers must understand and overcome.

Clients want personalized solutions aligned to their needs, and they want those quickly. The most appropriate customer-centric marketing approach begins by acknowledging that there is no such thing as an "average" customer. Each customer has different habits, preferences, and behaviours and this should be recognized as an opportunity to move past the "one-size-fits-all" style marketing approaches. Incumbent insurers should start looking at their customer base as their greatest and long-term asset. They must also make customer centricity a core tenet of their overall market strategy. Google gave some basic, but essential, pieces of advice destined for retailers in an article on micro-moments.[1] It highlighted that, to offer memorable experiences to customers, a retail brand must develop and cultivate three qualities:

1. They must "Be There" for their customers, meaning that they must show up when and where the customer has a need or desire.

2. They must then "Be Useful" and come up with valuable and relevant content.

3. They must "Be Quick", which means think and act fast or lose market opportunities and potential clients.

---

[1] Win Every Micro-Moment With a Better Mobile Strategy, 2015, https://www.thinkwithgoogle.com/marketing-resources/micro-moments/win-every-micromoment-with-better-mobile-strategy/.

To avoid losing a large portion of the digital generation, insurers must address these issues when reshaping their proposition and value chain.

The lack of a coherent and encompassing vision regarding online and offline sales channels and the integration among them should not even exist anymore but is a major handicap that customers can still experience when engaging with organizations. Insurance for the masses is becoming outdated, while newcomers are clearly moving towards offering context and utility.

These newcomers must not be overlooked. According to Venture Scanner, these InsurTech startups have received over US$18 billion of investment since 2004.[2] Bringing with them new business models and a breath of fresh "technological" air, they might be just what the doctor prescribes for keeping with the pace of change within a highly-connected world.

In this context, artificial intelligence (AI) and the Internet of Things (IoT) represent major trends that will impact the evolution of the insurance industry as we see it. And a number of InsurTech startups are already building solutions that enable carriers to propose innovative and customized insurance to their final clients.

Micro-policies or Short Duration Insurance: Approaches to Sell Timely and Distribute the Right Coverage at an Affordable Price

One of the first micro-policies purchasable through a cellular phone was made available in 2010 by Tokio Marine in partnership with NTT Docomo,[3] a mobile network operator, and remains an often-cited case study for insurance innovation regarding in particular the customer experience. Since then, a series of startups that offer micro-policies have appeared and they operate according to certain sales approaches and distribution models.

Some startups like Trov,[4] Cuvva,[5] or Back Me Up[6] are based on stand-alone solutions, which means that their solution does not rely on another party to make their insurance services available to customers. Each of these players has its own mobile app or website,[7] which is used to propose different types of micro-policies to customers, from gadget and home insurance to wedding and pet insurance. The opposite approach to the stand-alone distribution model is the plug & play approach, meaning that integration is needed with a third-party customer-facing website or app. This model will include examples such as Simplesurance,[8] Pablow,[9] and BIMA.[10]

The distribution model has a great impact on the potential reach and exposure of the new solution to final customers. Stand-alone solutions need to be researched by the potential clients directly, while plug & play solutions already benefit from a customer base supported by a partner. The sales approach instead could have direct impact on the challenge of adverse selection[11] and on delivering unique customer experiences.

---

[2] Venture Scanner data as of April 2017, https://home.venturescanner.com/blog.

[3] https://www.the-digital-insurer.com/dia/tokio-marine-partners-with-ntt-docomo-to-offer-one-time-insurance/.

[4] www.trov.com/.

[5] https://cuvva.com/.

[6] www.backmeup.co.uk/.

[7] Please see www.airsurety.com/ for a comparative model.

[8] www.simplesurance.co.uk/.

[9] www.pablow.com/.

[10] www.bimamobile.com/.

[11] "Adverse selection is a phenomenon wherein the insurer is confronted with the probability of loss due to risk not factored in at the time of sale. This occurs in the event of an asymmetrical flow of information between the insurer and the insured". Definition made available by The Economic Times, http://economictimes.indiatimes.com/definition/adverse-selection.

From our research, we can assert that there are InsurTech players that are deploying a "pull-based" sales approach. This is the equivalent of the customer having to ask for a specific insurance cover that he or she can access on a timely basis. The Trov app is one such example of how one can insure valuable objects at any point in time, at a reduced cost, and without paperwork. The app also works as a digital inventory, offering users the option to store and categorize items, while at the same time displaying the market value and description of each object.

The downside of the "pull-based" sales approach in general is that preventing fraud becomes difficult and foul play is not easily detectable. At the opposite end of the spectrum sits the "push" approach, meaning that the solution provider proposes insurance to the customer of its own initiative. A downfall of this approach is that insurance propositions could be overlooked by customers because they fail to arrive at the right time and within an appropriate and meaningful context for the customer.

I personally believe the two criteria that I mentioned earlier (sales approach and distribution model) are particularly relevant on the insurance market today in determining the success of selling micro-policies. I would also suggest that selling insurance via push notifications (compared to a "pull" approach) could be a better and more effective way of approaching customers who are not otherwise inclined to purchase non-compulsory insurance. This can help overcome the obstacle highlighted previously that "Insurance is sold, not bought". A challenge remains when sending insurance information: to approach a user in an intelligent non-invasive way. Intelligent in this context refers to having a system capable of understanding the customer's physical context, emotions, and preferences and even predicting his or her future actions to offer the right insurance products and services at the right time.

This is what Neosurance is trying to do. Neosurance uses artificial intelligence to enable insurance companies to sell limited-duration insurance covers via push notifications through a smartphone app used by a community of users (e.g. a runner's community app, or an amateur soccer player's community app).

The smartphone becomes a medium to push insurance propositions and to address existing challenges relating to closing the underinsurance and insurance protection gap,[12] as it has become the preferred research means, when searching for information, comparing products, finding best deals, and connecting with market brands.

As the sharing economy becomes more widespread, the market will not be lenient with those market participants that deny technological progress, especially when it comes to evolving future customer experiences. The market will demand niche products that are relevant for specific customers and ecosystem partners, digitally accessible at any moment. Then you'll be able to give them the right insurance coverage from their smartphones.

Micro-policies are at the beginning of their journey, particularly in industrialized markets. There are still uncharted territories for us to explore, and the potential to raise the industry's profitability

---

[12] "Underinsurance can be defined as the gap between the amount of insurance that is economically beneficial and the amount of insurance actually purchased. In non-life insurance, this phenomenon can be measured by a benchmarked insurance coverage ratio. This ratio is based on a country's non-life insurance penetration (premiums as a share of GDP), adjusted for differences in per capita income and natural catastrophe exposure. An alternative measure is the insurance gap, which describes the difference between insured and total economic losses as a share of GDP. In life and pension insurance, more specific measurements apply … In term life insurance, the aggregate protection gap of a country can be defined as the difference between the present value of income needed to maintain the living standard of survivors plus debt outstanding, and the present value of the sum of future pensions to survivors, life insurance in force and a certain share of financial assets." Definition made available by The Global Insurance Protection Gap: Assessment and Recommendations, November 2014, https://www.genevaassociation.org/media/909569/ga2014-the_global_insurance_protection_gap.pdf.

level through those is seen by some as significant. Investing in a digital sales force able to sell insurance in a smart way using AI and machine learning capabilities would be a good investment to reach these connected generations through their smart devices.

I am certain that micro-insurance policies will increase in the near future, because of the nascent needs of their buyers. The protection gap is reducing, because of the development of a more intimate customer-insurer relationship.

The huge amount of data out there combined with the ability to analyse it in such a way as to bring value to both customer and insurer leads me to believe that investments in this type of innovative solution will rise, taking advantage of the still emerging talents.

InsurTech: Refreshingly Different – Like Lemonade!

By Désirée Klingler
Senior Consultant, Roland Berger

"The most imminent effects of disruption will be felt in the banking sector; however, the greatest impact of disruption is likely to be felt in the insurance sector."[1]

This quote highlights that innovation across FinTech was and still is in the spotlight of the media and academia, but that the digital revolution across the insurance sector will slowly but surely step out of the dark. This chapter will review emerging models and innovations impacting the insurance sector and their somewhat disruptive potential, if any, on the industry.

Innovation along the Insurance Value Chain

To understand the impact and the degree of digitization and/or disruption across the insurance sector, we need to review the traditional insurance value chain and its five key elements:[2]

- Product management deals with the planning, forecasting, and marketing of a product at all stages of the product life cycle.

- Sales and distribution encompasses marketing channels and promotion means to bring the product to the customer.

- Underwriting and risk management is at the core of the insurance business where the insurance company evaluates the risk of potential clients and guarantees payment in case of damage or financial loss.

- Claims management offers the service to advise the client, compensate the loss, and cover litigation of the insured person.

- Customer service is the provision of service before, during, and after a purchase, which can also include the vital part of customer retention.

With the evolution of new technologies such as artificial intelligence (AI), blockchain, distributed ledger technologies (DTL), and data mining (DM), so-called InsurTechs have started to re-engineer these five elements and combine them in ways that make buying, claiming, and managing insurance intuitive and relevant for customers. For each element of the value chain (except the first one) a selection of most innovative startups[3] and their unique offerings are introduced.

Sales and Distribution

Look at ventures such as Lemonade, Guevara, and Friendsurance. This triad has come into business within the past seven years and has deployed similar peer-to-peer (P2P) insurance business models that shift the leads generation process from the direct-to-consumer insurer or broker channels to the insured themselves. Focused on selling low-cost renter insurance, Lemonade[4] is an

---

[1] World Economic Forum, The Future of Financial Services Report, June 2015, http://www3.weforum.org/docs/WEF_The_future__of_financial_services.pdf.

[2] See PwC, The Insurance Value Chain, http://www.pwchk.com/en/industries/financial-services/insurance/the-insurance-value-chain.html.

[3] Based on the Roland Berger Focus publication, InsureTechs and the Digitization of the Insurance Industry, to be published in 2017, and 33 Insurtechs To Know, 27 September 2016, http://fintechranking.com/2016/09/27/33-insurtechs-to-know/.

[4] *The Economist*, A New Yorker startup shakes up the insurance business – Is the future of insurance named after a soft drink? 9 March 2017, http://www.economist.com/news/finance-and-economics/21718502-future-insurance-named-after-soft-drink-new-york-startup-shakes-up.

insurance startup that started trading in New York and expanded to other US states. The way it distributes its products is fully digitized, intuitive, and fast. With its AI bot Maya one can get insured in seconds and claims settled in minutes. The UK-based startup Guevara[5] enables its users to meet and pool their car insurance premiums together online to save money. Providing a series of omni-channel property and casualty (P&C) insurance products, Berlin-based Friendsurance[6] rewards groups of trustworthy friends or users with a significant cashback bonus if they remain claimless. The US startup Ladder,[7] founded by alumni from Google, Dropbox, and Harvard Business School, offers individualized, fast, and easy access to life insurance by enabling customers to get a quote in seconds and be covered by a pure, term product without going through the hassle of high pressure sales tactics. The theme here is simple, faster, and relevant.

Underwriting and Risk Management

Today, scoring mechanisms require more advanced sources of data to improve underwriting precision and accuracy. The Californian startup Social Intelligence[8] uses and distributes social media and online presence data to the insurance industry to enhance underwriting. Trov[9] offers the first instant micro-durational P&C insurance where policies can be underwritten and priced in real time to allow users to switch on and off policies instantaneously.

[5] Rick Huckstep, Guevara, moral hazard and the future of P2P Insurance, 24 December 2015, http://www.mckinsey.com/industries/healthcare-systems-and-services/our-insights/how-discovery-keeps-innovating.

[6] See www.friendsurance.com/.

[7] See Business Insider, New insurtech Ladder is digitizing life insurance, 11 January 2017, http://www.businessinsider.com/new-insurtech-digitizes-life-insurance-2017-1?IR=T&r=US&IR=T.

[8] See www.socialintel.com/.

[9] See https://trov.co.uk/blog.

Claims Management

Claims innovation ranges from the digitization of the full claims process to specific enhancements of the customer engagement. The German startup Motionscloud offers end-to-end digitized claims management to insurance companies with a claim cycle that takes hours instead of days. To fast-track the claims process, customers can upload pictures of incidents through their phone.

In addition, the real music plays with the use of machine learning and predictive analytics to make claim decisions, prevent fraud, and spot litigation issues – such as offered by EagleEye Analytics – that has been recently acquired by Guidewire Software.

Customer Service and Retention

Swiss mobile-first insurance broker Knip[10] delivered increased policy transparency for users by moving insurance brokerage and policy management 24/7 onto the mobile phone, while South African venture Discovery[11] developed a collaborative business model that offers a series of third-party health benefits via a behaviour-linked loyalty program that tracks people's activities. It thus shifts the business model from protection towards prevention.

Innovation or Disruption?

Having a close look at these InsurTech examples, the question that comes to mind is whether these innovations have the

[10] Steve O'Hear, Swiss Mobile-First Insurance Broker Knip Pucks Up $15.7M Series B, 26 October 2015, https://techcrunch.com/2015/10/26/knip/.

[11] Adrian Gore, How Discovery keeps innovating, May 2015, http://www.mckinsey.com/industries/healthcare-systems-and-services/our-insights/how-discovery-keeps-innovating.

potential to disrupt the insurance sector or whether they will just digitize existing processes along the insurance value chain.

Coming back to basics, disruption represents the genuine change in traditional business models and their replacement with new ones, mostly driven through technological innovations. Digitization or innovation introduces new ideas, devices, or methods to run processes more efficiently. In Ryan Hanley's words: "Disruption changes the game, digitization simply improves the game."[12]

Based on the InsurTech examples shared earlier, two groups of innovations emerge.

One group of startups tends to introduce incremental change like automation or digitization of processes. For instance, Ladder allows faster and easier access to insurance products. Knip and Motionscloud transfer traditional insurance processes like policy and claims management onto digital means to deliver transparent and trusting relationships.

Some other groups of startups have developed alternative business models combining very specific parts of the insurance value chain. As noted, P2P startups Lemonade, Guevara, and Friendsurance drive value through social participation and group claim sharing. Trov's business model has itemized risk insurance and Discovery focuses on prevention instead of protection by its behaviour-linked loyalty program.

These examples are facilitating more efficient insurance processes – particularly where insurers fail – by means of advanced technology or redefining much-targeted elements of the insurance value chain, rather than disrupting or reversing the entire insurance industry.

---

[12] Ryan Hanley, SVP of Marketing at TrustedChoice.com and the Managing Editor of Agency Nation, 3 Reasons Why P2P Insurtech Start-ups Will Not Disrupt the Insurance Industry, 16 June 2016, https://www.agencynation.com/p2p-insurtech-start-ups-disruption/.

Is the Peer-to-Peer Insurance Model a Revolutionary Idea?

This brings me to the P2P insurance models offered by Lemonade, Guevara, and Friendsurance, which were celebrated as the new business model of the twenty-first century. But is the model really revolutionary or is it reviving an old market concept?

Most new P2P insurance propositions offer personal lines insurance against a flat fee, which represents the commission paid to the product provider. A group of people pays premiums into a claims pool. When an insured event occurs, claims payment is triggered first from the pool and then for larger claim incidents from reinsurance arrangements. If there is a premium surplus at the end of the insurance period, the money is returned or paid into a fund based on the agreed terms of the proposition.

This is a "refreshingly different" approach to insuring because conflict of interest during the claims process are minimized as the insurance provider is only paid from an agreed fee or commission and is therefore incentivized to pay claims.

Still, three critical remarks need to be made:

First and foremost, the idea of P2P insurance is not new. At the end of the seventeenth century "Hand in Hand Fire & Life Insurance Society" was established as the first mutual insurance office, that is a company owned entirely by its policy-holders. It was founded in London to protect its members from losses incurred by fire while Lloyd's of London, created slightly earlier, focused on ships and cargos. In the US, the first successful mutual insurance company, the Philadelphia Contributionship, was founded by Benjamin Franklin in the eighteenth century. This clearly means that P2P business models are not new.

Secondly, the only true "peer" element in the P2P insurance model is the sense of community it creates between friends and families, who are then connected through social media means. Peers merely pay the first low-value claims, before the reinsurance agreements step in to take over the larger bulk part. Furthermore, the P2P solutions do still involve brokers – the P2P insurer is acting as both broker (charging a flat fee) and carrier (paying the claims) at the same time.

Lastly, every hype levels off after it has reached its peak. My belief is that after a few years of business, P2P insurers may not be able to pay all claims incurred, and create disappointments among customers because every innovation reaches its plateau. Still, such startups can offer other useful value to customers.

In light of these remarks, Lemonade, Guevara, and Friendsurance's true benefits include fast and easy access to otherwise highly administrative and burdensome insurance capabilities, packaged and offered through fully-digitized and mobile means.

While innovation opportunities will come from shaping and remodelling the value chain, disruption opportunities will come from identifying truly revolutionary business models. However, it is likely that this change will be facilitated by disruptive technologies such as the blockchain and artificial intelligence/machine learning. Blockchain will deliver massive cost savings through smart contracts. These smart contracts will include the support of new intercompany transaction models, customer-led ID checks, or the launch of truly innovative and cost-effective microinsurance offerings. Artificial intelligence/machine learning supported by advanced analytics algorithms will provide a platform to create interesting pre-sales insights, deliver a multitude of refined and automated customer engagements, and reduce the potential risk of adverse selection.

Forget Peer-to-Peer, the Future of Insurance is Invisible and Parametric

By Jean-Charles Velge
Co-Founder, Qover

and Quentin Colmant
Co-Founder, Qover

The InsurTech wave has just begun and will fundamentally change the industry in the coming years. All parts of the insurance value chain will be challenged by InsurTech players and incumbent players will have to partner with innovative players to embrace these changes.

Although the revolution in place has not yet elected the winning business model(s) of tomorrow, we will focus in this chapter on what we believe will be the fundamentals of the insurance of the future rather than reviewing what we call the technological enablers of this soon-to-come transformation.

By referring to technological enablers, we mean all technologies and tools such as machine learning techniques, artificial intelligence (AI), the Internet of Things (IoT), distributed ledgers, etc. that are not an end per se, but a means that is already in use within the tech landscape, and which does not totally determine the fundamentals of the new paradigm of insurance.

Our assumption is that the new paradigm of insurance will be "invisible" and "parametric", enabled by several technologies including AI and the IoT.

The concept of invisible insurance mainly addresses the way insurance will be distributed. The direct consequence of being invisible is the need to shift operating models towards "Insurance-as-a-Service" infrastructures and the possible emergence of other types of giant risk carriers.

While invisible redefines the distribution of insurance by minimizing any possible friction, at the other extreme of the value chain we also see change throughout the claims management process. In our view, while several InsurTechs do focus in some shape or form on "solving" problems endemic across claims management in general, our belief is that the problem should rather be tackled at the source: by redefining the essence of claims management to create a situation where it does not need to be managed anymore. This will lead to the second fundamental that will define the insurance of tomorrow, which we call "parametric insurance".

Some readers might raise questions with regards to a possible third fundamental: "peer-to-peer insurance" (P2P). In our view, the new disruptive P2P business models tend to irritate insurance purists: the roots of insurance have always been in the mutualization of risk. The insurers are *essentially* an "escrow" account shared by all insureds (so it is already P2P), and some of them already share their profits. In short, "P2P" sounds just like a trendy synonym for traditional insurance.

So, let's review these fundamentals.

First Fundamental: Distribution Will Be Invisible

Most customers are not interested in insurance. Very few people wake up in the morning thinking about buying insurance. Customers, however, understand the value of it and are just seeking protection, each of them according to his own risk appetite. As a result, insurance should be viewed as a complementary feature to a product or a service rather than a core customer offering. This also means that it is extremely important that insurers consider the technological trends affecting the products and services they insure. Our society is currently shifting from "ownership to usage" with the sharing economy and business models associated to it. And technology enablers such as the IoT, "virtual and augmented reality", and the "blockchain" are going radically to change the way insurance can be priced, underwritten, and serviced.

Therefore, in a connected world, the insurance industry needs to rethink its distribution model. For example, the driverless car of tomorrow that picks you up should be able to get the right insurance coverage automatically, to protect you and your belongings according to the journey you intend to undertake or the estimated traffic. Once you step out of your home, your smartphone should take over this hassle for you. Those connected devices will invisibly source the most suitable insurance solution for you at any time, or may immediately cover you based on the agreement you made with your microinsurance provider.

Frictionless distribution implies that insurance must become somehow invisible for the insured, fully embedded within the core product or service, and perfectly tailored to the customer needs and very own risk appetite.

In such an "Invisible World of Insurance", it is paramount to leverage the existing technological enablers such as AI that define what and when you need coverage, IoT that enable connected devices and services to interact, and new ways of distribution to further reduce friction.

Furthermore, embedded insurance must undoubtedly be supported by a strong infrastructure for insurance (see Figure 1) or "Insurance-as-a-Service".

Insurance-as-a-Service offers a business the opportunity to leverage a digital layer that seamlessly integrates a series of complementary digital insurance coverages to their product offerings or services. The distributor simply deploys its insurance application programming interfaces (APIs), or widely used set of clearly defined methods of communication to accelerate integration among various software

components, to a digital managing agent, insurer, or even reinsurer. The distributor can also choose in real time from a library of online features that can turn them into truly digital insurance providers. The insurance coverage is either fully embedded in each product and service or can be purchased as an add-on.

Such infrastructure implies a shift in the distribution of revenues from "insurance providers" such as a direct website, brokers, or agents to the distributor of the core product/service, such as, for example, the driverless car manufacturer or the companies that build the key application used for car sharing. Using Insurance-as-a-Service, all businesses are given the opportunity to take the "fee" or "commission" part of the insurance value chain and offer their customers digital access to value-added capabilities now embedded within core insurance products and services.

However, the biggest challenge for InsurTech companies lies in building the digital infrastructure – meaning developing the digital, legal, and insurance framework to enable such an "Insurance-as-a-Service" distribution model to work. The hard part resides in bringing two fundamentally different worlds together: traditional insurance creation and new underwriting techniques, combined with digital/tech solutions.

Insurance product creation and underwriting require a wide variety of internal capabilities, which include: obtaining insurance licences, creating a legal framework, defining the pricing, dealing with the regulator, and obtaining the delegated authority from risk carriers. Building a product, creating the right

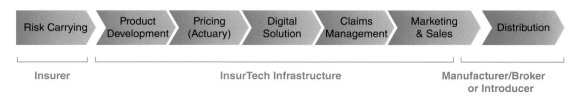

Figure 1: Insurtech infrastructure

pricing, and agreeing on a distribution method remain a gruelling process for an InsurTech startup.

The digital infrastructure needs to be built from the ground up starting with customer experience. Traditional insurers too often "digitize their own products, services, and processes" and simply integrate their inherent complexity into new digital solutions.

Finally, the natural consequence of Insurance-as-a-Service is the emergence of "giant risk carriers" that will directly provide cross-border capacity to InsurTech players that have built the infrastructure to sell insurance solutions digitally.

In such a connected world, with a frictionless distribution and integration model and a clear transparency on coverage and pricing, the premium paid by the customer will get closer to the real technical premium. In such a case, the intermediary will then disappear while some insurers will be at risk of extinction, as the infrastructure could directly source insurance capacity to the reinsurer. What a scary scenario! A wave of consolidation will then need to take place among insurers, while we shall witness the emergence of smaller players at the edge of innovation, partnering with "giant risk carriers".

Second Fundamental: The Rise of Parametric Insurance

While several InsurTechs are investing in a variety of domains, including developing Internet-first platforms or solutions that enhance the distribution, underwriting, claim handling, and assessment processes (e.g. video-based expertise, AI for fraud …), we believe that the fundamental change resides in redefining the fundamental notion of "what a claim is".

From our point of view, parametric insurance is the answer. It does not indemnify the loss, but instead an amount agreed ex-ante on the occurrence of a trigger event. Currently, parametric insurance

has effectively been used for large risks such as natural disasters and crop coverage, an example being The Climate Corporation, a platform that builds a massive data platform for agriculture in the US.[1] Parametric insurance is currently ideal for low-frequency but high-intensity losses. However, with the rise of the IoT, there is a unique opportunity to open parametric insurance to the whole Property & Casualty market.

Thanks to connected devices, parametric insurance will become the norm. Imagine if your connected car had a collision with a roadside object. The car, fully equipped with thousands of sensors, could automatically assess the damage and instantly evaluate the loss. The self-driving car could immediately be routed to an agreed repair shop and the loss would be instantly compensated.

The possibilities of parametric insurance are infinite but need to follow the pace of innovation of current products and services. The insurance coverage and indemnity will also need to be redefined. This would necessitate an iterative learning process leveraging machine learning insights and data recorded by billions of sensors and connected devices.

Conclusion

The industry will be reshaped through the emergence of two new fundamentals: the invisible and the parametric.

Invisible insurance will require the development of an Insurance-as-a-Service infrastructure that will propose traditional coverage. It will also require a more modular approach through sliced and on-demand coverage. It is about cutting traditional insurance products into smaller, non-overlapping coverage elements. These allow the customer to pick and choose options to build a personalized

[1] https://climate.com/
https://www.forbes.com/sites/bruceupbin/2013/10/02/monsanto-buys-climate-corp-for-930-million/#118b51b1177a.

insurance solution. Such infrastructure will redistribute the stream of revenues from traditional intermediary to any business owning a digital ecosystem. The final objective will be to reduce the remaining distribution-related frictions. This will lead to a wave of consolidation where insurers and reinsurers will become giant risk carriers.

While embedded insurance will become the norm, the final state of insurance would also integrate parametric insurance concepts. Rather than focusing on improving claim handling, the real asset will result from redefining the notion of the claim itself and what the associated loss really means. Parametric insurance is very promising, but it will require a more connected environment equipped with millions of sensors and a long learning curve to better attribute indemnity to each specific claim occurrence.

What happened in FinTech will happen in InsurTech with a vengeance. The InsurTech revolution has just begun and will fundamentally change the insurance industry in the coming years.

Behavioural Design and Price Optimization in InsurTech

By Bernardo Nunes, PhD
Head of Data Scientist, Growth Tribe Academy

Delivering effective pricing is still today a core challenge for many insurers. The main reasons are due to:

1. **Asymmetry of information.** Buyers of insurance products possess better information about their own desires, preferences, and behaviours than any insurer would ever do. As a result, insurers rely on predictive models to infer premiums that are based on a heterogeneous number of risk factors for each future potential new insured.

2. **Post sales risk profiling.** Once insured customers are on cover, insurers gain insights on their behaviour to better understand high-risk from low-risk profiles post sales, and hence use this information to refine future pricing strategies.

The good news is that these challenges can be addressed in a much more informative way due to the rise of InsurTech startups and the possibility to observe customer behaviour better through the digital footprints each customer leaves behind when using connected devices.[1] Based on individuals' behavioural patterns, insurers can develop personalization triggers to "nudge" them towards specific actions and test whether these interventions are effective to reduce potential claim incidences.

There are lots of InsurTech solutions out there, and many of the applications I have seen still seem to offer one-size-fits-all mechanisms, which very rarely consider customers' differences. Personalization, when it exists, is restricted to the onboarding process, to optimize product selection based mostly on sociodemographic characteristics and self-reported attitudes and habits. Alternatively, by collecting data from social networks and web applications, insurers can go beyond demographic segmentation and infer individuals' psychographic criteria, such as personality traits and non-cognitive skills that determine behavioural patterns.

When these factors are incorporated into customer analyses, the accuracy of risk assessments improves and, consequently, prices are optimized. In this chapter, I shall cover what these factors are and ways to identifying them across pre- and post-sales engagement processes, highlighting how to learn from customer behaviour and continuously improving ongoing price strategies.

InsurTech and the Role of Psychographics during the Pre-sale Process

Insurers' profitability is highly dependent on the way they price and identify relevant factors that are associated with claims. In theory, insurers should have strong incentives to go beyond demographic characteristics to profile customers and identify new factors that describe their customers' habits and ultimately their attitudes and behaviour. While demographic criteria are related to the structure of target segments, psychographic characteristics deal with individual personality, values, attitudes, and opinions[2] (see Table 1). These factors can be mined through large-scale observational data sets to feed better risk models. In fact, the search for user-level data is not specific to the insurance industry, it is in the mindset of many marketing departments that want to combine data collection and digital channels to

---

[1] M. Madden, S. Fox, A. Smith, and J. Vitak, Digital Footprints. Pew Internet & American Project, 2007, www.pewresearch.org/.

[2] A. Birkett, How Data-driven Marketers are Using Psychographics, 2017, https://conversionxl.com/psychographics/.

achieve personalization at scale. For example, today, the advent of automation and data analytics allow many companies to "learn and test" using a variety of tools.[3] As a result, these practices form part of some of the most advanced innovations that insurers can possibly use to redesign their value chain, improve their risk modelling techniques, and deliver significant new value-adding predictors.

THE VALUE CHAIN

Table 1: **Demographics and psychographics**

Demographics	Psychographics
Age	Personality
Gender	Interests
Income	Attitudes
Education	Opinions
Job class	Values

Note: psychographics are also referred in marketing as the "IAO" factors due to the acronym formed by the words Interests, Attitudes, and Opinions.

It is important to note that observational data can now be more easily collected because of the online social interactions and shopping habits we now more readily undertake through mobile devices. Such engagements generate large amounts of digital records that are changing the way behavioural scientists observe individual actions and determine statistical patterns supported by clearly defined principles.[4] For example, recent evidence on human personality traits has shown that computer predictions of digital behaviour are better predictors than judgements made by friends and family.[5] Personality

traits are one kind of psychographics defined as patterns of thoughts, feelings, and behaviour that serve as explanatory variables to predict a variety of social and economic outcomes.

The Big Five personality traits[6] created by Costa and McCrae provide broad dimensions of non-cognitive abilities and emotional skills that shape human behaviour and preferences (see Table 3 in Appendix). Such measures have been applied in empirical studies to explain, for instance, health-related outcomes,[7] risk propensity,[8,9] financial behaviour,[10] and lifetime unemployment.[11]

The body of evidence supporting these psychological factors as predictors of life outcomes has naturally led to

---

[3] M. Ariker, J. Heller, A. Diaz, and J. Perrey, How Marketers Can Personalise at Scale, *Harvard Business Review*, November 2015, https://hbr.org/2015/11/how-marketers-can-personalize-at-scale.

[4] R. Lambiotte and M. Kosinski (2014) Tracking the Digital Footprints of Personality. Proceedings of the IEEE, 102(12), 1934–1939, http://ieeexplore.ieee.org/document/6939627/.

[5] W. Youyou, M. Kosinski, and D. Stillwell (2015) Computer-based Personality Judgements are More Accurate than Those Made by Humans, PNAS, 112(4), 1036–40, http://www.pnas.org/content/112/4/1036.full.pdf.

---

[6] P. Costa and R. McCrae (1992) Revised NEO Personality Inventory (NEO-PI-R) and NEO Five-Factor inventory (NEO-FFI) professional manual, Psychological Assessment Resources, http://www.sjdm.org/dmidi/NEO-FFI.html.

[7] A. Caspi, D. Begg, N. Dickson, H. Harrington et al. (1997) Personality Differences Predict Health-risk Behaviors in Young Adulthood: Evidence from a longitudinal study, *Journal of Personality and Social Psychology*, 73(5), 1052–63.

[8] M. Zuckerman and M. Kuhlman (2000) Personality and Risk-taking: Common biosocial factors, *Journal of Personality*, 68(6), 999–1029, http://www.rgtinfohub.org.uk/wp-content/uploads/2014/09/Zuckerman-2000.pdf.

[9] N. Nicholson, E. Soane, M. Fenton-O'Creevy, and P. Willman (2005) Personality and Domain-specific Risk Taking, *Journal of Risk Research*, 8(2), 157–76.

[10] S. Brown and K. Taylor (2014) Household Finances and the "Big Five" Personality Traits, *Journal of Economic Psychology*, 45, 197–212.

[11] M. Egan, M. Daly, L. Delaney, C. Boyce, and A. Wood (2017) Adolescent Conscientiousness Predicts Lower Lifetime Unemployment, *Journal of Applied Psychology*, 102(4), 700–9

their application within digital ecosystems. For instance, the myPersonality project[12] addressed the relationship between personality and digital footprints. Like Facebook, it has collected data from millions of psychometric tests from users. Its database is available on the website of the Psychometrics Centre of the Cambridge Judge Business School.[13]

An insightful review of the opportunities and challenges of using Facebook as a research tool to infer psychometrics was done by Kosinski et al. in 2015.[14] The article follows the idea that the Internet of Things, through our smartphones and other digital devices, is operating like a psychological questionnaire, which we are constantly completing both consciously and unconsciously.

Among the psychometric measures currently available on myPersonality, there are proxies for personality traits and their facets, measures of cognitive skills (IQ), self-monitoring, and life satisfaction. Notable business applications are being developed in the area of behavioural micro targeting, one of which by the data science firm Cambridge Analytica.[15] They use psychographics to try to anticipate customers' needs and predict how their behaviour will change over time, to build relevant services that customers will engage and interact with.

In 2016, an attempt to use digital footprints was made by Admiral Insurance, a well-known motor and home insurer in the UK. It started to use an algorithm to identify safe drivers from Facebook "likes" and posts. First-time car owners who were identified as conscientious and well organized would get a discount on their insurance quote.[16] This assessment was based on research evidence showing that conscientiousness is negatively associated with the crash risk of newly licensed teenage drivers.[17] On the day of the launch, Facebook said that Admiral could not determine discounts based on its users' social media behaviour, but only as a login tool during its onboarding process. An optional personality quiz is promoted to first-time drivers who have received a quote, which they may like to reduce. Every customer who takes the quiz is given a discount ranging from 1% to 10% based on the responses they give.

Psychometrics is the field of behavioural science that is devoted to the measurement of these psychological metrics, where it can be combined with a variety of individual digital footprints. It is important to differentiate between active and passive digital footprints. An active digital footprint is generated when personal data is made accessible online, through deliberate postings or sharing of information by a user, while a passive digital footprint is obtained with no deliberate intervention from the individual. An analyst working on the data would still have to identify how some patterns in the digital footprints are related to selected psychographics. In summary, the process involves the use of unsupervised machine learning algorithms, first to discover patterns and relationships in the data, and second to validate the psychographics as predictors in a supervised algorithm.

[12] mypersonality.org.

[13] http://www.psychometrics.cam.ac.uk/.

[14] M. Kosinski, S. Matz, S. Gosling, and D. Stillwell (2015) Facebook as a Social Science Research Tool: Opportunities, challenges, ethical considerations and practical guidelines, *American Psychologist*, 70(6), 543–56, http://www.davidstillwell.co.uk/articles/AP_2015.pdf.

[15] https://cambridgeanalytica.org/.

[16] G. Ruddick, Admiral to Price Car Insurance based on Facebook Posts, *The Guardian*, 2 November 2016, https://www.theguardian.com/technology/2016/nov/02/admiral-to-price-car-insurance-based-on-facebook-posts.

[17] J. Ehsani, K. Li, B. Simons-Morton, and S. Klauer (2015) Conscientious Personality and Young Drivers' Crash Risk, *Journal of Safety Research*, 54, 83–7.

Behavioural Design in the Post-Sales Process

The identification of relevant applications of behavioural economics to the insurance industry is not something new.[18] Today, such applications can be enhanced through emerging digital ecosystems. Once a digital user has become a customer, insurers should continuously interact with him by understanding his usage of connected devices and sensor-based technology to unveil unspoken needs. Such interaction will mitigate the risk of losses for the insurer and the insured. Behaviour-led product design might help insurers reduce the risk of fraud and churn. From an insured viewpoint, this would lead to the reduced likelihood of claims through preventative triggers and recommendations. From such learning, insurers can improve pricing strategies deep-diving into customers' true behavioural patterns.

Because InsurTech relies on the ubiquitous utilization of social media and digital channels, insurers can enhance the results from their behavioural work through the study of computers as persuasive technologies, called captology.[19] These persuasive technologies might also be understood as devices that help users to monitor their risky choices in order to achieve a desired goal. For example, insurers can send timely nudges[20] to customers' smartphones and email addresses to influence the context-based determinants of decision-making and behaviour.

The MINDSPACE framework[21] provides a checklist of potential behaviour change techniques that insurers could potentially test. The options and commitments that result from the work could improve the effectiveness of an insurer's business model. Despite the heterogeneous nature of psychographic criteria, unique user experiences can be optimized through the delivery of personalized interventions.

We can find examples of ways digital technologies are used to create simpler and automatic customer interactions that improve data collection but also drive compliance (see Table 2). Renter insurance provider Lemonade uses timely pledges and moral reminders to reduce the risk of dishonesty within a peer group before a claim is paid. Daniel Schreiber, co-founder and CEO of Lemonade, talks at length about the behaviour economics that Lemonade uses within its algorithms and web pages. Among many other findings that apply to InsurTech startups, Ariely's research[22]

Table 2: Captology – computers as persuasive technologies

Computers/Digital Technologies	Persuasion
Mobile phones	Behaviour change
Websites	Attitude change
Smart environments (cities, homes)	Motivation
Videogames	Lifestyle change
Virtual reality	Compliance

Note: for more insights please visit the Stanford University Persuasive Tech Lab website (http://captology.stanford.edu/).

[18] M. Updike, Putting Behavioral Economics to Work for the Insurance Industry, *Genre Bulletin*, December 2015, http://media.genre.com/documents/bulletinlh1512-en.pdf.

[19] B. Fogg, Persuasive Technologies, *Communications of the ACM*, 1999, 42(5) 26–9.

[20] C. Sunstein, (2013) Impersonal Default Rules vs. Active Choices vs. Personalized Default Rules: A Triptych, 19 May 2013, SSRN, https://ssrn.com/abstract=2171343.

[21] P. Dolan, M. Hallsworth, D. Halpern, D. King, and I. Vlaev, MINDSPACE: Influencing Behaviour through Public Policy, Institute for Government, Cabinet Office, March 2010, https://www.instituteforgovernment.org.uk/sites/default/files/publications/MINDSPACE.pdf.

[22] D. Ariely, *The Honest Truth about Dishonesty*, HarperCollins Publications, 2012.

shows that when an individual signs up at the top of a web page, it is likely that the individual will be more honest with the information he or she discloses thereafter.

Aviva, the largest general insurer in the UK, launched in 2012 an app called Aviva Drive that records information on a driver's journeys with smartphone GPS geolocation. Once a driver has driven and recorded 200 miles of journey, the app gives a score (out of 10) based on the driver's cornering, braking, and acceleration skills. This information is later used to price car insurance and personalized future discounts. The app provides feedback on driving skills the driver needs to improve, while also utilizing rewards mechanisms through gamification techniques for safe driving, ensuring that the driver visits the app on a regular basis.

Both Lemonade and Aviva provide insightful examples of how InsurTech could exploit the opportunities brought by behavioural design in the development of their solution or platform, particularly during after-sales processes, such as claims prevention and servicing. Such practices help increase brand awareness for those using the techniques on a regular basis and scale up relevant and targeted customer communications.

Some Ethical Concerns

As we would expect, nudges need to be utilized carefully, specifically impersonal nudges, when segments are very heterogeneous or when the audiences cannot take decisions autonomously. If it is essential and feasible for a segment to learn new behaviour through educational mechanisms, it is more effective to produce informative digital content that improves the audience's competence while monitoring risky behaviour.

Delivering large volumes of personalization triggers might be perceived as invasive and raise questions about privacy and customer manipulation.[23,24] Nudges are supported by the majority of European countries,[25] but the US prefers that, in specific cases, these interventions be supported by the display of value-added information.[26,27] These very recent findings highlight the importance of evaluating users' satisfaction to ensure that the information they receive is not seen as manipulative.

Conclusions

The main idea of this chapter is that insurers should go beyond demographic segmentation and infer individuals' psychographics through the use of active and passive data collection. When these factors are incorporated into customer analyses, the accuracy of risk assessment is improved and pre- and post-sales engagements become more personalized on an increased scale. As insurers can optimize prices and users can better monitor their behaviour, value-chain interactions are enhanced.

However, even though users can gain benefits from sharing data to access better services and better prices, practitioners should expect an ongoing debate relating to the ethical concerns regarding the use of psychographics through persuasive technologies, and how invasive such technological advancement might become with the wide use of interconnected devices.

[23] C. Sunstein, Impersonal Default Rules vs. Active Choices vs. Personalized Default Rules: A Triptych, 19 May 2013, SSRN, https://ssrn.com/abstract=2171343.

[24] A. Arad and A. Rubinstein, The People's Perspective on Libertarian-Paternalistic Policies, 2017, http://www.tau.ac.il/~aradayal/LP.pdf.

[25] L. Reisch and C. Sunstein (2016) Do Europeans Like Nudges? *Judgement and Decision Making*, 11(4), 310–25, https://papers.ssrn.com/sol3/papers.cfm?abstract_id=2739118.

[26] C. Sunstein (2016) People Prefer System 2 Nudges (kind of), *Duke Law Journal*, 66(1), 121–68, http://scholarship.law.duke.edu/dlj/vol66/iss1/3/.

[27] J. Jung and B. Mellers (2016) American Attitudes Toward Nudges, *Judgement and Decision Making*, 11(1), 62–74.

Appendix A

Table 3: The Big Five model of personality

Broad dimensions	Examples of questionnaire items: *"I see myself as ..."*	Facets
Openness to experience	Open to new experiences, complex. Conventional, uncreative.	Aesthetics Fantasy Feelings Actions Ideas Values
Conscientiousness	Dependable, self-disciplined. Disorganized, careless.	Competence Order Dutifulness Achievement striving Self-discipline Deliberation
Extraversion	Extraverted, enthusiastic. Reserved, quiet.	Warmth Gregariousness Assertiveness Activity Excitement seeking Positive emotion
Agreeableness	Critical, quarrelsome. Sympathetic, warm.	Trust Straightforwardness Altruism Compliance Tendermindedness Modesty
Neuroticism	Anxious, easily upset. Calm, emotionally stable.	Anxiety Hostility Depression Self-consciousness Impulsiveness Vulnerability to stress

Note: Personality dimensions and facets from Costa and McCrae (1992). Examples of questionnaire items from the Ten-Item Personality Inventory-(TIPI) of S. D. Gosling, P. J. Rentfrow, and W. B. Swann Jr, A Very Brief Measure of the Big Five Personality Domains, *Journal of Research in Personality*, 2003, 37, 504–528. Measuring personality in one minute or less: A 10-item short version of the Big Five Inventory in English and German, Beatrice Rammstedt and Oliver P. John, Center for Survey Research and Methodologies (ZUMA), P.O. Box 12 21 55, D-68072 Mannheim, Germany; Department of Psychology, University of California, Berkeley MC 1650, Berkeley, CA 94720-1650, USA, available online 3 April 2006. Online link: http://citeseerx.ist.psu.edu/viewdoc/download?doi=10.1.1.588.1086&rep=rep1&type=pdf. The Big Five model is also referred to as the OCEAN model due to the acronym formed from each word's initial.

Data Changes Everything

By Visesh Gosrani FIA
Director of Risk and Actuarial, Guidewire, Cyence Risk Analytics

There is a Large Untapped Potential to Collect Relevant Data about Policy-holders and their Homes

A significant and ever-increasing amount of data is being generated by people and their homes. Whether you look at the TV, the washing machine, the fridge, your Google home or Alexa devices, data are everywhere and can be collected to better service home owners. These data have the potential to provide much more accurate details on a policy-holder's behaviours, but also their wants and needs as well as their risk profile.

This chapter seeks to describe the benefits for both the customer and the insurer of collecting and analysing a wider range of data sets to deliver personalized insights and services. The chapter sets out a few guiding principles and illustrates those principles with examples focused on home insurance. The same scenarios are equally applicable to other types of insurance offerings.

Helping Policy-holders Understand Actions or Characteristics that Put them at an Increased Risk of a Claim

No rational policy-holder desires the interruption caused by a claim. They may not understand how their behaviours or circumstances affect or increase their likelihood of suffering such an event. However, combined together, policy-holders' specific

data and more general environmental data can help an insured manage his or her risk better.

Policy-holders' specific data are captured during the quote process, where very specific questions are asked and then enriched with specific data services. Other mechanisms already exist to allow the policy-holders to share a wide set of real time data (e.g. personal and social data) with their insurer and others involved through this process.

It is fair to say that an applicant may not want to share his data because of the risk of being declined. Nonetheless, if he did, both the applicant and his insurer would derive clear benefits from the insights this provides.

It is also clear that the policy-holder and the insurer can benefit from ranges of data captured by a variety of data sources via Internet of Things (IoT) technology. Examples include home occupancy, alerts, and event indicators such as the triggering of a smoke alarm or the usage of a variety of smart home sensors, including energy management systems. And, while a policy-holder can use home automation to achieve the protection he or she seeks, an insurer using the same data sets to monitor large numbers of policy-holders can benefit from the iterative learning of optimizing pricing and claims support activities. Blending these resources can lead to improved series of outcomes when an actual or potential claim event occurs.

1. If a fire alarm is triggered in a smart home, and the devices have not registered a human presence in the home at the time of the incident, the home devices can still trigger internal fire alarms and could take greater steps to alert the home owners, the local fire brigade, and the insurer of the incident. While this may result in the production of false positives, the feedback loop would enable the increased accuracy over time of the algorithms used to perform those services.

2. Smart devices able to suspect, detect, and measure unusual uses of water (e.g. leaks or open taps) based on volumes,

velocity, location, and other patterns are known as leak bots. Devices functioning on their own can provide an alert to the policy-holder. Combining these bots with occupancy indicators could increase the accuracy assessment of potential home perils, ensure that actions are taken before they become disastrous, and increase the validity of the preventative actions taken – for example, halting a flow of water using an electronic stopcock rather than just notifying the insured.

Environmental data are not directly applicable to the policy-holder but are useful indicators. The amounts of data currently available can be used to enhance insurers' relationship with their policy-holders in many ways.

1. Historical measurements of climate factors could enable an insurer to link burglary events to changes in weather patterns – meaning temperature, humidity, and other key factors. An insurer that successfully interrogated its claims data to understand how the environment relates to incurred claims could implement a program of tailored messaging to reduce the risk of theft. A historical increase in property crime between June to August was identified by one study.[1] It is clearly possible that there may have been a strong correlation between opened windows and increased risk of night burglaries as policy-holders forget to close their windows. It could also be possible that the propensity for criminal acts increases during these summer months. Insurers could take the insight and recommend actions to ensure that their policy-holders are protected from the risk of a claim.

2. Monitoring real-time crime and fire event data within both local and wider communities can lead to early preventative actions. The limited insight provided by current open source crime reports allows month-by-month analyses of crime patterns in specific areas. An average policy-holder is unlikely to have the ability and time to monitor and analyse crime patterns with his or her own community;

---

[1] 21st Century Criminology: A Reference Handbook/Edition 1, by J. Mitchell Miller, p. 55.

however, insurers focused on enhancing prevention could provide alerts for policy-holders and wider communities, and not limit this to property crimes. The same analysis could lead to targeted forms of communication between policy-holders and their insurers in particular for areas prone to a variety of daily incidents and crimes. Such activities would shift the insurer–policy-holder relationship to a trusted advisory one from just post-event assistance.

Validating that Policy-holders Understand their Obligations

A number of exclusions and conditions exist within insurance policies to manage insurers' risk exposure and prevent negligent claims. Insurers can use data collected from IoT devices to identify potential scenarios where policy-holders might be prone to be acting within exclusion zones. By having the data to initiate a conversation, the insurer can ensure that the policy-holder is aware of the exclusions and understands the rationale behind them. This can reduce the likelihood of denied claims due to misunderstood terms, enhancing the overall customer experience. Insurers can use this mechanism to verify that the policy-holders have represented themselves, their risk, and exposure correctly.

Examples of how this can be of benefit include:

1. Making a policy-holder aware that their property seemed unoccupied for a long period of time and reminding them that their home can only be unoccupied for no more than an agreed number of days.

2. Making a policy-holder aware during winter months that their home temperature is too low and could result in burst pipes.

3. Leveraging electronic access to digitize asset inventories and assist in determining the true insured content value of a home.

Making policy-holders and people in general aware of home insurance risks can help them understand and manage their exposure better. However, the abundance of non-relevant information potentially extracted from IoT sources can lead to information overload and apathy. One way to overcome apathy is to personalize the information on risks through awareness and education campaigns. Using claims data from policy-holders with similar characteristics can help shape guidance parameters and result in greater attention paid to share recommendations.

Resolving the Issues Related to the Collection and Aggregation of Significant Pools of Untapped Data Sources

Organizations that want to lead the way in the access and usage of IoT-based data are facing a number of challenges arising from (1) the collection of new data sources, (2) the aggregation of these sources to deliver relevant new insight, and (3) the analysis of such insight to deliver new products and services that augment users' lives.

The issues we believe large enterprises will encounter are several as highlighted below:

- As no standard is yet available for IoT data, insurers will need to transform that data into forms that can be utilized for analysis.
- To easily incorporate external data sets and meet internal data security standards, systems will need to be upgraded.
- To satisfy policy-holders' privacy expectations, especially with respect to listening devices, such as Google Home and the

Amazon Echo, insurers will need to develop and share policies on connectivity and data usage.

- To avoid reputational risk linked with data usage and insurability, insurers will need to focus on prevention rather than identifying foundational issues that will make the policy-holder worse off than before. This issue is key.

The significant benefit that may result from using a variety of data sources for the purpose of providing preventative insights and guidance should outweigh the risk of making specific risk types uninsurable. However, a mechanism by which risks made uninsurable by new insights outside of the policy-holder's control or due to poor insurer interpretation may remain. This is where industry bodies, the regulators, and the law will increasingly be involved in such initiatives.

Conclusion

Data changes everything because policy-holders can now better understand their exposure and manage their risk themselves. For the insurer this means that increased transparency will drive a focus on more prevention-focused products and services. Such a scenario changes the nature of insurance from just financially indemnifying policy-holders to continuously managing and mitigating policy-holder risks for the wider good. These provide clear benefits to both stakeholder groups, because it educates the insured on the right behaviour to achieve peace of mind and reduces overall claims costs for the insurer. This also reduces the current focus on commoditizing insurance to providing more personalized servicing ranging from:

- tailored guidance to the policy-holders in respect of their risk profile such that policy-holders do not have to interpret advice and understand why it is applicable to them;

- confirmation that policy-holders' actions and characteristics are in line with the statements made explicitly or implicitly when taking cover;
- more effective triage of fraudulent claims, reducing the pain of the claims experience for policy-holders.

The key challenges to this brave new world are around consumer acceptance of sharing the data, the regulatory concerns that will arise from managing an abundance of personal and insightful data, and the protection of policy-holders that are deemed to be uninsurable by the insights available from the data collected.

Beware of GDPR – Take your Cyber Risk Responsibility More Seriously

By Eelco Ouwerkerk
Industry Director Wholesale and Retail, Aon

All organizations, whether businesses or government agencies, should be concerned with their cyber risk exposure at this very moment.

The connectedness among businesses, their operations, suppliers, and customers, due to the increasing use of digital technologies, means that every organization around the globe is vulnerable to potentially catastrophic losses resulting from electronic data theft and sabotage. This reliance among partnering organizations and the growing prevalence of the usage of big data, cloud computing, social media, "bring your own device" within corporate policies, and state-sponsored espionage have catapulted the number of risks resulting from cyber crimes into one of the top concerns of business leaders today.

And it is not just businesses. Local and national governments are catching up with this relatively new threat as well. Digital technology is more and more used for commercial purposes within those environments too. It is used to sell products and services, to optimize business processes, and/or to reduce operating costs. Known applications used across government agencies include cloud computing, email, the Internet, social media, mobile applications, as well as big data.

Whether in business or government, these technologies and new advancements play a major role in the realization of stakeholder value, whether this means optimizing profits or taxpayers' monies. But when there are opportunities there are also downsides. Indeed, the downsides from data usage and sharing are increasing every day. Organizations must not only protect *themselves* from cyber abuse, they also need to protect the data and records of their most precious asset: their customers.

Data Dependence Comes with a Price

Our increasing dependence on digital technologies and data exchange, and the heightened susceptibility of businesses and governments to specific electronic risks, bring new challenges to world economies. Human and system failures are rapidly increasing, partly due to the heavy commercial dependence among supply chain partners. Currently, regular criminals, digital first individuals, professionals, as well as (former) employees can all be guilty of major crimes, ranging from data theft, fraud, sabotage, and espionage to hacking.

The financial consequences and bottom-line results of such crimes can substantially impact profit and non-profit organizations across all industries. Imagine the impact of legal liability, reputational damage, and business disruption on your current business operations and on your future sources of incomes.

The 2016 Global Cyber Impact Report

The whole insurance market is deploying innovative digital solutions to address uncertainties arising from the increased inter-connectivity among business operations.

The 2016 Global Cyber Impact Report from the Ponemon Institute[1] highlights interesting developments across a variety of industries, some of which I shall share with you below.[2]

---

[1] Ponemon Institute 2016 Cost of Cyber Crime Study & the Risk of Business Innovation, October 2016,https://www.ponemon.org/library/2016-cost-of-cyber-crime-study-the-risk-of-business-innovation.

[2] http://ir.aon.com/about-aon/investor-relations/investor-news/news-release-details/2017/AonPonemon-report-Almost-four-times-more-budget-is-being-spent-on-property-related-risks-vs-cyber-risk/default.aspx.

- Nearly 65% of organizations expect their cyber risk exposure to increase in the next two years:
  - The impact of business disruption to cyber assets is 72% greater than to property, plant, and equipment (PP&E) assets.
  - Organizations valued cyber assets 14% higher than PP&E assets.
  - Quantification of probable maximum loss from cyber assets is 27% higher than from PP&E.
  - Organizations insure on average 59% of PP&E losses, compared to an average of 15% of cyber exposures.
- Information assets held by businesses and government are underinsured against theft or destruction based on their market value.
- Despite the increased risk digital undertakings have on businesses, companies are reluctant to purchase cyber insurance coverage.
- 69% of respondents to the Ponemon Cyber Survey believe their companies' exposure to cyber risk will increase over the next 24 months … However, only 15% of respondents confess their company has cyber insurance coverage.
- 57% of companies in the Ponemon Cyber Study experienced a material or significantly disruptive security or data breach one or more times during the past two years, and the average economic impact averaged US$2.1 million.

How do Organizations Transfer Cyber Risk?

Some exposures can be transferred contractually. The marketplace is evolving fast on this specific subject to provide more personalized services solutions, such as loss control resources, data breach coaches, dedicated claims resources, and pre-approved panels of vendors and service providers to ensure adequate responses to individual breaches. And many insurers provide cyber coverage on a primary basis, i.e. the breach response coverage offering varies based on insurer and policy structures.

Ask your Organization These Key Questions

Before addressing the issue of risk transfer and cyber insurance options, let's review why there is a need for these in the first place. The key questions that every risk officer should ask him- or herself are: "Can we identify and quantify the damages resulting from a successful cyber attack? And beyond the usage of readily available IT solutions, how do we protect ourselves from cyber risk?"

If your risk officer can answer these questions, it is likely that you have steps in place to create a safe cyber environment. However, organizations often struggle to answer these questions. In the worst-case scenario, many would not know what needs to be done in the first place.

General Data Protection Regulation (GDPR)

To create a safe cyber environment within your organization, you must first answer the questions we raised earlier, and then act on your findings as those choices will impact the safety of your employees and customers.

On 25 May 2018, the GDPR will come into effect. It is designed to ensure that every company within the European Union follows the same data safety regulations and every business should ensure that it takes the necessary steps to become compliant.

What does compliance under the upcoming GDPR mean?

An organization must:

- anchor privacy and data protection at the highest level within its business;
- perform a cyber-risk prevention analysis to identify privacy risks and control issues through appropriate techniques and measures;

- produce a register and record the usage of any sensitive data;
- classify the organization's personal information to comply with statutory data retention and deletion periods;
- evaluate existing contracts with third parties with whom the organization shares information. Each organization will be asked to put data privacy and security agreements in place with each of its data processors;
- set procedures to adequately anticipate and handle a data breach;
- increase privacy awareness of all employees through educational activities;
- set privacy regulation based on the GDPR or adjust existing policies accordingly;
- inform those concerned about what will happen to their personal data;
- determine if your organization must have a data protection officer.

Every business, large or small, must ensure that they have procedures in place to deliver on these measures. However, it is clear that many organizations do not have the manpower or expertise to deliver on these and will need to find a "cyber risk partner" to ease the burden brought on them.

Growing Responsibility for Organizations

The GDPR does not just provide guidelines. Under the new regime, companies will have obligations towards every personal data record. They will have to comply with the European privacy laws and demonstrate that they are compliant by implementing technical measures and documenting that appropriate actions took place. The Regulation is there to regulate organizations and impose fines when they fail to comply.

Power to the People

The GDPR strengthens individuals' privacy rights and gives individuals the ability to assert themselves when their data are misused. Post privacy law, organizations must get consent from every person to use any set of personal data. It must also be just as easy for any individual to withdraw his or her consent, and ask a business to delete any personal records they hold. It is also likely that organizations that pass data to third parties in a multi-party transaction will have to request that these third parties delete received data. And individuals wanting to change supplier(s) will be able to request that their personal data be shared with them or a third-party supplier in a standard format, to ease transactions with other sellers and service providers.

Consequences Beyond Reputational Damage and Disruption

It is simple. Businesses need to comply if they do not want to be fined. The best way to avoid a fine is to conduct a yearly Privacy Impact Assessment (PIA) and/or appoint a Data Protection Officer (DPO).

The penalty in the Netherlands for data breach is estimated to be a maximum of EUR 820,000 today. By 25 May 2018 the fines will grow: a two-tiered sanctions regime will apply. Businesses conducting breaches of specific types could incur fines of up to €20 million or 4% of global annual turnover for the upcoming financial year, whichever is the greater, which will be levied by the data watchdogs.

For other smaller breaches, the authorities could impose fines on companies of up to €10 million or 2% of global annual turnover, whichever is greater.

So Why Did we Start our Argument Focusing on Cyber Risk?

I must say that it is likely that any business out there will attempt to comply with GDPR. However, additional peace of mind will come for those that invest some time and effort in identifying the right cyber risk prevention and protection solutions that best suit them and their business.

Such insurance products would include coverage for the following:

- **Liability risk,** which provides compensation and legal support in the event of third-party claims resulting from loss of personal and/or business data;

- **Crisis costs** to undertake forensic investigations, reputational public repair, customer notification costs, credit monitoring, IT services, and cyber incident response services;

- **Fines** for research costs, legal assistance, and administrative fines;

- **Digital media breach** to cover compensation and defence costs related to third-party claims against you arising out of your multimedia activities (e.g. defamation, allegation, or plagiarism);

- **Cyber extortion,** including ransomware;

- **Network interruption,** loss of revenues, or net profits associated with network downtime.

Cyber insurance provides great assistance in the case of legal issues. Many of the products available will enable businesses to contact a team of lawyers to find answers for their data breach questions, and whom to inform in case of breach.

All in all, it is clear that businesses must start preparing their operations to avoid data-related claims. And if there is a data breach they must ensure that they have the right processes in place and that the business was protected by cyber insurance in the first place.

Why Claims Sharing? Innovating within the Business-to-Business Insurance Claims Handling Ecosystem

By Laimonas Stoncius
Founder and CEO, ClaimsControl

InsurTech disruption brings many positive changes into every aspect of the insurance industry including the insurance claims ecosystem. The claims sharing concept is based on digitizing the claims process through an automated exchange of insurance claims between Business-to-Business (B2B) customers, insurance service providers, and other claim process participants.

The necessity of integrating insurance claims data has always been on the minds of multiple claims process participants. The standardization of insurance data structure was successfully introduced by ACORD[1] in the US and this approach could potentially ease the insurance data integration attempts. However, the difficulty of connecting a vast number of claims process participants remained, so the proper way to ease the full integration of insurance claims data became technically realistic when an independent hub structure was introduced.

The basis of the concept is an Open Application Programming Interface (API) hub, where any claims system can connect to exchange data with other systems. The hub can also send all claims details via automated emails to the claims process participants who are not connected to the hub.

_____
[1] www.acord.org.

The hub should also have a web platform for entering claims data directly. Where the companies do not have their own claims system, they could use the hub to account for their claims. This option also enables them to amend/append the data if this cannot be done by their own system. The platform should allow for anyone to record and share an unlimited number of claims for free, and ensure that all key participants to a claim are involved.

This chapter aims to explain the practical aspects of our claims sharing concept and the proactive changes it brings within current claims handling practices.

Streamlining Claims Processing

One of the primary challenges affecting the digital transformation of current insurance claims processing practices is to ensure the automatic distribution of all originally recorded claims data, lodged within the databases of all claims handling participants. Once the claims data is entered by each participant, the need for repetitive data entries by other participants becomes irrelevant and should be fully eliminated – thus reducing tedious manual data entries, minimizing claim cycle time, and enabling efficient exchanges of large volumes of data.

Typically, any single insurance claim involves a fair amount of manual work and time for all participants involved in a specific claim process. In the event of an accident, the company claimant has to enter the claim data twice – into its own claim system or spreadsheet and then into another reporting system for the insurer or the broker. All additional updates and exchanges of claims data are also performed manually.

When insurers receive a First Notice of Loss (FNOL) by email or phone, they must enter the claims data into their system manually. The self-service platforms and apps enable insurers to minimize their own manual work, but they will not be able to refuse to accept mails from their clients – major B2B clients who send FNOL via automated emails.

The claims sharing hub will exchange the claims data with an insurer's claims system, similarly to the way various insurers' self-service platforms register and process claims data. Therefore, the hub will not interfere with the usual tasks of claims adjusters but ensure an automated 100% claims data entry.

The burden of double manual entry work also falls upon insurance brokers, as discussed later, as well as on transport leasing companies, garages/workshops, loss adjusters, and other claims process participants. In some cases, a certain type of claim is processed without an insurer's involvement, for example, freight forwarders often handle complaints between transport carriers and cargo owners.

Leveraging Apps and the Internet of Thing (IoT) for Real-time B2B Insurance Claims Data

On the one hand, during the course of the past few years, insurers started investing into artificial intelligence and machine learning technologies to improve underwriting, enhance fraud prevention, and automate sales and claims processes. They knew that the more accurate, precise, and detailed data they got access to, the more efficient the results could be. Real-time data collection became more effective with the use of telematics in vehicles and various autonomous sensors able to measure speed, airbag deployment, cargo temperature, and so on.

On the other hand, insurers were, and are still, looking for ways to simplify and speed up the claims process while raising customer experience and satisfaction to new levels. The automation of exchanges among claims data feeds is a potential option to solve the contradiction arising from the need for accessing increasing volumes of claims data while simplifying the claims process.

There are multiple IT solutions available to insurers including FNOL and claim settlement apps that can be used directly by private

customers. However, such apps do not work well for business customers. For example, a company truck driver is not empowered to send claims-related accident data directly from his mobile app to the insurer, because the decision to report a claim must be made by his company, the owner of the insurance contract. The direct integration between the claims systems of the insurers and their B2B customers will never take place. Therefore, a claims sharing hub seems to be the best option to solve this data collection problem.

There is also a major issue standardizing data formats. Every app, IoT device, or provider of data sources today tends to have very specific data structures that must be accepted by different data systems. The hub is an ideal place to coordinate seamlessly multiple data formats and sources.

The Revised Role for the Broker

When it comes to insurance claims handling, brokers fall into two types – those who handle claims and those who don't. The first type of broker requests their clients to report all claims directly to them, with the majority of claims being fairly standard. More than 90% of brokers' work consists of just forwarding the claim information from the client to the insurer and back. This also slows down the claims processing. Integration of brokers' and insurers' claims systems would save a great deal of time for every single broker, but, in reality, such integrations are costly and not very common.

The second type of broker does not face the abovementioned problems; however, in this case, they do not have access to any claims information under the insurance policies they service, which means that they are unable to improve the quality of the customer service they deliver.

In both cases, the brokers' practices are flawed. They are unable to speed up their service delivery or serve their clients appropriately. The insurance market would benefit from a broker-focused solution that can be managed via the hub.

A hub that eases the exchange of claims will provide B2B clients with an opportunity to share claims data, whether complex or simple, at their own discretion simultaneously with the insurer and the broker, and it will relieve brokers from the need to enter claims data into a multitude of systems. As a result, all brokers will have equal technical opportunities to monitor claims.

Uberization of Claims Surveying

Insurers will always need to inspect a damaged property or the site of an accident. Creation of a large surveyors' network does not provide an effective solution. InsurTech technologies, like Rescue Lens,[2] offer solutions to insurers to capture details of accidents directly from a site with the help of the apps used by their customers. However, there will always be cases when the insurer will need to send their representative to review the claims. The Uberization of the claims experts' structure is imminent. Actually, one startup organization located in the US is focusing its effort just on this.[3] The insurer must know which independent surveyors are located near the accident site and be able to select the most relevant and skilled expert based on availability. The hub platform and its exchange principles are both the right environment to provide access to the expert network as the hub contains all the details about experts, key accident data, and claims.

Blockchain Technology for Reliable Data and Fraud Prevention

Even though the blockchain is still emerging in insurance, it has been utilized for user cases in the intracompany challenge areas in the banking sector.

To provide a B2B customer with an insurance quote, an insurer must analyse the customer's loss history. Bearing in mind that some losses relate to self- or uninsured cases, the B2B customer becomes the only information source for his full loss records. Insurers and insureds understand that insurance rates depend on the loss history. Therefore, in a situation where insurers do not have an opportunity to verify loss records, there is no trusted data exchange and transparency between parties. In addition, financial losses caused by dishonest and fraudulent clients lead to increased rates for the whole insurance sector.

This problem can be solved by a claims sharing platform, able to provide any company with the opportunity to keep correct records of claims/losses in one place, the credibility of which is validated by a blockchain-based technology. Such platform enhancement will not violate privacy rules: the company will decide which data point can be shared with whom.

This solution can be especially useful for the smart enablement of developing countries' economies. For example, in the absence of compulsory motor third-party liability insurance and due to the lack of trust between insurers and business customers, a vast amount of commercial transport has been left uninsured. Blockchain validation will reinstate the trust among parties. This will result in the increase of volume in the insurance market.

We at ClaimsControl have designed such a platform.

---

[2] www.logmeinrescue.com.

[3] https://wegolook.com/.

Reinsurers Need Backward Innovation

By Vaughan Jenkins
Independent Consultant, Meta Finance

A Story from the Industrial Revolution

21 April 2017 was Britain's first ever working day without coal power since the Industrial Revolution.[1] If we think about the advanced technologies that old infrastructure has been powering, it is clear that the pace of change can vary significantly across value chains. It is also illustrative of how a core supply can be substituted by new power sources that have adapted to new demands and a different regulatory context.

What about Reinsurance?

Reinsurance has changed relatively little in its fundamental form since it emerged from the Industrial Revolution. It fuelled economic growth by facilitating effective risk transfer. Swiss Re and Munich Re emerged as dominant players in a marketplace built on a combination of trust, underwriting expertise, and a cost-to-income ratio model that rode the cycles of hard and soft pricing. The market has not been without its problems. Similar in characteristics to the later banking crisis, the Lloyd's of London market crumbled because of the punitive damage issues of the 1980s, where a number of Lloyd's investors went bankrupt due to their lack of understanding of asbestos liability claims.[2] In banking, issues were

related to failed electronic trading initiatives, and despite market failures and a series of major natural catastrophes, the reinsurance market seemed built to weather the storms.

This resilience has recently been fundamentally challenged by technological changes and new business models, making some traditional reinsurance practices look as obsolete as coal powered electricity generators. Reinsurers have scrambled to partner and realign themselves with InsurTech startups and alternative risk transfer methods, and the struggle to remain relevant has never been greater.

The foundation of the reinsurance market is based on consensus-led pricing and the diversification and specialization that support a largely effective, if not wholly efficient, market that translates risk into a market tradeable instrument. It is a market that has displayed some incremental innovation over time and now has to address some new structural changes. The development of alternative risk transfer mechanisms, notably Insurance Linked Securities (ILS), with a resulting margin erosion and accelerated industry consolidation with implications for market capacity, pricing, and insurance covenants.

Market Reality

As in any market, economies of scale and economies of scope support large and niche participants. New market entrants from capital markets and a concentration of power have impacted the historic rhythms of the loss and recovery cycles. The ILS deals tend to be fully collateralized and should in theory offer better security than conventional reinsurance.

However, there is no clear correlation between the losses effectively sustained by the reinsurer as the result of a catastrophe and what they might recover from a bond. Catastrophe-related bonds can in turn drive down prices for conventionally written business. What capital markets represent is what the insurance

---

[1] https://www.theguardian.com/environment/2017/apr/21/britain-set-for-first-coal-free-day-since-the-industrial-revolution.

[2] http://www.telegraph.co.uk/finance/newsbysector/banksandfinance/insurance/8463871/How-asbestos-brought-Lloyds-of-London-to-its-knees-in-the-90s.html.

business refers to as "innocent capacity". I can tell you that sooner or later some of these investors are going to face huge losses and will then wish that they had stuck to treasury bonds, however low the yields. In a worst-case scenario, the disruption of an old model could see the reinsurance market repeating the shortcomings of the subprime mortgage market collapse.

Reinsurance as a Service

If we turn to the insurance market and especially the distribution aspects of personal lines, InsurTech is driving new concepts of digitized mutual risk sharing through peer-to-peer insurance, microinsurance, usage-based services, and a heap of technologies to support digital transformations at different levels of processing – underwriting, distribution, claims management, customer servicing – and stages of the value chain. A buzz of excitement can be heard from China to the US, especially related to non-risk bearing distributors. Whether that is Lemonade, Zhong An, Friendsurance, or Ladder,[3] respected commentators as far back as 2014[4] envisaged that we would be witnessing a transformation driven by InsurTechs that is similar to the time when the PC stack replaced the mainframe. We moved then from vertical integration (where mainframe vendors controlled the whole stack) to horizontal layers (namely Intel, Microsoft, PC manufacturers, and applications).

In this scenario, reinsurance is reimagined as a service from a platform that combines capital, regulated status, geographic reach, and the data and models to support pricing. Some firms, notably Munich Re, have started to work more closely with InsurTech startups and others have followed suit. Reinsurers have also started to explore blockchain applications, notably the B3i consortium including Aegon, Allianz, Munich Re, Swiss Re, and Zurich, among 15 participants in total.[5] But in engaging in this open interoperability, with insurers and brokers able to talk to one another through open platforms (demonstrating a strong resemblance to the changes occurring in the banking sector), reinsurers could be planting the seeds of their own demise. To borrow a phrase from Bill Gates, the market may need reinsurance but not reinsurers going forward.[6]

The Impact of InsurTechs on Reinsurers

The InsurTech shift is encouraging shorter value chains between innovative distributors, shifting risk directly to reinsurers and cutting out friction and cost from middlemen, including insurers.

Reinsurers bring not only capital but also intellectual property through their underwriting and product knowledge. In theory, the breadth and depth of knowledge can provide distributors with more support than a single insurer.

Reinsurers can also be a drag on innovation, if they and their shareholders cannot adapt quickly enough to enter new markets and support new risk types.

In *Making a Market for Acts of God*[7] the authors describe a distinct "reinsurance-underwriting" market culture, comprising underwriters acting within "densely-nested relationalities" that extend across geographic regions and across firms. The culture is made by practices and it exists despite having no common IT (e.g. there is no common trading platform), no universal

---

[3] www.ladderlife.com/.

[4] Bernard Lunn, Daily Fintech News.

[5] http://www.insurancejournal.com/news/international/2017/02/06/440629.htm.

---

[6] Bill Gates quote modified, https://channels.theinnovationenterprise.com/articles/bill-gates-said-that-banking-is-necessary-banks-are-not-but-banks-are-still-around-today.

[7] P. Jarzabkowski, R. Bednarek, and A. P. Spee, *Making a Market for Acts of God: The Practice of Risk Trading in the Global Reinsurance Industry*, Oxford University Press, 2015.

common risk-calculation algorithm (though catastrophe risks, also called CAT models, are held in common), and no overarching regulatory regime.

The sector is not only opening up to alternative sources of capital to take on new risks, but also new players are emerging and engaging with unusual and unfamiliar risk types. This makes the reinsurers' data and practices become less relevant, while other actors are prepared to adopt more powerful and accurate data analytics capabilities.

There is no shortage of capital trying to find the shortest route to the best risk receivers. Reinsurers are alert to the threat that they may appear to gain access to market opportunities faster by bypassing traditional ceding agents. However, a changing distribution strategy may fail to highlight and prevent reinsurers being substituted by alternatives such as ILS and capital markets, or even big tech companies that have access to more sophisticated data models, able to price risk at least as well as them.

This is actually a present issue, not a speculation.

Emergence of New Risk Trading Platforms

According to data from Willis Re,[8] insurance-linked securities and alternative reinsurance capital continued to grow in 2016, rising by over 7% from $70 billion to $75 billion, or nearly 17% of the total reinsurance capital, while at the same time the underlying return-on-equity (RoE) of the reinsurance sector continued to shrink.

The data also showed that reinsurers seem unable to control their expense ratios, "despite the pressure they face and the fact the

industry has been aware of the need to increase the efficiency of its underwriting capacity for a number of years now".[9]

Pressure on margins has been increasing, as capacity has increased. Reinsurers are now operating business units close to break even, with Willis Re's tracked group running at an RoE of just 8%. In the new normal, rates are less likely to harden following major risk events as the industry recapitalizes more quickly than previous historic cycles of underwriting results.

In a military analogy, this is like attempting a radical change in formation while under fire and running out of ammunition. Cost increases due to investment in new technology, speculation on emerging ventures, and the design of products that cover new risks run against the need for immediate operational efficiency and effectiveness. But one way forward, to the benefit of InsurTechs and capital markets, has been the development of new risk trading platforms – these are intermediaries that can "auction" blended risk packages. These include ILS and traditional reinsurance models and act as a portal for risk trading.

When Aon Benfield launched its ABConnect platform in 2016 it commented:

> Collaborating with our reinsurer partners through this next generation platform will result in more real time information to share with clients and enable them to make more informed placement decisions.[10]

Other new platform players are emerging. These would include the likes of Extraordinary Re, which is planning a $1bn launch[11] in

[8] 20 April 2017.

[9] http://www.artemis.bm/blog/2017/04/20/ils-capital-up-7-while-underlying-reinsurance-roes-shrink-further-willis/.

[10] http://www.businessinsurance.com/article/20160405/NEWS06/160409906/Aon-Benfield-launches-online-reinsurer-trading-platform,-Aon-PLC,-ABConnect-Plac.

[11] http://www.trading-risk.com/reinsurance-trading-platform-tests-ahead-of-1bn-target-launch.

2018. It is aimed at new and underserved classes of risks, such as "contingent business interruption and cyber". New risks mean new solutions.

As fast moving FinTech and InsurTech players develop new sources of data leveraging the Internet of Things to drones and biometrics, the input of data to underwriting models will inform new risk profiles and the ability to price new and emerging risk types more accurately. This backward innovation from distributors to reinsurers and capital markets, or alternative risk takers, will see specific market segments become more commoditized at one extreme, and others run their business on dynamic real-time risk pricing models.

Platforms will better facilitate competition and provide hubs for risk trading and knowledge sharing. This will break away from traditional consensus-based profiling and inefficient relationship-led supply chains. These could, however, provide a new infrastructure that is suited to engage in new business relationships in our dynamic twenty-first century.

Business Models

7

It Is All About Disruptive Innovation

There are three types of innovation a corporation can focus on:

1. **Core Innovation** – optimizes products for today's customers. Represents 70% of a corporate's innovation portfolio

2. **Adjacent Innovation** – enters adjacent markets or customer segments. Represents 20% of a corporate innovation portfolio

3. **Transformative/Disruptive Innovation** – creates new markets, and targets new sets of needs. Represents 10% of a corporate innovation portfolio.

While most businesses focus money and effort on secure core innovation (that delivers c.10% of the long-term cumulative return of a company's innovation investment), transformative innovation which is riskier, brings far higher long-term returns.

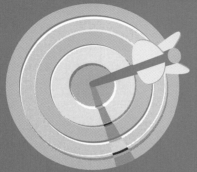

Emerging market and business models

- Estimated transaction revenues generated by the sharing economy businesses:
  - Today ⟶ $20bn
  - By 2025 ⟶ $335bn

- While sharing economy related businesses will expand by 30% per year over the next 10 years, in 2016 only 10% of insurers had in place a sharing economy offering, 35% were at design or pilot stage, 55% had no strategy in place.

A new reality?

Everything will be smart and connected within the next 10 to 15 years

- As sensors and cameras are becoming smaller, smarter and 24/7, your home, your car and your assets will be monitored 24/7 through the use of a simple apps.

- Wearables and devices will continuously be connected and the data transmitted from those will help deliver better services and prevent risks.

- Intelligent machines will automate and operate systems without human intervention resulting in increased level of accuracy and efficiency.

  - **Wearables** – will monitor our health and eating habits, prevent illnesses and diseases.

  - **Mobile devices and smart chips on humans** – will connect to other devices, transmitting data points to augment service level.

  - **Self-driving cars** – will get rid of thousands of road traffic fatalities and claims caused because of speed and drunk driving.

In this part, our authors are tackling business models, an important topic to determine the future sustainability of InsurTech startups. The authors have reviewed patterns that have emerged during the course of the past four years and looked through their crystal balls to define or identify the most relevant business models of the future.

The business of insurance has not actually changed for many years. From core, adjacent business models to transformative options, InsurTechs are dabbling across the range to exploit the growing imbalance between customer expectations and the service offered by insurers. Their intent is to deliver relevant quality alternatives to cater for new generations and evolving customers' needs.

At its most conceptual level, a business model is no more than the strategic configuration of components that makes a business whole and able to make money. And while emerging business models may list smart or connected, peer-to-peer, credit-based, preventative, or sharing economy approaches as the new ways of doing business, each of these models resides at the intersection of a few major fundamental changes.

Change number 1 includes the use of unique data sets pushed through highly sophisticated models to deliver competitive insights relevant to better acquire, retain, and service customers as well as deliver unique experiences.

Change number 2 relates to being digital-first or able to automate and provide online, social, and secure interactions to address a variety of lifestyle choices, making offline propositions more difficult to sustain without a digital presence. It is also about making trust and transparency essential parts of the transaction model.

Change number 3 focuses on the development and acceptance of new partnership and alliance models, which involve many new parties formerly non-existent across the insurance value chain. They often reposition the role of the insurer as white-label insurance enabler, underwriter, or claims handler depending on the context of the new propositions. The new business models that are emerging are more data-driven and collaborative-focused. They are built on an ecosystem of relevant partners and services that are willing and keen to adopt more preventative behavioural approaches.

It is recognized that while innovation opportunities will come from shaping and remodelling the value chain, disruption opportunities will come from identifying truly revolutionary business models.

Business Model Innovation – From Incremental to Disruptive

By Dan Smith
Co-Founder and Managing Partner, Exponential Ventures

"The worst place to develop a new business model is from within the existing one."

Clayton Christensen

At its most conceptual level, a business model is no more than a strategic configuration of the various components constituting a business and the logic of how this business intends to operate and make money. The application of technologies permeates all aspects of each business model and holds the potential to reconfigure existing business models or create entirely new ones, in a quick efficient manner leveraging the context of the consumer. In order to provide a sense of where the focus is across innovation models, we categorize them according to Nagji and Tuff's[1] three-tier innovation ambition framework (see Figure 1):

1. **Core** – optimize existing products for existing customers (not the focus of this chapter);

2. **Adjacent** – entering adjacent markets and customer segments;

3. **Transformative/Disruptive** – creating new markets, and targeting new needs.

McKinsey's three horizons framework, if you are familiar with this, is equally interchangeable.[2] Most companies anecdotally strive

for the "golden balance" of 70-20-10 split for core, adjacent, and transformative initiatives in terms of innovation asset allocation. However, research has consistently identified that the financial returns are broadly the inverse of this, with core innovations returning around 10% of the long-term cumulative return on innovation investment.[3] Given this, it's important to highlight the current state of play in insurance innovation to ensure that we are channelling innovation efforts appropriately.

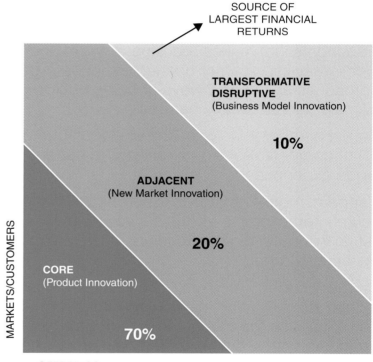

Figure 1: Nagji and Tuff's three-tier innovation ambition framework

---

[1] Tendayi Viki, Frameworks for building innovation portfolios: Three horizons and disruptive innovation, 17 April 2016, https://medium.com/the-corporate-startup/frameworks-for-building-innovation-portfolios-8e189b4d4189.

[2] http://www.mckinsey.com/business-functions/strategy-and-corporate-finance/our-insights/enduring-ideas-the-three-horizons-of-growth.

[3] https://www2.deloitte.com/content/dam/Deloitte/us/Documents/strategy/us-managing-your-innovation-portfolio-07102013.pdf.

Core (or incremental) innovations are really focused on delivering product innovation improvements to existing markets and customers. A lot of the innovation coming from InsurTech during the course of the past two formative years has been targeting the optimization of online distribution (including price comparison and aggregators) and the digitization of inefficient processes, with startups building digital capabilities to augment the existing value chain. There is already a well-versed body of research on this area (value chain unbundling and digital distribution plays). As a result we won't be revisiting this specific topic within this chapter.

Adjacent innovation is about stretching existing capabilities/products to serve adjacent markets or consumers. Notable business model trends in the adjacent innovation space include:

Product disaggregation – InsurTech businesses such as Trov are tackling the short-term/on-demand insurance opportunity through a combination of new pricing strategies and new product features to create a great user experience and frictionless way to create a digital asset vault. This storage of digital assets is a powerful tool for client retention, which helps explain the emergence of startups focused on owning the digital vault, such as CBien or AssetVault. This presents adjacent opportunities like asset (digital and physical) life-cycle management. Qover are taking product customization further through personalization of both product term *and* specific non-life coverage options, white-labelled to commercial clients. Creating these insurance building blocks will be critical to driving Insurance-as-a-Service and could rapidly open up new non-insurance distribution channels as companies looking to cross-sell insurance can be as granular as designing insurance propositions for the customer "segment of one". For on-demand propositions, a key consideration is to build sufficiently sophisticated techniques to avoid fraud as it is difficult to track/prove that users haven't "turned on" insurance coverage after the event. Fundamentally, however, the core product is the same.

"Robo broker" – insurance advice and broad risk assessment is a clear extension of price comparison and automation of the role of the broker (e.g. Wrisk or Brolly). In effect it enables a digital consolidation of siloed insurance products into a single orchestrated view. Over time this should extend to catch up with the robo investment business model innovations that are heading towards generating insights that are timely, contextual, relevant, and personalized. It's not difficult to envisage even predictive insights about an individual's insurance requirements or risk profile. Artificial intelligence (AI) and neuro linguistic programming techniques can be used to understand consumers' risk appetite and compare policy wording, which is critical to identifying and appropriately communicating risk overlaps/gaps. This baseline understanding sets the stage for robo insurance advice and appropriate product recommendations. This is already happening in the commercial space with offerings from RiskGenius, leveraging technology to identify wording gaps, and much more. Many consumer-facing robo investment models have struggled to gain sufficient initial traction and so have pivoted to business-to-business distribution, creating a hybrid robo platform that enables, rather than replaces, the broker to profitably serve the long-tail of clients – important given the customer acquisition costs, churn rates, and combined ratios of insurers today.

Embedded "pull" insurance – Adjacent distribution/product bundling – these models are starting to emerge across the InsurTech landscape. Commercial partnerships with banks, telcos, and ecommerce providers have existed for some time – good old-fashioned affinity models. The innovation opportunity is in deeply embedded insurance, effectively as a business-to-business insurance API or application programming interface, invisible to the end-user. For example, Tesla are embedding auto insurance in their cars in partnership with AXA, packaged as an extended warranty. Tikkr are seeking to embed on-demand sports activity insurance within the various sports apps on the market. These embedded models shift insurance from a mandatory purchase/sales push effect to an invisible or embedded purchase or sales pull effect – part of the package that creates a frictionless end-to-end experience. Creating this frictionless integration and a seamless user experience for the distribution channel partner to sell to their end-users are quickly becoming hygiene factors. Successful propositions will be those that can offer deep-embedded individualized offerings with minimal manual data inputs, leveraging AI/machine learning (ML) techniques and bringing together relevant open accessible data, as they establish higher switching costs, margin protection, and improved customer loyalty.

Preventative risk management – these models are about creating user engagement or monitoring services proactively before risks arise. This opportunity is only now becoming possible at scale and in a cost-effective manner by leveraging data, the Internet of Things (IoT), and ML – bringing all of these together to add material value to the customer and reduce the insurer's risk. Great initial examples are emerging such as automated vehicle or driving behaviour diagnosis (e.g. Amodo), tracking health and activity status (e.g. LifeQ, Quealth, Fitsense), monitoring household water leakages (e.g. Leakbot, by Homeserve and Aviva), or industrial machine monitoring with Hartford Steam Boiler. This model requires an adjustment to the existing value chain as you build out the ecosystem of relevant service providers and adopt a preventative operating and underwriting model – one that is based on real-time/forward-looking, and potentially even predictive, data; a very different world from most incumbents today. MMI Holdings'[4] "Multiply" or Discovery's "Vitality" products are well-established insurance propositions in South Africa that have pioneered preventative models in the life/health insurance markets. For the incumbent, such business models drive user engagement and a positive impact on customer acquisition, retention, and cross-sell rates, but also could dramatically change the risk pools as we know them today. The challenge for startups is that replicating these ecosystems often requires a critical mass to bring together various service providers so the entry point may be to enable incumbents to adopt preventative models, as Sureify is doing, for example.

---

[4] http://www.mmiholdings.co.za/en.

A key consideration for the insurer is to avoid too stringent risk screening that leads to adverse selection. Abusing the asymmetric information advantage that the insurer holds on the basis of client-permissioned data sharing (i.e. unknowingly using client data against them for ulterior motives), while balancing the insurers' growth trajectory, is a difficult tension and conflict that will need to be actively managed. It will be a cost-benefit trade-off between acceptable balance sheet risk and overheads associated with proactive risk management actions. Equally, adverse selection would have a regulatory or political risk too if you create pools of uninsurable, or risks that are out of access stopping people being able to get to work, or cover their homes.

Transformative (or Disruptive) Innovations are about creating new markets and solving (sometimes latent) customer needs. Typically, such innovations are difficult to achieve as the dominant business model design is not predetermined so it is a highly risky form of innovation. It will eventually cannibalize revenues and market shares of incumbents as many disruptive innovation strategies start by gaining a toehold in an adjacent or underserved customer segment deemed unattractive to the large incumbent insurers. However, they quickly move into prime customer segments with product extensions. These sorts of innovations may also appear too small or too slow to value to meet investment criteria of traditional (larger) businesses, which are often more interested in innovations that hold the potential of a bigger financial contribution to the bottom line faster (and at apparently less risk). This thinking often closes the door to the consideration of low or new market disruptive ideas. Examples include:

P2P or "digital mutual" models. These are deemed to be disruptive as they remove insurance incumbents from the equation in many cases and democratize access to insurance, potentially acting as an investment asset class over time for institutional and retail investors. The irony with P2P models that they have existed for many years in an offline version called ROSCAs (Rotating Savings and Credit Associations) and have been used to great effect in Africa. However, technology has empowered these models to seek scale. Various digital models have developed, such as relying on shared insurance requirements of similar groups of people to negotiate better terms (e.g. Bought By Many) or platforms that are self-governing, self-selecting risk pools (aka risk pool unbundling) of individuals who typically rely on affinity groups and some form of user engagement to make the unit economics work in terms of customer acquisition costs or keeping fraudulent claims down (e.g. Insure-a-thing, Friendsurance, Guevara, So-sure, etc.). Users typically pay monthly into a risk pool and are rewarded through some form of incentive (commonly cashback) if no/minimal claims are processed.

An enabler for this trend is the granularization of risks (enabled by IoT/smartphone data). A key hurdle is the inherent self-selection bias as many of these platforms rely on affinity groups and trust between members to help keep fraudulent claims to a minimum, which is difficult to do at scale. These also require some level of user engagement, which is hard to achieve outside of customer segments that are extremely price-sensitive as insurance is not an engagement-driven product today.

Preventative models 2.0. This evolution sees a transition to real-time data and proactive suggestions/remedial action in a mobile-first distribution channel. The shift is from an IoT infrastructure "connectivity" focus ("connected home", "connected car") to a focus on "outcomes" via platform-enabled ecosystems. However, what if we imagine a broader preventative model, for example encompassing all forms of transport in an ecosystem model? A consumer could buy one travel insurance policy, "Citymapper v2.0", with an insurer orchestrating an ecosystem of transport options (car/bike rental, taxi, public transport) in the event that your primary mode of travel isn't available to get you to your destination. You are automatically presented with a pre-funded alternative transportation option based on the best risk-reward ratio or your policy tier. So, in effect, the user is buying peace of mind that they'll reach their destination. Companies that can help enable this model include Concirrus.

Two-sided platforms. Health insurers already adopt the structure of a two-sided platform model, albeit not in a digitally-enabled manner. Platform models work most effectively when they impact at least two variables positively – typically price and availability/variability of an offering. There is wider applicability of two-sided markets in general insurance as there is a market-wide under-utilization of balance sheet capacity that creates an opportunity to aggregate the supply of capital on the "producer" side, from a wide range of institutional investors. Global digital platforms (Facebook, Google, Amazon, etc.) can also compete given their massive online distribution and reach. Reinsurers are also actively experimenting with digital to customer propositions through a managing general agent (MGA)[5] proxy. The differentiation is mostly needed on the consumer side of the platform to address poor customer satisfaction and product innovation efforts, otherwise consumers will remain price-sensitive and such a market with one variable (price) will drive commoditization and margin erosion. To limit commoditization risk on the platform supply-side (producer), a critical success factor is exposing the buy-side (consumer) to differentiated solutions, perhaps with advisory layer/personalized recommendations to avoid becoming an aggregation play and just competing on price.

Freemium models. The insurance model is effectively a reverse freemium model as everyone pays for the benefit of the few (who claim). An interesting example is the Tigo and Bima partnership in Ghana, scaling to over 1 million users before offering a paid upgrade option to double their coverage. A user's mobile phone credit was the proxy for their assessment of risk. With an initial 60% conversion rate, this has proved to be an attractive model. Low acquisition costs make this an attractive growth model but a key consideration is ensuring you have the balance sheet

---

[5] A specialized type of insurance agent/broker that, unlike traditional agents/brokers, is vested with underwriting authority from an insurer. Accordingly, MGAs perform certain functions ordinarily handled only by insurers, such as binding coverage, underwriting and pricing, appointing retail agents within a particular area, and settling claims.

capacity to cover the claims risk exposure and well-defined upsell/cross-sell strategy.

Open platform business models. Insurers can expose parts of their business to the open market to benefit from talent, specialized skills, or IP (outside-in) or expose any world-class capabilities to the market for them to collaborate or build upon (inside-out). A good area of opportunity for startup collaboration is to enable insurers to conduct an assessment and quantification of new forms of cyber risk threats and incorporating new forms of data into existing risk and pricing models. EigenRisk are an established independent software vendor in this space with startups AdaptReady and ThreatInformer offering useful risk assessments already.

In summary, there are broader trends that will influence future business models:

- **Asset sharing.** As we move to a world of asset sharing, the complexity of managing risk between parties can become more complex, specifically who and what you are sharing and when.

- **Data ubiquity.** Proliferation of real-time will eventually shift focus to forward-looking risk models and will enable more companies to move from mono to multi-line insurance. Ultimately the most important thing here for insurers is the shift from product-centric to customer-centric cover. Insurers will likely need help making sense of how to assess/score risk from unstructured data sets/IoT.

- **Alternative risk models.** Insurance industry barriers to entry fall as the dependency on long-term historical risk models declines and the focus moves to forward-looking, data-driven models. When we reach this inflection point, insurance becomes an investable asset class for many institutional investors seeking alpha. Hedge funds are well placed, as modelling risk-adjusted returns on a diversified portfolio of policies based on geography and peril bears similarities to hedge fund portfolio construction. A recent partnership between quantitative hedge fund Two Sigma and insurers AIF and Hamilton suggests we're already seeing the line blur between credit risk and insurance risk pricing.

- **Future of mobility.** Self-driving cars/fleets remove human error and will make auto insurance largely redundant. Business models will need to evolve to create B2B commercial insurance-warranty hybrid or microinsurance products. The nature of risk also evolves to one that is systemic and down to technology system errors.

- **Future of work.** The gig economy continues to grow, placing stress on credit products, insurance, and pension schemes. Future products need to reflect a blend of personal and commercial liabilities for these "businesses of one" – a massive opportunity to get SME right.

- **AI and automation.** The opportunity is the automation of increasingly complex tasks, e.g. underwriting, which provides potential for cost savings and lower risks. The threat takes the form of AI-enabled cyber risks, coupled with IoT, that present macro-systemic risks for which we as society are not prepared. As an example, IoT and automation technologies applied to smart city use cases (e.g. monitoring the structural health of city buildings/bridges, providing access control to restricted areas, and controlling traffic flow) offer great benefit to society but present a real threat if visibility of this data and control of automation protocols fell into the hands of individuals with malicious intent.

No matter what the future holds, there are some fundamental changes we can be certain of – given what we've seen in other consumer-focused industries. Insurance will be data-driven and there will always be a need to manage risk even if the characteristics and bearer of the risk evolve. As digital weaves its way into insurance, adjacent industries will converge and value chains reconfigure. The pace of change enabled by technology means the biggest global insurance companies and new business models are unlikely to exist as they do today. Ultimately, whichever companies and dominant business models win, they will need to delight the consumer, influence behaviour, and solve for the original intent of insurance – peace of mind and financial resiliency. Whether we call it insurance or not is a different debate!

The Future of Insurance – From Managing Policies to Managing Risks

By Dr J.H.F. Onno Bloemers
Head of Insurance Transformation, Delta Capita

The End of the Current Model

The classical insurance business model, with insurers offering financial compensation or stability to clients through a contract represented by a policy, is under attack.

Today's customers expect seamlessly-working digital solutions across more and more aspects of their lives, as well as in many of their dealings with insurance companies. Both convenience and relevance are essential in today's competitive environment, where new business and architectural standards are dictated by rapidly-evolving technologies and rapidly-crumbling industry boundaries.

Insurers struggle to respond to these ever-increasing expectations. Often quoted reasons for this struggle are the increase in regulatory pressures, which is absorbing a large part of available change capacity within incumbent organizations. And, of course, it doesn't help either that many insurers still run on a myriad of legacy applications. Obviously, these circumstances form important, difficult, and very real obstacles, but there might be a more fundamental reason for the difficulties insurers face with organizational transformation and innovation.

On this more fundamental level – and notwithstanding the drive and energy of the countless insurance professionals I've met over the years – it seems that incumbent insurance organizations do not hold all the capabilities needed to effectively design and implement an updated, future-proof business model. The reason for this could be quite straightforward: insurance organizations simply never had to do this before. It is the result of the existing insurance business model being tremendously successful over a long period of time.

By providing a safety net for individuals and businesses alike and through their collection and investing of capital, insurers have contributed on a global level to stable economic growth. But while insurance organizations are equipped to manage a lot of different things, this does not seem to include fast, disruptive change. By and large, organizations lack structure, skills, and experience to transform their business effectively. Now, these incumbents suddenly have to catch up in a short period of time on all those changes affecting the industry. This means that facing disruptive change is going to prove quite difficult. And likewise, this is one of the key reasons why innovation labs are flourishing and why they are positioned at some distance from their parent organizations.

InsurTechs Fill the Gap

InsurTech startups are keen to exploit the growing imbalance between customer expectations and insurance services offered, providing new solutions or improvements for specific aspects in the insurance value chain. A growing range of business concepts offers improved customer interactions, introduces new pricing models based on usage or behaviour, and provides a fully digital claims experience or reorganizes supply and demand in peer-to-peer platforms. These solutions provide clear advantages where they replace old-fashioned, cumbersome, bureaucratic procedures.

Confusing Aims and Means

The real innovation, however, must take place at a much more fundamental level. Remember the great American railroads at the beginning of the twentieth century? The classic railroad companies believed their core business was building railway infrastructure and operating trains.[1] If they had formulated their mission statement differently – e.g. our business is to transport people and freight – then they might have made different choices and invested more in upcoming forms of transportation in order to maintain their relevance, instead of losing the large part of their business to planes and automobiles. Over time, they confused aims and means.

Insurers find themselves in a similar situation. For a long time, insurers have redistributed risks and balanced premium income using the insurance policy as their instrument. Incumbents have developed great capabilities to manage these policies through their life cycle. Product development, pricing models, risk management, and claims processing have evolved over the years, and – to some extent – reflect advancements in technology.

But the key problem here is that a policy is far from an optimal solution for managing risks, the original core business of insurers. Firstly, providing financial compensation to customers after an unforeseen event only covers part of the loss. You will never be able to compensate for stress, trauma, or lost family valuables after a fire, not to mention the tremendous impact of accidents on people's lives. For businesses, the effects can be similarly severe, with customers turning to other suppliers when a business must shut down temporarily after an incident.

Secondly, a policy doesn't provide a lot of options for regular, meaningful customer contact. If interaction with customers is limited to policy renewal and premium payments, there is not much opportunity to build a more solid customer relationship.

And lastly – let's be honest: there is not much attractiveness in an insurance policy. People are not looking for a policy because they want to, but because they must, due to legal requirements, or for lack of alternatives.

---

[1] Theodore Levitt, Market myopia, *Harvard Business Review*, first publication 1960, reprinted July/August 2004.

A New Paradigm

However, with the rise of the connected world of sensors, big data, and the Internet of Things (IoT), a completely new paradigm arises where offering a policy to manage risks is much like the tail wagging the dog.

The opportunity insurers face is to take a step back from their policy-driven business model and revisit the original reason for their existence: providing solutions for customers to manage their risks.

Combining existing internal data with new data sources, real-time sensor information, and their deep understanding of risk, insurers now have the option to dramatically increase their relevance with each one of their customer segments.

Taking customer risk as a starting point, insurers can build analytical capabilities to refine and personalize customer risk assessments. These data offer new ways for getting to know your customers, including their tolerance for risk and their preferences for handling these risks.

Once they understand your individual customer's risk profile and preferences, insurers can use these insights to position themselves as expert risk managers offering a range of solutions that fit individual customer situations. Depending on lifestyle and risk appetite these solutions may include accepting a certain amount of risk. Or they might include solutions or services reducing the probability or impact of risks. Risk reduction measures may range from applying sensor technologies (smart homes, self-driving vehicles, IoT) to maintenance services, training, and education. Of course, leveraging new technologies may themselves introduce new risk types, such as cyber and privacy risks, which should be considered by all insurers. Once insurer and customer have identified, reduced, neutralized, or accepted the full set of risks that affect them, a policy might only come in to cover any residual risks, e.g. the risk that remains after applying technologies or services that reduce or eliminate the risk.

This new approach offers several key benefits over the traditional policy-driven approach. Firstly, it makes more sense to support your customers to improve their safety – prevention is always better than cure, particularly if that cure is only partial.

Secondly, using real-time sensor data and IoT technologies provides the basis for regular and relevant customer contacts. Insurers can design frequent customer touchpoints and become an integral part of daily customer life in a positive way.

Lastly, over time the revised risk profiles may result in substantial reductions in both claims frequencies and amounts as risk management measures in larger populations gain effect. Estimated reductions in home claims range from 40 to 60%.[2]

Making it Happen

Enhancing policies with relevant services offers clear opportunities across different insurance lines. There is a growing number of initiatives where insurers partner with suppliers of smart devices to offer home automation in combination with a modest discount on policy premium. With connected sensors for water, fire, or intrusion to prevent damage in your home an instantaneous response is possible when the need arises.

In life and health insurance, we see the rise of connected wellness devices, reducing premium costs and providing incentives to customers to become more active. Policy-holders are collecting rewards through their activity trackers and earning discounts on their life insurance. A fall detection sensor provides seniors with a virtual safety net.

Safer driving can be induced by rewarding the right behaviour, measuring speed and g-force, enabling emergency assistance when needed.

In business-to-business insurance the same principles apply. While businesses may already be subject to mandatory safety measures and inspections, there is a world to be gained by improving awareness and changing behaviour at work. Next to their policy offering we see the first insurers starting to offer services through a subscription model. Businesses sign up for a set of services (e.g. checking electrical installations or expert risk analyses), security systems, or sensors on a subscription basis, eliminating large investments in equipment upfront.

Many of these examples are in a proof of concept stage, providing a point solution for a specific risk using connected technology as an add-on to an insurance policy. Soon, we'll see a turning point where this is going to be the other way around: technology as the primary solution with an insurance policy to manage the residual risk. Developments in this area may go quickly as more and more consumers are expected to take up smart devices in the coming years.

Conclusion – The Way Forward

Insurers need to evolve into organizations offering a much broader set of risk management solutions. Asking the right questions internally is critical. Instead of answering the question "How do we sell more policies?" this is the time to ask "In which business are we?"

InsurTech, as a theme, will be a critical component in this by integrating itself into a larger ecosystem of capabilities and by enhancing or replacing traditional policy offerings. Companies that

---

[2] Morgan Stanley/Boston Consulting Group, Insurance and Technology, Evolution and Revolution in a Digital World, September 2014.

excel at analysing risk patterns and translating these into attractive customer value propositions, whether business-to-consumer or business-to-business, will become dominant.

A key capability required for insurers will be to develop and manage cross-industry partnerships with technology providers or service suppliers. By building these strategic alliances insurers may be able to maintain a competitive edge over new entrants. An insurance company knows about risk like no other. The future playing field will be dominated by insurers contributing to their customers' safety, wellbeing, and peace of mind. Traditional policies will not disappear, but they will not remain a decisive factor for competitive strength and company value anymore.

Seeing through the Hype – A Closer Look at Key Smart InsurTech Business Models

By Karolina Burmeister
Senior Relationship Manager, OP Financial Group

Working in the insurance industry, it is impossible to avoid the ongoing hype around the industry's digitalization, commonly called #fintech or #insurtech. According to believers, new insurance startups will rapidly emerge and rule the world, based on superior customer experience. Alternatively, will new technologies reduce the need for insurance altogether? Based on my 20+ years' experience of evaluating business models, I decided to comment on some themes that frequently emerge. I also wanted to look at it all specifically from a European perspective.

Many of the proposed InsurTech business models are not new, but instead they take advantage of technology that was not previously available. Superior customer experience is an advantage in itself, if it helps people to buy insurance cover. Reduced risk levels are a great advantage to society. Still, in many cases technology will merely shift risks from end-users to service providers. For example, all service providers will desperately need cyber insurance to cover liability and data breaches. There are many steps to go before a startup becomes a sustainable and profitable business.

Smart Health Insurance

The idea: "Heart rate and blood pressure can be monitored by biometric sensors and smartwatches. This provides real-time data and incentives to consumers."

Insurers may want to use customers' health data for underwriting purposes. Maybe health problems can be avoided and prevented altogether when individuals are monitored in real-time? This would most certainly bring down the cost of insurance, and, even more importantly, increase the customer's health and life expectancy. The disadvantage is obviously that for an individual consumer, the gadgets and monitoring costs may well exceed the premium discount.

It is also important to notice that unlike the US, nearly 100% of Europe's population is under automatic or mandatory primary health coverage. Thus, supplementary health insurance (SHI) is not the first thing on which consumers will spend their money. Finnish researchers recently concluded that SHI was purchased by people with a higher level of education, better health, and higher household income than the average consumer. Currently around 23% of Finnish adults have some sort of SHI, and many of those schemes are actually provided by employers.[1,2]

Smart health insurance may be highly interesting for those consumers who are already buying SHI, but the market size might be disappointing for insurers and startups, especially in markets with solid automatic health insurance. On a side note, employers might just be more interested in smart health than they would like to admit. However, the EU's general data protection regulation will make it costly for service providers, employers, and insurers to manage health-related data going forward. If anything, they will certainly need cyber insurance to cover potential data breaches.

---

[1] OECD Health Working Paper no. 50, http://www.oecd-ilibrary .org/social-issues-migration-health/health-systems-institutional-characteristics_5kmfxfq9qbnr-en;jsessionid=1fprpv7ukaqo.x-oecd-live-03.

[2] H. Valtonen, J. Kempers, and A. Karttunen. Supplementary health insurance in Finland, consumer preferences and behavior. Kela Working Papers 65/2014.

Smart Homes and Property Insurance

The idea: "Homeowners and insurers can take advantage of sensors and monitoring systems to control major risks."

This is highly interesting. Monitoring equipment that has been in use at industrial sites for decades has now become inexpensive and adapted to consumer properties. Your house can be monitored 24/7 through a simple app, some sensors, and cameras. Typical claims like flooding, theft, and fires can be detected more rapidly. Maybe someone would like to install sprinklers? Underwriters may be able to reward consumers for the increased safety, as they are now rewarding industrial companies for their good risk management.

As with smart health equipment, property monitoring and security systems are also costly. Not all industrial clients have invested in protection despite available technology and their insurer's recommendations to do so. Overall, monitoring technology will certainly help prevent many property claims going forward. The impact on insurance pricing will come with a few years' lag, when the installed base is large enough to provide a solid claims history. It is important for startups to have sufficient funding to build up their installed customer base and track record.

We will also see a shift in insurable risks, from the end-user to the service provider. For example, what will happen if the IoT sensor system is faulty, or worse, hacked so that burglars can enter your house freely? Software companies will see an increasing need for cyber liability insurance, which hopefully will be provided to them by the established insurance market.

Driverless Cars and Car Insurance

The idea: "Driverless cars will decrease the number of accidents significantly, and motor liability insurance will become obsolete."

Yes, the advantages will be enormous! Just think of the roughly 26,000 yearly road traffic fatalities in the EU – mostly related to speeding (30% of all deaths) and drunk driving (25%). Just getting rid of speeding and drunk driving would save 14,000 lives! Of course, there would be big repair cost savings from all the spared vehicles. The brave new world of self-driving cars, buses, trucks, and utility vehicles would certainly look very different, and the traffic-related risks would be extremely low, with driving motor liability insurance down.

The only disadvantage is that this will not actually materialize just yet. The transition time span here is so long that even the slowest of the incumbent insurance companies will be able to adjust without much effort: when the entire car fleet is self-driving, all current auto insurance underwriters will be long since retired. The EU's car fleet numbers 291 million vehicles, so with the current pace of 15.8 million new registrations per year, replacing the entire fleet would take more than 18 years. And we are still waiting for the first self-driving cars to go live in traffic.[3]

In the meantime, car insurance might not get much cheaper after all. On the contrary, the cost of motor hull insurance has been on the rise over the past decades due to ever more complicated technologies driving sums insured and repair costs upwards. During the same decades, road safety has improved significantly in the EU.

But when the first self-driving cars do emerge, car producers and their software providers had better have some top-notch cyber insurance in place! Car thefts can suddenly be performed by hacking into the driving system. It is also

---

[3] European Automobile Manufacturers Association, 2015.

important to note that legislative issues related to self-driving cars still remain open. Insurance products will be based on the evolving legal liability framework going forward.

Person-to-Person Insurance

What if a group of people agree on a risk-sharing scheme and compensate each other in the event of a claim? In fact this is one of the oldest business models in insurance, also called cooperative or mutual insurance. According to ICMIF,[4] the 5,000 mutual and cooperative insurers represent 27% of the total global insurance market. I see the difficulty for new peer-to-peer (P2P) schemes to build sufficient trust and capital buffers. Trust is essential: clients need to be sure that no-one is making false claims, that the client's claims will be fully paid, and that the decisions are fair and transparent. And some of these startups are providing an excellent user interface and customer onboarding experience, making them highly attractive potential acquisition targets for incumbent insurers.

In the meantime, I consider the best new P2P insurance so far to be crowdfunding. Just take a look at the "Accidents & Emergency Fundraising" part of gofundme.com. Tens of thousands of dollars are being crowdfunded for uninsured families who have lost their homes in floods and fires, thanks to this "second chance" service.

Capacity and Specialization

It is normal that many InsurTech startups will develop solutions around lines that are familiar to young entrepreneurs such as car, health, and home insurance. But these consumer lines are just a fraction of global insurance needs. Will we see startups around large global risks? Natural catastrophe? Product liability? Terrorism? Epidemics? I doubt that will be the case because of the large amount of capital and specialty knowledge needed.

Across all sectors and times, capital and specialization have protected businesses from competition. Incumbent insurers and reinsurers with sufficient capacity will most certainly be able to survive the technology shift by adapting their customer experience, investing in digitalization, and acquiring bolt-on technologies.

Specialization will be another winning concept, as technology will shift risks in unforeseen ways. Building up expertise is not easy. All of this requires hard work and strategic patience for incumbents.

On the other hand, startups will also require hard work and a lot of patience before they will be able to acquire the customer base, specialty skills, and capital needed for large-scale operations. There simply are no free lunches.

---

[4] International Cooperative and Mutual Insurance Federation.

Assessing the Long-Term Viability of the Insurance Peer-to-Peer Business Model

By Damiano Pietroni
Management Consulting Manager – Insurance, Accenture

Background

The peer-to-peer (P2P) insurance sector is enjoying significant growth because of the linearity of its business model:

- Customer premiums are pooled by the P2P insurer into risk-specific pools; for example, motor risk or mobile phone risk pools.

- Customer claims are paid from the pool; where the pool is insufficient to cover a claim, the P2P insurer acts as reinsurer.

- Funds remaining at the end of the year after all claims have been paid are either returned to customers or carried over into the next year.

- The P2P insurer makes a profit by extracting a percentage of the funds in the risk pools to cover costs and margin.

This type of business model is the focus of this chapter. We will first cover how the business model of three major P2P insurers (Lemonade in the US, Friendsurance in Germany, and Guevara in the UK) compares to the business model of three large general insurers (Allianz, AXA, and AIG), before listing and analysing key advantages and limitations between the two groups. We will then determine the long-term viability of the P2P insurance model.

Comparing Business Models – Common Elements

Lemonade, Friendsurance, and Guevara leverage the same risk pooling mechanisms as Allianz, AXA, and AIG.

Comparing Business Models – Differing Elements

- With 2016 revenues of €122 billion (Allianz),[1] €100 billion (AXA),[2] and US$55 billion (AIG),[3] the three general insurers are significantly larger than Lemonade, Friendsurance, and Guevara.

- The business lines transacted are more diversified and therefore generate greater opportunities to attract customers (see Table 1):

Key Advantages of the P2P Insurance Business Model

1. **Fraud risk is minimized.** Customers are disincentivized to commit fraud due to three factors. Firstly, P2P insurance risk pools are significantly smaller than general insurance risk pools, and as such the connection between claims paid from the pool and premiums paid is more obvious, prompting customers not to fraudulently claim knowing that doing so would increase their own end-of-year premiums and impact the relationship they have with other pool participants. Secondly, P2P insurance has a social element, lowering fraud levels as defrauding other individuals is perceived as less acceptable than defrauding insurers.[4] Thirdly, where premiums, in excess of claims paid, are returned to customers, as is the case for Friendsurance, the benefit of claims fraud is reduced, as the payout from the fraudulent claims is partially offset by the reduced returned premium at end of year.

---

[1] Allianz, Annual Report 2016, https://www.allianz.com/v_1489492630000/media/investor_relations/en/results/2016_fy/ar-2016-annual-report-allianz-group.pdf.

[2] AXA, Annual Report 2016, https://www.axa.com/en/about-us/key-figures.

[3] Marketwatch, AIG Financials 2016, http://www.marketwatch.com/investing/stock/aig/financials.

[4] Capgemini, Top 10 Trends in Insurance in 2016, https://www.nl.capgemini.com/resource-file-access/resource/pdf/insurance_trends_2016_0_0.pdf.

Table 1: Insurers and their business lines

Company	Lines of business
Allianz + AXA + AIG	<ul><li>Personal (motor, home, travel, pet, equine, musical instruments, legal expenses, personal liability)</li><li>Life (annuities, critical illness, life assurance)</li><li>Commercial (small/large business, directors, engineering)</li><li>Specialty (space, energy, marine, aviation, Alternative Risk Transfer)</li><li>Reinsurance (Allianz Re, AXA Partners, AIG-Ascot Re)</li><li>Asset management (Allianz Asset Management, AXA Investment Management, AIG Asset Management)</li></ul>
Lemonade	<ul><li>Personal (home, renters, condo, co-op)</li></ul>
Friendsurance	<ul><li>Personal (home, electronics, personal liability, legal expenses)</li></ul>
Guevara	<ul><li>Personal (motor)</li></ul>

2. **Digital-first.** The P2P insurance business model is Internet-first and leverages automated online interactions with customers to underwrite risks, manage policies, and pay claims, leading to:

a. Lower payroll costs; once the automated underwriting and claims handling systems are functioning the human effort required to run the operation is limited.

b. Lower acquisition costs due to its disintermediation; selling directly to the customer via web or mobile means that broker fees and white label distribution costs are both avoided. Furthermore, the direct engagement with the customer allows P2P insurers to build a brand that resonates with the customer.

c. Lower system maintenance costs; front-end applications powered by lean back-end systems are significantly less expensive to maintain than complex, often legacy-based, IT architectures that insurers use to service multiple business lines, to deliver single customer views, and comply with regulation.

Key limitations of the P2P insurance business model, and how they can be addressed, are shown in Table 2. Key limitations of the P2P

Table 2: Key limitations of P2P insurance business model and solutions

ID	Limitation	Solution
1	Smaller risk premium pools cannot cover black swan claims events, namely events that deviate from what is expected and have a significant impact; this is particularly an issue for P2P insurers covering cars, such as Guevara, as claims can exceed £1m where an insured faces permanent disability through the materialization of a liability risk.	It is key to purchase reinsurance cover to overcome weaknesses of the model (e.g. Lemonade reinsures with Everest, Hiscox, Munich Re, Transatlantic, and XL Catlin).[5]
2	Whereas in P2P lending the trust burden is on the customer, who must repay the loan, in P2P insurance the onus is on the P2P insurer, which must indemnify customers' valid claims. This implies that P2P insurers require significant trust "equity" to operate, as customers will not transact business with any P2P insurer that they believe is unlikely, beyond reasonable doubt, to trade over the long term.	To make this work P2P providers must:<ul><li>highlight the experience and calibre of the P2P insurer's leadership team</li><li>demonstrate the stability of the organization by reviewing the financials</li><li>gather and display the positive feedback provided by customers</li><li>have the organization's business model reviewed by authoritative bodies (e.g. the Chartered Insurance Institute).</li></ul>

[5] Insurance Journal, Leading reinsurers line up for Lemonade, the P2P Insurer, http://www.insurancejournal.com/news/national/2016/02/09/398087.htm.

3	Specialty lines of insurance such as energy, satellite, and political risks cannot be covered by the P2P models because the current P2P insurance business model relies on commoditized risks for automated underwriting.	Extend the P2P insurance business model to cover specialty risks by pooling them in the same way personal lines risks are pooled. The business model could be designed as follows:
		
		• The P2P insurer enlists enough specialty risks operators for digitally-led mutual insurance to be feasible, finding, for example, eight satellite operators willing to mutually insure.
		
		• The P2P insurer collects premiums from the operators, and in exchange both purchase reinsurance cover and provide technical expertise to the risk pool in the form of:
		  • large claims adjusters
		  • technical underwriters
		  • maintenance experts
		  • specialist lawyers.
		
		• Where for a given pool for a given year premiums are in excess of claims, the subsequent year's premiums are adjusted to compensate.

4	Due to its short lifespan in the UK, P2P insurance as a framework for transactions and next generation mutualized agreements is not yet supported by a legal framework or volumes of legally binding contracts sufficient to provide some level of certainty for delivered outcomes. Examples of grey areas: 1. Do the concepts of subrogation, namely the substitution of a party by another with regard to an insurance claim, accompanied by the transfer of relevant rights, obligations, and contributions, namely the principle that two or more insurers, each liable for a claim, should participate in indemnifying such loss, apply to P2P insurance contracts in the same way they do for standard insurance contracts? 2. Can P2P insurance disputes in the UK be handled within the small claims procedures, or must they follow the procedures determined by the P2P insurance platform? 3. In the event of a cross-border dispute, such as a German motorist insured by a German P2P insurance scheme raising a claim following an accident with a French driver in France, who determines what law is applied to the claim? 4. Is the standard of disclosure concerning material facts for P2P insurance customers aligned to the principle of utmost good faith, or is it regulated by platform-specific guidance?	The best solution here would be to: • set up a work group composed of insurance P2P executives, representatives from the Financial Conduct Authority (FCA), and insurance-focused lawyers, with the aim of providing authoritative answers to open questions through written guidelines relating to the application of UK legal frameworks to P2P insurance contracts • instruct a group of legal professionals to track and document the progress of disputes relating to P2P insurance through the UK courts, and then create a website that specifically calls out such information, ensuring in doing so that P2P insurance legal doctrine can be easily retrieved.

insurance business model mapped against limitation's severity and each solution's complexity are shown in Figure 1.

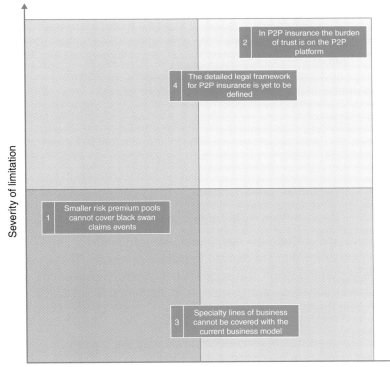

Severity of limitation

| 2 | In P2P insurance the burden of trust is on the P2P platform |

| 4 | The detailed legal framework for P2P insurance is yet to be defined |

| 1 | Smaller risk premium pools cannot cover black swan claims events |

| 3 | Specialty lines of business cannot be covered with the current business model |

Complexity of solution

Figure 1: Key limitations of the P2P insurance business model – mapped against limitation's severity, and solution's complexity

Conclusion

The P2P insurance business model relies on three key advantages. Firstly, it is linear and easy to understand, leading to increased interest from customers. Secondly, it discourages fraud through premium payback mechanisms, and should inherently attract less fraud due to the social nature of the interactions occurring among peers. Thirdly, the P2P insurance business is digital-first, leading to lower staff costs due to the automation of underwriting and claims handling. The model reduces acquisition costs due to direct interactions with customers, and maintenance costs due to the lack of legacy IT architectures.

That said, the P2P insurance business model has four key limitations, which need to be addressed to support its growth. First, smaller risk pools cannot accommodate black swan claims that are today overcome by reinsurance. Second, P2P insurers require significant trust equity to operate. This is addressed by investing in trust-building exercises. Third, the current P2P insurance business models do not accommodate specialty risks. This is tackled by extending the existing model to cover more complex risks. Last, the legal framework for P2P insurance is not yet fully established, which can be addressed by partnering with regulators and courts to agree both new operating frameworks and precedents.

Overall, the P2P insurance business model is viable. It is a simple response to a group of customer needs for transparency. It has inherent advantages over the traditional insurance model, which means that it could grow to the point of becoming an accepted alternative. However, for this to occur key limitations must be addressed as a matter of priority, by focusing first on building trust within the P2P insurance model. This is the most important and complex step in this process. Then a legal framework able to accept specialty risks must be established and accommodated, supported by reliable reinsurance solutions.

You Said … Sharing Economy?

By Sabine VanderLinden

CEO, Startupbootcamp InsurTech, Rainmaking Innovation
InsurTech, The Proposition Circle

Insurers beware: there are ventures out there that are challenging traditional market practices across business-to-consumer and business-to-business markets. From freelancing platforms changing the way we work (SkillShare[1]), to food-sharing platforms changing the way we share and connect to local communities (Shareyourmeal[2]), or ridesharing platforms (BlaBlaCar[3]) that allow groups of individuals to travel from A to B at a very low cost, leveraging spare spaces in drivers' cars.

Collaborative, also called sharing or gig, economy businesses are leading new economic and social interactions across Europe and the world as a whole.

The number of people taking part in it has skyrocketed. Businesses such as Uber, Netflix, Airbnb, Zipcar, and TaskRabbit are competing with successful incumbents, entertainment companies, hotel chains, and car rental services by enabling each and every individual to outsource day-to-day activities to other qualified parties. And all this thanks to the ubiquity of digital technologies.

Collaborative consumption is no longer an unknown phenomenon for consumers and businesses. It provides economies around the world with sustainable opportunities for growth. At the same time, it is clear that it poses significant challenges for policy-makers and regulators to keep up with.

_____

[1] https://www.skillshare.com/?via=header.

[2] www.shareyourmeal.net/.

[3] www.blablacar.co.uk/.

Not an Insignificant Market

Like many people out there, I have asked myself whether the collaborative economy is a passing fad. The more I see and live within it, the more I realize that it must be much more than that. We see its growth across the globe as the result of several mega-trends,[4] powered by rapidly changing customer needs and emerging technologies, which are colliding to disrupt fundamentally the way we create and deliver value.

The sharing economy is today facilitating billions of euros of revenues and transaction values. The platforms that are emerging have allowed anyone to become a producer and to connect with others, disintermediating many traditional organizations in the process. Blockbuster, among others, was an early casualty of such models.

With that in mind, there are five recognized segments of the sharing economy that are delivering sizable revenues. These include accommodation, transportation, household services,[5] professional services, and finance. And insurance is gradually permeating these various segments.

PwC[6] estimated that revenues generated by the sharing economy are estimated at US$15–20 billion today. The sector

_____

[4] Billee Howard, 11 Business trends entrepreneurs need to be aware of, Forbes, 22 September 2016, https://www.forbes.com/sites/billeehoward/2016/09/22/11-business-trends-entrepreneurs-need-to-be-aware-of/#58e2d0924aad.

[5] https://www.raconteur.net/business/house-sharing-is-shaking-up-uk-hotel-sector.

[6] PwC Consumer Intelligence Series, The Sharing Economy, 2015, https://www.pwc.com/us/en/technology/publications/assets/pwc-consumer-intelligence-series-the-sharing-economy.pdf.

will expand by 30% per year over the next 10 years, generating £18 billion of platform revenues and £140 billion of transactions revenues in Europe by 2025. This will represent US$335 billion revenues too, capturing missed opportunities within consumers and businesses.

Why is this Happening?

Interest in the sharing economy is increasing because of a variety of factors:

- **Digital literacy.** Remember those pictures of digital natives, with digital devices in their hands at the youngest age? As we all know, this is becoming the norm.

- **Ease of accessing digital technologies.** Any entrepreneur today can set himself up with limited funding. Digital technology is ubiquitous and can be accessed at a very low cost.

- **Entrepreneurial spirit.** Working for a large corporation was the norm some time ago. Today, many young graduates decide to take the entrepreneurial route and start their own project and company.

- **The acceptance for emerging creative skills.** Expertise in design thinking has become one of the most prized skills to address major customer engagement challenges across industries.

- **The incubation of young businesses.** Thousands of startups are entering incubation programs to accelerate their business like Uber, Airbnb, and Dropbox did.

- **The acceptance of sharing economy ventures.** Whether for pleasure or for business, some of us use such services every single day for travel (Uber), to eat (Deliveroo), or to stay (Airbnb).

What is the Sharing Economy?

So, what is the sharing economy? As highlighted by Alex Stephany in *The Business of Sharing*,[7] "The sharing economy is the value realized in taking under-utilized assets and making them accessible online to a community, leading to a reduced need for ownership of those assets."

What Alex means by that is:

- **Value.** Sharing economy businesses realize value from reciprocity. Often goods are swapped or exchanged and monies generated from affiliate deals and ecommerce transactions. While gifting is part of the process such models also intend to monetize things.

- **Under-utilized assets.** Even when they are idle, sharing economy assets can generate cash. It is about turning a resource's downtime (meaning intangible or tangible assets) into revenue. This can be done through purchase, sharing, and rental too.

- **Online accessibility.** To be accessible the resources need to be made available online. This includes a variety of revenue models.

- **Community.** The asset needs to move within a community. Often communities are built around interest groups. This means that they must engage beyond any transactional need through discussion forums, reviews, messaging, and blogs.

- **Reduce need for ownership.** Once individuals access the good or service through the online platform there is a reduced need for ownership. Whether you look at Uber or Zipcar, there is no reason today to own a car.

---

[7] Alex Stefany, *The Business of Sharing: Making it in the New Sharing Economy*, Palgrave Macmillan, 2015.

The sharing economy enables assets that are not used to be sold or rented out between a supplier and a consumer through the use of digital online platforms able to show available alternatives. For participants, this means more flexibility, accessibility to products and services 24/7, efficient use of resources, and a more sustainable way to consume market offers.

The Key to this Market Economy is the Platform

A sharing economy marketplace involves three important sets of players: *the platform* – which provides the marketplace, *the buyers* – also referred to as consumers, riders, or renters, and *the sellers* – also referred to as suppliers, providers, or hosts.[8]

The buyers and sellers are typically individuals or small entities who transact over a platform, which provides a discrete set of services to the parties using it, facilitating their efforts to transact effectively and efficiently, including searching for potential transacting partners, agreeing to terms with them, and performing contractual agreements.

The platform must:

- **attract large numbers of participants on both sides of the marketplace,** so that each participant has a substantial number of potential matches on the other side of the market from which to drive value. This results in two-sided network effects.

- **enable potential business partners** to search for one another, find a match, and complete a transaction. To be successful,

a platform must reduce friction that otherwise would make transactions costly or more cumbersome.

- **make transacting between strangers safe and reliable** enough that buyers and sellers feel confident that their transactions will proceed as agreed even when dealing with smaller and unknown suppliers. New platforms seek to address this need by implementing trust mechanisms such as social media ID checks, reputational rating, experience rating, feedback scores, incentives, and geolocation-enabled personalized services.

So, What Does all this Mean for Insurance?

In a special report on The Future of General Insurance 2016,[9] Marketforce interviewed many insurers and ascertained that "the vast majority of insurers have made little headway in delivering solutions for the sharing economy: just 10% already have an offer in the marketplace[10] and another 35% are only at the pilot or strategy stage. *55% have taken no steps* towards meeting these new insurance needs, potentially missing out on a significant new line of business."

The opportunity though is that people do not comprehend that there are risks when engaging with sharing economy platforms. Users are often uninsured or underinsured, and standard insurance policies are usually not fit for periodic sharing practices. Then, there is a need to understand what the "insurable interest" is when there is no owned inventory.[11]

Let's review of few sharing economy business models.

---

[8] Federal Trade Commission, The Sharing Economy: Issues facing platforms, participants & regulators, an FTC staff report, November 2016, https://www.ftc.gov/system/files/documents/reports/sharing-economy-issues-facing-platforms-participants-regulators-federal-trade-commission-staff/p151200_ftc_staff_report_on_the_sharing_economy.pdf.

[9] Marketforce, A special report, The Future of General Insurance, 2016, https://www.slideshare.net/NickMeijvander/marketforce-te-future-of-general-insurance-2016.

[10] Esther Val, Meet the insurers of the sharing economy, 1 March 2017, https://www.sharetribe.com/academy/insurance-sharing-economy/.

[11] BIBA, A BIBA brokers' guide to insuring the Sharing Economy, Issue 4, 2016, www.biba.org.uk.

Peer-to-Peer: Friendsurance

Friendsurance[12] is one of the first peer-to-peer insurance propositions, which has experimented with the sharing economy since 2010 by applying the principles of social networking and risk pooling among friends. The company rewards small groups of users that insure similar sets of products with a cashback bonus at the end of each year they remain claimless. It operates as an independent broker in the German market with over 60 domestic insurance partners, which offer car, home, electronics, legal expenses, and personal liability coverage to hundreds of thousands of customers. Friends that come together expect the group to be trustworthy and caring for their peers.

The vision of Friendsurance is to make insurance easier, more transparent and affordable, and less expensive for customers, helping them to save money.

Large claims are still covered by traditional insurance carriers but small claims and deductibles are covered by the group. At the end of the period, if claims are small or non-existent, the group gets a refund. Premium payback can reach up to 50%.

Business-to-Consumer: BlaBlaCar

Founded in 2006, BlaBlaCar offers its services to over 20 countries. It is a business-to-consumer long-distance ridesharing platform, which connects drivers who are travelling between cities and who also have empty seats, to individuals looking to travel the same way. Drivers typically use the platform to share costs of taking long journeys, to meet new people, and have some company. It can cost as little as £12 to travel between London and Manchester with BlaBlaCar's ridesharing service. With over 25 million users in 2015,

it allows over 10 million people to travel together each quarter, three times more travellers than on the Eurostar.

The high cost of owning and maintaining cars often pushes individuals to consider such options, which are more pleasant, convenient, and price efficient than using existing transport alternatives, particularly when travelling to underserved areas.

To protect car sharers, BlaBlaCar collaborates with AXA[13] to provide sharing economy ridesharing insurance based on the usage of the car, with the purpose of protecting drivers and passengers alike. Often, drivers assume that their cars, even when not used for profit-generating purposes, are insured. However, this is unlikely to be the case with personal injury and breakdown risk claims, and new products are being designed to overcome just that.

Business-to-Business: CBien

Created in 2013, CBien, a French double entendre between "Your assets" and "It is great", enables individuals to create an inventory of those possessions that are the most precious in their lives. The assets could include, for instance, a watch, a smartphone or a laptop, a motorbike, wine collections, or designer clothes. Most people think of CBien as an asset management platform, but its visual display enables users to do much more than that. Consumers can scan, upload, and manage their valued assets in one place. Insurers can insure each item and handle claims in near real-time, leveraging the tech the platform provides. CBien developed first their business-to-business model working primarily with insurers and helping them become more relevant for their customers. Today, they are expanding into the business-to-consumer markets, designing more relevant consumer experiences across a series of direct interactions.

---

[12] www.friendsurance.com/.

[13] https://www.blablacar.co.uk/axa-partnership.

How to Thrive in this New World

The process of sharing is based on multi-party transactional exchanges. The three examples highlighted in this chapter include interesting economy models that are gradually impacting the business of insurance. New business models are now emerging more regularly. To thrive in such an environment, new entrants have realized that they must develop customer models that are, at their core, based on trust, authenticity, and transparency. These are indeed very similar principles to where insurance started 300 years ago.

While authenticity and transparency are currently addressed with digital tools (response, persuasion, and exchange mechanisms), trust remains the fundamental pillar of the sharing economy and insurance can play a greater role in reinforcing it. Indeed, in the opinion of many thought leaders, insurance represents the next frontier for the sharing economy and many insurers are now gradually investing significant sums of money to understand this emerging engagement system better. Getting it right will be critical for reaching a wider number of reluctant observers who still believe the business of sharing involves too many risks.

From Claim Settlement to Claim Prevention – How Insurers Can Make Use of Predictive Analytics to Change their Business Model

By Bert F. Hölscher
Partner, ARKADIA Management Consultants GmbH

The main purpose of insurance is for insurers to settle claims caused by accident or damage. Big data and predictive analytics have the potential to change this operational expectation by predicting and preventing claims. New technologies such as the Internet of Things (IoT) offer a completely new approach to the business model of insurance companies. By collecting, analysing, and using all sorts of data sent by insured customers or insured assets, insurance companies have a much better chance to prevent damages or accidents even before a claim occurs.

An insurer's ability to process and analyse large amounts of varied data and data sources like Google does, to generate deeper business insights, is an emerging and fast growing mega-trend. Other industries such as retail banking, telecommunications, and energy have already shown how they are reshaping their business models by leveraging new data sources. For example, energy providers use smart metering to collect energy usage data of private households to improve energy efficiency. Independent Internet applications such as "smappee"[1] will turn private households into smarter, more energy-efficient homes, by providing real-time energy readings as well as consumption costs to allow appliances to be switched on and off remotely. By combining key mega-trends including "Industry 4.0" and emerging digitization capabilities, insurers have enormous potential to optimize their existing operating environment and business models.

Industry 4.0 is a trend that combines automation and data exchange with manufacturing technologies. It includes cyber-physical systems, the IoT, and cloud computing, and supports a concept called a "smart factory". In short, cyber-physical systems integrate computation, networking, and physical processes and enable physical processes to affect computers. Smart factory environments converge virtual and the physical worlds through cyber-physical systems allowing the fusion of technical and business processes, key to delivering a new industrial age – the Industry 4.0 concept.

Within modularly structured smart factories, cyber-physical systems monitor physical processes and create a virtual copy of the physical world. This allows them to make decentralized decisions. Cyber-physical systems communicate and cooperate with one another in real time. The basic principle is that by connecting machines, material, and systems, businesses are creating intelligent networks along the entire value chain that can control each other autonomously. Some examples include machines that can predict failures and trigger maintenance processes autonomously, or self-organized logistical systems that react to unexpected changes in production. These emerging system interactions offer some great potential to turn business logics in the insurance sector upside down.

Enormous Potential for Insurance Companies to Gain Profitability

While existing business logics in the insurance industry are focused on innovating primarily across the claim settlement processes, future opportunities will concentrate on technical improvements to prevent claims from occurring in the first place. Following Insurance Europe's report from the European Insurance

---

[1] http://www.smappee.com.

and Reinsurance Federation, European non-life insurers paid out €313 billion in claims to insureds in 2014. Of that amount, €98.8 billion was for motor insurance, €94.1 billion for health insurance, and €53.7 billion for property insurance claims.[2] These figures show the enormous potential for insurance companies to optimize their financial balances and gain profitability by using innovative technologies to prevent claims.

The change of business models will also require a shift in current business logics. In the existing business models, premiums are the main focus to generate profits as insurance companies collect insurance premiums to invest on the capital market. With current ongoing low interest rate policies, this revenue model is at stake. With the appearance of innovative business models, insurance companies need to turn their gaze towards the very beginning of the process chain as it needs to avoid claims to retain profitability. It is a change from a backward-oriented approach towards a forward-oriented approach. This business approach requires a new alignment with all sorts of manufacturers to allow the provision of relevant data.

Big Data Technologies Enabling Data-driven Business Models

Big data analytics is the technique that automates the process of collecting, processing, contextualizing, and analysing large sets of data, commonly referred to as big data, to uncover patterns that help a business make better decisions. Big data analytics differs from traditional data analytics because it can capture and analyse data sets that are very large, move fast, and lack a common structure. In modern digital businesses, data is the currency that guides all decisions and actions. Complete and accurate

analysis empowers insurance companies to develop data-driven business models. Unfortunately, the analytics tools and processes most insurance companies rely on are not designed to analyse the volume, velocity, and variety of big data in today's modern business. To harness the opportunities of big data, insurance companies must adopt a big data analytics platform that is optimized to handle high volume and real-time data streaming.

With new data analytics tools in place, insurance companies can analyse multiple sources of data, from weather patterns to social media, which can help them to profile customer's behaviour and to streamline costs, be more targeted with the risks they want to underwrite, predict fraud, or identify claims that have the potential to become very expensive. Furthermore, data providing insights on the usage of products or the lifestyle of an insured customer deliver even greater value to insurance companies. Insurance companies will be able to monitor and analyse maintenance cycles and repair statuses of machinery via intelligent sensors, security and safety measures of private homes via smart home devices, as well as health-checks cycles of insured customers via smart watches.

Identifying Sources to Collect and Analyse Relevant Data

Technology and innovative analytics algorithms are one thing. To reshape the existing business models of insurance companies, we also need to find ways to collect data relating to the state of customers' insured assets as well as causes of damage at every possible point and event within that insured's life. While more and more physical assets are fitted with sensors and network connectivity, insurance companies need to create new business processes to get hold of these important data sets. While it is in their best interest to improve the reliability of their machinery, manufacturers will take the opportunity to equip their products and facilities with sensors and network connectivity to control and maintain on-premise running assets. Manufacturers can monitor

[2] European Insurance – Key Facts 2015, August 2015, page 22, https://www.insuranceeurope.eu/sites/default/files/attachments/European%20Insurance%20-%20Key%20Facts%20-%20August%202015.pdf.

current machinery conditions as well as maintenance cycles to ensure the timely high reliability and availability of all kinds of assets.

This trend will help insurance companies to gather all kinds of relevant data once connected to the manufacturer's databases. The information collected through big data technology is of high value to insurance companies as it delivers insights into the way policy-holders are taking care of their insured assets. Insurance companies therefore need to find an approach to align their interest with those of the manufacturers and get hold of the analysed usage and maintenance information. This will lead traditional insurance companies to innovate and become a "smart insurance provider". Insurance companies therefore need to create dynamic business networks with all sorts of organizations such as car manufacturers, machinery suppliers, smart home technology providers, as well as health institutions to collect and analyse all kinds of relevant data (see Figure 1).

This business approach will have a deep impact on the business logic of modern insurance companies. Collecting, analysing, and interpreting big data requires new competencies within the industry and new roles, such as network managers and big data analysts. Network managers will be responsible for organizing and orchestrating the new insurance ecosystems to ensure a constant flow of data from all kinds of data sources. Data analysts, however, will take charge of extracting relevant data points and translating

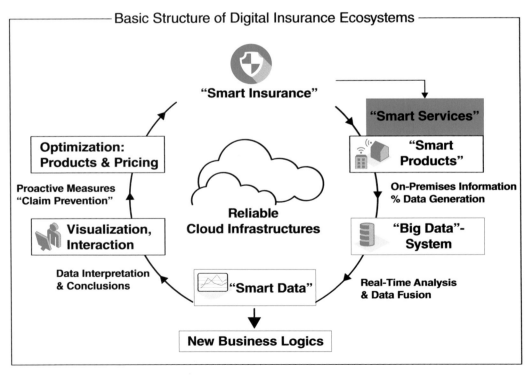

Figure 1: **Business logic and data infrastructure of "smart insurance"**

them into pricing decisions. This will help insurance companies to improve their claim statistics and dramatically reduce claim volumes. This approach landmarks a forward integration of insurance companies to make use of digital technologies and significantly increase profits.

Individualized Offerings Based on Prevention Efforts

When collecting machinery and customer data to reduce claim volumes, insurance companies can offer much better terms and conditions to their customers, helping them to prevent accidents or damages. Insurers can also develop completely new individualized pricing models based on the prevention efforts undertaken by the insureds. The more the insureds take care of their assets, the more likely it is that claim volumes will decrease. This means that insurers will be prepared to calculate and offer far more attractive premium rates. This will finally lead to a win-win situation for customers and insurance companies.

But existing insurance companies need to watch out carefully, as this innovative business approach is likely to bring new competitive threats. It allows aggressive startups and data specialists to step into the market and redefine existing business logics. For example, UK-based insurance company Drive like a girl[3] offers premiums that are connected to the driving style of the insured. The company fits a telematics box about the size of a mobile phone into the customer's car. Telematics technology allows the gathering of accurate information about the individual driving profile of each customer, so the insurance company can calculate individual premiums instead of just offering gender-neutral premiums based on group statistics. Established insurance companies are well advised to start their data activities right now and learn how to profit from using big data to extend their current business model and prevent newcomers from gaining significant market share.

---

[3] www.drivelikeagirl.com.

True Business Model Innovation – a Credit-Based Approach

By Tobias Taupitz
Co-Founder and CEO, LAKA

Status Quo

The Financial Services sector is facing an unprecedented level of innovation. Business models are constantly challenged: from banking to payments, and capital markets to lending and saving, culminating in the term FinTech. Numerous challenger brands were established, which forced incumbents to rethink their offerings, to the benefit of consumers.

The insurance sector, however, has *successfully* avoided deep transformation and seems to be largely driven by corporate needs (capital requirements, pressure on investment yields, large loss events, etc.), rather than the desire to improve the customer proposition.

In the General Insurance space, customers are frustrated with high premiums and cumbersome processes, while insurers are suspicious of overstated or fraudulent claims. It is a vicious cycle.

Thinking about the mechanics behind an insurance contract, the conflict of interest is clear: one additional claim paid reduces the (underwriting) profit of the insurer. Equally, a delayed payment allows the insurer to generate another day, week, or month of investment income. Customers are rarely regarded as a key stakeholder on par with shareholders. Premiums charged during a period are the maximum revenue that an insurer can generate for providing cover for the risk of loss. It is therefore inevitable to manage the underlying parts closely.

To date, claims are still predicted on the basis of proprietary knowledge (though with ever-increasing accuracy) and margins are added on top: risk buffer, operating expenses, and profit. Profit margins are largely dictated by shareholders' demands while costs continue to increase. Between 2005 and 2015, commissions and expenses grew annually by 1.5% and 0.8% for motor and property insurance, respectively.[1]

Settling claims appears to be the only part of the equation that is not fixed. The fewer claims that are settled, the higher the profits for the insurer. The willingness of an insurer to settle claims has become an increasingly heated discussion. The mantra of an insurer being bound to act within the agreed terms and conditions, and as such a legally binding contract, is a poor one from a customer's perspective.

It is a business model designed to cause friction and results in conflict of interest. It will require a tremendous effort to move back to a time where protection for an uncertain outcome was regarded as a service to society.

Signs of Change

Today, the product offering in the life insurance sector is already shifting, moving away from underwriting to fee-based income. This shift is being driven by external factors such as increasing asset management activities. A company formerly known as The Standard Life Assurance Company claims to be "building a world-class investment company" – and with around 92% of their total income being fee-based in 2015, they may rightfully claim so.[2]

[1] Association of British Insurers; own calculations.

[2] Standard Life, Annual Report 2015.

However, one might argue that the shift from traditional guarantee-based to unit-linked products, where the customer bears the investment risk, predominately helps the insurer, not the customer.

Turning to the dynamics in the General Insurance space, significant change to the centuries-old operating model has yet to come. The focus tends to be on improving operational efficiency with general insurers increasingly looking for collaboration with InsurTech startups to enhance their traditional service.

If a business model has not changed materially over the course of several centuries, it either means that the best model was chosen outright or that the sector in question has so far successfully avoided transformation. If the latter is the prevailing situation, one should expect to see alternative models emerge that might better cater for customers' specific needs – it's just a matter of time.

To date, we have seen attempts to enhance the traditional model through solutions commonly referred to as peer-to-peer insurance. Most of these firms recognize the inherent conflict of interest between customer and insurer, and have developed their own solutions to this problem, such as returning excess premiums to customers or donating them to charity.

One might argue, however, that the answer to the industry's problems cannot be derived from a deviation of the existing actuarial model. At the end of the day, if premiums are paid back in part at the end of the year, it simply means that too much was taken from the customer in the first place.

A New Credit-based Approach

Regulators recognize the need for new approaches and have set up innovation hubs and sandbox initiatives in cities such as Abu Dhabi, London, and Singapore. A changing regulatory landscape acts as the catalyst for change and enables firms to deviate from known paths and allows them to challenge every single component in the value chain.

What is more, one can let go of an operating model that is based on the actuarially predicted level of losses, with the main risk being the underwriting risk. This paves the way for a new avenue: a credit risk-based offering. A credit risk-based model means customers will pay at the end of a period, with the benefit of knowing the exact value of claims settled. Customers can join a group of peers who are like-minded risk takers and are looking to protect similar items. At the end of a period, the group will share the cost of all claims settled equally.

Linking revenues to the actual value of claims handled and paid, by adding a fixed fee per claim, aligns with the interest customers. The firm generates revenue when acting in the best interest of customers: settling their claims. The monthly payments that customers make in this new model will vary, as they are directly correlated to the number of claims. However, customers will be protected from an extreme circumstance through an aggregate Excess of Loss agreement provided by re/insurance partners.

From a customer perspective, they receive two benefits during the onboarding process: the maximum price they will ever have to pay in the period, and the much lower average price they can expect to pay.

Requesting payment at the end of the month based on the true cost of claims will result in a direct correlation between a group of customers and their payments. This fixes a common issue in today's insurance landscape: accountability. The fewer claims that occur in a month, the less the affinity group will have to pay. A group's behaviour directly correlates to their payments. It is therefore essential to group customers into similar risk pools. Risk education and prevention will play a crucial role in this proposition to help reduce negative experiences before they even occur.

True, a cost-plus model introduces credit risk where there is little at the moment. The real question is which can be managed better, underwriting or credit risk. With the deep expertise from credit card and lending space, managing the latter should be feasible.

Credit-based models are the new reality and will come to market soon. One example of a company using this type of model is my venture, UK-based company LAKA[3] – our goal is to support the development of a new world.

---

[3] www.laka.co.uk.

From Event-Focused Insights to Coaching

By Benjamin Von Euw
Enterprise Architect, iA Financial Group

According to the Cambridge Dictionary, insurance is defined as the agreement, between two parties, in which the insured pays a company money to gain access to security, and the company pays the costs if the insured suffers an accident, sustains injury, or endures loss. This, by default, means the event has happened, or is occurring randomly rather than according to plan. Whether you're talking about life insurance or Property & Casualty (P&C), individual or group insurance, insurers collect premiums and issue unilateral contracts that will be executed if a random event occurs. The traditional business model relies on random facts and events, but are they truly random or just out of control today?

Traditional Insurance Business Relies on Lack of Knowledge

For centuries, humans believed in spontaneous generation, coherently synthesized by the well-respected Aristotle. Aristotle explains that lives generate spontaneously from non-living sources such as a piece of tissue. However, in 1859, thanks to a more rigorous experiment, Louis Pasteur inhibited bacterial growth and proved that life wasn't generated spontaneously from non-living sources. Biogenesis, the generation of life from existing life, was born. Later we discovered that it was much more efficient to heal people by giving them a pill than performing bloodletting; which human characteristics were transmitted from parent to child via DNA; and, more recently, studies are demonstrating how ancestral climates may have shaped the human nose.[1] One day we will probably know how to treat cancer and maybe learn that the gender of a baby is not that random either.

In fact, after investigation, most random events can be explained as non-random. For example, an airplane crash is usually the consequence of technical or human failure that can be avoided or weather that can be anticipated thanks to meteorology. Even a toast landing butter-side down might not be that random, but depends on its weight, shape, and the table height. For years, companies worked hard to analyse and understand car crashes. Their self-driving cars have already driven millions of kilometres. They can potentially save lives and make traditional insurance less relevant.

The traditional insurance business model for the most part still assigns randomness to death, sickness, or accidents but this must change to a more deterministic criterion as our knowledge increases.

Digital Ecosystems Lead a New Era of Knowledge

Data generated by digital ecosystems is the key component for new knowledge. We now generate and record more data than we have for whole generations passed. This evolution improves our ability to acquire knowledge faster especially when we can make the data "talk" to deliver data-driven insight. Data collection has also become much easier since most is automatically generated, recorded, and shared without needing human surveillance or input.

Whether your data is shared by you or by someone else, digital ecosystems live track and record our entire life and its environment: habits, location, weather, health, wealth, family, friends … They know what we say, listen to, write … and some technology has even been announced to be working on reading our thoughts.[2] Finally, it's becoming almost impossible for people to lie, cheat, commit fraud, or be fully anonymous when data are cross-checked: for

---

[1] https://www.nytimes.com/2017/03/16/science/ancestral-climates-may-have-shaped-your-nose.html.

[2] https://www.facebook.com/zuck/videos/vb.4/10103661167577621.

example, according to Facebook[3] insights, even if your status is set to "single", the number and content of discussions will lead to the conclusion that you are dating someone.

The power of digital ecosystems is that they not only focus on specific industry data. They allow the user to use approaches and technologies such as business and artificial intelligence to analyse a huge amount of open and private data from a variety of applications, systems, industries, and government, which helps them to identify more and more sophisticated patterns. At first it might appear to be way too much information but they are not limited to a few characteristics to create groupings that can perfectly describe a person, an event, or an item to reduce margins of error. Even if only a very low percentage of those data are analysed today, they will later help to find new patterns and relationships between facts we ignore today. Compared to traditional insurance companies, big tech companies are much more advanced because of their access to this data and they can compare it over billions of customers.

Data doesn't lie, but it only delivers the right insight when you know how to handle it. Insurance companies might have been one of the first industries to analyse data, life tables, and statistics to determine premiums with the help of actuaries. However, in this new race to data, knowledge, and sophisticated patterns, they must become data specialists, rely on data-driven insight, and become part of digital ecosystems if they don't want to be bypassed by new players.

The One who Knows can Anticipate and Influence the Future

Analytics helps to understand what happened and improves knowledge. This knowledge forms different patterns, and can be very powerful: not limited to the past, it can lead its owner to anticipate and influence the future. Vaccines you get to avoid being sick is a good example of something that has been observed, analysed, and is now anticipating and influencing your future health. While some companies are looking to ship you a package before you even buy it,[4] it's easy to imagine many cases where data gives insight on what you want before you even ask for it.

Later, patterns might reveal that the formula used to calculate life expectancy can be replaced by a much more complex, accurate, and personal equation of life derived from a series of parameters including your DNA, eating habits, physical activity levels, location, employment, friends, happiness, and health conditions. We still have lots to discover, but remember that thanks to progress, increased knowledge, and better control on events we now live much longer. Crazy science fiction stories from books such as *From the Earth to the Moon* by Jules Verne or movies like *Minority Report* have become scientific fact. More recently, by watching eight factors, we discovered that artificial intelligence can predict heart attacks more accurately than the doctor can![5]

Industry should also use knowledge and anticipation to improve its own processes: why ask people to fill out forms and require exams to get a quote when you can collect it? Why ask them again to claim when you can anticipate it? Those activities have no value for the customer and are "mudas":[6] meaning that the client is not willing to pay for that, doesn't want to wait, and is already too busy or shocked, dealing with the loss of a relative, an accident, or a house fire. Data insight gives insurers the opportunity to anticipate a client's expectations, bypass forms, process claims in seconds,

---

[3] https://www.facebook.com/notes/facebook-data-science/the-formation-of-love/10152064609253859.

[4] https://blogs.wsj.com/digits/2014/01/17/amazon-wants-to-ship-your-package-before-you-buy-it.

[5] https://www.engadget.com/2017/04/16/ai-can-predict-heart-attacks-more-accurately-than-doctors.

[6] A Japanese word and key concept of Lean manufacturing, meaning useless or non-value added activity, waste.

or even "auto-claim" with smart contracts. This might mean more operational spending because more claims are processed, but it also means better customer satisfaction and less fraud. How high would customer satisfaction be if the customer received coverage without having to apply and get their refund and support without having to claim it?

The biggest value of data and knowledge is not understanding the past but anticipating and shaping the future. Knowledge will not only help to serve clients better, but will lead to big changes in the insurance industry's business model, pivoting it to anticipation, streaming, real time, and automation.

Coaching, the Future of Insurance

Prevention is more effective than detection and reaction. Clients would be happier if insurers helped them to live longer, healthier, richer lives, while avoiding fire, robberies, and other incidents. For example, instead of paying the life insurance policy to your beneficiary after your death, your insurance company could send you to the hospital right before you had a heart attack. To make it possible, insurers will act as coaches: develop a strong and close relationship with the client, analyse their behaviour, give them instant feedback, and offer rewards to influence behaviour. They will share their knowledge to help others making better products such as food, drugs, cars, and tools, and influence the environment with strategic investments in organic food and healthy activities.

Do people want a personal coach? How will people react if they are tracked 24 hours a day and we tell them what to do? Do they want to know everything rather than preserve a bit of randomness and mystery in life? Coaching can train a bad driver but how do you react when genetics play a role, for example, with chromosome abnormality? What will be the consequence if a client refuses to follow coaching recommendations? Will it remain a recommendation or become mandatory? How will insurer robots deal with racism, sexism, and handicaps? Who will be responsible for decisions?

Moreover, any coach can make mistakes. As with spontaneous generation and many other theories "proven" … before being proven to be wrong. For decades, to prevent people developing potentially deadly peanut allergies, allergists recommended that the young avoid consuming them for as long as possible. However, a study conducted recently demonstrated[7] that sustained consumption of peanuts beginning in the first 11 months of life was more effective in preventing the development of allergies. Worse, though, is that the previous recommendation of allergists might have contributed to the rise of peanut and other food allergies. How would insurers react if for decades they promoted a lifestyle choice that is then known to have a negative impact on the lives of those people? Beyond the legal challenges, the industry must address a lot of ethical issues.

Insurers should not be limited to only helping clients during the life event, they should also influence the whole life ecosystem. This new value proposition requires insurers to answer new questions, redefine the traditional business model, including key partners, activities and resources, customer relationships, segments, and channels.

Conclusion

Finally, insurance has been considered a good way to transfer and mitigate risks, but is now becoming good at limiting and even avoiding them. The traditional business model focuses on the reaction to adopt in case of a random event but it will not survive the techs. Because of their capacity to find relationships and patterns in the most random data and bring disruptive changes, the traditional insurance business model will be replaced by coaching. It will become a more proactive partnership where an insurance company will be well connected to ecosystems, to support its clients in accomplishing their personal goals, avoiding random risk, and influencing its environment. It will evolve and deal globally and to do so it must be based on trust and address important privacy and ethical questions.

---

[7] http://www.leapstudy.co.uk.

One of the most unique attributes of InsurTech is its ability to harness technology from other industries

Adopting a "Tech-First" Mindset Is Non-Negotiable

- Millennials will soon be dominating the workforce

- Younger workers demand more meaningful roles in their company. Insurers need to start viewing employees as partners instead of workers

InsurTech's big question: why the customer is still always right?

- For Insurers to harness the power of AI today – they need: data, capital and know-how

- IoT has already scored notable successes in the insurance sector with motor insurance

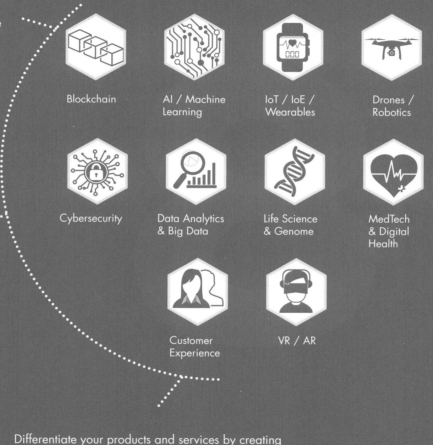

Blockchain

AI / Machine Learning

IoT / IoE / Wearables

Drones / Robotics

Cybersecurity

Data Analytics & Big Data

Life Science & Genome

MedTech & Digital Health

Customer Experience

VR / AR

Differentiate your products and services by creating beautiful and delightful experiences that elicit an emotional connection with customers

The InsurTech's Action List

- Many claims processes are routine, so can be successfully completed through robotic automation

- GDPR, present challenges for the industry as a whole by shifting the burden of proof and reliance on insurance contract language when dealing with claims

- Platforms now interrogate social media and find patterns that claim investigators would struggle to identify through video and voice stress analytics

Blockchain start-ups – Unlikely heroes for the insurance industry?

- 10% of global gross domestic product will be stored on blockchain technology by 2025
- Blockchain can provide better data provenance, faster and more reliable claims handling via an accurate register of all assets, and the automation of policy enforcement

InsurTech and AI

Goal-based insurance is a way of trying to better understand customers

The smart journey: from contract hype to insurance reality

A smart contract as "code deployed to a distributed and replicated ledger, with an ability to control its own state and assets

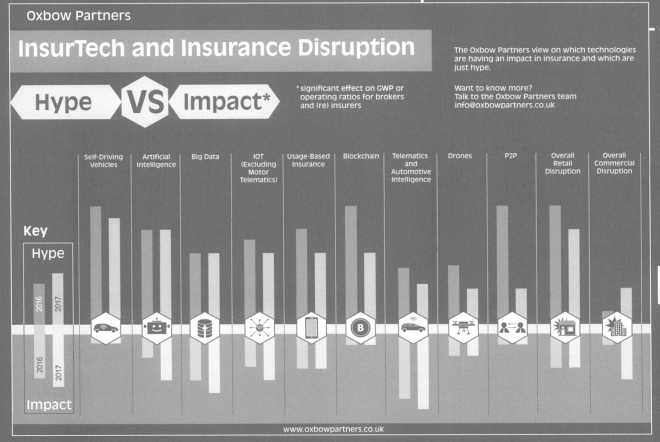

Oxbow Partners

InsurTech and Insurance Disruption

Hype **VS** Impact*

*significant effect on GWP or operating ratios for brokers and (re) insurers

The Oxbow Partners view on which technologies are having an impact in insurance and which are just hype.

Want to know more?
Talk to the Oxbow Partners team
info@oxbowpartners.co.uk

Key

Hype
2016 2017

Impact
2016 2017

Chart categories: Self-Driving Vehicles · Artificial Intelligence · Big Data · IOT (Excluding Motor Telematics) · Usage-Based Insurance · Blockchain · Telematics and Automotive Intelligence · Drones · P2P · Overall Retail Disruption · Overall Commercial Disruption

www.oxbowpartners.co.uk

Robots are taking over the world – the global robotics market will be worth +£100bn by 2020

As with the broader FinTech market, the debate continues about the power of technology shaping InsurTech. This is not just about the hyper-relevant role of data in predicting risk and disaster but equally about the changing technology-inspired business models provided by new entrants.

The topics covered in this part are broad:

- The connected insurer (IoT)
  The growth in IoT and the connected world means that we are witnessing data growth that is unprecedented. The data collected and processed daily from external sources is a key factor in enabling better risk modelling and predicting disaster.

- AI/machine learning
  AI and machine learning algorithms reduce company expenses, expedite daily operations, and lead to bigger opportunities in the marketplace.

- Augmented reality (AR)/virtual reality (VR)
  Using techniques such as virtual or augmented reality to model scenarios for commercial and personal risk are vastly empowering for insurers who are able to use scenario modelling to equip them better in dealing with disasters, claim handling complexity, and growing areas of risk such as those related to climate change and terrorism.

- Cyber security
  We are exposed to news headlines of a new cyber breach daily. Cyber-security crimes have increased globally and have created demand for an entire new area of insurance products. The cover is challenging given the digital nature and hence unpredictable contagion caused by cyber hacking or fraud.

- Drones
  This technology is advancing in leaps and bounds and serving as aerial "guards", delivery, and fulfilment as well as emergency support tools in natural disasters.

- Blockchain and smart contracts
  These support the ability to speed up service-level fulfilment in the claims handling process and with the traceable/ immutable nature of the blockchain can ensure that fraud is minimized.

- Data, data, data
  Insurance is underpinned by data captured historically and stored but then not used to its full potential. The world of InsurTech has offered up groundbreaking innovation in the areas of predictive modelling, IoT, and machine learning in ways that mean that historic data could become an obsolete way to measure future risk. New insurance policy structures are possible using predictive, external, and unstructured data.

Becoming Tech-First – Why Adopting a "Tech-First" Mindset is Non-Negotiable

By Julien Breteau
Head of Content Marketing, Intrepid Ventures

By 2025, the consumer landscape will be predominantly digital; insurers refusing to adapt to new workplace trends won't make the transformation and will eventually perish.

Adopting new technologies and digitizing the business is important. But an equal pillar to the company's success is helping employees become tech-first and educating them on how technology makes processing insurance (and their work) easier.

Instead of waiting days for a response, policy-holders now get instant access to important information like claim reimbursements, health scores, and reports at the touch of a button. However, instant feedback isn't only a must for customers, it's a must for employees too.

Most incumbents today are focusing on digitizing the customer experience. But that's a tiny piece of the puzzle. Almost as important, if not more important, is digitizing the employee experience.

By focusing on building for the employee as much as the customer, and by building an innovation-valuing company culture, where anyone is welcome to participate and contribute, incumbents can cement their future position in the industry.

Creating the Right Workplace

Productivity and innovation are stifled by corporate structures and complex systems. Although stringent legacy models persist in most industry giants to this day, refusal to change gears directly impacts their ability to invest in (and become a part of) the growing digital economy.

Currently, the tides favour digital-born companies, who can capture markets without being held back by legacy systems. Removing rigid structure makes room for flexible business.

Using technology to streamline operations enables them to:

- hire fewer employees, and report higher market capitalization per employee
- develop agile programs and designs in days, instead of months or years
- fill important roles by quickly finding the right people
- boost time for innovation and research on new projects
- rapidly respond to market changes.

In order to create the right workplace for employees, insurance companies need to understand that employees expect a digital experience as much as any customer. Far too many insurance companies are still pushing paper. Outdated and rigid legacy systems are still in use. This not only affects the customer journey, from enrolment to claims processing, but also frustrates employees and forces the best people to find new jobs.

Attracting the Best Talent

Millennials will soon be dominating the workforce. Across the globe younger workers demand more meaningful roles in their company. Insurers need to start viewing employees as partners instead of workers.

Begin first by understanding the millennial mindset. The millennial workforce:

- value flexibility in work schedules
- want lots of feedback (to stay on track and up-to-date)
- believe integrating technology is unavoidable
- expect to be listened to and have opinions respected.

Having a reputation for growing and nurturing talent is a big attraction to the most ambitious candidates across Gen Z and Gen Y. These generations are hungry for growth and big learning experiences and relish opportunities to travel, experience new cultures, and build their skills.

One approach to this is to ask fast-track candidates to spend time across different functions in different locations before promoting them to management positions. This approach not only better prepares your best talent by experiencing the digital transformations each aspect of your business is going through, it also helps attract them.

Millennials are drawn to the entrepreneurial experience. Companies known for giving these opportunities will be the ones able to attract the best talent from around the world.

However, sending employees across to experience different functions or countries isn't enough. Companies have to ensure that the environment and feedback loop is in place to make this a valuable experience for both the company and the employee. Maintaining a partnership approach in the employee's career track is vital. Companies can ensure managers maintain a positive relationship with the best talents by:

- acknowledging their merits
- providing feedback on completed tasks
- encouraging them to speak up and be involved

- communicating face-to-face even in a digital world. Newer generations prefer personal meetings when discussing important matters
- rallying the entire team to be decisive and strategic.

In similar fashion, we can burgeon innovation in the following ways:

- **Introducing new technologies**
  AI and machine learning algorithms reduce company expenses, expedite daily operations, and lead to bigger opportunities in the marketplace.
- **Examining relationships between products/services**
  Pinpointing human behaviours that lead to good and bad outcomes during interactions with applications, websites, and salespeople.
- **Challenging teams to help individuals achieve their goals**
  Complement applications with offers to minimize unhealthy behaviours among employees and policy-holders.

The sooner the incumbents adopts a tech-first mindset, the sooner they'll be attracting, hiring, and retaining the best talent available.

Change is Inevitable

Currently, there are several well-known companies making bold advances with new technologies (machine learning in particular). For instance, Google has been researching algorithms and their relationship to "problem-solving" since they've started, but they've only recently *really* put the pedal to the floor in regards to AI.

Google's star of the show is none other than DeepMind, the research program responsible for AlphaGo, a highly-competitive AI system that, in late 2015, beat the world champion of Go (a game that requires complex multi-level cognition) – a task many had sworn impossible.

AlphaGo's success still sends ripples of concern to those who fear that AI may become uncontrollable. To combat this, John Giannandrea, Google's head of search and its AI chief, believes machine learning research should become Google's top priority over any other venture.[1]

Smarter algorithms for information processing are being worked on every day, but companies who fail to innovate won't be capable of accommodating newer machines and applications – leaving only a small window of opportunity to catch up before losing their place forever.

Change is inevitable … don't get left behind.

For the Greater Good

As companies begin to adopt a tech-first mindset, the most important thing to remember is to keep testing, keep refining, and keep building. Most players are still learning how to approach these new technologies. But the shift doesn't have to happen overnight. Companies need to:

- perform extensive research and develop proof-of-concepts
- consult with employees for their opinions and insights
- launch, test, and repeat.

There are countless emerging technologies such as blockchain, wearables, and AI that insurance companies should be looking

at. The technology is already there for these large incumbents to reduce their operating costs by 60–70%.[2]

What's important to remember is that this overhaul requires an end-to-end transformation. Both the front end (customer experience) and the back end (employee experience) are vital to a company's success. Digital platforms for claims, online enrolment, and accessing medical networks that service the customers must also translate into digital processing for the employees. Too often we're seeing a digital platform on the customer side and a manual, labour-intensive platform on the employee side.

The changes the industry is about to experience are unprecedented and are required on a massive scale. But it doesn't have to start on a massive scale. We know the technology is there for insurance companies to build end-to-end digital insurance platforms that make use of blockchain, AI, machine learning, chatbots, etc. with the capability to automate several aspects of the insurance experience. So why not start there? By building an end-to-end platform and testing it.

Large incumbents are focused on trying to collaborate with and integrate new platforms, however as they often operate on overly complex and workforce reliant legacy systems, this poses a big "risk".

Ideally insurers should be spending an equal amount of time building new platforms top to bottom – starting afresh – and building an insurance platform that's separate from the constraints of corporate structures. Somewhere where innovation and flexibility are not stifled by silos and never ending hierarchies.

---

[1] Backchannel, "How Google is Remaking Itself as a Machine Learning First Company" by Steven Levey, 23 June 2016, https://backchannel.com/how-google-is-remaking-itself-as-a-machine-learning-first-company/

[2] McKinsey & Company, "What drives insurance operations costs?" by Björn Münstermann, Georg Paulus, and Ulrike Vogelgesang, April 2015, http://www.mckinsey.com/industries/financial-services/our-insights/what-drives-insurance-operating-costs

Start there, and slowly grow. I'm not talking about running a PR exercise where every month the company gets to announce it's working on "X" technology. This is about building a real business, from the ground up. Give the best and most eager employees the chance to participate in the process. Let them learn from a tech-first team. Let them come up with their own ideas and give them the opportunity to build on them.

Maybe then we'll start to see empowered employees who are creative and take initiative, freed from the constraints of corporate legacy culture.

Research. Build. Test. Launch. Repeat.

It's a simple process.

Practical Robotics in Insurance – The Future is Here Already

By Tony Tarquini
Director of Insurance EMEA, Pegasystems Limited

Robots are taking over the world. They are no longer sci-fi fantasy and today robots powered by artificial intelligence (AI) can clean your house, educate the young, care for the old, and fetch your wine and slippers. Reports suggest that the global robotics market will be worth £100 billion+ by 2020.[1] This chapter concentrates on the specifics of robotics, rather than the full spectrum of artificial intelligence (AI), which incorporates neural networks, data science and machine learning, and the many other categories in between, which constitute the world of AI.

Robotics is a powerful, tactical tool that, utilized correctly within a clear architecture and roadmap, can deliver significant, immediate cost and quality benefits, particularly against repetitive, manual tasks and legacy connectivity. However, robotics is not a strategic, enterprise-level transformation tool nor a silver bullet.

Today the insurance industry is just starting out on the robotics journey and very little is understood about what robotics can do for insurance and how. Even less is known about what is commercially viable today and what is still a pipe dream.

This chapter discusses the different forms of robotics available to insurers and when to use them, what is commercially viable, and why some projects fail. It will also consider the importance of people and robots working together, with governance and oversight over the robots. Six key areas are examined.

_____
[1] http://fortune.com/2016/02/24/robotics-market-multi-billion-boom/.

When to Deploy Robotics in an Insurance Organization

The main characteristic of a robotics-ready environment is where the concept of quality prevails over quantity, volume, and cheap labour. In a successful robotics environment, productivity increases by relegating non-value-added (NVA) work to robots and concentrating human activities on intelligent work in parts of the business process that are customer-centric.

Robotics can have significant impact when people are obviously doing things by rote in order to fill in the gaps or when business is moving too quickly for standard solutions. It is particularly effective in situations where:

- legacy systems and processes (particularly multiple legacies) inhibit productivity;
- APIs or services don't exist;
- service/API integration is too slow or too expensive to deliver ROI;
- problems are currently solved through training, documentation, and process outsourcing.

In all these situations, it is external customer demand that has overtaken traditional interactions and processes from where and how they originated, often prompted by more agile competitors and InsurTech startups redefining industry practices. The traditional insurer is left behind and has to race to catch up, otherwise others will step in and their customers will disappear.

However, robotics does not significantly re-engineer business processes enough to deliver the full benefit of transformation and these tactical quick wins should be recognized as valuable only within a long-term strategic transformational plan.

What are the Typical Benefits Robotics Can Deliver?

The benefits that can be derived from using robotics within an insurance environment centre on operational improvement, productivity increases through efficiency and effectiveness, increased quality of execution, performance recording, and improvement in customer and staff experience.

- The first benefit insurers gain from robotics is an improved operational resilience through an ability to manage resource capacity during operational peaks and troughs.

- Typically a robot produces three times the output of one full-time employee and works 24/7 without benefits at 50% of the cost of an off-shore human resource. As a result, average time to complete a process can be reduced by 40–60%, both in terms of elapsed time and man-hours, thus reducing costs by 30–80%.

- Instilling 100% accuracy and consistency eradicates the costs associated with errors and omissions and rework.

- The creation of a full audit trail eases regulatory compliance and facilitates risk management.

- Robotics enhances customers' experience by reducing wait times and accuracy of execution.

- Simultaneously, it raises staff satisfaction by reducing monotonous working practices.

- By using robotics, insurers can accelerate time to value and return on investment. A reasonable expectation is for a robotics process to be designed, configured, tested, and deployed in around six to eight weeks and ROI to be realized in three to six months: not the timescales associated with traditional project business cases.

The Different Types of Robotics and When and How to Use Them

The world of robotics is rapidly evolving: in the products available, the terminology used to describe them, and the burgeoning list of vendors in the market. No one product is the answer to all situations, and insurers should ensure they carefully consider the applicability of any one tool or type of technology when establishing a business case for a project. It is also crucial to establish how it integrates with other technologies such as business process management, case management, and AI and exploit what they bring, rather than trying to recreate them. In many cases it is the integration with these other technologies (and the ongoing maintenance) in a larger transformation that can determine the strength of the robotics business case. A unified architecture is a major advantage.

Virtually all recognized robotics vendors maintain that the majority of their revenues come from customers in the US$1 billion+ or even US$10 billion+ turnover category; the economics of robotics is very much about scale and its geography is mainly large international insurers.

However, while it is certainly true to say that the established market for robotics is larger insurers, vendors are almost always either small (organizations with <US$20 million turnover) or smaller autonomous divisions of larger technology vendors. Careful due diligence is a watchword for larger corporations putting strategic reliance on the capabilities, R&D, future direction, and commercial stability of considerably smaller vendors, some with exposed commercial futures.

As the established analyst companies focus on the robotics market, some conformity of terminology is emerging to facilitate better comparisons and the opportunity to explain the application of different tools to different business problems.

Chatbots

Increasingly deployed and increasingly sophisticated, tools in this area are coming fast and furious. However, what is crucial here is that the digital business model for customer service should be able to maintain customer conversations both online and offline, ranging from an AI-based neuro-linguistic programming (NLP) chat (including sentiment analytics) either direct or embedded in something like Facebook Messenger, to a virtual chat with a customer service agent, to the traditional face-to-face interaction.

The really tricky bit is handling the context, and continuing the conversation outside the silo of the chat channel. Insurers must provide that continuum of context, and be able to go from machine learning and predictive analytics-based interactions, to chat-based conversations, to robotic process automation, and be able to transition the conversation to a human when and if needed. People and robots working together and passing the Turing Test, with governance and oversight over the robots, will be considered a crucial objective and likely to be a key differentiator for many years for any insurer planning to enter this arena in the near future.

Robotic Process Automation (RPA). RPA maps processes for the robot to replicate in order to move data between screens and databases, execute actions and calculations, create audit trails, and trigger further robotics processes or functionality from other tools and technologies. RPA essentially falls into two main categories: Unattended and Attended.

A. Unattended
  Normally cited on a server, Unattended RPA tends to replicate full end-to-end processes and give close to 100%

improvement across smaller groups of workers on more simple processes such as fraud detection and AML checks. However, the history of robotics is littered with Unattended RPA failures because it does not suit many situations. Also, where significant numbers of process exceptions exist, overambitious business cases do not stack up. Unattended RPA technologies tend to be based predominantly on screen scraping and OCR.

B. Attended (also called Robotic Desktop Automation – RDA)
  Normally cited on a user's desktop, Attended RPA tends to replicate smaller task automation for individual employees and gives 10–20% improvement across larger groups of workers on processes such as address change, payment change, and fund transfers. The incidences of success are far higher with Attended RPA and the time to value is far faster. Attended RPA tends to be based predominantly on injection technologies that sit between the applications and the operating system. Many consider this to be the future of RPA.

Workforce Intelligence Systems

The old adage that "what is not measured cannot be managed" is never truer than in robotics. Most insurers are blissfully unaware that they operate at approximately 40% productivity. By measuring, managing, and applying the correct technology this can be increased to 60%+, indeed probably up to 70%. At 80%, intensity is too high to be sustainable and if measurement is not maintained, productivity falls back rapidly (Pegasystems Customer Guidance in Operational Performance Improvement 2017).

Measurement tools, which continuously assess activity, point out to management where productivity can be improved and whether a "fix" has been adopted. They are fundamentally central to a balanced, rational, and focused robotics strategy. This is technology that should be deployed as a cloud solution, mainly due to the need for fast reporting, peaks and troughs in activity, and the need to store significant data.

Identifying which Processes are Viable for Robotics

As described previously, the correct technology has to address the correct business problem. To maximize success, there are some key minimum characteristics to look out for when selecting the business process to be addressed:

- It should be predominantly rule based and not depend on human judgement.
- It should be supported by digital, preferably structured data.
- It should be functioning and stable.
- It should save significant time and complexity.
- It should be reusable and scalable across the business, including multiple geographies, with little or no adaption.
- For a proof of concept project, it is key that the process leverages the key systems of the company.

Examples of Processes that Can be Automated with Robots

Process selection typically falls into two categories: generic activities that can usually be undertaken in all organizations and those specific to the insurer. The former category includes processes such as users logging onto systems and applications, data extraction activity (e.g. from forms or websites) and the creation of an audit trail for operational and regulatory compliance purposes.

Processes specific to insurance might typically include:

- Address or payment changes and fund transfers
- Policy amendments
- Compliance checks
- Background validation, e.g. credit checks, fraud detection
- Data capture and triage for underwriting, particularly with extensive schedules originating in spreadsheets
- Autogeneration of documents
- Payment reconciliation
- Month end consolidation.

The Human Factor and the Role it Plays in Success

There is no doubt that robotics, alongside AI, elicits the same concerns over livelihood protection as with Luddites of the Industrial Revolution. Although replacing humans with automation technology has continued unabated since the nineteenth century, robotics, by its very name, raises particular human concerns and a successful program has to address these issues very thoughtfully.

Insurers must carefully explain the strategy of "taking the robot out of the humans", which will focus their staff on more complex, intellectually challenging activity and ensure humans and robots work in harmony together. Redirecting staff to activities with a higher requirement for judgement and an emphasis on interacting with customers rather than repetitive, rote activity, not only drives up NPS[2] scores with policy-holders but empowers staff and improves morale.

---

[2] NPS – the Net Promoter Score – is an index ranging from −100 to 100 that measures the willingness of customers to recommend a company's products or services to others. It is used as a proxy for gauging the customer's overall satisfaction with a company's product or service and the customer's loyalty to the brand.

Success is achieved through a bi-directional approach to achieving buy-in across the business. The biggest failure for any project is lack of committed top-down sponsorship, so this has to be very visible to all concerned. This, together with strong governance and the deployment of reusable standards across the business, is an essential component to achieving objectives.

However, this has to be combined with bottom-up behavioural change programs. These powerfully emphasize the personal benefits accruing to staff to prevent a negative attitude to adoption. Alongside expert team coaching on new skills and the celebration of success, they raise the probability of success at the grass roots level.

Summary

Robotics is not the answer to every problem and cannot deliver enterprise transformation. It is a rapidly evolving technology with enormous potential to shape businesses quickly. Care must be taken in choosing vendor partners, the right tools, and the correct targets for robotic deployment. However, with sensible strategy, informed execution, and a strong communication plan, robotics can add significant business improvement, future agility, and overall value to the operations of every traditional insurance organization operating today.

Frictionless Insurance in a Land of Utility

By Nigel Walsh
Partner, Deloitte

Imagine a world where "it just works". A phrase that was made famous by the world's most valuable company and most identifiable organizations – you would argue the two are not a coincidence!

"It just works" is a phrase that needs no introduction for most and it is usually delivered with such precision and poise that by default comes with a lifelong guarantee that even just reading it out loud brings most of us a warm smile. We know what it is and we trust it by default.

Of course this refers to an object that most happen to spend a lot of time on, but it won't necessarily save your life or be there for you in a crisis. It may of course play a material part in that journey – more on that later, should you ever need it.

No one wanted a music player, a phone, and an Internet device all in one (no one was ever asked!), or ever imagined these three unique things coming together until you gave it to them. Now you would find it hard to buy a device that wasn't this smart by default.

Devices that now can cost nearly £800, described with words that ooze empathy and feeling. It's never about what they do per se, more what they enable the owner to do with them. Equally, you open the box, there's no terms and conditions and no manual. It's intuitive so that almost anyone can work their way through it in no time at all. This for me can be summarized as *simplicity*.

Moving away from this to what I consider to be one of the world's best organizations at delivering on its promise – they are simply great at delivering. We have come to know that when we order something it's usually a great price and with us next day or in the hour, depending on what level of service we have signed up for. You know it's something you can lean on when you need it. This for me can be summarized as *execution*. In the UK, we have widely adopted contactless payments. It wasn't so long after Chip and Pin saved you the hassle of having to sign for your transaction and have the staff challenge you with two signatures that would never match. The next stage was the move to contactless cards that soon were enabled on most mobile devices and some watches. Now the sheer effort of having to take out my wallet, put in my card, and punch in my four digit pin is just another friction point I no longer expect. This for me can be summarized as *pace*.

Now, of course, I choose these organizations as almost everyone can relate and there's a high chance that we have experienced one, if not all, of them personally. Equally there are thousands of other firms that deliver great experiences day in day out. And that's what we do day in day out when we buy other things, be it a financial product or physical asset. We make comparisons, so by default every interaction we have sets the bar for what we expect regardless of what or who we are buying from. Now nine times out of ten these experiences follow a happy path and just work.

However, taking these three examples, simply put – table stakes just get higher and higher and the pace at which we expect and integrate change into our everyday life never ceases to amaze me. Today's innovation is tomorrow's baseline expectation.

So How Does all this Relate to Insurance Organizations?

Whether we are paying for goods, using a mobile device, or ordering something online – there is a lot for us to learn in all of these instances and how we specifically bring them together to match or exceed these ever-increasing table stakes relationships that are being defined and enhanced every single day.

For years, innovation was about breaking these parts down and making them more efficient, digital, and seamless (think marginal gains from Sir David Brailsford of British Cycling) of which there is still lots of mileage to go, specifically for legacy insurers. However, in many cases, good enough will no longer be just that. However, if you comb all of these three themes together (simplicity, execution, and pace), all of a sudden, you move from incremental (and still hugely important) change and benefit to exponential change for the end customer, be it personal lines, commercial lines, or enabling a broker in the middle of the two.

There are many reasons why we can and absolutely need do this now – importantly our attitude to doing and trying new things is now much more open. However, the downside is that our attention span has decreased at the same rate. It's an opportunity that insurers cannot miss out on, the alternative being that someone else will take advantage of this moment in time and own the client engagement going forward, an existential threat that has been identified again and again for insurers. So if we compare our phone, music player, and Internet device to financial services, addressing the unmet needs of consumers simply becomes tomorrow's default goal – let's not ask what customers want, but instead create something so desirable they can't live without it.

For random run-of-the-mill products, this is just fine. However, what happens when your product is a regulated contract that one day you or your family's life, someone else's life, your home, or your livelihood may need to depend on, and in a way that you never really wanted to find out just how good it is.

This, however, goes back to my original point: how and what we enable customers to achieve must be shared in the most appropriate way. An organization's most valuable asset these days is fast becoming its ability to tell a story, bringing customers on a journey – even if they may never use it or hope never to cash in on its promise. For mandatory products such as motor insurance, there is a base enablement, but then there are all the features that enable you to do so much more – breakdown cover, legal support, backup car should you need it, and much more. These are often provided by multiple different parties, orchestrated by an insurance brand. Can we truly tie all of these together in a frictionless experience for the end consumer?

Comparing this to my first example of a phone or even the motor manufacturer itself is quite interesting. In my examples, the brand itself owns the end-to-end promise or expectation with the customer, whether it's assumed or direct explicit responsibility for execution of the promise, even if others do the delivery. In the world of insurance, this is often not the case and may create additional friction points that the consumer is forced through.

There is a parody in the UK that goes along the lines of "computer says no" – or in my world, someone taking no accountability and blaming the process. We should apply the most simplistic approach and think like a customer. How as an organization do we empower front line staff to counter any friction points?

Legacy systems/processes and regulation are often used as reasons why things can't be done for the customer, while at the same time they are reasons we seek investment – either to remove legacy systems or to simplify and modernize them. These perceived barriers create the right ambition to drive change – it's all about how we look at them. Are we a large insurer with lots of legacy technical debt that means new regulation is painful and costly to adopt, or a small agile player than can turn quickly and use this to our competitive benefit in the race to win the customer?

When I Look at Simplicity, I Often Refer to this Quote: "Perfection is achieved not when there is nothing more to add, but when there is nothing left to take away"

Finally, simplicity is as important to our internal customers as it is to external end-users. The alternative is that we end up creating environments in which it is near impossible to do what people want most, i.e. deliver great experiences. Only the superhuman survive through a series of heroic swivel chair integrations while at the same time multitasking with a customer at the end of the phone. Efforts should be firmly focused here, as making life straightforward here will pay material dividends. If we take the end-to-end process and look at all the engagement and interaction points, be it broker, third-party supplier, or otherwise – then what would our world look like if we were to design from scratch a beautiful frictionless experience? That means interventions now to mitigate against issues later. I believe that this is what we have to do to make our environment a great place to work too!

Moving beyond simplicity, we need to focus next on how we execute, regardless of where or when we are in the perceived value chain – customers really don't care in their time of need. Ultimately, when a customer calls, we need to have all the processes, people, and capability laser focused to execute flawlessly and make them feel like they are the one and only thing on our mind.

We know why they call us and often when they will call us, e.g. the first frost of the year and so many other predictable events, so let's get one step ahead and when we call it's "Mr Walsh, we have been expecting your call" – or, better still, two steps ahead. In today's connected world, don't wait for the call: "Mr Walsh, we are expecting frost this week, these are the steps you can take now to avoid an event." Delivering experiences that mean the customer will never need to call changes the relationship and materially increases trust and value.

Pace is practically the only thing not slowing down! It feels as though for every day that passes, two actually go by. How traditional carriers keep up with this is an ever-increasing challenge. Startups and newer insurance organizations are not constrained by these rules and often play on this as an advantage. Their ability to offer product speed to market, or service new clients or new products in an entirely different way, quite simply changes the traditional relationship that we have come to loathe and expect.

Each of these on their own adds incremental benefit to an insurer. However, bringing together simplicity, execution, and pace creates the opportunity for truly disruptive and exponential benefit. As consumers we can emotionally engage; we become fans, advocates, and champions of the brand that has delivered for us and not let us down.

Meeting the unmet needs of clients should be our sole purpose, delivered effortlessly through a frictionless, usage- (utility) based experience. It still has to be beautiful by design. It's something that should be so intuitive that my mum or my kids could use it with ease!

Although less the case in recent years, one final tag line that always instilled a level of surprise and delight was "one more thing" – made famous by the late Steve Jobs. Whatever he said after these three words was sure to leave the audience in a positive state of mind, full of excitement and positive anticipation. How do we deliver this experience for insurance customers at their time of need?

I'm not saying we will immediately get to a place where there are zero friction points – in some cases we may design these in on purpose. If a customer is looking to leave, let's at least have the conversation with them! So any friction points that are left need to be there by design.

I've never imagined an insurer that doesn't just work, or is not there (intentionally) when we need them. However, sometimes the cogs need a little more pushing and oiling. To create frictionless experiences we need to go beyond the product offered, creating immersive brands that customers and employees can relate to and exude passion and pride when describing them. Once we have you hooked, we need to keep things (as) simple as possible and execute the hell out of it. Looking east, we need only see some of the providers such as WeChat that are doing this flawlessly and at scale – a messenger and communication platform that allows you to do everything you need from the comfort of your own walled garden. We can easily see that most of the InsurTech investment has focused on this area, taking out friction points (and cost) from distribution – it's the closest part to the customer and the best opportunity to build engagement.

Insurance is your platform for building services beyond insurance as we know it today. Perhaps frictionless is more than just evolutionary fixes to broken processes, but instead, revolutionary leaps that deliver delight. Ultimately, to get to frictionless we need to be brave, bold, and get used to being comfortable with being uncomfortable.

The Smart Journey – From Contract Hype to Insurance Reality

By Akber Datoo
Partner, D2 Legal Technology LLP

Blockchain technology and "smart contracts" are often accused of hype. Yet multiple industries continue to search for the opportunities to unleash their inherent innovative and disruptive potential. Given the fundamental mechanics of insurance and the pervasive issues with contract management, one could argue that the industry truly needs the potential of the smart contract.

What is this Blockchain that Underpins the Concept of Smart Contracts?

Blockchain is a database, recording transactions, forming a "block" across a peer-to-peer network. Participants install the application locally and all the "nodes" hold a copy of the database, i.e. there is no central entity that holds control. The database is structured as a ledger of transactions into the blockchain, which is replicated in full by each participant's computer, and therefore consists of blocks that hold "time-stamped" batches of valid entries. Each block includes the "hash" of the prior block, linking the blocks together. The linked blocks form a chain, with each additional block reinforcing those before it. Transactions are passed from user to user, or node to node, on a best-effort basis. If any data in any block in the chain is later altered, the hash of that block will no longer correspond to the later blocks' hash of that "tampered" block, so the change will be clear to participants. The result is an indelible record operated on a distributed basis.

So What is a Smart Contract?

Smart contracts are computer protocols, embedding the contractual obligations of the contract into source code, which is compiled into executable computer code that can then be automatically executed per the terms and conditions of that contract. The distributed ledger architecture of blockchain is used by adding the code that makes up the smart contract into part of an entry to a blockchain application. One can define a smart contract as "code deployed to a distributed and replicated ledger, with an ability to control its own state and assets, with an ability to respond to the input of external information". The trust aspect that is fundamentally built into the blockchain means that smart contracts can be entered into between two parties unknown to each other. The participants of the blockchain (which could be party to the smart contract, or have an interest in it) have access to the block within which it is contained. The relevant block can be public (with an ability for all to view) or accessed on a "permissioned" basis.

Smart contracts can be fully automated and self-enforcing. Once the computer code representing the contractual obligations is set, the contract will run its course and the terms will be executed impartially by the computer on the basis of the code and the external information that the contractual obligations are dependent on. This automation, combined with the lack of traditional trust-building costs, significantly decreases transaction costs, making such exchanges much more profitable.

However, drafting a contract that takes into account all possible contingencies and states all their desired outcomes is difficult, especially in the real world of commercial contracts – hence the need for courts and judges to help in cases where circumstances unforeseen by the parties arise. In such cases, it is important that the smart contract's coded outcomes should not occur automatically. There is a drive to use artificial intelligence for the drafting, managing, and enforcement of smart contracts – however, it has to date been a challenge to embed the concepts required by key industries such as fairness and good faith. This means an interim state where smart contracts are open-ended and rely on input from non-automated actors.

The Issues with Semantic Information and Smart Contracts

Information can be divided into two types: syntactic and semantic. The former are the rules about the relationship between symbols, whereas the latter relates to the meaning attributed to such symbols (i.e. "intent"). Syntactic information can be parsed and measured (as famously shown by Shannon and Weaver in their seminal work *A Mathematical Theory of Communication*), and is open to mathematical proof.

Semantic information, however, is what we as humans attribute to the meaning of a symbol. Normalizing semantic information, such as natural language, making it processable, and representing its meaning are difficult tasks. Legal notions of "good faith" commonly used in contracts to deal with circumstances unforeseen by the contractual parties, for instance, are particularly complex, especially in the context of insurance contracts.

Given the smart contract automatic execution of the outcome upon the meeting of pre-set conditions, and the immutability through blockchain implementation, there is significant danger in an incorrect determination of a condition that is semantic in nature. Various solutions have been mooted, such as the concept of an "escape hatch": a pre-programmed way of changing the terms of a smart contract.

Deterministic versus Non-Deterministic

There are two types of smart contract that need to be considered: deterministic and non-deterministic. The primary differentiator is whether the network would have sufficient information to determine an outcome, or whether outside information is required. The ideal is to decentralize such a service in order to reduce the potential issues of trust and improve transparency.

Where non-deterministic, there isn't sufficient information on the distributed network itself to make the required decision – so an external source/party is required – an "oracle". The parties to the smart contract will need to agree a trusted source as the oracle, to submit the outcome that is a key part of the condition for a payout. Accordingly, the reliability and trustworthiness of the source is key. Some have approached this issue by implementing carefully thought-out processes to reduce the potential for undesired behaviours, e.g. federating oracles or an arbitration process. Principal component analysis can be used to reduce the risk of fraud/manipulation to break out the sources of the data and make the computation harder to "game".

Insurance Contracts: Opportunities for Smart Contracts

UK insurance contract law has its foundations in common law and was codified into the Marine Insurance Act 1906, designed to protect an insurance market from exploitation by customers who knew their business better than the insurers, giving the insurers draconian powers to avoid insurance claims at any sign of wrongdoing by the insured, imposing on them a higher standard of utmost good faith (*uberrimae fidei*).

In *Prudential Insurance Co v IRC*, Channell J held that the essential requirements of a contract of insurance were:

- The payment of a premium in return for the other party undertaking to pay a sum of money upon the happening of a specified event;

- The specified event being one that is adverse to the interest of the policy-holder, over which the policy-holder has no control (i.e. there is an element of fortuity); and

- The presence of an insurable interest (i.e. the insured has a legal or equitable interest in the subject matter of the insurance cover and would either be prejudiced by its loss or benefit from its safety).

The UK Insurance Act 2015, which came into force in August 2016, has created a different balance, representing a significant change to insurance contract law as it has stood for over 100 years. For business contracts, it forces cooperation between insured and insurer at the pre-contract stage. It does this by introducing a new obligation on an insured to make a fair presentation of a risk to the insurer. This greatly assists the use of smart contracts, encouraging a transparent discussion of the code conditions at its heart, based on this fair presentation of the underlying facts known.

With the explosion of data required in the assessment of a payout of an insurance policy being available from social media and the IoT (the Internet of Things), there is also the ability to objectively assess the occurrence of the event at the heart of the insurance policy. Provided the underlying data can be trusted and protected from fraud and manipulation, a major issue for insurance – fraudulent claims – can be significantly mitigated by the smart contract. Moreover, given the ease of the claims process for the insured due to the automatic payout, it is likely that customer satisfaction can also be improved.

Another challenge for the insurance industry is the control of costs relating to claims, for example, trying to limit the medical professional panel that must be used in the case of injury, or the garage used for repairs in respect of a car accident and the repairs to the vehicle. In the latter case, the condition in a smart contract could be met through a connected car, whose data clearly validates the occurrence of an accident. The smart contract code could limit any payout to specific designated third parties who are also on the relevant blockchain underpinning the smart contract.

Concern as to whether the insurance company will view an event as one caught within the coverage of the policy is also an area that the smart contract can assist with. A quick glance at a critical illness insurance policy shows a long list of exclusions that raise the concern of whether the policy provider may try unfairly (in the eyes of the policy-holder) to exclude an event. Frequently, the policy-holder is at an informational disadvantage to the insurer in terms of understanding the true coverage of the policy. In many ways, a smart contract would just codify the conditions and list of exclusions; however, the fact that the execution of the payout would be automatic, based on the data logic that has been coded (and agreed between the parties), means that it at least forces the removal of subjectivity that the insurer might use to its advantage (albeit with reputational risk).

The Next Steps to the Smart Contract Transformation of Insurance Policies

Bearing in mind the issues we have discussed, and given the breadth of the insurance sectors, it is clear that smart contracts are able to transform some areas of insurance more readily and sooner than others, typically where the conditions of the policy can be determined objectively and verifiably through data that has a low risk of being fraudulent.

The reliance on oracles cannot be underestimated, and, going forward, social networks and IoT will be the cheapest and most commonly used data feeds for various different insurance applications, making for the cheapest, most reliable, oracles for all types of future claims validation efforts. However, there are rightly significant concerns over the use of this data in relation to rights of data privacy and protection. How the industry manages this within the context of the smart contract will be a key determinant of its adoption.

But is it Still Insurance?

One of the essential requirements of an insurance contract is showing loss to the insured. Without it being present, some would argue that it is in fact a derivative contract, rather than one of insurance (and the regulatory requirements around the treatment therefore differ significantly). Accordingly, unless one can get comfortable on the objective determination of loss to the insured, there is a more fundamental question thrown at the heart of the insurance smart contract. That said, if it meets the desired commercial objectives of the contractual parties, should we really worry about the form (rather than the substance), assuming the regulation can keep pace with the transformative change potential of the smart contract?

Smart contracts certainly are on the way to helping the management of uncertainty better than the current traditional contractual forms and regulation will simply be forced to keep up as the potential of insurance smart contracts is realized.

InsurTech and AI – You Can Run but You Cannot Hide from the Future

By Richard Turrin

Artificial Intelligence | FinTech WealthTech | InsurTech
Professional and Chief Innovation Officer, Singapore Life

Artificial intelligence (AI) is the largest single disruptive technology impacting InsurTech. I work with AI every day and know that you can run, but you cannot hide from the fact that AI is going to change the insurance industry fundamentally.

While it's intuitive that AI can break the paradigm of how users interact with our systems, I want you to imagine with me what else AI technologies can do for InsurTech. Selling insurance and settling claims are the easy parts. AI is going to do far more, it's going to give us new kinds of insurance, new ways to look at risk and allow us to look at data at a scale far beyond our human limitations.

Cognitive Computing

Cognitive computing – computers that understand the intent of conversation – will own the future. These computers will also be imbued with the ability to understand that we're human and have sentiments and personalities. Cognitive computing will give us unprecedented advances in automation that will provide non-stop services from sales to claims. AI's most powerful feature will be the system's ability to understand who we are as customers, what we do with our lives, and what insurance we need. The future of insurance isn't depersonalized as some may fear, in fact, AIs are going to make it more personal than it has ever been before.

Chatbots Change how Humans Interact with Machines

Chatbots are the hottest topic in InsurTech with good reason; they are the first real technology that changes the paradigm of how humans interact with machines. Chatbots are designed to be the interface that gives technology a voice so that we can talk or text in natural language with a machine. It is a foundation technology upon which more sophisticated automated advisors will eventually be built, so ignore chatbots at your own peril. You probably couldn't ignore them if you tried, as they are already in our living rooms and allow us to play music, turn on the lights, or buy detergent when key words are detected. InsurTech chatbots are coming online now that will allow us to buy coverage, check coverage features, and do many of the simple jobs done either by FAQ sections of the Internet or call centres.

While chatbots are still a long way away from having a full-on conversation with a human, the simple tasks they perform can bring dramatic increases in efficiency and significantly alter how we interface with insurance platforms. They provide an instantly scalable interface that can be seen as an intermediary between a call centre and a website. Most importantly, they allow 24/7 access to information in a delivery mechanism that can be rolled out and integrated into insurance platforms in months. They will be the constant companion of your customer and allow you to serve them better throughout their customer journey. The most significant benefit is that they can be configured to help educate the user and allow them to do more by themselves. Think of this as AI giving humans greater capability to handle their own affairs rather than having to wait for a human agent to act as an intermediary. Does this scare you? How many of you still want to call your airline and talk to an agent to select a seat rather than booking it on your phone with an app?

Advances in chatbots now allow the "bot" not only to converse with us, but to determine the tone of the discussion through a process called sentiment analysis. This is where bots become personal in their responses as they can detect the client's emotional state and deal with them according to their level of satisfaction. If chatbots let you communicate with a computer, sentiment analysis is what will give the computer a heart. In the most simple use case the bot can determine when the client isn't satisfied with the service provided by the bot by understanding the tone of their response. Just as the user starts to sound frustrated the bot can volunteer to transfer the call to a human agent. In more complex uses, sentiment analysis can be deployed to see how users are interacting with a new system. You can actually compare the users' sentiments to the prior version and get unambiguous results of customer satisfaction with system improvements.

Even if we integrated chatbots with a heart into every part of an insurance company it still would not resolve the problem that we continue to sell product by silos such as health, auto, and life. This is hardly the view of the future that any of us have but we seem stuck to this view of the world because, for now, our products are each covered by a unique contract. What this fails to do is to relate to the customers based on their needs or goals.

Artificial Intelligence and Goal-based Insurance

Goal-based insurance is a way of trying to understand customers' needs better based on what they want to do or achieve in the year ahead, or potentially with their lives. If you ask a customer whether they need supplementary foreign medical coverage you are likely to get the answer "no". If you ask the same customer if they plan any wonderful holidays abroad this year you will probably get a "yes". Customers tend to think in terms of what they want to achieve, or do, rather than which silo of insurance is applicable to them. Goal-based insurance is a means of mapping out the customer's life journey in a way that uncovers potential areas for insurance rather than probing the need for individual policies.

AI and goal-based systems are the perfect combination of technologies for creating a major disruption in how we sell insurance. Goal-based systems are just now being developed that "gamify" the process of understanding a client's goals. Gamification is a way to simplify the process of understanding the client's goals without frustrating them by asking tedious questions. First-generation goal-based systems are going to use chatbots alongside gamification to make the experience interactive. Second-generation systems will unleash the full potential of AI, vastly simplifying the process so that the system only needs to ask two questions: "Who are you?" and "What can I do for you?" AI connected to big data will do the rest. It will understand who you are as a customer, where you are in life, and your optimal insurance coverage based entirely on analysis of your big data footprint. It will then have a discussion with you to refine the coverage better and provide optimal insurance just for you.

Sound far-fetched? First-generation chatbots are now in service at a number of insurers providing customer service that never sleeps and the first chatbot selling travel insurance on Facebook Messenger was launched in Singapore in 2017. While most of the bots built right now will not fool you into thinking that you're talking with a human, don't dismiss the simple things they may do like answering questions or helping guide customers through sign-up or claims processes. It may seem like the leap between first- and second-generation systems that know about you is a big one. It isn't, the technology is actually already here, the problem is gaining access to data sources that link you unambiguously to your data. This is changing quickly since governments spurred by "Know Your Customer" (KYC) regulations are putting directories of citizens and taxpayers online to reduce fraud. Singapore is launching its KYC system for Singapore residents in early 2018. Once these KYC systems come online, the personal data can be crossed with social media platforms to provide you with everything you need to put together a basic customized insurance program. We'll see the first of these systems by 2022/3.

If AI is going to help make policies more personalized, the natural fallout is that insurers will need to learn to blend our policies into a more goal-based view of coverage rather than selling a series of disjointed policies. Successfully underwriting these new policies will also require AI as they will be priced upon multiple dimensions of risk characteristics that will be taken from the client's actual behaviour. Take auto, for example, where each client will have a customized risk spectrum based on five to ten dimensions, each with a differing risk score. It's easy to imagine a risk spectrum composed of days used, miles travelled, region, speed, telephone usage, passenger numbers, braking force, and any other data on-board telematics may give us. Now take this auto profile and add it to similar metrics collected on the insured's health, property, occupation, and hobbies and you can build a policy that gives your clients more personalized coverage than ever before. Just as importantly, you're going to reallocate your clients' money to areas where they need the most protection and better underwrite their "real" demonstrable risks. It's a future that I look forward to.

The Next Generation of Insurance Will be Built on AI

So far, we've only considered what AI is going to do to our existing systems to improve the customer experience and access behavioural data more easily. The next step for AI will be to help us design new types of insurance coverage for risks that can only be defined with use of AI. The most obvious place for AI to do this is in cyberspace since humans aren't equipped to monitor or respond to threats in cyberspace until after the damage is done. Cyber security is really a new frontier for the insurance world and an area where AI can monitor, mitigate, and quantify risks faced by our customers. They can scan our cyber-life for signs of malicious attack, raise alarms, and give a clear unambiguous view of the severity of the attack or even potential damages. The threats monitored by AI will be subtler than data theft or loss due to malicious activities currently covered in cyber policies, but go to the root of insuring our cyber-life and that this life has value beyond the data. Access to granular data on health, life, loss, driving behaviour, and personal habits will shatter actuarial norms. Just as significantly, AI's access to new data from our cyber-life will give us new quantifiable dimensions of risk that we can price and manage.

I know some of you are thinking that this is going to happen in the distant future and that it won't affect you. You're mistaken. These changes are happening now. AI is going to make insurance easier, cheaper, more personalized and will manage more kinds of risks than we can currently conceive. It will change how we interact with our customers and improve the overall customer experience. Paper and PDF forms are the cement and bricks that built our industry. The next generation of insurance will be built on AI. So start thinking more like an AI company and less like an insurer if you want to survive this paradigm shift.

Blockchain Startups – Unlikely Heroes for the Insurance Industry?

By Becky Downing
CEO, Buzzmove

Blockchain technology is often touted as the latest Holy Grail for the insurance industry. It has the power to simplify the claims process, alleviate high premiums, and help insurers create niche coverage. That all sounds very impressive. But just how big an impact could this new technology have?

According to a paper published in September 2015 by the World Economic Forum, "ten percent of global gross domestic product will be stored on blockchain technology by 2025".[1] This is very significant. Yet blockchain is never going to realize this potential if it can't find a fan base beyond the technically-minded.

Many in the insurance industry think the technology is completely overhyped. Arguably, this is the result of a lack of real understanding of what the blockchain is and what it does. If a new technology or innovative concept can't be understood and consumed by the layman, many will view it as unworthy of their time and attention.

But that doesn't mean it's better for insurance companies to sit back and wait for the blockchain to reach a certain level of maturity. Even less so, to wait for the general public to catch up. Waiting too long will allow competitors to innovate their way into permanent competitive advantage and condemn the late adopters to a game of permanent catch-up.

Now is the perfect time to embrace and understand the technology, while it's still the "new kid on the block" (pun intended). It may be a cliché that those who learn to understand and embrace blockchain now will secure a valuable advantage, but that doesn't make it any less true. Particularly since blockchain could solve so many of the urgent problems currently facing the insurance industry.

Does the Glove Fit?

Setting aside blockchain for a moment, most would agree that the industry needs help. It currently spends 10% to 15% of premium income on claims handling.[2] It remains slow to respond to claims due to unreliable data passing between participants requiring armies of back office staff to check and recheck information on mutable databases. The industry also loses 5% to fraud,[3] due partly to the lack of data transparency. The current inability of the industry to combat fraud also makes the claims process slower and more complex than it needs to be.

Ouch. That's a long list of misdemeanours. Could blockchain be the solution? Blockchain can provide better data provenance, faster and more reliable claims handling via an accurate register of all assets, and the automation of policy enforcement. All of this will lead to better fraud protection, reducing risk and exposure.

Nevertheless, compared to the broader FinTech market, insurers have been apprehensive about adopting blockchain. This is understandable given the clunky, prehistoric legacy systems that insurers contend with. Not to mention inherent bureaucracy and organizational resistance to change. The business culture of most

---

[1] World Economic Forum: Deep Shift: Technology Tipping Points and Societal Impact – Survey Report, September 2015.

[2] Association of British Insurers, UK Insurance Key Facts 2014.

[3] http://www.monitor.co.ug/Business/Insurers-lose-5---revenue-to-fraud---industry-official/688322-3828736-hel6vu/index.html.

insurers values consistency, reliability, predictability, and short-term profitability. These values have served insurers in the past. But they are ill-suited to an industry that is being disrupted by newcomers with the ability to move fast. As with FinTech, the innovation that will radically change this industry will come from new entrants and startup players unencumbered by corporate process, finance committees, and red tape.

Working with Startups

Of course, that doesn't mean incumbents are powerless to innovate. But it does mean they need to harness this energy. Partnering with trail-blazing startups as trusted third parties will enable insurers to integrate into the blockchain ecosystem more quickly, reduce the costs of their global platforms, improve customer and market reach, and develop new propositions.

There are a number of reasons why it can be exponentially more beneficial to work with blockchain startups rather than funding blockchain projects internally. Some are well known and have been cited often. Others are not acknowledged as frequently, but may be even more important.

No legacy systems. Startups are not shackled by legacy systems. They can start from an idea without the technology constraints an incumbent faces.

Speed and agility. Startups are faster than incumbents at testing and learning. Even if many InsurTechs fail, some will change the insurance sector beyond recognition.

Internal bias. Most incumbents in any sector, not only insurance, are led by people for whom short-term sales and marketing targets are the top priority, rather than engineering or technology. The incumbent is focused on meeting each quarter's figures, rather than how innovative products can be brought to market to secure the company's success in five to ten years. The newcomer can begin with a clean sheet of paper, focus on the customer, and build efficiently from the outset.

Startups are led by visionaries. There is a key reason why it is even more important to work with startups when we talk of blockchain. Most InsurTech startups seek to redesign part of the insurance process (such as improving the distribution channel, or using big data to reduce risk), whereas blockchain startups are more visionary. They need to be, because it takes a visionary to see how technology that most don't understand will shape and change an industry in the future. These people are often mavericks who are not afraid to think very differently – even audaciously – about the product and services they deliver. Think Steve Jobs or Elon Musk. When such visionaries execute successfully they can be dangerously disruptive and effective. It is essential to have such forward thinking individuals lead blockchain projects.

Startups have more skin in the game. There is an age-old business fable involving a chicken and a pig. In the story, the chicken proposes a business partnership with the pig to open a restaurant offering bacon and egg breakfasts. The pig's response is: "No thanks. I would be committed whereas you would only be involved." Similarly, most startup founders have taken great personal risks and have sacrificed a great deal to build their company. It follows that their drive to succeed is likely to be substantially higher than that of any internal employee within an incumbent – or an external consultant, for that matter. This commitment can be a powerful force in delivering innovative, disruptive concepts to market fast.

Better teams. It's easy to think that a startup's edge derives solely from the technology they build and dismiss the critical role that culture and a varied team can play. Many InsurTech startups have thriving, vibrant, and innovative cultures that attract talent and best-in-class skills from across industries.

Startups lead with passion. Startup founders and employees (particularly the early-stage team members) did not leave their secure (and often well paid) jobs for nothing. They took a risk because they truly believe in – and are passionate about – what they are building and are trying to achieve. When this filters through to their products and customer care, it can lead to a powerful competitive force. One which is very hard to recreate.

Restricted budgets. Yes, this is actually an advantage! Having a massive budget is often counterproductive. It can engender complacency, whereas a finite budget and short runway forces startups to think much more creatively. The most effective growth strategies are often born from this level of discipline.

Startups embrace failure. It sounds counterintuitive, but you cannot have innovation without failure. This doesn't mean the total and final failure that leads to closing up shop, of course. It means constantly experimenting. Most experiments will fail, in order to find the few that will succeed that much faster. Those that do succeed have the potential to birth robust and successful customer value propositions. Insurance companies are not designed to handle such an approach. They are fundamentally risk averse and consistent failure is a fast track to the job centre. Granted, several of the most progressive have built internal innovation labs and accelerators, and this is big a step in the right direction. But on its own it's not enough. An innovation lab without the right mindset is never going to break the mould.

A Way Forward

Quite simply, innovation is better off in the hands of startups built by passionate, visionary founders who are driven by a sense of urgency and the need to succeed. An incumbent's quickest path to securing its future is to partner with such startups.

Incumbents can, and should, invest in building teams and forging close links with blockchain businesses to get access to knowledge. They should develop, test, and build prototypes that can be scaled and deployed. To do so, they will need to position themselves to enable efficient co-working with the startup.

There are a number of ways of doing this. Creating a sandbox environment is one of them. That would enable chosen startups to perform meaningful experiments with the incumbent, and to share learnings throughout. Should a proof of concept or strategic partnership prove to be successful, the incumbent can choose to continue the partnership or even acquire the startup.

For the blockchain to fulfil its potential for the insurance industry, more partnerships between startups and incumbents are vital. The faster the benefits of blockchain are explored and exploited, the quicker the technology will enter the mainstream. Partner the long-term experience and underwriting abilities of an incumbent with the innovation, passion, and drive of a startup, and you have an unstoppable combination to speed up adoption. Then the blockchain really could become the Holy Grail, and not just "pie in the sky".

Alexa, Can You Get me an Insurance? A Structured Approach to the Hyped Technology of Voice-Based Assistants

By Tobias Becker
Manager, Diconium Strategy

and Tobias Troendle
Management Consultant, Diconium Strategy

Relevance of Voice-Based Assistants – From Touch to Talk

The rise of voice-based assistants has not occurred unexpectedly. For years, interfaces have been changing to adapt to our habits – from smaller screens over concepts like Amazon's dash button up to sensors woven into clothes, as Google demonstrates with Project Jacquard. In the hunt for the pole position in every customer's life, nothing seems impossible. Additionally, messenger commerce is on the rise and will further increase its relevance with a more natural way of closing transactions – especially for younger generations. Fuelled by these trends as well as others like smart home technology in the need for one single control unit and the new possibilities from artificial intelligence (AI), voice-based assistants are on the rise. Furthermore, as we seek to maximize convenience in our homes, there is still room for innovation as touch might not be the all-time best input method.

As companies like Lemonade exemplify by combining AI and messenger technology, innovation is also possible in the insurance sector. Currently, this is almost exclusive to InsurTechs, while established players struggle to foster an innovation culture. For a sector offering consulting-intensive products and dealing with

long customer journeys, the value proposition of voice-based assistants sounds promising. While customer acquisition through online channels is already expensive, advertising through voice-based assistants is (almost) untouched territory in terms of less competition and therefore being cheaper. Additionally, insurers hope to create a more personal connection and offer added-value services to their customers using voice-based assistants, as shown in Figure 1.

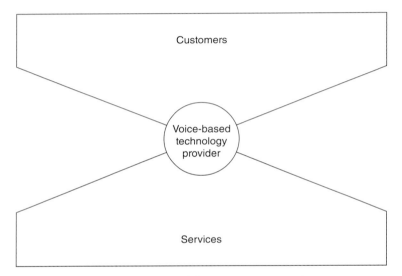

Figure 1: Technology providers act as gatekeepers between companies and their customers

Even though the opportunities sound promising, using voice-based assistants comes at a risk. While tech companies offering voice-based assistants are supportive when developing skills for their platform, long-term lock-in effects are created and dependencies emerge. Furthermore, companies lose control over the customer touchpoints and can only decide within the boundaries of technology functionality. Due to the early stage of this technology there is also no clear answer yet as to which kind of services will work. While the number of services increases, customers mostly show interest for built-in functions such as weather, traffic, news, and reminders.

Especially for insurers, additional risks arise around data security. Not only is voice-based authentication currently an unsolved problem, but also the data transfer between user and insurer, as there is always a technology provider in between. As insurance deals with sensitive personal and financial information, a secure way needs to be found for communication. Additionally, informational duties are difficult to handle, especially when insurers want to sell their products via voice-based assistants. Therefore, intelligent solutions need to be found to comply with different laws around the world.

Technology Snapshot – Players and their Strategies

As new players are still entering the market, competitors are moving at a fast pace. Nonetheless, different strategies and approaches can already be recognized. First-mover Amazon acts fast, focusing on market penetration with low pricing, company partnerships, and easy-to-use development tools. While Amazon could already establish partnerships with brands like Volkswagen, Ford, LG, and Mercedes, Google is still trying to catch up. Struggling on internationalization and other issues, it will be interesting to observe whether their exclusive access to Google Search can bring the competitive advantage over Amazon Alexa on the long run. Besides that, there are other B2C-focused companies following with their assistants like Apple's Siri, Microsoft's Cortana, and Samsung's Bixby. Even though they lost the race for the pole position, there are still opportunities for them as they all come on multipurpose hardware and don't have to be bought separately.

Achieving the How To

We are certain that voice-based assistants will generate real business potential within the insurance sector. To make use of this potential insurers need to think about what they want to achieve using voice-based assistants.

The key question to ask would be: "Do I want to support my existing business model or do I want to establish a completely new business model using voice interfaces?" (see Figure 2).

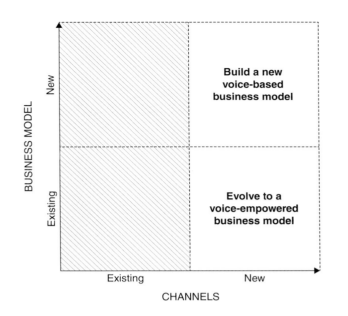

Figure 2: Differentiation of the use of a new channel by business models

Source: diconium strategy, "Established banks and their business models are existentially threatened by agile digital players" by Tobias Becker and Ingmar Berger, published in February 2016

Creating a complete new business model is very complex, due to certain restrictions that come from the voice-based assistant landscape.

The user scenarios are limited to the interface – the voice – and the context of use – e.g. at home, sitting on the couch. Currently, the potentials of utilizing voice-based assistants are limited to the supported scenarios. All the traffic from using services on voice-based assistants is routed through the operating system. The interface is completely owned by the operator, e.g. Amazon or Google. Therefore, every interaction is known and tracked by the operator and the voice-based business model is fully dependent on the strategy of this operator.

Minimal revenue streams are generated via the respective app stores, e.g. Amazon Skill Store. The limitation in user scenarios makes single transactions for generating revenues without any other touchpoints very hard, too.

Supporting an existing business model by providing an additional service through voice-based assistants is much easier. It serves as the best playground to test potential and build capabilities. Considering specific voice-based user scenarios, an existing value proposition can be enriched with additional customer benefits.

1. Know your customer

For the first step, you need to know your customer and his or her problems. Use Osterwalder's Value Proposition Canvas[1] to visualize the customer jobs you are solving with your existing business model (see Figure 3). Based on the customer jobs, you are now able to find pains and gains the customer may perceive during the journey.

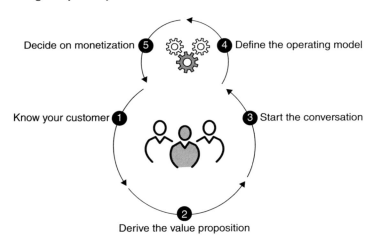

Figure 3: Structured approach based on Osterwalder's Business Model Canvas

[1] A. Osterwalder, Y. Pigneur, G. Bernarda, and A. Smith, *Value Proposition Design: How to Create Products and Services Customers Want*, John Wiley & Sons, 2014.

2. Derive your voice-empowered value proposition

With the collection of customer jobs, pains, and gains you have the right base to define your voice-empowered value proposition. The key question here should be – "Where can voice-based assistants help to solve jobs, support gains or mitigate pains?"

It might be helpful to write down your existing value proposition before starting from the customer perspective. This will ensure your focus and will provide a more transparent view on additional aspects from the voice-based perspective.

3. Start the conversation

After you've defined your value proposition you should be able to prototype your voice-based service. Just sketch a dialogue with Alexa or make a video, faking a conversation with a voice-based assistant. With an early demonstration, you are perfectly equipped to get out of the building and talk to potential customers. Get their feedback to optimize your value proposition and the respective voice-based service. Don't forget to find out whether your customers are willing to pay for using your voice-based assistant's service or whether they expect to have that service for free.

4. Define the operating model

Once you have your voice-based service defined and tested you can dive deeper into the operating model. Your service needs to consist of the key features essential to provide the defined value proposition. A key feature may be "return current account balance". After you have defined your initial set of key features, you should be able to derive key resources you need to realize your service – e.g. the customer database. You may need external services to provide your value proposition – e.g. weather data. Therefore, define your key partners outside your organization.

5. Decide on monetization

Based on the customer feedback you have gathered in the third step you should now decide on what revenue model you want to go for. Consider the limitations described earlier: monetizing a single transaction performed at a voice interface is complicated and may not be used by the customers. The "premium model", where the use of your service is part of a premium package a customer needs to book, may be a better choice, depending of course on existing revenue streams.

The Crystal Ball: Future Potentials of Voice-Based Assistants

The journey of innovation in this area has just started and we do not even know where it will take us. Amazon has proven with the introduction of Echo Look that voice-based assistants do not need to be blind and new potentials can arise from technological innovation. Within the area of technological innovation, AI plays a crucial role, as there is huge potential from intelligent assistants. In a couple of years, they will become ultimately fully context-aware and will judge, anticipate, and forecast which information becomes relevant for the customer at which point in time.

Innovation will also arise from partnerships between technology providers and other players. Especially within our homes, voice-based assistants will emerge to become the preferred input method for several tasks and activities, as they act as a new kind of universal remote for services from different providers. Furthermore, as automotive companies demonstrate how voice-based assistants can increase their customers' experience aside from their primary use at home, there will be potentials for insurers as well. As voice-based assistants become more important, gain new functions, and become a fundamental part of customers' lives, not only will digital commerce change in general, but especially digital commerce for consulting-intensive products like insurances will evolve.

Therefore, it is crucial for every company that plans to participate in this market to foster curiosity and start using this new technology as soon as possible. Since there is a learning curve for customers as well as for companies, it is essential to plan for several iterations to meet customer needs exactly.

InsurTech's Big Questions – Why the Customer is Still Always Right

By Janthana Kaenprakhamroy
CEO and Founder, Tapoly

Way back in 2009, a man had an idea that would change the world. Having spent US$800 hiring a private driver, Garrett Camp came to the conclusion that it must be possible to do things more cheaply. After much ruminating and long chats with friends, Camp came up with a simple solution: why not reduce the cost of rides by sharing them? From this, Uber was born.

In 2012, Uber unveiled another of its innovations with the creation of Uber X. Now, by using their own cars, Uber drivers could actually undercut regular taxis. Instead of frequently slow, late, and overpriced taxi services, consumers could now easily order a cheaper option, which would usually arrive within minutes, and even follow the cab's progress on the Uber app. It was a formidable combination, and one that, for all Uber's much-publicized recent problems, has created a global tech juggernaut valued at an astonishing US$70 billion.

Now imagine Uber had taken a different route. Imagine that, instead of just creating a service that made cabs cheaper and more accessible, Uber had begun by adopting a visionary, long-term strategy of embracing driverless cars. It would be difficult to argue against the assertion that, at some point, this investment would pay off handsomely. But if, in 2009, Garrett Camp had concluded that the best way to improve taxis – at that moment – was to work towards replacing drivers, how many people would have heard of Uber today?

Tomorrow's Tech, Today's Problems

The question, of course, is impossible to answer. Yet it is one that may have some relevance to where we are with InsurTech. Because while genuinely thrilling technologies promise to upend the insurance industry, they may not be answering the questions consumers have *today*. Questions like, why can't I get insurance for my Airbnb property? Why do I have to buy full-contents insurance for just a few items in my home? And where can I find a really flexible, user-friendly insurance service online?

Before going any further, it's worth looking at some of these groundbreaking technologies and why, despite their vast potential, they may not be best placed to underpin a transformation in the insurance world – especially for startups – just yet.

1. **Artificial intelligence**

    For all AI's recent headline-grabbing successes – and its clear potential to disrupt the insurance industry – formidable medium-term barriers remain to its widespread adoption in InsurTech. For such a transformative technology, the operational risk in tightly regulated industries like insurance is, for most companies operating today, unacceptably large. And, crucially, insurers have to be able to interact meaningfully with human beings, something that remains a long way off for even the most sophisticated AI software or chatbots.

    Of course, things are changing quickly. But for companies to harness the power of AI today, they need vast amounts of three things: data, capital, and know-how. Almost by definition, startups (at least to begin with) are deficient in all three, making it very difficult to create a business focused primarily on the customer experience, rather than AI for its own sake.

2. Internet of Things

Given that it could ultimately bring thousands of everyday items online, the IoT has been widely touted for its potential to transform the insurance sector.

Indeed, the IoT has already scored notable successes in the insurance sector with motor insurance. But, paradoxically, rather than signal IoT's imminent widespread adoption in InsurTech, this success more likely underlines the technology's particular effectiveness in specific sectors. The widespread adoption of everyday devices linked to the Internet is some way off, meaning that, for now, adopting IoT technology would be extremely burdensome and slow for bigger insurance companies, and prohibitively expensive for startups.

3. Blockchain

Perhaps the most eagerly anticipated technology in the world of finance, it would be easy to believe that blockchain is an idea whose time has come. As a public digital ledger of all transactions, blockchain promises a world of transparent and secure transactions that are practically impossible to hack.

But in insurance, at least for now, the public nature of the ledger brings problems of its own – both for companies, who need to retain a customer base, and for consumers themselves, who will have concerns about personal data. What's more, unlike, say, stock markets, the insurance market is far from being fully digitized and continues to rely on human interaction and physical transactions. This will undoubtedly change, but, for now, attempts to force the square peg of insurance into the round hole of blockchain seem unlikely to help optimize the customer experience.

Where the Customer Leads…

If these impressive technologies aren't necessarily the ideal match for most InsurTech startups today, which ones might be? As I've suggested already, this could be the wrong question. As is well documented, InsurTech is among the hottest areas of FinTech today, because its long-established (and relatively unchanged) business models are increasingly seen as ripe for disruption by innovation and venture capital money. But also, as with the best FinTech ideas, the best InsurTech is being driven by a relentless focus on solving customer problems, taking away pain points, and answering needs that aren't being catered to elsewhere. Consequently, the key question surely is, which technologies can create the ideal customer experience in the InsurTech sector?

Before answering that question, let me share exactly what it was that inspired me to start an InsurTech company. Like millions of other people, I decided that I wanted to generate a little extra income by letting out part of my flat via Airbnb. I knew that getting the right insurance would be crucial so I got cracking on what I thought would be a 10-minute job. I thought wrong. After literally hours on the phone, I found the sum total of one insurer that was prepared to offer the cover I wanted – for a king-sized fee. I was staggered that in a time when we think nothing of booking a room, office, or cab with a few clicks, it was next to impossible to find a decent insurance option for transactions in the sharing economy.

Going through this experience made me understand what it was to be a frustrated insurance customer – because I was one! It also made me see just how underserved by insurance the sharing and gig economies are, despite the phenomenal growth and even greater potential of those sectors.

Companies like Airbnb, BlaBlaCar, and, of course, Uber have thrived precisely because they've retained a razor-sharp focus on identifying a customer need and then, crucially, continually refined their services to match customer behaviour. How ironic, then, that insurance for these sectors has remained so stuck in outdated models, concerned far more with the insurers' operational efficiency or long-established risk models than with the actual needs of customers. It may seem an obvious point, but this is exactly why InsurTech is so exciting: being driven not by technology but by customer needs, the sector's potential to create a business every bit as dynamic and successful as the likes of TaskRabbit or Uber is huge.

Savvy Startups

Fortunately, some technologies, being used by incredibly smart startups, are already helping InsurTech companies meet those customer needs.

Take Leakbot. Already being offered by Aviva to its customers, this gadget attaches to pipes near the stopcock to detect leaks from pipes or taps, information it then relays to users via their smartphone. The early detection of leaks can help customers avoid the much greater expense and strife of serious damage should the problem continue unattended.

Another example is Jolt, an app that turns smartphones into dashboard cameras. While helping prevent fraud, so clearly a welcome development for the industry, Jolt can also help customers prove the authenticity of their claims, thereby making the claim process faster and fairer. Better still, by helping reduce fraudulent claims, the makers of Jolt believe that it could lead to significant savings in premiums for good drivers.

Across the InsurTech sector, numerous startups are creating slick, intuitive user interfaces that take so much pain out of the whole process of searching and applying for insurance – companies like Buzzmove and Fabric (and soon my own company, Tapoly). Yes, excellent user experience can be considered a minimum requirement but it is in precisely these fields that insurers have for so long lagged the wider financial industry, creating unnecessary headaches for consumers.

Eight years on from Uber's tentative first steps into providing taxi services, the company – and the industry – are unrecognizable from what they once were. And having led a transformation of taxi services, the company now finds itself at the forefront of the push towards driverless cars, a technological change that, when it happens, will have truly earned the right to be called revolutionary. Crucially, though, Uber reached this point not by first focusing on radical technological change, but by improving the customer experience to something so much better that it was transformational. As InsurTech takes centre stage in the world of FinTech and creates new, exciting innovations, I hope this is a lesson the sector continues to embrace.

ClaimsTech – The InsurTech's Action List

By Craig Polley
Director, Digital Risk Services Limited

More often than not, it will be a claims process that most defines the customer experience and whether to buy or stay with one insurer or intermediary over another. The InsurTech player in the insurance claims value chain should aim to excel at claims, exceed expectations, and delight customers. This chapter proposes an Action List for InsurTech in Claims, and focuses on:

- private motor/auto

- personal effects

- owner/occupier private dwellings.

For context, the focus is generally accepted practice, without a particular focus on laws or regulations.

The following are common elements of the claims process:

1. Incident occurs

2. Incident notified, recorded, and acknowledged

3. Claim validated

4. Repair, replace, or pay

5. Final settlement

6. Subrogation, recovery, or third-party aspects.

It is important to distinguish first party from third party as a claim: the first party is the (named) insured, and the third party is anyone else who may be entitled to or otherwise seeks redress from the insured party. If an insured driver impacts another vehicle and is at fault, then the insurance policy should indemnify the policy-holder against claim(s) from the third party where fault is established with the first party. This chapter does not delve into areas of third-party liability, contribution, or subrogation. In fulfilling the claims promise, the following most basic rules contribute to the customer experience:

1. Ease and availability to report a loss

2. Communication, communication, communication

3. Meticulous record keeping

4. Managing expectations (see 2. above)

5. Efficient management of external suppliers

6. Time/speed to settle.

Where do InsurTechs wish to sit in the overall value chain? Some may simply want to sell somebody else's product and move on, equivalent to box shifting as seen in price-comparison space. InsurTech firms selling insurance products underwritten by an insurer, reinsurer, or Lloyd's underwriter will need to establish (a) which party will be managing claims and (b) which suppliers could be involved. For an InsurTech, managing the whole claims process is unlikely but there are many opportunities to introduce platform offerings that simplify, accelerate, and optimize the claims handling process.

Claims also have a tendency to occur at inconvenient times. Similarly, many claims can come all at once, something the insurance industry refers to as a *surge*. So, careful orchestration, planning, and processing with respect to claims must not be left to chance. Similarly, it is inevitable that not every claim will have a 100% satisfactory outcome for a policy-holder so it is important to have superior complaints handling processes. Complaints processes may often be a key component of regulatory applications and subject to ongoing supervision. Thus, a documented process/procedure that includes robust record keeping is required.

The Supplier Landscape

Sometimes claims handling is best done by the underwriters of the actual policies. This means claims control will largely be in the hands of other party(s). Insurers commonly outsource claims, involving a specialist third-party administrator (TPAs or claims management firms). Many of these companies operate a full suite of services with authority to settle claims without reference to the principal company (called "delegated authority"). They are paid a fee and provided with cash funds to pay claims directly, often up to a certain limit. Similarly, many law firms have administration units to process claims, usually specializing in injury and liability matters. While securing underwriting capacity and products is a key objective of many InsurTechs, this claims supplier landscape is important.

If controlling claims is desired *and* the indemnity provider is satisfied that an InsurTech is well positioned to administrate claims *and* grants settlement authority, then one must assess how much of the process one can manage and consider whether to build, or buy, a claims management platform. It is a "buyer's market", so in evaluating options, be sure to understand the scope of services available, how these are delivered, and differentiators in terms of value-added services. Then there is the issue of pricing and who picks up the costs.

After considering all of these factors, should it be determined that your InsurTech business could embrace claims or, better still, make claims a key differentiator for competitive advantage, then there is a broad and rich stream of opportunities to improve the value chain. And a multitude of options to introduce incremental improvements within established enterprises.

CX in claims

The Customer eXperience in claims remains broadly operated by telephone and form filling, either paper or digitized. Firms *are* expanding capabilities to add mobile and other channels, increasing the options on how customers choose to initiate a claim or handle correspondence, validation, and so forth. Lightweight, mobile-first, responsive design is key. If regular interaction and customer engagement with an insurance product app forms a key part of the business objectives, then adding efficient claims reporting and processing tools to the menu makes sense. Many companies still require policy-holders to download, print, and submit a form, perhaps reflecting the disconnect between back-end policy, claims, and customer platforms, respectively.

Analytics in Claims

The spreadsheet is still perhaps the most widely employed tool in the claims manager's toolbox, possibly supported by some additional management information tools. Aggregating structured and unstructured data alongside multi-channel capabilities capturing client communications, artefacts, and data is where InsurTech has potential to move the needle. Incumbent firms have vast silos of claims data in many forms (usually archive boxes!). Demarcation between personally identifiable information, when all information that could be used, directly or indirectly, to identify an individual is an obvious necessity. Everything else, ingested into modern and capital efficient platforms, introduces the ability to move the claims paradigm from the realms of hindsight and insight to *foresight*. In some cases, claims might even be automatically validated and settled. In other cases, forecasting on time to settle, cost to settle, and deaccessioning on complex liability based on historical claims experience or propensity can be achieved.

Robotics … Arise the Claim Machines

Software and machines, chatbots, and robo-advisors are now being programmed to learn through conversational experience with humans. Natural language processing, the ability to command and control processes with one's voice and get answers, are now becoming commonplace. Chatbots have the advantage of capturing routine data more efficiently than humans and triggering automated processes that are resource consumptive if done manually.

Many claims processes are routine, so well-refined processes developed by humans can be successfully completed through robotic automation. The most obvious example is in the routine of First Notification of Loss (FNoL), the Q&A between insurer or broker and policy-holder when a claim is discovered and onboarded. The what, where, why, and how (much) can be captured and input to core systems and related incident response teams where required. Capturing and analysing in this manner builds data continuously and is scalable to meet the demands of the largest enterprise.

IoT Applications in Claims

With the washing machine or refrigerator becoming "smart" and the likelihood that anything that can be connected *will* be connected, IoT will also find applications in the claims process. Connected cars can notify of adverse events via wireless networks; sensors in the home, factory, and farm field can instantly raise an alarm that may indicate (or evidence) a claim admissible under a policy of insurance. In fact, centrally monitored security and fire detection was introduced decades ago, and many insurance policies contain warranties to this day that stipulate the usage and maintenance of such devices to mitigate risk. Plant and machinery breakdowns, and indeed their consequences, often become claims in commercial insurance. The speed of containment of a claim can mitigate the consequences for policy-holder and insurer. Wind turbines and photovoltaic solar panels, both domestic and commercial, not only need repair or replacement when damaged but may also cause financial losses and *both* may be recoverable. If adverse weather, hail or storm conditions, for example, were to be forecast, preventative measures could lessen or eliminate the risk of damage.

Digital Evidence and Thwarting Claims Fraud

How InsurTech firms maintain digital records with respect to client interaction is an area that needs careful consideration. The UK Insurance Act (which came into force in August 2016) and other EU Directives, including the *General Data Protection Regulation*, present challenges for the industry as a whole. The concept of "treating the customer fairly" shifts the burden of proof and reliance on insurance contract language when dealing with claims. When dealing with multi-channel communications, how and what information is exchanged in the process of a claim must be captured and retained to whatever extent may be required for class and jurisdiction of business, which can vary considerably. Conversely, industry supervisors may need to see evidence that fraud is being routinely and robustly monitored. This is not an optional item that a regulated firm can decide upon. It is usually mandatory because, in the eyes of the regulators, fraud is a threat to other policy-holders and the broader financial system. Accordingly, anyone involved in handling claims will need to demonstrate and may become reliant on methods employed to counteract fraudulent activity.

Fraud detection is not merely a claims matter, but part of broader fraud prevention. It is also applicable at point of sale, where information is obtained from the policy-holder during the proposal and underwriting stage. The use of technology and data in the fight against insurance fraud is not new. However, new techniques like behavioural analytics that operate in real-time are more advanced. Many platforms now interrogate social media and find patterns that claim investigators would struggle to identify. Video analytics and voice stress analytics are being combined and trialled by US and Canadian immigration at the time of writing. A platform developed by the University of Arizona, called AVATAR, (Automated Virtual Agent for Truth Assessments in Real Time) offers a glimpse of what is happening presently. It is multilingual too! InsurTech firms should liaise closely with insurance partners and experts to develop strategies and procedures to detect and tackle fraud. Many are well resourced in this area and have a common interest in mitigating fraud risk.

Technology is Not Enough

By Harry Williams
Business Designer, Fjord

With insurance being the latest industry to be enriched by technology-driven investment, there are risks arising. There's a risk that technology will be used for the sake of it. There's a risk that technology will lead to even more complexity. And there's a risk that technology will result in overwhelming uniformity, changing the dynamics of competition.

Design can provide the answer. To make sense of this, it's essential to look beyond any misconceptions that design is just about making stuff look good. The fundamental reason why design is such a powerful tool is the emphasis that's placed on people – whether that's your customers, employees, or the rest of society. In this chapter, we'll look at three ways design can be used to create products and services that users love, and your competitors hate.

Design as a Problem Solver

Focusing purely on how technology can be used to create a new service is the first step on a journey to creating a service that nobody wants.

Following a design-led approach overcomes this by thinking about the user and their needs first, not some cool new technology. The first stage of any product development process should be figuring out the problem you're going to solve. This should involve talking to your users to understand their behaviour and feelings throughout their insurance journey. By mapping this out, you can begin to understand the highs and lows of your user's experience. And, importantly, you'll see opportunities to create new services that will improve their overall experience. You may observe that your users feel that the process of making a claim on their insurance is time-consuming and complicated. From this, you can start creating a service that solves this problem. By starting with identifying the

problem your technology will be solving, you reduce the risk of spending 12 months working on your fancy "robo-advisor-chatbot-assistant-driven-by-artificial-intelligence" customer engagement platform, then releasing it into the market to find out nobody wants it.

This is not to say that a relentless focus on the needs of your users should be at the detriment to your business. Once you've found a problem worth solving, and a solution that solves it, you can work with other areas of the business to ensure a service that makes commercial sense. The key is finding the balance between a service that's desirable for the user, will make money for the business, and is technically feasible.

Design to Differentiate

We live in a world of abundance. Markets are more competitive than ever. And with the decreasing cost of technology and the free access to information, the market barriers to entry are lower than we've seen for a long time. Now, students graduating from university can start their own InsurTech business. We have moved on from a time where a lack of information, and a lack of choice, meant that adequately functional products, at a reasonable price, were enough to attract customers. In this age of abundance, appealing only to rational, logical, and functional needs is insufficient. To differentiate your offering in this overstocked marketplace, you need to create a beautiful and delightful experience that elicits an emotional connection with your customers.

Now, that sounds rather fancy and complicated. But one way to achieve this is by following some principles of good design. Design can be used as a tool to solve complexity, delivering the simplest experience to your customers. Striving for simplicity may sound a bit straightforward if you're aiming to create a magical experience and achieve differentiation from competitors, but it has long been a fundamental principle underlying some of the most successful products, services, and businesses in the world. Consider the phone, computer, or maybe even the watch you use. If it has the infamous Apple logo, you're experiencing this principle in action. When Steve Jobs returned to save Apple in 1997, one of his guiding principles was "simplicity is the ultimate form of sophistication". And it's Apple's relentless focus on staying true to this principle that has contributed to them becoming one of the most successful businesses ever, creating products and services loved by millions across the world.

With complexity rife in the insurance industry, making things simple is more powerful than ever. Insurance is complicated. Customers find it hard to compare policies, they struggle to understand what they're covered for, and making claims is painful. Beyond a poor experience for the customer, this complication can fuel distrust. If a customer doesn't understand the four policy documents they've been gifted, how can they trust their insurer to have them covered at a time of need?

A great place to start simplifying your experience is by rethinking the way you communicate and present information. Firstly, you'll need to rethink how you talk to your customers. Imagine you were describing something to a friend in the pub; that is the type of language you should be using. Cutting out the jargon and overly complicated words that most of your customers won't understand. A great way to give your brand personality through your tone of voice is by thinking of a person in real life that you feel embodies your brand. It might be a trusted friend, a caring family member, or an authoritative colleague. Think about the characteristics of this person, and ensure these are influential in all communications that come from your business. The result is a friendly, human-like connection with your brand and an element of simplicity that cuts through the complexity of the industry. A second way to solve complexity is in how you present information. In an era of disappearing images, and 280-character tweets, your average customer doesn't have the time or inclination to focus long enough to work out what all of this insurance stuff means. By simplifying the key information a customer really needs to know into a visual summary, customers are more likely to understand what you're providing them with and believe you have their best interests at heart.

With the issue of complexity common across the entire insurance industry, it will be the insurers who are able to overcome this issue that will take the first step towards differentiation. Riding a wave of attention, and with US$60 million backing,[1] the US insurer Lemonade is proving how a focus on simplicity and transparency can provide clear differentiation in the market. Their communication style is fun and light-hearted. Their business model is simple and displayed proudly on their website for all to see. And the experience they provide is quick and enjoyable, meaning you can be covered in 90 seconds, or complete a claim in three minutes. It will be the industry players who are able to adopt these key design principles and put them into action who will achieve sustainable differentiation from competitors.

Simplicity is one example of a design principle that can differentiate your service in the market. There are plenty of others to explore, from practicality and functionality to elegance and honesty. The key is identifying the principles that will have the biggest impact on your service and working with talented designers to execute them.

Design Beyond the Design Department

From this chapter, it should be clear that the value of design goes beyond making stuff look good. Design is a tool for problem-solving, and a tool for achieving sustainable differentiation. But to realize these benefits, a mindset change is key. Taking design out of the design department doesn't mean placing designers within your finance and compliance teams; it's about changing the way all employees approach and solve problems. The key is to place the customer at the centre of everything you do, making sure the solutions you're coming up with are not just solving a business need, but solving a user's need. Because without the user, there will be no business.

---

[1] Source: Lemonade.

Changing the behaviour of everyone within an organization is a big challenge. Airbnb has a great approach for promoting this "design way of thinking" throughout their organization. In every team, the project manager has the role of representing the customer.[2] This ensures that every discussion considers the impact on the customer, and every solution delivers value to them. If design is to have a positive impact on your organization, you need to make a change and run with it. Whether that's ensuring the "voice of the customer" is heard within your team, or you run "design thinking" training with your team, the best response is action.

So, to Conclude

If you're to build a successful InsurTech business, technology alone is not enough. If you want to create products and services that customers love, and are differentiated from competitors, design is a tool to help. So, remember: place the user's needs at the centre of the problem you're solving, follow design principles to create an experience with a sustainable competitive advantage, and create a culture where a design approach is valued throughout your organization.

---

[2] Source: Wired.

InsurTech Futures

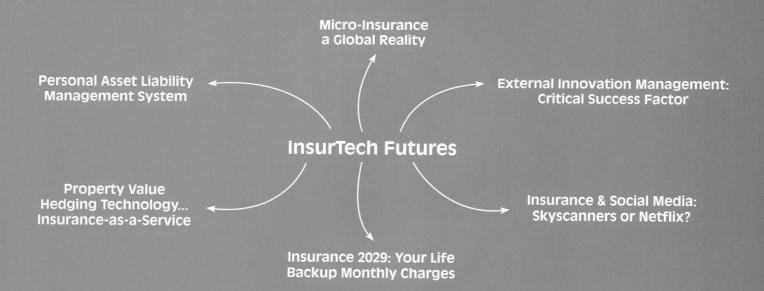

Micro-Insurance
a Global Reality

Personal Asset Liability
Management System

External Innovation Management:
Critical Success Factor

InsurTech Futures

Property Value
Hedging Technology...
Insurance-as-a-Service

Insurance & Social Media:
Skyscanners or Netflix?

Insurance 2029: Your Life
Backup Monthly Charges

Our contributors for this part took on the brief of imagining the InsurTech futurescape with real gusto. Six writers from around the world present their interpretations and visions of what's in store, and, for us, the variety of perspectives here is almost as fascinating as the chapters themselves.

For Ulrich Kleipass, it is obvious that innovation in insurance is far from new – but what *is* new is how the sector is no longer totally inward looking, but actively externally focused (on partners, customers, and even peers) to get innovation and digitalization done. This makes getting "external innovation management" right absolutely critical, and Kleipass offers up a practical eight-point action plan for insurer incumbents to do just that.

Pauline Davies' powerful arguments for the new world of "connected customer" to actually mean the acceleration of microinsurance hit home. Davies' detailed analysis of the current state of non-insurance, especially in Africa, and examination of how digitalization and InsurTech can change this situation is down-to-earth yet inspiring. Many will feel that enabling microinsurance is, of itself, a rationale for InsurTech worth rallying around.

The third piece in this part comes from Ming Chiu and Yawei Cui. They analyse the future of InsurTech as a means of both "demand-side", i.e. customer, understanding and control, and "supply-side" innovation, i.e. providers having fully applied Big Data and AI to internal structures and efficiencies. Chiu and Cui propose a Personal Asset Liability Management System encompassing every type of insurance (health, P&C, etc.), as well as personal finance, wealth management advisory, and execution.

No consideration of InsurTech futures would have been complete without a discussion of social media, and Erik Abrahamsson unsurprisingly writes engagingly and persuasively of two possible outcomes for the future of insurance through this lens: Skyscanners and Netflix representing his "worst-" and "best-case" scenarios, respectively, and ZhongAn as the exemplar for the successful social media-enabled insurance company of the future. (He does not say which scenario he believes most likely: see what *you* think.) A common thread for all our contributors (not just for this part but throughout *The InsurTech Book*) is that InsurTech is really *not* all about technology, but much more about what you do with it – and why.

Mindset shift is also the key to Gilad Shai's "take" on the future. He envisions incumbents (early adopters, fast followers and all) choosing *not* to solve "the technology issue" themselves, instead re-imagining insurance as "Insurance-as-a-Service", i.e. risk services delivered in partnership with specialized, tech-enabled partners (InsurTechs).

Insurance professionals in the UK will recognize some of Shai's examples of what this might mean as "Schemes" by another name – the UK broker has historically been valued for being specialized in finding new risks, and new customers for those new risks, and working with insurers to productize protection quickly but Shai is really challenging us to view InsurTechs not simply as useful, a necessary evil, or even an unavoidable threat. His challenge to incumbents is to make InsurTech partners a core part of your business, an Opportunity and a Strength in the ubiquitous SWOT analysis. Shai does not have the space to consider how InsurTech startups, fired up as many are with the urgent desire to disrupt or destroy the status quo, should view his ideas, or how they would shape their own offerings and approach. Perhaps next time?

And finally, George Kesselman's rich and informative piece takes us to January 2029, and our monthly Life Backup Bill, detailing the payment required for this month's activities, our precisely calibrated and costed individual "riskiness", and consequent usage of Life Backup protection across every aspect of our lives. This is a tour de force of sustained argument, and whether or not you find Kesselman's future personally appealing, all readers will find this contribution thought-provoking and a most original take on the "insurance as a utility" idea. Taken as a whole, this part weaves strands and ideas that feel simultaneously known *and* unfamiliar; logical *and* infeasible; obvious *and* inspired. A fitting completion, then, to a volume dedicated to InsurTech at this stage in its evolution.

Digital Transformation and Corporate Innovation Management – an Incumbent's Action Plan

By Dr Ulrich Kleipass
Head of Innovation Berlin, ERGO Group

Digitalization has become of increased strategic relevance: insurance companies have to digitalize their existing businesses and at the same time innovate through new processes, products, markets, and business models.[1] This raises the question of how such an innovation process can be organized. Although not as prominent as in other R&D-intensive industries, innovation isn't exactly new to the insurance industry. However, what *has* changed is that a more inward focus in sourcing new ideas has shifted to leveraging external partners, peers, and customers to make advances in innovation. So which guiding principles should be followed?

1. Look beyond incremental innovation

Incremental innovation is foreseeable and easy to consider in strategic planning. Exponential developments and disruptive innovations on the other hand are much harder to cope with through existing systems. Nevertheless, drivers from the Internet of Things to improved data availability influence how disruptive innovation comes to the insurance industry:[2] it might be at the customer front end, in the underwriting process, or another function. Consequently, insurance companies need

to adapt to become more open to more radical approaches. The goal of innovation should not solely be to drive efficiency further, and sell more of the same at lower cost to more of the same types of customers. Insurance companies should start experimenting even more outside their comfort zones as the competitors of tomorrow might not even come from within their own industry (e.g. car manufacturers selling car insurance products).[3]

2. Towards a fully digital insurance value chain

Other industries such as banking have already shown what happens when startups stir up an industry: they accelerate the decomposition of the value chain.[4] In the last three years we've witnessed many so-called InsurTech companies attacking the insurance industry through offering customers more attractive digital front ends by acting as a digital broker. European players such as Knip and Clark have pioneered contract administration tools that have a much more "digital feel" than anything that traditional insurance companies have provided so far.[5] In fact, these examples only mark the first generation of InsurTech companies: founders had to learn that in order to be a real threat to existing insurance companies they have to integrate further back into the value chain and not just concentrate on one piece of the value creation process. This means that, for instance, they also have to offer a fully digital claims process and (co-)design

---

[1] McKinsey & Company, The Making of a Digital Insurer, 2015, pages 3ff.

[2] A. Sen and D. Lam, PineBridge Investments – Insurtech: Disruptions and Opportunities in the Insurance Industry, 2016, https://www.pinebridge.com/insights/investing/2016/10/insurtech-disruptions-and-opportunities-in-the-insurance-industry.

[3] D. Muoio, Markets Insider – Tesla wants to sell future cars with insurance and maintenance included in the price (TSLA), 2017, http://markets.businessinsider.com/news/stocks/tesla-cars-could-come-with-insurance-maintenance-included-2017-2-1001777951.

[4] The Geneva Association, Digital Transformation in Insurance, 2016, https://www.genevaassociation.org/media/940832/digitisation-in-insurance_hk-insurance-ceo-summit_fabian-sommerrock.pdf, page 10.

[5] Oliver Wyman, The Future of Insurtech in Germany – The insurtech-radar, 2016, http://www.oliverwyman.com/content/dam/oliver-wyman/v2/publications/2017/jun/Oliver-Wyman-Policen-Direkt-Global-InsurTech-Report-2017-Final.pdf.

products that are optimized for a digital customer journey.[6] Otherwise, customers will be disappointed in the end, finding a nice customer front end with a traditional analogue product.

3. Innovation for corporates is an evolutionary process

Insurance firms need to go through an innovation learning cycle. Most start with a phase of experimentation, where different formats can be tested and new processes are set up. Investing in startups is not something that all corporates have experience with, and spending €80 million as part of an M&A transaction may be familiar where investing €100,000 through a convertible note may not. This phase should be understood as a period of professionalization. This can mean that innovation topics are picked more selectively, and partnered projects organized more efficiently. Lastly, we observe pressure mounting to move to performance orientation where, in order to survive as a corporate function, corporate innovation needs to show KPIs that convince on real business impact. Metrics here can range from business goals such as improved online conversion rates, to fulfilling cultural goals, to reputational gains.[7]

4. You need to concentrate on the right innovation topics

The concept of Gartner's Hype Cycle gives a good first point of orientation for deciding on which topics of innovation to address.[8] It can be argued that the early hype cycle topics are at too early a stage to realize any business impact soon. For example, blockchain in 2016 was still in its infancy and so most insurance companies had trouble finding profitable use cases for the foreseeable future. Here, joint industry initiatives such

as the B3i are a solid foundation to lay groundwork before an actual go-to-market. At the other end of the scale are topics that are already established in most organizations (e.g. SEO, SEA[9]). Here, it can be argued that these topics too should not be the prime focus of an innovation function as they should be "business as usual" for relevant business units. So what is left? A lot! From "smart home" to "connected car" – customers will judge which innovations are here to stay.

5. Use scouting to partner up with innovative startups

Scouting can be described as the systematic process to "identify new opportunities for partnership, co-development, licensing or acquisition".[10] How do you pick the right targets, and approach them? Scouting has many parallels with a sales function: leads are generated through different channels (e.g. demo days, conferences, desk research); startups are approached via scouts (sometimes the other way around); collaboration potential is discussed and joint ideas are developed until both parties agree to do a proof of concept … sometimes followed by a project that scales.[11]

However, to steer this process efficiently:

a. Know what you are looking for! You need a clear picture of what is interesting for your organization. Without the buy-in of the business unit, collaborations will stay in the sphere of the innovation management function, and rarely scale.

---

[6] BCG and Google, Insurance @ Digtial-20X by 2020, 2014, http://image-src.bcg.com/BCG_COM/Insurance-at-Digital-20x-2020-Mar-2014-India_tcm21-28795.pdf, page 20.

[7] E. Milsbergs et al., Innovation Metrics: Measurement to Insight, White Paper, http://www.innovationmanagement.se/wp-content/uploads/pdf/Innovation-Metrics-NII.pdf, pages 4ff.

[8] Gartner, Hype Cycle for Digital Insurance, 2016, https://www.gartner.com/doc/3355217/hype-cycle-digital-insurance-.

[9] SEO (Search Engine Optimization) increases your website's visibility in organic result lists. SEA (Search Engine Advertising) increases web traffic to your site through digital advertising.

[10] Nerac, Scouting for Innovation: Global Benchmarking Study, 2009, https://www.nerac.com/scouting-for-innovation-global-benchmarking-study/.

[11] Mills, H. and Tubiana, B. (2013) Innovation in insurance: the path to progress, Deloitte University Press, https://dupress.deloitte.com/dup-us-en/topics/innovation/innovation-in-insurance.html.

b. Get the right technologies in place to support your process. This means on the one hand internal tools (e.g. tracking databases), but also technologies for cooperation (e.g. APIs that allow startups to play with some test data).

c. Get processes in place to be able to move quickly on pilots. Your startup partners don't have the same amount of time and money as you think you do.[12]

6. Go where innovation happens

Innovation does not necessarily come to you – you have to go where innovation is. Your HQ may be in Hamburg, but if InsurTech startups locate in Silicon Valley, London, and Berlin, you have to work out how to connect with them there. Although they are resource-intensive, especially for smaller insurance companies, there are clear gains in installing innovation scouts in major locations to be close to where "the magic happens".[13]

7. Partner with the best

Partnering with established accelerators (e.g. Startupbootcamp[14]), company builders (e.g. FinLeap), or venture capitalists to have good access to the latest trends, startups, and people is an alternative, saving on set-up and operational costs, and offering quicker impact and opportunities to learn from others.

8. Invest in startups

This is growing,[15] but is arguably still a novel activity for many incumbents. An investment can increase mutual commitment; and business units will always prioritize innovation projects differently, when an equity investment is involved. An investment is a very good chance to get to know a partner/industry/technology in depth relatively cheaply. You might secure important technology at the expense of a direct competitor. While you do not want to limit the growth trajectory of your startup partner, you still have more influence this way.

External innovation management – i.e. leveraging external partners, peers, and customers to make advances in innovation – can be a major lever to advance an established insurance company in its digital transformation process. The author is an active investor and has worked with 250+ startups, and from this deep experience, this chapter has concentrated on the drivers that are important to implement external innovation management successfully, and as part of a digital agenda. The "silver bullet" to make it all work has not yet been found, but corporate innovation management *can* make a lasting contribution to the success of an insurance company. No guarantees – but trying and failing will take you much further than sitting it out.

[12] M. Blake, Insurtech – an Industry Dilemma, KPMG, 2017, https://home.kpmg.com/au/en/home/insights/2017/03/insurtech-dilemma-insurance-technology.html.

[13] R. Huckstep, How the Incumbents are Responding to the InsurTech Evolution, 2016, https://www.linkedin.com/pulse/how-incumbents-responding-insurtech-evolution-rick-huckstep?trk=mp-reader-card.

[14] https://www.startupbootcamp.org/blog/2017/01/startupbootcamp-insurtech-kicks-off-2017-program/.

[15] CB Insight, Insurance Tech Startups Raise $1.7B across 173 deals in 2016, 2017, https://www.cbinsights.com/blog/2016-insurance-tech-funding/.

The New World of the Connected Customer – The Future of Microinsurance?

By Pauline Davies
Partner, Fee Langstone and CEO, InsuredHQ

The world's population is connected today in more ways than it has ever been, thanks to the Internet and the rapid rise over the last thirty years of web-based methods of communication – except in areas where it is barely connected at all. Internet usage estimates current as at March 2017[1] indicate that Europe contributes 10.9% of the world's population, of which 77.4% has Internet access. In North America, which holds 4.8% of the total population of the world, the number rises to 88.1%. It is probably fair to assume that on both of those continents, the Internet is available (on some basis) to virtually anyone who wants it. The same, though, cannot be said of other regions of the world, with Africa being the most extreme example. Africa holds 16.6% of the global population at almost 1.25 billion people, and only 27.7% of that number are Internet users, i.e. just over one in four.[2] If those numbers are broken down a little further, the discrepancies between Africa and Europe/North America become even more pronounced. While Kenya is the leading light, at 77.8% population penetration, only one other country (Mauritius) exceeds 60% and 19 countries are below 10%. Those at the bottom of the list are Eritrea at 1.3% and Niger at 2%. Interestingly, the availability of the Internet in African countries appears to be only loosely reflective of the financial strength of those countries. Kenya, for example, has only the 22nd highest GDP per capita and it is 150th in the world, despite having greater Internet penetration than Europe.

Eritrea has the 34th highest GDP per capita (of 53 countries) in Africa, and Niger has the 48th.[3]

So, if money is not necessarily the reason for low connectivity, what other reasons might there be?

The stark reality is that in many African countries there simply is no Internet, particularly in rural areas. There is a significant lack of investment in the necessary infrastructure, such as broadband cables. In some areas that do have Internet, there can be a lack of content in the local language, and there may also be education issues with potential users not able to use such technology as might be available.[4] Overall estimates put the number of people worldwide without Internet access at around four billion,[5] being around 60% of the world population. All of this, though, is changing. Facebook's Free Basic program, which allows mobile users to access Facebook without paying data charges, is now available in 42 countries, of which over half are in Africa. Facebook also has in development a satellite and a solar-powered drone to give Internet access to rural areas without the need for broadband cables.[6] Google's Project Loon, run by X (formerly Google X), has the goal of using a network of solar-powered balloons to achieve global Internet coverage. This project has been under way since 2013[7] and in 2015 was named in MIT Technology Review's list of Top Ten Breakthrough Technologies for that year.[8]

---

[1] Internet Users in the World by Regions – March 25, 2017, Internet World Stats Usage and Population Statistics, http://www.internetworldstats.com/stats.htm.

[2] Ibid.

[3] List of African Countries by GDP per Capita, International Monetary Fund Economic Outlook, October 2016, http://www.statisticstimes.com/economy/african-countries-by-gdp-per-capita.php.

[4] https://www.theguardian.com/world/2016/aug/01/facebook-free-basics-internet-africa-mark-zuckerberg.

[5] http://www.digitaltrends.com/web/4-billion-people-lack-internet-access/.

[6] https://info.internet.org/en/approach/.

[7] http://www.businessinsider.com/how-google-makes-project-loon-balloons-2016-8/?r=AU&IR=T/#the-goal-of-project-loon-is-to-use-a-network-of-solar-powered-balloons-to-beam-broadband-to-areas-without-internet-access-1.

[8] https://www.technologyreview.com/s/534986/project-loon/.

Even discounting these advances, and starting from a very low base, Africa still leads the way in growth rates for Internet penetration. Penetration improved by over 7,700% in the years 2000–2017, compared to the already well-serviced North America, which grew by only 196% in the same period, and Europe (500%).[9]

What's this got to do with insurance generally, and microinsurance in particular?

Microinsurance can be generally defined as insurance for low-income people who are not served by social security, and which is characterized by low premiums and coverage limits.[10] The most common types of insurance products offered to this market segment tend to be accident, health, and life covers, with some agricultural and property risks being insured. It can readily be understood that this sector of the world community is the most at risk when catastrophe strikes, and it has also become apparent that it is the poor who will be disproportionately adversely affected by climate change.[11] Insurance mitigates against risk and hence reduces vulnerability. Those who are better equipped to recover from financial adversity are also better contributors to national economies, as opposed to being drains on national resources. Hence, the delivery of insurance products to this market is a priority for many countries, particularly in India, Africa, Asia, and South America. The delivery of microinsurance remains a significant challenge, though. Many factors come into play here including delivery costs that make the premium too high; customers being insufficiently savvy on the benefits of insurance; the limited range of products available; lack of access to remote communities; and the lack of bank accounts from which to pay premiums and receive claim benefits. The result is that, despite annual growth rates in microinsurance of around 30%, coverage rates remain woefully low – estimated at 5.43% in Africa for 2014.[12]

---

[9] Internet Users in the World by Regions, Internet World Stats Usage and Population Statistics, 25 March 2017, http://www.internetworldstats.com/stats.htm.

[10] http://www.microinsurancenetwork.org/brief-history.

[11] https://openknowledge.worldbank.org/bitstream/handle/10986/22787/9781 464806735.pdf.

[12] http://worldmapofmicroinsurance.org/.

Technological advances have certainly assisted in improving the distribution rates. Mobile network operators have for some years now been seen as ideal insurance partners because of their reach into otherwise unconnected sectors of the population for marketing, client acquisition, and premium payment. Mobile technology does though have its own limitations in the context of insurance delivery. Many insurance products, particularly in markets where insurance is a novel and not well-understood concept, are sold as "freemium" products, i.e. policies that are incorporated as an additional benefit to users of the telco's service. Not only does this give rise to the challenge of converting customers into those who pay a premium, it can mean that customers don't even realize that they *have* the insurance – which means that they then don't claim when they need to. There is also no sales agent in the sales chain, so no product explanation or assistance with enrolment. Premium collection for paid cover can also be an issue, with premium generally taken by way of mobile wallets or by deductions from air-time credit. Mobile wallets are not held by all mobile users so this is a definite limiting factor; and deductions from air-time have the downside of using credit so that customers may need to top up before they can make calls. Despite all this, mobile phone networks offer one of the most successful means currently available to sell insurance outside the developed world.

What, then, if we look ahead a few years to focus not on what is achievable now, but what may be achievable in the future?

The Internet will be a game-changer because it will solve so many of the problems currently besetting the delivery of microinsurance. Once people have access to Internet-enabled smartphones, let alone PCs and tablets, multiple possibilities emerge:

1. The delivery of meaningful education about insurance and risk management, in the language (including the dialect) of the user can be made available. This will not be limited to

written material either: video and audio will give access to the same information, for those who struggle with the written word.

2. Of course, those who can't read will not be able to write either so there is likely to still be a role for sales agents, at the very least because they may well be a trusted member of the community who can also explain the nature of the product being purchased. But imagine the credibility of a sales agent with a tablet who can help a client to complete an online proposal, receive immediate acceptance (or otherwise), and generate and print the policy documents on the spot. At the same time, the client data and the financial implications of the cover being purchased are automatically loaded into the insurer's cloud-based policy management system, so there are never any questions over when the risk commenced, and where the paperwork may have got to after having been sent by mail.

3. Premium can be paid by online means and will not be bank-account dependent. PayPal is an obvious example. WhatsApp announced in early 2017 that it is soon to launch online payments as well. And, of course, if money can be sent it can also be received, which will assist with the movement of claim payments.

4. The fact that the insurer will be running a cloud-based policy management system means that it will have reduced its overhead costs and therefore made low-premium insurance more viable. No servers, no IT department, no double-handling of items for processing.

5. The range of insurance products available to consumers will not only be able to be greatly expanded, but policies will be able to be tailored to individual need. Online auto-rating will enable much greater flexibility in terms of sums insured, levels of policy excess, the range of property that can be covered, and so on. At the same time, the insurer will be better able to assess (automatically) individual risk.

6. It will be possible to process online, assisted by the uploading of photos of damage or receipts and invoices.

7. Then, of course, there is data analytics. Once information is online it becomes available to be used by insurers in ways that may not currently be possible. It will become a tool for understanding risk and customer behaviour and as a means for fraud detection.

What is particularly interesting about all of this is that all the technology described here already exists and is gaining some traction in the developed world. Online sales channels are increasingly being seen as essential, particularly as a means of reaching the so-called millennials who expect to be able to do everything online, without having to visit an office or sit on hold with a call centre. While insurers, to a large extent, are not yet using cloud-based policy management systems, that is certainly changing.

It may yet be some time before the less-developed areas of the world start to see the use of the Internet as an essential part of daily life in the same way as is the case in Europe, North America, and countries such as New Zealand and Australia, but in many ways, they will start ahead of the game, with technology that is no longer in its infancy and which can deliver real benefits at significant pace.

Personal Asset Liability Management System

By Ming Chiu
CEO, Actuarial Financial Group

and Yawei Cui, PhD
Senior Academic Director, Moody's Analytics

The first wave of InsurTech innovations in the period 2010–17 have already made profound impacts on the traditional insurance value chain. Internet-based innovations in insurance prior to the invention of the term InsurTech concentrated on the product price comparisons and broadening product distribution channels through the Internet, for example, Policybazaar in India[1] illustrates the importance of price comparison portals in more price-sensitive markets while the rise and fall of InsWeb in the US shows the limitation of pure Internet insurance distribution channels. The key features of this wave of InsurTech innovations (starting in 2010) are the disaggregation of the insurance value chain and connected insurance – anywhere anytime. Traditional retail auto product design and pricing have been changed by the availability of telematics, and pricing algorithms based on usage-based insurance and behavioural-based insurance.[2] Underwriting processes are being enhanced by ubiquitous smartphones and big data algorithms running on the cloud.

China's ZhongAn insurance, with a strong Internet startup gene since its founding in 2013, utilized cloud computing and real-time pricing to issue over 100 million package transportation insurance policies during the 11 November 2015 ecommerce big promotion day.

Drones and aerial images are being used to underwrite properties and accelerate property damage claims. Cape Analytics uses machine learning to identify the property risk level based on aerial imagery. Dropin has developed a platform for live streaming video from drones or smartphones to help insurers adjust claims remotely. Wearable devices can bring rewards to policy-holders who practice healthy lifestyles by lowering their healthcare costs. In 2016, Springbuk, a healthcare analytics firm, published a research finding claiming that over a two-year period, employees using wearable fitness monitoring devices had an average US$1,292 lower healthcare costs than employees in the control group.[3] UK-based Neos provides a home insurance product, underwritten by Munich Re, which comes with eight sensors and a camera to help detect potential issues in a home. When your home becomes safer because of connected smart devices and enhanced driving technology continuously pushing driving risks lower, personal risks become more standardized and commoditized.

While these innovations help insurers innovate on the *supply side* of insurance business, it is widely accepted that policy-holders have difficulties in understanding the features of these insurance products and appreciating the cost/benefit of the offerings. We see an important and emerging opportunity to combine traditional actuarial pricing and reserve models with more innovative arsenals, such as big data and artificial intelligence, to create sophisticated analytics for visualization and product customization on the *demand side* of insurance business.

We should not overstate the capability of big data and artificial intelligence in predicting the probability of occurrences of unforeseen events such as illness, disability, car accidents, or even deaths that individuals and families may encounter, over traditional actuarial methods. Mobile apps and online platforms

[1] KPMG and H2 Ventures, 2016 FINTECH100 Leading Global Fintech Innovators.

[2] Nino Tarantino, Octo Telematics, How to Implement UBI and Telematics Programs.

[3] Chris O'Malley, Can Wearable Fitness Devices Lower Healthcare Costs?, http://www.crains.com/article/news/can-wearable-fitness-devices-lower-healthcare-costs.

developed by independent InsurTech startups help policy-holders or potential insurance purchasers better understand their risk exposures and insurance needs. Swiss company FinanceFox claims to be the first completely independent service platform for insureds' needs with access to all one's insurance contracts anytime anywhere and policy exchange with one click. Moreover, we envision that the next wave of innovation for online finance platforms will push the demand side of financial services analytics to a much more sophisticated level. Individuals and families will have access to an online real-time 360-degree view of all physical and intangible assets, liabilities, and unforeseen event risks and solutions. Personal finance platforms such as Mint and Personal Capital have pioneered the concept of comprehensive personal asset and liability analytics with a focus on the cash flow analysis. China's Ant Financial pioneered the concept of "digital life", which consolidated customers' payments, insurance needs, and wealth management activities into one platform.

Institutional asset liability management practices have evolved from cash flow analysis to economic valuation of financial statements to scenario-based economic projections. In the US, life insurance companies are required to perform cash flow testing while European Solvency II is a comprehensive principle-based insurance regulatory framework that requires economic value simulations. An updated personal asset liability management system may extend its capability beyond cash flow analysis of bank deposits, salaries, mortgages, car loans, credit card payments, and various liability payments.

For the emerging Chinese middle class, getting "real-time" valuation of their real estate holdings, cars, investment portfolios, and deducting the liabilities to arrive at their net worth is a welcome utility. Several Chinese FinTech startups, such as WaCai and 51 Credit Card, incorporated comprehensive personal finance book-keeping functionality in their apps. Demand will also increase for projections of future personal asset and liability cash flows and valuations, as well as various insurance needs and coverage by life cycle stages. For instance, recent hot topics among Chinese middle-class families include the financial impact of having a second child, increased tax-advantaged savings for retirement, and long-term care insurance

for ageing parents. A sophisticated asset liability projection system with user defined "what-if" scenarios will facilitate making better decisions. Such a high-value sophisticated financial analytical toolkit was not available on the individual level before the emergence of FinTech and has yet to appear in the personal apps marketplace.

The rise of robo-advisory[4] addresses individual asset accumulation for long-tail customers in the wealth management industry. In order to apply asset allocation optimization algorithms, the investor's risk appetite and risk tolerance must be evaluated. The spending pattern and attitude toward saving or borrowing can be accurately depicted by analysing one's bank statements, thus providing a powerful predictor for one's risk aversion.

However, we argue that InsurTech should serve as the core of a 360-degree, personal asset liability management system as opposed to an aggregation of parallel functional modules dealing with deposits and credits, investments, book-keeping, investments, and insurance. When we consider the most important needs and protection that a person or a family encounter, we see healthcare services, retirement savings, protection against accidental mortality, primary resident damage, and many unforeseen events as the truly life-changing contingencies. Insurance companies already collect the most sensitive data – on health status, retirement needs, life coverage, property value, and more. InsurTech, utilizing embedded traditional actuarial models for evaluating contingent event probabilities as well as big data predictive analytics, can paint a much clearer picture of an individual's unforeseen event risks, and provide better cost, and benefit, analysis for insurance coverage. Important insights can also be gained into credit rating, and annuity payment projections for annuity contracts, risk coverage for illness and disability, the

---

[4] FINRA, Report on Digital Investment Advice.

cost of insurance for mortality, expected motor vehicle premium rates, and agents' commission structure. These suggestions make insurance products more transparent and easier to understand, and can create a new personal asset liability system that connects the demand side of financial services to the supply side.

A cloud-based automatic pricing and underwriting solution can be developed to provide straight-through processing. Truly customized insurance solutions for individuals or families therefore become a reality because the parameters needed for actuarial pricing are uploaded directly from the policy-holder to the insurance company with almost instantaneous underwriting and insurance issuance. Insurance coverage plays a vital role in optimizing a personal or family utility function by providing certainties surrounding personal wealth. We predict that an integrated personal asset liability platform can effectively lower the liability cash flows by lowering mortgage rates, car loan rates, and credit card rates for the customer, while enhancing the risk appetite on the investment side.

We are working towards the next generation of comprehensive personal finance platform with InsurTech as the centre of the architecture with full asset liability analysis capabilities delivered by key functional modules including the WealthTech-enabled investment module, the LendingTech-enabled deposit and borrowing module, a book-keeping module, and a social networking module to connect with the financial advisory supply side. Welcome to the Personal Asset Liability Management System.

Social Media in Insurance

By Erik Abrahamsson
Founder and CEO, Digital Fineprint (DFP)

Social media has earned a place in the life of almost every single person on the planet. There are now 1.97 billion active Facebook users as of April 2017.[1] As of June 2017, the world population was 7.5 billion, meaning a quarter of the world's population is on social media.[2] Because of this, one would have expected insurers to start using this omnipresent technology much faster than is currently the case. But using social media for insurance is hard, and expert guidance is needed when navigating the technical, legal, and ethical landscape of social media analytics. In this chapter, I will explain some of the main challenges, and propose ways for how we as an industry can solve them. There will also be examples of insurers getting it right, and wrong, and two alternative scenarios for the future of insurance. Ready? Let's get into it.

We can start by agreeing on the fact that social media is ubiquitous in almost all other industries. We use Facebook to login to our Spotify accounts and get music recommendations. We order flowers and groceries directly from our WhatsApp or WeChat accounts. And even banks have woken up to the massive opportunities inherent in analysing social media data, and use it for marketing and for helping users to a smoother customer journey. The birth of FinTech in the late 2000s has accelerated the development of social into financial services, and we are now starting to see the beginning of the same trends in insurance.[3]

When we started Digital Fineprint, an InsurTech company based in London, we identified three key challenges to using social media in the insurance industry, arising from the idiosyncratic nature of insurance. Understanding each of the three challenges is highly important for any industry player attempting to enter the space, so let's go through them one by one.

First, insurers need to convince their customers to share their social media profile (often by clicking "Connect with LinkedIn" or "Log in with Facebook"). If there is not a clear customer benefit, users are less likely to do so, and insurers will not have sufficient data to analyse.

Secondly, the platforms themselves need to be aware and approve of the way insurers use this sensitive data. In a rapidly changing legal environment, platforms such as WeChat, Twitter, LinkedIn, and Facebook are all updating their privacy policies, and only the fastest moving technology companies are able to keep up with and stay ahead of the changes. Insurers lack the technical capability and expertise to deal with this very dynamic data landscape.

Finally, even if users and platforms agree to share data with an insurer, there is a challenging technical difficulty inherent in distilling insights from massive amounts of unstructured data. Predicting insurance needs, giving insights to insurance agents, and calculating risk classifications from social media data is extremely difficult, which is why even social media analytics companies working with banks have not yet moved over to insurance (as of the time of writing). It seems that only by focusing solely on insurance and solely on social media data can this technical challenge be overcome.

When Admiral launched "FirstCarQuote", targeted at first-time drivers or car owners in November 2016, they were planning on using data from a user's Facebook profile in order to set the price of their car insurance. This would be based on things like what posts they had "liked" and the way they spoke online – whether they wrote in short, concise sentences and used lists. Their launch failed, but three problems were painfully illustrated. First, customers saw no benefit in sharing their sensitive Facebook data

---

[1] https://www.statista.com/statistics/272014/global-social-networks-ranked-by-number-of-users/.

[2] http://www.worldometers.info/world-population/.

[3] http://www.bbc.co.uk/news/business-37224847.

with Admiral, and the insurer did not do a good job of communicating the benefit to the user. Secondly, Facebook's developer agreements were not followed, which led to the access being revoked on the same day the initiative launched. Thirdly, media reports from several sources indicated that Admiral was not technically ready to analyse the relevant data, and thus would not have been able to make sense of any collected data. As a result, FirstCarQuote ended up being a PR failure and Admiral was forced by Facebook to pull the product less than two hours before it was due to launch.[4] More insurers are now instead getting help from external vendors instead of building in-house solutions for using sensitive social media data.[5]

It is perhaps then no surprise that insurers have been slow to adapt to the social media revolution, despite a few attempts. In 2014, AXA announced a strategic partnership with Facebook and it was seen as a brilliant, innovative move by industry observers and insiders alike.[6] But after almost three years, what has actually happened? Can customers buy insurance on Facebook yet? Is social media being used to augment underwriting data? Surprisingly, all the massive resources invested by insurance companies have not led to meaningful innovation in the niche field of using social media in insurance. This, I believe, is due to the three key challenges, which have yet to be overcome by the incumbent insurers. We therefore now see significant innovation and development from startups in the niche field of social media analytics for the insurance industry. One example is Common Easy, which allows users to create a "safety net" with their social network; Friendsurance, which uses an online P2P insurance combining social networks with well-established insurance companies; and Inspool, which uses social networks to let drivers connect with family and friends to form their own insurance groups.[7]

So what does all this mean for the future of insurance? I'll take the daring approach and suggest two alternative futures for the industry, which will contrast two ways in which insurers can respond to the growth of social media. Let's call them the "Skyscanner scenario" and the "Netflix scenario". In short, I think that incumbent insurers will either end up as travel companies did in the mid-2000s, or, if things go well, as the Netflix of the 2010s. Let me explain how: when the travel industry started seeing online sales on comparison sites, direct-to-consumer plays and more, the industry as a whole closed their eyes and let innovative players scoop up the entire online market. Price became the key differentiator, and suddenly comparison sites became the key venue for booking especially airline tickets. Here, the industry missed out on an amazing opportunity to use social media data to give travel recommendations, build a trusted relationship, and create massive value for its customers. It is only now, ten years later and ten years too late, that the travel industry has started using, for example, Instagram to spread its message. The insurance industry is today, unfortunately, travelling on the same trajectory, with more and more comparison sites leading to commodification of personal lines of insurance.

Contrastingly, when Netflix started seeing its DVD rental business dwindle in the face of online streaming, they realized that by taking its most valuable resource – its database – it could completely turn around its fate. It therefore took its customer database and combined it with aggressive social media marketing, personal recommendations, and a great use of analytics.[8] As a result, it became the leader in online streaming, and is now vastly more profitable than it could ever have been if it had relied on a DVD rental base. Insurers now have the exact same opportunity, and all they need to do is to take advantage of the innovative work being done in social media analytics. By combining customer insights with social

[4] http://www.bbc.co.uk/news/business-37847647.

[5] https://www.fca.org.uk/publication/thematic-reviews/tr15-07.pdf.

[6] https://www.the-digital-insurer.com/axa-facebook-creating-stir-digital-insurance-implications/.

[7] https://letstalkpayments.com/101-insurtech-startups-revolutionizing-the-4-5-trillion-dollar-insurance-industry/.

[8] https://hbr.org/2011/09/netflix-bold-disruptive-innovation.

media targeting of advertising, or by linking risk scores to online profiles, a whole new world of opportunity is there for the taking.

The use of social media in the insurance industry is inevitable. The data is too valuable and too useful for it not to be used by insurers. As an industry, we will simply have to agree on how, not if, it can be used in a way that benefits the customer. By overcoming the challenges already mentioned, we can take a first step towards a social media-enabled insurance company.

To have a look into the future, we can look to the east. Many industry observers have watched Chinese InsurTech ZhongAn grow from nothing since its inception in 2013, to offering 200 different insurance products and underwriting 3.6 billion policies for 369 million customers by the end of 2015.[9] This is a growth journey that has absolutely astounded the industry. Observers are wondering what could have enabled it to grow so quickly, and already reach profitability.[10] The author's view is that everything so far discussed is represented in ZhongAn, as they managed to get everything right and overcome the three challenges. They took a "Netflix" approach to innovation, and created more lessons than any other InsurTech for the rest of the world to learn from. Incumbent Chinese insurers were left gaping in horror and in awe at the massive growth, and are now struggling to replicate the steps ZhongAn took to achieve its success.[11]

So what did ZhongAn do differently to make all this happen? They integrated their entire insurance offering with WeChat, the largest Chinese social media platform.[12]

[9] https://www.wsj.com/articles/chinas-first-online-only-insurer-zhong-an-plans-up-to-2-billion-ipo-1455790288.

[10] http://insuranceasianews.com/news/chinas-zhong-an-online-portal-posts-us30m-net-profit-in-2015/.

[11] https://www.bcgperspectives.com/content/articles/insurance_roadmap_winning_insurance_goes_digital/.

[12] http://www.scmp.com/news/china-insider/article/1441962/wechats-latest-viral-hit-china-health-insurance.

InsurTech and the Promise of "Property Value Hedging Technology"

By Gilad Shai
Founder, InsurTech LA

What is InsurTech? For the tech entrepreneur, it's the dreaded and perennial question: what does your company do exactly? The answer only gets tougher when it comes to insurance – often seen as a slow-moving and stale industry that lacks innovation. Yet InsurTech, when made geeky-cool, is "property value hedging technology". Now, the advancements that InsurTech is bringing to the insurance industry are what Airbnb and Uber have brought to the housing and transportation industries – even as hedging risk and value recovery remain key insurance foundations. InsurTech is any company, or product, that leverages technology to provide value in the insurance value chain.

The Insurance Value Chain

A customer's relationship with an insurance company has three – sometimes four – stages: policy purchase, premium payment, claim filing, and recovery. An insurer maintains many processes and operations, out of the customer's view, to sustain this relationship and keep its profits growing. The first stage of the relationship typically consists of exposure, education, discovery, decision, qualification, approval, and purchase. The second stage entails interactions with the customer to collect payments, deepen the relationship, and cross-sell. In the third and final stage: if damage is incurred, the insured submits a claim – via an agent, customer service, or online – which is then reviewed, checked for fraud, adjusted, approved, and potentially paid out to cover the loss. Each of these functions – the links of the insurance value chain – carries frictions and thus opportunities for improvement via technology. Such opportunities can be seized via ad-hoc technological add-ons or smart exploitation of the latest technology trends.

Technology Trends

Five key technology trends are shaping insurance (and other industries):

1. Big data and modelling
2. Automation
3. Connectivity and mobility
4. IT infrastructure
5. Telematics and Internet of Things (and drones).

These trends are the basis of much of the innovation by insurance companies in the strategic dimensions of customer engagement, marketing and distribution, insights, productivity, and risk. Currently, insurance companies mainly compete with each other in the marketing and distribution dimensions, with the goal of increasing market share, or up-selling, via customer engagement. This approach is straightforward. When successful, it yields growth. But is it enough? Or should insurers be doing more technological innovation within their businesses?

If they did, incumbents could pick low-hanging fruit by adapting existing technologies to their systems and processes. They might, for example, harness big data to enable commercial underwriters to better assess risk; let claims adjusters use pictures, captured by drones, to help process claims; or allow body shops to bid automatically on claims and agents to manage their business from their mobile devices. However, in the long term, the landscape of the industry will change. The incumbents need to decide if they are going to determine the direction of this change actively, as they have done in the past, or if they will be forced to adjust passively to it.

Opportunities for InsurTech

Historically, insurance companies' competitive advantage has always been strong brand, distribution channel, and vendor management. Recently, insurance companies, brokerages, and agencies have recognized the advancement in technology and the emerging need for an on-demand, on-the-move, tailor-made coverage with a modern user experience. Alas, they are not technology companies and technology is not part of their DNA. To make things worse, in the past they identified IT as cost and outsourced the majority of their operations and know-how, making themselves heavily dependent on offshore service providers. This conservative culture left the insurance companies vulnerable and without a technological competitive advantage. Now, because the playing field is shifting towards technology and the insurance companies are not equipped with the right gear, mindset, and expertise, there is an opportunity for entrepreneurs to found InsurTech startups as:

1. Facilitators

2. Enablers

3. New kinds of insurers.

Each of these three buckets can be categorized with one or more of the following attributes: policy aggregator, coverage compare engine, Platform-as-a-Service (PaaS), data aggregator, data modelling, IoT, customer engagement, risk management, productivity tools, office management, digital insurer, digital broker, and digital agency. Facilitators primarily offer or develop customer-facing applications that simplify the search for an insurance policy. They started servicing customers prior to the 2015 surge in InsurTech startups. A common example is a policy-price compare engine. Most facilitators monetize on affiliate or brokerage fees, and they have become a major source of customer acquisition flow in the digital age. Enablers are companies that develop technology to help insurers offer new lines of business (LoB) or improve operations. Importantly, they do not provide coverage. Instead, they work with other companies –

either incumbents or new entrants – whose existence is made possible by the enablers' technology. Some enablers, for example, permit insurers to offer usage-based insurance (UBI). Others collect data and assist with fraud detection. Enabler entrepreneurs have the largest pool of opportunities in the insurance value chain. One caveat: only startups able to endure a long procurement process will be able to enjoy those opportunities.

Finally, the new insurers. They provide coverage and offer new lines of business or familiar insurance products with better user experiences and cheaper and scalable infrastructure. It will take years before, say, mobile-first P&C insurers threaten the market share of incumbents. But, in the short term, they will likely be bellwethers for the industry, providing proof of concept for new means of customer engagement and claims processing and new sorts of insurance products.

The main investors in InsurTech startups are venture capital (VC) firms and angel investors with reinsurers and insurer corporate venturing arms. The InsurTech entrepreneurs together with the VCs and the angels will have several possible exits to gain a return on their investment. They may take a company public, sell it, or grow it to a substantial size. The motivation behind the reinsurer and insurer venture arms is similar to the VC's return on investment (ROI) goals and usually their investment portfolio serves the strategic need of the sole limited partner, the reinsurer. The expectation is that the portfolio startup will have a guided opportunity to be acquired for a market segment, or get acquired for a technology stack. When planning the long-term goal and possible exit of an InsurTech startup it is important to consider the different opportunities and challenges that a core system, for example, a policy system, and an auxiliary system, for example, an AI-powered insurance agent chatbot, bring to the table. Furthermore, peripheral product relies on the assumption that insurers can integrate new product with their legacy system. In many cases, replacing an old core system is probably easier than just reforming it, though recognizing this and making such a change is likely to be a large cultural obstacle for many companies. So, will insurance companies disappear? No! They will just be better.

Insurance as "Property Value Hedging Technology"

Insurance is an important financial tool. It is an economy enabler that lets people make larger bets on the risks they want by hedging away the risks they don't want. When we take a step back and look at the evolution of P&C insurance, we see that insurance enables transportation of people and goods; it guards trade, exploration, and discovery. It hedges the risk for construction of homes, commercial buildings, and infrastructure. In other words, it empowers individuals and businesses. Innovative ideas can be adopted from other industries and business models.

Software-as-a-Service (SaaS) changed the way that businesses procure and utilize software. The next step in evolution, PaaS, reshaped how businesses develop software. PaaS reduces cost of entry, reduces operational costs, shifts maintenance responsibility, and is scalable and available on demand. The same way PaaS powers companies to build and deliver better products, Insurance-as-a-Service (IaaS) powers insurance companies to develop new products.

IaaS Will Propel the "Property Value Hedging Technology" Story

When applying the general concept of SaaS to the insurance industry, one can imagine various insurance processes being turned into services, including underwriting, claims, and even the overall insurance process itself. By making these processes generally available in an easy manner, these services are likely to spur innovation by reducing the barriers to entry for new and more creative firms.

Ideally, a company will be able to recognize a demand for a coverage, or risk hedging, and supply a new insurance product within a short period. Say, for example, that an insurer notices that newly-married couples would like to hedge their risk of having their honeymoon ruined by bad weather. A nimble startup might be able to go to market quickly with a server-less technology stack that integrates IaaS and SaaS components.

IaaS is not Limited to the First Movers

Companies that define themselves as fast followers should harness IaaS to secure InsurTech as a factor in the Strength and the Opportunity quadrants of their SWOT analysis instead of the Weakness and the Threat quadrants. InsurTech has the potential to radically improve the insurance industry's failure to innovate. Collaboration between large insurance providers and InsurTech startups will benefit both sides. The former will bring the customers and brands, and the latter will bring the innovative energy, new ideas, and culture.

Insurance 2029 – Life Backup Companion

By George Kesselman
President and Founder, InsurTech Asia Association

What if you knew the precise possibility of things going wrong today, including falling sick, having a freak accident, and anything happening at home? Imagine waving off Nikola (your personal AI companion) who is telling you about a few things particularly to watch out for on that day, alongside your morning briefing. Having an absolute certainty that, as annoying as any of those risks are, it would not be the end of the world if it happened: you will receive absolutely the best medical treatment and any of the assets will be quickly and seamlessly replaced. You tell your AI companion: "Stop being such a worrier, Nikola!" In response you hear a light chuckle in your ear: "George, I'm here to worry so you don't have to." That's the world of tomorrow for insurance, where, in a not so distant future, this will become completely integrated into our everyday lives to the degree that it will fade away into the background. In the same way we don't think of an Apple iCloud subscription as insurance for our phone and computer data, we will stop thinking of insurance as a product and just start relating to it as our everyday-life backup, which will have an impact on our monthly insurance bills as shown in Figure 1.

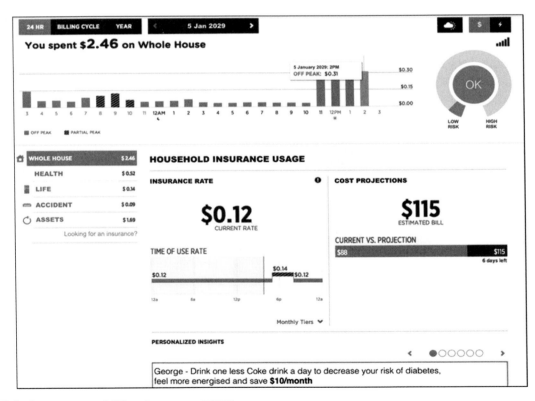

Figure 1: Your monthly insurance bill – January 2029

Welcome to the future where the proliferation of data about each and every one of us and our environment, together with a deep understanding of that data using machine learning, means the world becomes a lot more predictable. As we speak, our civilization is advancing quickly in the understanding of human genetic coding and how that might increase our predisposition to certain diseases. That understanding, combined with an explosion in data from IoT, wearables, and things that surround our everyday lives, does mean that we can pinpoint exact risk probabilities. It's not as far-fetched as it sounds. Companies have already started using data to predict certain events like an individual's risk of heart attack hours before it happens and elderly fall rates even weeks before they occur.

The first question that comes to mind when most people think about that future possibility is whether we'd be open to sharing all this private data. It is likely to become a societal norm in the same way we get used to the idea that Google has the potential to scan our emails and web searches while Facebook can control our social media status. What used to be taboo less than ten years ago has become something that we have got used to. This data surveillance will not only take the form of real-time monitoring and management of risk but will be an indispensable day-to-day companion. It certainly sounds like an attractive future and one that can bring insurance back to its purpose of acting as a social safety net.

Let's take a step back and look at where insurance is now and how it will get to this future.

Back in Time: Back to Reality

Imagine a time when oil lamps dimly lit up streets. If you had the privilege of having one of those contraptions outside your home, you could be forgiven for not feeling overly joyous the majority of the time. While it certainly had an important purpose, it was difficult to service and oil had a nasty tendency to catch fire during storage and transport. Moreover, it needed someone to light it up and put it out on a daily basis, apart from regular cleaning. At that time, manufacturers were coming up with ever better and safer oil lamps but the "benefit" had a high overall ownership cost. It would have been very difficult for oil lamp manufacturers to realize that society needed the "utility of light" and not a better oil lamp. As a result, it wasn't lamp manufacturers that enabled the revolution of electricity and electric lighting that most of us now take for granted. The story of insurance is not dissimilar to the story of the transition from oil lamps to electricity. There are a lot of parallels and using this story is a powerful step change as a proxy that will give us a useful reference on how things could potentially evolve for the insurance industry on the way to becoming a utility.

The Power of a Utility

Over the years, insurance has evolved into the equivalent of a "complex oil lamp contraption". Complexities are profound in the need to address the inherent structural limitations of the current risk transfer model.

The only way forward for insurance is for it to become a utility, just like electricity or water. As a consumer you want insurance for exactly the same reasons that you want electricity: to enable greater joy, safety, and productivity. In the same way we do not think about electricity, insurance is something that is at the core of societal needs. Furthermore, similar to electricity, which expanded from the original purpose of lighting to powering everything from the Internet to transportation, once insurance becomes a utility there's a world of opportunities for insurance to impact our society positively on a much broader scale (see Table 1).

Table 1: Insurance vs. oil lamps

	Oil Lamps	Insurance Now (Oil Lamp Age)	Insurance Future (Utility)
Sales	Door to door	Door to door	On demand/instantaneous on/off and choice of few utility partners
Servicing	Regular manual cleaning	Mostly manual	Fully automated changes
Use	Fires, oil refills, manual lighting, and putting on and off on daily basis. Limited light, dirty, and smelly	Highly manual claims that take a very long time to initiate and settle. Quite common to have settlement different from expectations	Seamless system of lodging, settlement, and accident prevention
Fraud	People stealing oil during transport and operation	At least 10% of all claims are fraudulent	Integrated system with no loopholes or fraud
Pricing vs. Value	High price	High price	Closely matched

Insurance has been trying to solve its own problems incrementally for a long time. Despite all the investments and resources that have been thrown at it, insurance has only managed to move marginally in the past 20 years. There are challenging constraints together with powerful lobby groups that have continued to side-track progress.

Journey to the Future

As we progress from the day of "oil lamp" insurance to the future of insurance as a utility, there are going to be broadly three major phases of industry InsurTech transformation:

1. Optimization
2. Product redesign
3. Insurance as a utility.

This transformation will take place over the next 10 years and will see a combination of significant industry job losses as well as redistribution of value across the value chain in the history of the insurance industry. As we discuss the value redistribution, it's going to be important to keep in mind the current "value stack" as it will give us a good reference point in terms of how things are likely to progress.

Insurance Value Stack: Quick Refresh

The insurance value stack (see Table 2) is the average allocation of a dollar of customer insurance premium across broad areas of insurance expenses. This has been validated across an array of industry stakeholders and appears fairly uniform across major product lines of general insurance, life insurance, and commercial insurance.

First Phase: Optimization

The first phase is focused on introducing operational and distribution efficiencies to insurance firms, by applying digital solutions. Prime candidates include low hanging fruit like

Table 2: The insurance value stack

WHAT	SALES	CORE RISK	BACK OFFICE	RE-INSURANCE	FRAUD
VALUE	20%	55%	12–22%	5%	5%
WHY	SOURCING CLIENTS	ACTUAL LOSSES (CLAIMS)	OPERATING EXPENSES	INSURANCE OF INSURER	INFLATED & FRAUDULENT LOSSES
WHO	AGENTS BROKERS BANKS	CLIENTS	INSURERS	RE-INSURERS	CRIMINALS

Source: Data from Pivot Ventures "The Insurance Value Stack" by George Kesselman. Published on 29 Mar 2016. https://www.slideshare.net/GeorgeKesselman/value-stack-29-march-2016

auto-underwriting of simple risks, self-servicing policy changes, instant claims handling, sophisticated fraud detection, social marketing, and process automation for 80% of back-office tasks. While the application of technology is bringing costs down across sales, risk evaluation (underwriting), policy servicing, and claims, the released benefits will not be redistributed equally across the value chain. Distribution partners are expected to retain a disproportional share of the value while customers will likely see a modest increase in value in the form of discounts and expanded coverage. Value improvements combined with a step improvement in the service and sales experience encourage consumers to buy more insurance. Still, the scalability is challenged as customers are likely to struggle when trying to understand off-the-shelf insurance products and their inherent technical complexities.

Phase 2: Product Redesign – Closer Mirror Risks and Needs

The next phase will focus on digitizing insurance products. Conventional products will go through a redesign to simplify them. The granular nature of the products, both in terms of their size (sum assured) as well as their term, will mean that they can be custom-packaged to match customer's actual risk profile closely.

This will pave the way for mass tailoring of insurance. Based on an understanding of customers' unique risks, technology will allow us to create a package that will precisely address their needs. Think of the Uber driver who just needs insurance for his or her passengers during a trip. An Airbnb host now only needs coverage for that one night a month when he rents out one of his rooms. Risks that were previously non-insurable will become understood and insurable (e.g. food poisoning, epidemics, pre-existing medical conditions, and traffic delays). Being niche and digital as a channel will be the only way to distribute these products.

Value redistribution will accelerate through this phase with customers seeing a significant 25% boost, which, together with simpler, mass-tailored products, helps insurance to regain consumer trust. This in turn will help insurance to enter an exponential growth phase.

Phase 3: Insurance as a Utility – Welcome to the Future!

In the next decade, as both insurance products and operations undergo a profound transformation, insurance will start to resemble a utility. On the supply side you have risk capital and on the demand side there's a customer consumption of risk capital. Rather than pre-buying insurance, insurance will move into a realm to real-time consumption where risks are mitigated appropriately. Customers will be charged based on the exact protection provided to them on a usage basis. For example, if you played a risky sport on a Thursday and chose to eat unhealthily on the next Friday evening, you might find your insurance charges would spike over that micro period. In this last phase, value redistribution happens and the ecosystem achieves equilibrium with customers gaining 60%+ in extra value through the three phases. The boundaries between insurers and reinsurers could blur to the point where they become indistinguishable. At this point, insurance could go viral and quickly achieve the status of a universal Life Backup Companion, there to either help you identify and avoid risks or quickly fix whatever does goes wrong.

Table 3 shows the new insurance value stack.

"Hello, Nikola, how much did you say that ski trip is really going to cost me?"

Table 3: **The new insurance value stack**

TIME/VALUE	CORE RISK (CUSTOMER)	SALES (DISTRIBUTION)	BACK OFFICE (INSURER)	RE-INS (RE-INSURER)	FRAUD
NOW	55%	20%	15%	5%	5%
Phase 1 Y:2020	60%	18%	10%	5%	2%
Start Phase 2 Y:2025	75%	13%	5%	4%	1%
Start Phase 3 Y:2030	90%	4%	{———— 6% ————}		~0%

List of Contributors

All chapters are included in this book, all abstracts can be read online at http://fintechcircle.com/insights/.

Jeremy Abbett
General Partner, InsurTech.vc
www.linkedin.com/in/jeremyabbett
www.twitter.com/jeremytai

See abstract:
The Children of Tomorrow

Erik Abrahamsson
Founder and CEO, Digital Fineprint (DFP)
www.linkedin.com/in/boerik
www.twitter.com/abrahamssonerik

See chapter:
Social Media in Insurance

Anne Amlot
Media Relations Manager, Pitney Bowes
www.linkedin.com/in/anne-amlot-382b268
www.twitter.com/AnneAmlot

See abstract:
Insurance for millennials

Dimitri Anagnostopoulos
Partner, True North Partners
www.linkedin.com/in/dimitri-anagnostopoulos-97589a7b/

See chapter:
Think InsurTech Culture Before InsurTech Adoption

Steve Anderson
President, The Anderson Network
www.linkedin.com/in/taareport/
www.twitter.com/stevetn

See abstract:
Using Machine Learning for an Annual Account Review Process

Marguerite Arnold
Founder, MedPayRx
www.linkedin.com/in/marguerite-arnold-1b09a311b
www.twitter.com/FinTechGal

See abstract:
Insuretech – What the Heck

Tamer Ayasli
Senior Finance and Controlling Professional, InsurTech Consulting Partners
www.linkedin.com/in/tayasli
www.twitter.com/AyasliT

See abstract:
Open Exchange Platform Utilizing Distributed Ledger Technologies for Collateralized Reinsurance

Tobias Becker
Manager, Diconium Strategy
www.linkedin.com/in/tobiasbecker1/
www.twitter.com/tobiasbecker

See chapter:
Alexa, Can You Get me an Insurance? A Structured Approach to the Hyped Technology of Voice-Based Assistants

Melike Belli
Market Development Manager, Cybertonica Ltd
www.linkedin.com/in/melikebelli
www.twitter.com/melikebelli

See chapter:
InsurTech in Turkey – Challenges and Opportunities

Tom Benton
VP, Research and Consulting, Novarica
www.linkedin.com/in/tombenton
www.twitter.com/@T_Benton

See abstract:
Incumbents and InsurTech: Working together

Jesús Bernat
Chief Technical Officer and Co-Founder, Drivies
www.linkedin.com/in/jesus-bernat-vercher/

See chapter:
Disrupting Car Insurance – Drivies App Makes Driving More Fun, and Insurance Fairer

Patrick Bibas
CEO, Ellis-Car The Data Driven Company
www.linkedin.com/in/patrick-bibas-86927a1a/
www.twitter.com/elliscarvl

See abstract:
AI Will not Change your Life but Will Probably Save it!

Nick Bilodeau
Head of Marketing, Insurance, Canada, American Express
www.linkedin.com/in/nickbilodeau/
www.twitter.com/FinMktg

See chapter:
"INSoT" – The Insurance of Things and the Proliferation of Protection

Dr José Luis Blanco
Chief Data Officer and Co-Founder, Drivies
https://www.linkedin.com/in/jose-luis-blanco-murillo/

See chapter:
Disrupting Car Insurance – Drivies App Makes Driving More Fun, and Insurance Fairer

Dr J.H.F. Onno Bloemers
Head of Insurance Transformation, Delta Capita
www.linkedin.com/in/onnobloemers/
www.twitter.com/onnobloemers

See chapter:
The Future of Insurance – From Managing Policies To Managing Risks

Dylan Bourguignon
Founder and CEO, SO-SURE
www.linkedin.com/in/dylanbourguignon/
www.twitter.com/DB_entrepreneur

See abstract:
Why is Disrupting Insurance so Hard?

Joshua Bower-Saul
CEO, Cybertonica Ltd
www.linkedin.com/in/joshua-bower-saul-29209a6
www.twitter.com/JBowerSaul

See abstract:
AI and the Future of InsurTech

Yvonne Braun
Director of Long Term Savings, ABI
www.linkedin.com/in/yvonne-braun-92368919/
www.twitter.com/YvonneBraun4

See chapter:
The Potential of a Pension Dashboard Infrastructure for UK Pension Savers

Julien Breteau
Head of Content Marketing, Intrepid Ventures
www.linkedin.com/in/julienbreteau/
www.twitter.com/jmbreteau

See chapter:
Becoming Tech-First – Why Adopting a "Tech-First" Mindset is Non-Negotiable

Karolina Burmeister
Senior Relationship Manager, OP Financial Group
www.linkedin.com/in/kaburmeister/
www.twitter.com/kaburmeister

See chapter:
Seeing through the Hype – A Closer Look at Key Smart InsurTech Business Models

Jehangir Byramji
Strategy and Innovation Professional, Lloyds Banking Group
www.linkedin.com/in/jbyramji
www.twitter.com/jehangir_b

See abstract:
Predictive Insurance New Opportunities, New Competitive Landscape

Dan Callahan
Director of Communication, GWG Life
www.linkedin.com/in/danielcallahan
www.twitter.com/@gwglife

See abstract:
The search for a better life expectancy predictor leads an insurance company to a science lab

Donatella Cambosu
Editor, InsuranceUp
www.linkedin.com/in/donatella-cambosu-3851724
www.twitter.com/@janazond

See abstract:
An Italian InsurTech story – When a technology changes the market mindset

Louis Carbonnier
Digital Agency Co-Founder, Euler Hermes
www.linkedin.com/in/louiscarbonnier
www.twitter.com/@LCarbonnier

See abstract:
How InsurTech will eat into the value chain

Martin Carroll
Co-Founder and Partner, Information IQ Ltd
www.linkedin.com/in/martincarroll/
www.twitter.com/theiiqview

See abstract:
New Distribution Models

Juan Cartagena
CEO, Traity
www.linkedin.com/in/juancartagena
www.twitter.com/jc2go

See abstract:
The future of insurance is assurance

290

Tolga Ceylantepe
Country Manager, AXA Partners
www.linkedin.com/in/tolga-ceylantepe-887580a

See abstract:
Digital evolution in Turkish Insurance Market

Allen Chen
MBA Candidate, PKU National School of Development
www.linkedin.com/in/allenlchen/

See abstract:
Just Do it – a Case Study of SCF in China

Alberto Chierici
Co-Founder and CPO, SPIXII
www.linkedin.com/in/albertochierici
www.twitter.com/ChiericiAlberto

See chapter:
Insurance Expertise, Family, and Integrity – the Story of SPIXII's Founding Team

Susanne Chishti
CEO and Founder, FINTECH Circle and FINTECH Circle Institute
www.linkedin.com/in/susannechishti/
www.twitter.com/SusanneChishti

See abstract:
How the Combination of InsurTech and WealthTech Can Soften the Global Pension Crisis

Ming Chiu
CEO, Actuarial Financial Group
www.linkedin.com/in/ming-chiu-1606bb4/

See chapter:
Personal Asset Liability Management System

Peter Clarke
Managing Director, Insurercore Ltd
www.linkedin.com/in/peter-clarke-40420b56
www.twitter.com/@insurercore

See abstract:
Are intermediaries zombies?
Sabotaging the insurance industry – from the inside

Simon Cocking
Senior Editor, Irish Tech News
www.linkedin.com/in/simon-cocking-20540135
www.twitter.com/@SimonCocking

See abstract:
What the future could look like for InsurTech, and how soon it might happen

Robert Collins
COO, Crossbordr
www.linkedin.com/in/robertcollins2
www.twitter.com/doingchinabiz

See chapter:
Insurance in China

Quentin Colmant
Co-Founder, Qover
www.linkedin.com/in/quentin-colmant-89b0697/

See chapter:
Forget Peer-to-Peer, the Future of Insurance is Invisible and Parametric

Mica Cooper
CEO, Aisus.com – InsureCrypt
www.linkedin.com/in/mica-cooper/
www. twitter.com/InsureCrypt

See abstract:
Lingua Franca for Insurance

Denisse Cuellar
FinTech and StartUps Partnership Manager, Banco de Credito BCP
www.linkedin.com/in/denissecuellar
www.twitter.com/denissefintech

See chapter:
InsurTech in Latin America – The Promise of Insurance for Everybody?

Yawei Cui
Senior Academic Director, Moody's Analytics
www.linkedin.com/in/cuiyawei
www.twitter.com/CuiYawei

See chapter:
Personal Asset Liability Management System

Prof. Dr Bjorn Cumps
Professor of Financial Services Innovation and Fintech, Vlerick Business School
www.linkedin.com/in/bjorn-cumps-298b111
www.twitter.com/bjorncumps

See chapter:
Dating InsurTech Startups

Paolo Cuomo
Co-Founder, InsTech London
www.linkedin.com/in/paolocuomo/
www.twitter.com/pgc_at_work

See chapter:
A Cartographer's Dream: Exploring, and Mapping, the New Unknown

Richard Dallas

CEO and Founder, Growth Unlocked Limited

http://linkedin.com/in/richard-dallas-1b34983
www.twitter.com/richarddallas35

See abstract:

Insurance – Simple, Frictionless, or Pointless?

Akber Datoo

Partner, D2 Legal Technology LLP

www.linkedin.com/in/akber-datoo-1105911/
www.twitter.com/akber_datoo

See chapter:

The Smart Journey – From Contract Hype to Insurance Reality

Pauline Davies

Partner, Fee Langstone and CEO, InsuredHQ

www.linkedin.com/in/pauline-davies-591507/

See chapter:

The New World of the Connected Customer – The Future of Microinsurance?

See abstract:

*The Future of Microinsurance? The New World of the Connected Customer
The InsuredHQ Story: Innovation, Disruption, Enablement*

Ofer Deshe

CEO, Tobias & Tobias

www.linkedin.com/in/deshe
www.twitter.com/tobias_tobias

See abstract:

Are Innovation and Regulation Incompatible?

Charles d'Haussy

Head of FinTech, InvestHK

www.linkedin.com/in/charlesdhaussy
www.twitter.com/hongkongFinTech

See abstract:

Insurers are ready for an upgrade

Gavin Dobson

Head of Marketing, Hood Group

www.linkedin.com/in/gavindobson
www.twitter.com/@GDobson_HG

See abstract:

How will the insurance sector change?

Becky Downing

CEO, Buzzmove

www.linkedin.com/in/beckydowning/
www.twitter.com/BeckyDowning1

See chapter:

Blockchain Startups – Unlikely Heroes for the Insurance Industry

Dominic Evans

Global Insurance Fund Investment Analyst, Polar Capital Global Insurance Fund

www.linkedin.com/in/dominic-evans-540a438/
www.twitter.com/DomEvans_Insure

See abstract:

InsurTech Has the Potential to be Central to the Building of a Resilient Society in The Fourth Indus

Sam Evans

General Partner, Eos Venture Partners

www.twitter.com/Sam_C_Evans

See abstract:

*It may be early but the pace is picking up
Partnership approach is still key*

Michael Fitzgibbon

Chief Underwriting Officer, Slice Labs Inc

www.linkedin.com/in/michael-fitzgibbon-757aaa30
www.twitter.com/@FitzDrum

See abstract:

The Digital Insurer

Laura García García

Chief Product Officer and Co-Founder, Drivies

www.linkedin.com/in/lauragargar/
www.twitter.com/lauragargar

See chapter:

Disrupting Car Insurance – Drivies App Makes Driving More Fun, and Insurance Fairer

Greg Gladwell

Owner and Founder, Gladwell Enterprises Ltd

www.linkedin.com/in/greggladwell

See abstract:

Tractable Revolutionises Insurance Estimating

Wynthia Goh

Chief Digital Officer, Asia, Aviva

www.linkedin.com/in/wynthia
www.twitter.com/verydeepsleep

See abstract:

*Death to Pooling
People need insurance, not necessarily insurers*

Yakir Golan
CEO, myDRO
www.linkedin.com/in/yakirgolan
www.twitter.com/@myDROsecurity

See abstract:
The future of cyber risks modeling

Terry Golesworthy
President, The Customer Respect Group
www.linkedin.com/in/terrygo
www.twitter.com/terrycrg

See abstract:
Insurtec – Friend or Foe

Visesh Gosrani
Director of Risk and Actuarial, Guidewire, Cyence Risk Analytics
www.linkedin.com/in/vgosrani
www.twitter.com/v15esh

See chapter:
Data Changes Everything

Jean-Stéphane Gourévitch
CEO and Founder, Mobile Convergence Ecosystems
www.linkedin.com/in/jeanstephanegourevitch
www.twitter.com/@jsgourevitch

See abstract:
Data are forever: A brief journey into strategic, market and public policy issues in the data economy

Ant Gould
Communication and Engagement Specialist and Director of Facilities, Chartered Insurance Institute
www.linkedin.com/in/antgould
www.twitter.com/insurancebod

See abstract:
New Money, Old Ways, New Solutions

Matthew Grant
Founder, Abernite
www.linkedin.com/in/matthewjggrant
www.twitter.com/@matthewjggrant

See abstract:
Bring on the big guns – what future for Insurtech in commercial and Wholesale insurance

Kris Grgurevic
Partner, goetzpartners
www.linkedin.com/in/grgurevic
www.twitter.com/@krisg1107

See abstract:
Anyone can do InsurTech – just understand your customers!

Ivan Gruer
Associate Manager, Accenture Technology
www.linkedin.com/in/ivangruer/
www.twitter.com/ivangruer

See chapter:
A Four-Step Practical Guide to Build InsurTech Value Chain Ecosystems

See abstract:
Strategic Positions towards Disruptive Startups

Max Gutbrod
Principal, Baker McKenzie
www.linkedin.com/in/max-gutbrod-2109a210
www.twitter.com/maxgutbrod

See abstract:
Revisiting Insurance Regulation

David Györi
CEO, Banking Reports Ltd
www.linkedin.com/in/davidgyoribankingreports/
www.twitter.com/DavidGyori

See abstract:
There is No Insurance Against InsurTech

Tshidi Hagan
Program Director, Startupbootcamp InsurTech
www.linkedin.com/in/tshidihagan/

See chapter:
The Corporate Collaboration Opportunity in InsurTech

Tim Hardcastle
CEO, Instanda
www.linkedin.com/in/tim-hardcastle-6016092
www.twitter.com/@instandaF2X

See abstract:
How to architect for disruption

Dr Rebecca Harding
CEO, Coriolis Technologies
www.linkedin.com/in/rebecca-harding-b639832
www.twitter.com/@RebeccaAHarding

See abstract:
Understanding risk through big data

Fuad Hendricks
Advisory Services, Accenture UK
www.linkedin.com/in/fuad-hendricks
www.twitter.com/ftotheh

See abstract:
The Impact of Segmentation [Un]relevance

Achim Hepp
CDO, Virado
www.linkedin.com/in/achimhepp/
www.twitter.com/achimh

See abstract:
A View on how InsurTechs Will Address the New Risks of the Sharing Economy Needs

Bert F. Hölscher
Partner, ARKADIA Management Consultants GmbH
www.linkedin.com/in/bert-hoelscher-482bb4a9/
www.twitter.com/bert_hoelscher

See chapter:
From Claim Settlement to Claim Prevention – How Insurers Can Make Use of Predictive Analytics to Change their Business Model

Susan Holliday
Principal Insurance Specialist, IFC
www.linkedin.com/in/susan-holliday-86516a10/
www.twitter.com/hollidsu

See chapter:
Increasing Access to Insurance in Developing Countries

A.J. Hough
Consultant, Hough Enterprises
www.linkedin.com/in/ajhough/
www.twitter.com/A_J_Hough

See abstract:
Renewable Energy – What Does it Have to do with Insurance?

Jonathan Howe
Partner, PwC UK
www.linkedin.com/in/jonathanhowepwc/
www.twitter.com/@JonathanHowePwC

See abstract:
Insurtech and the Internet of Things

Rube Huljev
CEO, Kingdon
www.linkedin.com/in/telcosales
www.twitter.com/@getkingdon

See abstract:
Millennials. Insurers worst nightmare or growth opportunity?

Ashley Hunter
Managing Director, Touriga Risk Partners
www.linkedin.com/in/ashleymhunter
www.twitter.com/hmriskgroup

See abstract:
Five Steps to Launch

Sebastián Inchauspe
Strategy and Innovation Partner, Auren Argentina
www.linkedin.com/in/inchauspe
www.twitter.com/@sebasincha

See abstract:
Focus on needs not products

Michael Jans
CEO, Michael Jans Advisory
www.linkedin.com/in/michaeljans/
www.twitter.com/michaeljans

See chapter:
InsurTech – Problem or Solution for Agents and Brokers?

Vaughan Jenkins
Independent Consultant, Meta Finance
www.linkedin.com/in/vaughan-jenkins-489563/amrfvr

See chapter:
Reinsurers Need Backward Innovation

Maria-Jose Jorda
Customer Experience Transformation, BBVA
www.linkedin.com/in/maria-jose-jorda-garcia-38000635
www.twitter.com/mariajosejorda

See abstract:
Cross Industry Perspectives for Disruption in InsurTech

Janthana Kaenprakhamroy
CEO and Founder, Tapoly
www.linkedin.com/in/janthana-kaenprakhamroy-0b73546b/
www.twitter.com/JanthanaK

See chapter:
InsurTech's Big Questions – Why the Customer is Still Always Right

Yuri Kartashov
CEO, Euclid Research Centre
https://www.linkedin.com/in/ykartashov/

See chapter:
InsurTech Trends – Why Regionalization Matters

Dror Katzav

CEO, Atidot

www.linkedin.com/in/dror-katzav-98103465

www.twitter.com/AtidotIsrael

See abstract:

Making the Impossible Possible
Turning the Paradigm Upside-Down / The Path Towards Data Driven Solutions

Christina Kehl

Co-Founder and Managing Director, Swiss Finance Startups

www.linkedin.com/in/christinakehl

www.twitter.com/extrablatt

See abstract:

Insuring Survival – InsurTech is not the Driver of Change it is the Answer to it

James Felton Keith

Author and Founder, Accrue Inc

www.linkedin.com/in/jfkii

www.twitter.com/@JFKII

See abstract:

Cyber Ecosystem Designing Cyber Insurance

George Kesselman

President and Founder, InsurTech Asia Association

www.linkedin.com/in/gkesselman/

www.twitter.com/mr_insurtech

See chapter:

Insurance 2029 – Life Backup Companion

Robin Kiera

Thought Leader and Founder, Digitalscouting.de

www.linkedin.com/in/dr-robin-kiera-33536931/

www.twitter.com/stratorob

See chapter:

Seven Things Insurers and InsurTechs Need to Know about the German Insurance Market

Alex Kim

Founder, Inku Ventures

www.linkedin.com/in/alexanderkim

www.twitter.com/alexkim

See abstract:

The MVP Gap

Dr Ulrich Kleipass

Head of Innovation Berlin, ERGO Group

www.linkedin.com/in/dr-ulrich-kleipaß-0b9b8728

www.twitter.com/ukleipe

See chapter:

Digital Transformation and Corporate Innovation Management – an Incumbent's Action Plan

Désirée Klingler

Senior Consultant, Roland Berger

www.linkedin.com/in/désirée-klingler-50046689/

See chapter:

InsurTech: Refreshingly Different – Like Lemonade!

Serhiy Kozlov

CEO and Founder, Romexsoft

www.linkedin.com/in/serhiykozlov/

www.twitter.com/SerhiyKozlov

See abstract:

How P2P is Changing the Future of Insurance

Erika Krizsan

Managing Director, Insurance Factory

www.linkedin.com/in/erika-krizsan-29705088

See abstract:

Pressure to be innovative!?

Dr Sören Kupke

Head of Division Customer and Sales, Allianz Lebensversicherungs-AG

www.linkedin.com/in/soerenkupke

www.twitter.com/SoerenKupke

See abstract:

Redesign of Term Life Application Process

Nicholas Lamparelli

VP, CAT Modeling, QBE

www.linkedin.com/in/nicklamparelli

www.twitter.com/Nick_Lamparelli

See abstract:

InsurTech – Hiding in Plain Sight: How CAT Models Have Disrupted Insurance for 30 Years

Matthias Lange

Managing Director, FinLeap

www.linkedin.com/in/matthiaslange

www.twitter.com/@matthiaslange

See abstract:

Revolution from the back – what changes are needed in the insurance backend

Mike Lawrenchuk

Project Manager, Fox Lake Construction

www.linkedin.com/in/mike-lawrenchuk-039655123

www.twitter.com/mikelawrenchuk

296

See abstract:

Blockchain in Insurance – Quantifiable Benefits, Practical Examples, Real Challenges

Pritesh Modi

Director and Chief Actuary Asia, LeapFrog Investments

www.linkedin.com/in/pritesh-modi-a0198419

See abstract:

InsurTECH – at the Bottom of the Pyramid

Paul Morgenthaler

FinTech and InsurTech Investor, CommerzVentures

www.linkedin.com/in/paulmorgenthaler

www.twitter.com/@morningdollar

See abstract:

Investing in InsurTech

Susanne Møllegaard

CEO and Co-Owner, Process Factory

www.linkedin.com/in/susannemollegaard/

www.twitter.com/SusMoellegaard

See chapter:

Six Mega-trends that Will Take Insurance Back to the Future

Daniel Morgan

Founder, Dino

www.linkedin.com/in/daniel-j-morgan

www.twitter.com/dinoinsurance

See abstract:

How InsurTechs are Using a Niche Position in the Market to Drive Change

Mahalingasivam Muhunthan

Student, Temasek Polytechnic

www.linkedin.com/in/mahalingasivam-muhunthan-809718135

See abstract:

Crop Insurance in Emerging Markets

Ravindra Muley

AAO, LIC of India

www.linkedin.com/in/ravindra-muley-a4909034

www.twitter.com/@Ravindra_Muley

See abstract:

InsurTech: Collaborating across the chain

Roan Murray

CEO, Switching House

www.twitter.com/roanmurray

See abstract:

Creating Ecosystems through problem solving

Alex Nechoroskovas

Founder, FinTech Summary

www.linkedin.com/in/alexnechoroskovas

www.twitter.com/@fintechsummary

See abstract:

5000 Year Old Industry Reinventing Itself

Alejandro Nino

Co-Founder and COO, Above & Beyond

www.linkedin.com/in/alejandro-nino

See abstract:

The Year of Integration

Bernardo Nunes, PhD

Head of Data Scientist, Growth Tribe Academy

www.linkedin.com/in/bernardofn

www.twitter.com/ThisIsBernardo

See chapter:

Behavioural Design and Price Optimization in InsurTech

Max Odlum

Product Manager, Artificial Labs

www.linkedin.com/in/max-odlum-a588b447/

www.twitter.com/maxodlum

See abstract:

Lack of innovation in Lloyd's of London

Telly V. Onu

Impact Ecosystem Innovator and Managing Director, Prohaus Group

www.linkedin.com/in/tvonu/

www.twitter.com/teval

See chapter:

Internationalizing InsurTech – A Global Phenomenon in Different Markets

Jaco Oosthuizen

Co-Founder and Chief Wellbeing Officer, Exponential Ventures

www.linkedin.com/in/jaco-oosthuizen-86314911/

www.twitter.com/@Jaco87654321

See abstract:

Back to basics

Eelco Ouwerkerk

Industry Director Wholesale and Retail, Aon

www.linkedin.com/in/eelcoouwerkerk/

www.twitter.com/EelcoOuwerkerk

See chapter:

Beware of GDPR – Take your Cyber Risk Responsibility More Seriously

Jennifer Overhulse
Principal Owner, St. Nick Media Services
www.linkedin.com/in/stnickmedia
www.twitter.com/@stnickmedia

See abstract:
The Long Tail of the Insurance Buying Cycle

Dan Padbury
CEO, Only Policy
www.linkedin.com/in/danpadbury/
www.twitter.com/@onlypolicy

See abstract:
A long winding road!

Rashee Pandey
Marketing and Communications Manager, Bankable
www.linkedin.com/in/rasheepandey/
www.twitter.com/@rasheepandey

See abstract:
Unravelling one of the least understood industries at the edge of disruption

Karl Heinz Passler
Product Manager and Startup Scout, Basler Versicherungen
www.linkedin.com/in/karlheinzpassler
www.twitter.com/insurtechtalk

See chapter:
"Real" InsurTech Startups do it Differently

Emma Pegg
Marketing Executive, SPIXII
www.linkedin.com/in/emmapeggmarketing/

See chapter:
Insurance Expertise, Family, and Integrity – The Story of SPIXII's Founding Team

Roger Perevelli
Partner, VODW and Connector, Digital Insurance Agenda
www.linkedin.com/in/rogerpeverelli
www.twitter.com/rogerpeverelli

See abstract:
Matching InsurTechs against the Key Challenges Insurers are Facing

Willie Pienaar
CEO, NuvaLaw
www.linkedin.com/in/willie-pienaar-12631526/
www.twitter.com/WilliePienaar

See chapter:
Altered Attitudes, Altered Outcomes – Collaborating for a Better Future

See abstract:
Altered Attitudes, Altered Outcomes. Insurance Gets a Shakeup

Damiano Pietroni
Management Consulting Manager – Insurance, Accenture
www.linkedin.com/in/damianopietroni
www.twitter.com/PietroniDamiano

See chapter:
Assessing the Long-Term Viability of the Insurance Peer-to-Peer Business Model

Vesna Planko
CEO, Habitual
www.linkedin.com/in/vesnaplanko/
www.twitter.com/@VesnaPlanko

See abstract:
Peer-to-peer Insurance for modern ages

Yuri Poletto
Co-Founder and Head of Business Development, Darwinsurance Srl
www.linkedin.com/in/yuripoletto/
www.twitter.com/@yuripoletto

See abstract:
The Darwinsurance manifesto

Craig Polley
Director, Digital Risk Services Limited
www.linkedin.com/in/craigpolley/
www.twitter.com/DigitalRiskServ

See chapter:
ClaimsTech – The InsurTech's Action List

Ruth Polyblank
Head of SME and Digital, Chubb Insurance Company of Europe
www.linkedin.com/in/ruth-polyblank-18575513/
www.twitter.com/RuthPolyblank

See chapter:
Not too Big to Learn not to Fail

Jens Prichenfried
Adviser/Shareholder, MEP Mobile Equity Partners GmbH
www.linkedin.com/in/jens-prichenfried-4809861
www.twitter.com/@JPrichenfried

See abstract:
Emerging Insurance Markets

Ed Pugh
Sales and Marketing Director, Red Crake
www.linkedin.com/in/ed-pugh-5573652
www.twitter.com/@redcrake_ed

Alex Ruthemeier
InsurTech Facilitator and Co-Founder/Operations, ONE Insurance
www.linkedin.com/in/alexanderruthemeier/
www.twitter.com/ruthemeier

See chapter:
Digital Transformation in Insurance – Four Common Factors from Other Industries

Jon Sabes
Life Epigenetics and CEO, GWG Holdings, Inc
www.linkedin.com/in/jonsabes/
www.twitter.com/jonsabes

See chapter:
Genomics 101 – The Search for a Better Life Expectancy Predictor Leads GWG Life to a Science Lab

Daniel Saksenberg
Co-Founder, Emerge Analytics
www.twitter.com/@dansaksenberg

See abstract:
How AI will transform insurance

Christopher Sandilands
Partner, Oxbow Partners
www.linkedin.com/in/csandilands
www.twitter.com/@consultilands

See abstract:
InsurTech is alive – but will change direction

Dr Florian Schreiber
Project Manager and Post-Doctoral Researcher, Institute of Insurance Economics – University of St. Gallen
www.linkedin.com/in/florian-schreiber/

See abstract:
Which business model patterns are inherent in InsuranceTech startups?

Paul Schulte
Founder and Editor, Schulte Research
www.linkedin.com/in/paul-schulte-43420262/
www.twitter.com/PaulSchulte88

See abstract:
The InsurTech Asteroid: Is Extinction of Traditional Insurance Inevitable?

Jannat Shah Rajan
Venture Capital Investor, AXA Strategic Ventures
www.linkedin.com/in/jannatshah
www.twitter.com/jannatshah

See chapter:
The Best InsurTech May not be InsurTech

Gilad Shai
Founder, InsurTech LA
www.linkedin.com/in/giladshai/
www.twitter.com/gilad_shai

See chapter:
InsurTech and the Promise of "Property Value Hedging Technology"

Andrea Silvello
Co-Founder, Neosurance, Founder and Managing Director of Business Support
www.linkedin.com/in/andrea-silvello-52240210/
www.twitter.com/SilvelloAndrea

See chapter:
Sell Your Insurance at the Right Time – Consider Micro Policies

Ian Simons
Marketing Director, The Chartered Insurance Institute
www.linkedin.com/in/ian-simons-a08b5b6
www.twitter.com/iantsimons

See abstract:
What is 'good' innovation?

McKenzie M. Slaughter
Founder and CEO, Prohaus Group
www.linkedin.com/in/mckenziemslaughter/
www.twitter.com/kenzieslaugh

See chapter:
Internationalizing InsurTech – A Global Phenomenon in Different Markets

Antonie Smaal
CEO and Co-founder, InsureMyTrans AB
www.linkedin.com/in/tonsmaal/
www.twitter.com/tonsmaal

See abstract:
The Mental Framework of InsureMyTrans

Dan Smith
Co-Founder and Managing Partner, Exponential Ventures
www.linkedin.com/in/dan-smith-562343b
www.twitter.com/finw3ll

See chapter:
Business Model Innovation – From Incremental to Disruptive

Lex Sokolin
Global Director Fintech Strategy, Autonomous
www.linkedin.com/in/alexeysokolin
www.twitter.com/@LexSokolin

See abstract:

How to pivot from B2C to B2B and why it's necessary

Vasyl Soloshchuk

CEO and Managing Partner, INSART

www.linkedin.com/in/vsolo/

www.twitter.com/vsoloINSART

See chapter:

InsurTech Trends – Why Regionalization Matters

Christophe Spoerry

Co-founder, Euler Hermes Digital Agency

www.linkedin.com/in/spoerry

www.twitter.com/@spoerry

See abstract:

Reinventing a 100-year-old Insurance Service with APIs

Catherine Stagg-Macey

Founder, Executive/ Team coach, Belgrave Street

www.linkedin.com/in/staggmacey

www.twitter.com/@staggmacey

See abstract:

Why an unexamined life is the downfall of a founder

Laimonas Stoncius

Founder and CEO, ClaimsControl

www.linkedin.com/in/stoncius/

www.twitter.com/claims_control

See chapter:

Why Claims Sharing? Innovating within the Business-to-Business Insurance Claims Handling Ecosystem

Gabriel Swift

Senior Marketing Adviser, NTT Data Inc

www.linkedin.com/in/gabrielswift/

www.twitter.com/GabrielSwift1

See abstract:

Swinton Insurance – search optimisation and interaction design
Tokio Marine tests new blockchain-based insurance policy

Eunice Tan

Local Principal, Baker McKenzie Wong & Leow

www.linkedin.com/in/eunice-tan-9232417/

See abstract:

Singapore racing ahead to become the InsurTech hub

Brian Tang

Managing Director, Asia Capital Markets Institute

www.linkedin.com/in/brian-w-tang-7131293

www.twitter.com/CapMarketsProf

See abstract:

AI in InsurTech – Opportunities and regulatory challenges

Tony Tarquini

Director of Insurance, EMEA, Pegasystems Limited

www.linkedin.com/in/tony-tarquini-2b92a/

www.twitter.com/TarquiniTony

See chapter:

Practical Robotics in Insurance – The Future is Here Already

Tobias Taupitz

Co-Founder and CEO, LAKA

www.linkedin.com/in/tobiastaupitz/

www.twitter.com/tobsnt

See chapter:

True Business Model Innovation – a Credit-Based Approach

Stewart Taylor

Head of London Market Modernsation and InsurTech, HFG

www.linkedin.com/in/stewarttayloruk/

https://twitter.com/stewarttayloruk

See abstract:

Why DINO-insurers will be killed off by the InsurTech meteor

Sylvain Theveniaud

Managing Director, Allianz Accelerator

www.linkedin.com/in/sylvaintheveniaud

www.twitter.com/sylvainth

See abstract:

Accelerating start-ups: From interactions to shaping frameworks for success

Periklis Thivaios

Partner, True North Partners LLP

www.linkedin.com/in/periklisthivaios/

See abstract:

Insurance is not a Business Model. InsurTech Could be

Denis Thomas

Associate Director, KPMG

www.linkedin.com/tdenisk

www.twitter.com/tdenisk

See chapter:

Competition vs. Coopetition in the Insurance Market

Neil Thomson

Strategic Sales Director, Freelance InsurTech Consultant

www.linkedin.com/in/neil-thomson-b92b379/

www.twitter.com/_NeilThomson

See chapter:
InsurTechs – Magical Thinking and Other Secrets of Success

Tuan Trinh
Founder, InsurTech Consulting Partners
www.linkedin.com/in/tuan-trinh-b81b3419
www.twitter.com/trinhanhtuan247

See abstract:
On the Creation of an Online Social Insurance Platform

Tobias Troendle
Management Consultant, Diconium Strategy
www.linkedin.com/in/tobias-troendle-07413890/
www.twitter.com/TobiasTroendle

See chapter:
Alexa, Can You Get me an Insurance? A Structured Approach to the Hyped Technology of Voice-Based Assistants

Steve Tunstall
CEO and Co-Founder, Inzsure
www.linkedin.com/in/stevetunstall
www.twitter.com/inzsure1

See chapter:
Why is Insurance Failing?

Richard Turrin
Artificial Intelligence | FinTech WealthTech | InsurTech Professional and Chief Innovation Officer, Singapore Life
www.linkedin.com/in/turrin/

See chapter
InsurTech and AI – You Can Run but You Cannot Hide from the Future

Igor Valandro
CEO, Air
www.linkedin.com/in/igor-valandro-1010b16

See abstract:
Enabling Usage Based Pricing: Airs Business Model

Sabine VanderLinden
CEO, Startupbootcamp InsurTech, Rainmaking Innovation InsurTech, The Proposition Circle
www.linkedin.com/in/sabinevanderlinden/
www.twitter.com/SabineVdL

See chapter:
You Said ... Sharing Economy?

See abstract:
The New Customer Reality: AI Is Everywhere

Jean-Charles Velge
Co-Founder, Qover
www.linkedin.com/in/jean-charles-velge-4345131/
www.twitter.com/velgejc

See chapter:
Forget Peer-to-Peer, the Future of Insurance is Invisible and Parametric

Shwetank Verma
Managing Partner, Leo Capital
www.linkedin.com/in/shwetankv/
www.twitter.com/shwetankv

See abstract:
5 Cs of Opportunity

Koen Vingerhoets
Blockchain Adviser, KBC
www.linkedin.com/in/koenvingerhoets
www.twitter.com/IthronKoen

See abstract:
Blockchain: A matter of life and death

Gerben Visser
Founder, FinTech Consortium
www.linkedin.com/in/gerbenvisser
www.twitter.com/fincon

See abstract:
Into South East Asia's InsurTech Ecosystem

Henrique Volpi
Author, InsurTech Entrepreneur and Co-Founder, Kakau
www.linkedin.com/in/henriquevolpi/
www.twitter.com/VolpiIT

See chapter:
Seamless Insurance: The Time is Now

Igor Volzhanin
CEO, DataSine
www.linkedin.com/in/ivolzhanin/

See abstract:
Serving Customers

Benjamin Von Euw
Enterprise Architect, iA Financial Group
www.linkedin.com/in/benjaminve/

See chapter:
From Event-Focused Insights to Coaching

Nigel Walsh

Partner, Deloitte

www.linkedin.com/in/nigelwalsh
www.twitter.com/nigelwalsh

See chapter:

Frictionless Insurance in a Land of Utility

John Warburton

Founder, Konsileo

www.linkedin.com/in/johnwarburton1/
www.twitter.com/broking_john

See chapter:

Where Does InsurTech Leave the People who Work in Insurance?

MIchael Weinreich

Venture Partner, Finleap GmbH

www.linkedin.com/in/michael-weinreich-35038b12
www.twitter.com/@MWFintech

See abstract:

Solving the 'unsolvable equation' – decrease cost yet increase customer satisfaction

Ronald Weissman

Partner, Circini Innovation

www.linkedin.com/in/ronald-weissman-36a3841

See abstract:

UBI: The New Paradigm Disrupting Auto Insurance Today and Other Lines Tomorrow.

Harry Williams

Business Designer, Fjord

www.linkedin.com/in/harryewilliams/
www.twitter.com/_harrywilliams

See chapter:

Technology is Not Enough

Paul Wilson

Insurance Digital Marketing Technologist Lead, Capgemini

www.linkedin.com/in/mymarketer
www.twitter.com/paulwilson

See abstract:

Using Behavior-Modification Gamification to Bring Insurers into the Connected World

Selim Yazici

Co-Founder, FinTech Istanbul and Professor, Istanbul University

www.linkedin.com/in/selimyazici/
www.twitter.com/SelimYazici

See abstract:

Digital Transformation in Insurance and the State of InsurTech in Turkey

Dorota Zimnoch

Founder and MD ZING Business Consulting, Strategic Advisor, The Heart

www.linkedin.com/in/dorotazimnoch
www.twitter.com/D_Zimnoch

See chapter:

Incumbent and InsurTech Collaboration via Open Innovation Strategy

Michael Zoelzer

Co-Founder and COO, WearHealth

www.linkedin.com/in/michaelzoelzer
www.twitter.com/michaelzoelzer

See abstract:

Merging claims data with data from wearables

Moran Zur

CEO, SafeBeyond

www.linkedin.com/in/moran-zur-46038057
www.twitter.com/@Safe_Beyond

See abstract:

The World's First Emotional Life Insurance Platform

Index

INDEX